Complete Encyclopedia *of the*

Freshwater Aquarium

Complete Encyclopedia *of the* Freshwater Aquarium

John Dawes

FIREFLY BOOKS

A FIREFLY BOOK

Published by Firefly Books Ltd., 2001

First Printing 2001

Canadian Cataloguing in Publication Data

Dawes, John, 1945–
   The complete encyclopedia of the freshwater aquarium
Includes bibliographical references and index.
ISBN 1-55297-544-4
1. Aquariums. 2. Aquarium fishes. I. Title.
SF457.D38 2001   639-34   C2001-930716-0

U.S. Cataloguing in Publication Data
   (Library of Congress Standards)
Dawes, John.
   The complete encyclopedia of the freshwater aquarium/John Dawes. –1st ed.
[304] p. : col. ill. ; cm.
Includes index.
Summary : A comprehensive guide to setting up and maintaining a freshwater aquarium at home.
ISBN 1-55297-544-4
1. Aquariums. 2. Aquariums – Equipment and supplies. I. Title.
639.34 21 2001   CIP

Published in Canada in 2001 by
Firefly Books Ltd.
3680 Victoria Park Avenue
Willowdale, Ontario M2H 3K1

Published in the United States in 2001 by
Firefly Books (U.S.) Inc.
P.O. Box 1338, Ellicott Station
Buffalo, New York 14205

Conceived and produced by Andromeda
Oxford Limited
11–13 The Vineyard, Abingdon
Oxon OX14 3PX
www.andromeda.co.uk

PROJECT DIRECTOR Graham Bateman
MANAGING EDITOR Shaun Barrington
EDITING AND DESIGN D & N Publishing,
           Marlborough, Wiltshire

EDITORIAL ASSISTANT Marian Dreier
INDEX Janet Dudley
PICTURE MANAGER Claire Turner
PRODUCTION Clive Sparling

Printed in Poland

CONTENTS

PICTURE CREDITS AND ACKNOWLEDGMENTS 6

INTRODUCTION 8

NATURAL HISTORY OF FISH 10
- What is a Fish? 12
- Natural Habitats 17
- Fish Conservation 20
- Commercial Breeding of Aquarium Fish 23

FISH CARE IN THE AQUARIUM 26
- Aquarium Setup and Maintenance 28
- Nutrition and Feeding 54
- Breeding Fish 57
- Health Management 62

AQUARIUM PLANTS 68
- Plants Listing 77

AQUARIUM FISH 82
- Cichlids 84
- Catfishes 128
- Cyprinids 164
- Characoids 188
- Loaches and Suckers 226
- Gouramis and Relatives 232
- Rainbows and Blue-eyes 248
- Sunfish and Darters 254
- Sleepers and Gobies 258
- Killifishes 262
- Poeciliids and Close Relatives 270
- Goodeids and Their Relatives 284
- Miscellaneous Species 288

GLOSSARY 298

BIBLIOGRAPHY 299

INDEX 300

P. 1 CLOCKWISE FROM TOP LEFT: *BRILLIANT RUMMY-NOSED TETRA (HEMIGRAMMUS BLEHERI); RUBY BARB (BARBUS NIGROFASCIATUS); FLORIDA FLAGFISH (JORDANELLA FLORIDAE); REDFIN OTOCINCLUS (PAROTOCINCLUS MACULICAUDA); ARCHER FISH (TOXOTES JACULATRIX); INDIAN GLASSFISH (PARAMBASSIS RANGA). PP.2–3: SOUTHERN PLATY (XIPHOPHORUS MACULATUS VAR.). THIS PAGE, TOP TO BOTTOM: BURNISHED GOLD SUNSET PLATY (XIPHOPHORUS MACULATUS VAR.); BIG-FINNED BRISTLENOSE (ANCISTRUS DOLICHOPTERUS); CATEMACO LIVEBEARER (XIPHOPHORUS MILLERI).*

PICTURE CREDITS AND ACKNOWLEDGMENTS

The Author and Publishers would like to thank in particular Frank Schäfer of the Aqualog Archive for his tireless cooperation—and knowledge—in finding illustrations; and also the incomparable aquarium fish photographer Max Gibbs.

Andromeda Oxford Limited 34tcl, 34tcr, 34tr, 34cl, 34cr, 46, 52, 53; Phil Jane/Andromeda Oxford Limited 257b; Aqualog Archive 1bcl, 86, 87, 88r, 89, 91b, 92c, 92b, 93, 96b, 130b, 131b, 132, 134c, 136–138, 139t, 140, 141, 142c, 144l, 145b, 146b, 147, 148b, 190–196, 197b, 199c, 200–205, 207, 209tr, 209c, 209b, 210, 211c, 212t, 213b, 214–218, 219b, 220–227, 228b, 229t, 230t, 231t, 268, 277t, 278t, 280b x3, 286–289, 290t, 291–297; Aquarian Fish Foods 20; Staffan Widstrand/BBC Natural History Unit 17; Dennis Barrett 5b, 6, 59; Dieter Bork 7b, 268b, 269; Jane Burton/Bruce Coleman Collection 12; Andrew Davies/Bruce Coleman Collection 19; D.J. Lambert 283; Max Gibbs/Photomax 1tl, 1cr, 1b, 1bcl, 1tcl, 2–3, 5t, 5c, 7t, 10–11, 13–16, 21, 23–31, 34tl, 37–39, 41–45, 48, 50, 51, 54, 56–58, 61–85, 88l, 90, 91t, 92t, 94, 95, 96t, 97–129, 130t, 131t, 133, 134b, 135, 139b, 142b, 143, 144r, 145t, 146c, 148t, 149–177, 178t, 179–189, 197t, 198, 199t, 206, 208, 209tl, 211b, 212b, 213t, 219t, 228, 229b, 230b, 231b, 232–256, 257t, 258–267, 270–276, 277c, 278b, 279, 280t, 281, 282, 285, 290c; M. Sandford 35, 55; W. Tomey 1tr, 9, 18, 22, 40, 49, 178b.

THIS PAGE: (TOP LEFT) *CELEBES HALFBEAK* (*NOMORHAMPHUS LIEMI*); (TOP RIGHT) *SPOTTED GOODEID* (*CHAPALICHTHYS ENCAUSTUS*); (ABOVE) *PIKE TOP LIVEBEARER* (*BELONESOX BELIZANUS*). OPPOSITE PAGE: (TOP) *PEPPERED CORYDORAS* (*CORYDORAS PALEATUS*); (BOTTOM) *BAR-TAILED RIVULUS* (*RIVULUS MAGDALENAE*).

INTRODUCTION

Little could I have guessed when I took up aquarium keeping about 50 years ago, that I was choosing one of the most absorbing, interesting and colorful hobbies in the world. Equally, there was no way I could have known then that those initial, exciting, error-riddled steps would lead to a lifelong involvement that has taken me almost round the world.

Seeing Cardinal Tetras (*Paracheirodon axelrodi*) for the first time in a flooded Rio Negro forest; netting Mosquito Fish (*Gambusia holbrooki*) in swamps in Florida; collecting Ornate Paradise Fish (*Malpulutta kretseri*) for a captive breeding project in the jungles of Sri Lanka; observing Threadjaw Halfbeaks (*Hemirhamphodon pogonognathus*) in a tiny stream in Malaysia—these, along with so many other experiences, have contributed to a fascination that continues to deepen with every passing day, fueling my enthusiasm to continue to search for knowledge about fish and aquatic plants. The more I have traveled, and the more people I have had the privilege of meeting, exchanging experiences with and learning from, the more I've come to appreciate that we all share the same "affliction"—we are all crazy about fish!

My teachers have been many. Sará—an Amazonian caboclo—taught me how to "call" cardinals out of hiding; Dharmadasa taught me, likewise, how to call *Rasbora vaterifloris* in Sri Lanka; Yong taught me how to spot Snakehead fry among water plants in Malaysia; Marco showed me just how tough some species of molly, such as *Poecilia vivipara*, can be (they thrive in the often-polluted waters of Lago Rodrigo de Freitas in Rio de Janeiro). Countless other unselfish people—including many hundreds of fellow aquarists—have generously given me their time and shared their hard-earned knowledge with me over the years. So while the pages that follow may have come from my pen, the information they contain bears witness to innumerable invaluable contributions made by many. To each and every one of them, I extend my respectful and most sincere thanks.

What I have attempted to do is present an overall picture of the modern hobby, outlining some of the latest thinking in aquarium management techniques and philosophies, and presenting an extensive selection of fish and plants. I also hope to have highlighted the tremendous responsibility that all of us who keep fish need to shoulder.

The fish section—the largest in the book—is arranged in families. There are some families, though, that are represented in the hobby by only one or a few species, and these have been grouped together in the final section. Owing to the large number of species featured, allied to space and other limitations, it has not been possible to illustrate every single fish. Readers are therefore encouraged to consult the specialist literature cited in the Bibliography for further illustrations.

Within the families, species are listed in alphabetical order of scientific name. The common name for the species is given on the first line. Common names vary from country to country—or even within a single country—and, in some cases, one common name may be applied to more than one species, something that does not, or should not, apply to the scientific equivalents. Therefore, *Dianema longibarbis* precedes *D. urostriata* in this book, even though this means that their respective common names, Porthole Catfish and Flag-Tailed Catfish, do not appear in alphabetical order.

Although, at any one time, there is (or should be) only one valid scientific name for each species, complications can, and do, occur. For instance, opinions may differ between scientists, with some claiming that two or more species are sufficiently similar to each other to warrant their inclusion within a single species. Alternatively, a variable species may be deemed by some to consist of not just one but several very closely related species. Further, one authority may deem an individual species to belong to a particular genus while others disagree and assign it to another. Genera may be considered members of different families or subfamilies, and so on.

Intimately associated with taxonomy (the science of classifying living organisms into hierarchical groups, i.e. subspecies, species, genera, subfamilies, families, and so on), is the science of systematics, which attempts to classify organisms according to their "natural" relationships by taking into consideration matters relating to their evolutionary biology. The end result is that, while universal agreement may exist regarding the identity and therefore, the name, of numerous species, there are also areas of disagreement and debate. Even when, or if, a consensus is reached, it may take some time (years) before the latest, agreed, valid name becomes accepted. Consequently, a particular species may be listed under one scientific name by some authors and under a different one by others.

A good example of this complex and "fluid" situation exists with the beautiful and highly variable African Rift Lake cichlid commonly known as the Zebra Cichlid. Traditionally this species is listed as *Pseudotropheus zebra*. In 1997, it was renamed *Metriaclima zebra*, but this move has yet to receive universal acceptance. To complicate matters further, some authors regard this species as *Maylandia zebra*.

Where such situations exist, I have highlighted some of the issues concerned and have listed such species according to how convincing, or otherwise, the arguments for and against appear to be, or how widely accepted, or otherwise, the various names have become. As a result, some species in this book, such as the Dwarf Rasbora (*Boraras maculata*) are listed differently than they are in some other literature. In the case of the Harlequin, which is still regarded as *Rasbora heteromorpha* by many authors, the new name, *Trigonostigma heteromorpha*, erected in 1999, is also listed and acknowledged because, in the foreseeable future, the new name is likely to replace the old one.

The above examples help to illustrate that, far from being a static science, fish classification is dynamic and "changing." To some, i.e. those who like their science presented in neat little packages, this situation causes problems. To many others (and I include myself in this group), problems are challenges in disguise. To us, the dynanism, subjectiveness, openness and everevolving nature of the subject is one of its major attractions.

Fish classification, aquarium science, and every single aspect of our hobby and the industries that service it, will continue to evolve apace, and we need to grow and adapt accordingly. New areas of debate and controversy will continue to challenge us, and all need to be faced openly and honestly. Two issues that have been "bubbling" for some time, and that have been gradually gaining momentum to the point that they are making headlines worldwide, are biopiracy and genetically modified fish. Both are of obvious and direct relevance to the hobby, as well as to the ornamental aquatic industry, and both will, undoubtedly, play significant roles in years to come. They are an integral part of aquatics in the new millennium—a millennium that will see us attain new levels of success in areas of activity that we don't even know exist yet. The ride will be exciting, though not always easy. Welcome aboard!

John Dawes
Sabinillas, Spain

THE RED PARROT, A RECENT ADDITION TO THE HUGE RANGE OF FISH THAT ARE TODAY KEPT IN AQUARIA.

NATURAL HISTORY OF FISH

Fish are fascinating creatures, but what is a fish? It is actually difficult to define the term "fish" concisely and unambiguously. The pages that follow therefore begin with a discussion of this important topic. They then detail the various characteristics of fish. Some of the most important habitats from which aquarium fish originate are also described. This is important because a better understanding of the conditions that fish encounter in the wild can help us to cater to their needs in aquaria.

Also of great relevance to aquarists is the status of fish species in the wild. Some are extinct in nature, but exist in captivity; others are close to extinction, while many are threatened. Efforts to save many such species are, however, under way, both at national and international levels, and some of these measures are described. Finally, the commercial aspects of ornamental fish breeding are examined.

WHAT IS A FISH?

There are well over 24,000 species of fish known to science, a number that appears to be increasing as quickly today as it did during the early period of plant and animal classification. However, although research may be more meticulous now, and communications are certainly more efficient—minimizing the risks of double, or even multiple, naming—there are still instances of the same fish (or other organism) being described and assigned different names by different scientists.

With so many thousands of species in existence, from whale sharks to minnows, we should all know what a fish actually is. We do not. It would be fair to say that there is no categorical definition of the term "fish." While we can all identify, say, any variety of goldfish as a fish, when it comes down to listing all the characteristics that would identify any fish as a fish, we immediately run into difficulties. It is, for example, quite ridiculous to say that an animal is a fish if it lives in water. Dolphins, whales, leeches, lobsters, sea cucumbers, sponges and numerous other aquatic organisms do likewise. Fish have scales on their bodies, but so do reptiles (crocodiles, turtles, lizards and the like). Conversely, not all animals that we definitely regard as fish have scales: catfish belonging to the family Pimelodidae are, in fact, quite naked, and there are numerous other examples of scaleless fish. Matters do not improve much when another fish characteristic—gills—is considered. Newt larvae and salamander tadpoles, including the incredible neotenous axolotl, all possess gills, yet they are amphibians—definitely not fish.

Combining fish characteristics, such as an aquatic lifestyle, and the possession of gills and fins might, at first sight, bring a definition a little closer, but not when you consider that other animals such as cuttlefishes (*Sepia, Sepiola* etc.) and squids exhibit the same characteristics. One important difference (there are others) is that in cuttlefishes and squids, which are both mollusks, the internal organs are found inside a mantle cavity. Fish do not possess a mantle cavity. Fish have an internal skeleton, but, then again, so do cuttlefishes and squids (the cuttlebone and pen, respectively), starfishes, and their close relatives the urchins (their skeleton consists of calcareous plates overlaid with thin surface tissue). What cuttlefishes and urchins do not possess is a cranium (braincase or skull). However, not even this apparently unassailable criterion is

sufficient to distinguish fish from other marine organisms. If it did then lampreys and the other "jawless fishes," the hagfishes, would also be "true" fish, but they are not. They do have a skull of sorts, even though it is largely a covered cartilage "trough" (particularly in hagfishes), but they also have many other "nonfish" characteristics, such as the absence of a backbone, two (instead of three) semicircular canals in the ear, and gills that are arranged almost back to front when compared with "normal" fish (in jawless fishes they are directed internally). In addition, jawless fishes (Agnatha), unsurprisingly, do not possess jaws. Therefore, even combining characteristics, the term "fish" is still impossible to define concisely and unambiguously.

Keith Banister, in *The Encyclopaedia of Underwater Life* (*see* Bibliography) puts the matter succinctly. Referring to the four groups of "fishes" that exist today, namely the lampreys, hagfishes, cartilaginous fishes, and bony fishes, he says that classifying all these under the common heading of fish is like "lumping all flying vertebrates, i.e., bats, birds and even the flying lizard, under the heading 'birds' just because they all fly."

If we consider the relationship between say, a lamprey and a guppy, we come to the conclusion that

THE POSSESSION OF GILLS DOES NOT DEFINE AN ANIMAL AS A FISH. THE AXOLOTL, A SALAMANDER, KEEPS GILLS THROUGHOUT ITS LIFE, WHICH IS UNUSUAL FOR AN AMPHIBIAN.

they are as different from each other as a bat from a chicken. It must be inappropriate to refer to them both as fish. Quoting Banister again, "'Fish' is simply a shorthand notation for an aquatic vertebrate that is not a mammal, a turtle, or anything else."

In practice, when we use the word "fish," we refer to those species of aquatic vertebrates identified as fish by Banister, some of which are eaten, some of which are maintained in aquaria and ponds. (Despite the fact that lampreys are eaten in some parts of the world, they are not included.) Common usage of the term "fish" is restricted to members of two large groups:

1. Cartilaginous fishes (Class Chondrichthyes)
   Sharks, rays and chimaeras (approximately 700 species).
2. Bony fishes (Class Osteichthyes)
   A large class of species from guppies to seahorses (over 23,000 species).

▲ CUTTLEFISH SHOW SOME FISHLIKE CHARACTERISTICS BUT ARE ACTUALLY MOLLUSKS.
◄ BABY CUTTLEFISH WITHIN ITS EGG.

Of these two categories, the one that is encountered almost (but not quite) exclusively in aquaria and in ponds, is the Class Osteichthyes, or bony fishes. It is possible, with difficulty and numerous exceptions and qualifications, to list the characteristics that, in combination, allow us to recognize a bony fish as such. Bony fish:

- Possess a braincase and limb (fin) skeleton consisting, at least in part, of bone
- Possess fins, usually with spines and/or rays
- Breathe through outwardly directed gills covered by an operculum (gill cover) that, externally, appears as a slitlike aperture
- Have bodies totally or partially covered in scales (with some important exceptions)
- Possess an air/gas/swimbladder used in buoyancy control (with a few exceptions)
- Possess a sensory mechanism called the lateral line system, which runs in a head–tail direction
- Are poikilothermic (cold-blooded): their body temperature is determined by that of the environment. (Again, there are some significant exceptions, such as tuna, which are capable of raising their body temperature above that of the surrounding water.)

THE SKULL

The skull or cranium of bony fishes is made up of two main parts: the neurocranium and the branchiocranium.

The neurocranium consists of the part of the skull that encloses the brain itself, plus the associated bones that make up the top half of the skull and extend forward to the "internal" upper tip of the snout (ending with the ethmoid and vomer bones). The neurocranium is subdivided into two further parts: the chondrocranium, which is the original cartilaginous braincase that ossifies (changes into bone) during development, and the dermatocranium, which consists of components that are ossified from the outset.

The branchiocranium consists of five separate composite components, referred to as arches, which include the maxillae (jaws) and the operculi (gill covers). One of the bones of the upper jaw, the premaxilla, covers the ethmoid and vomer bones mentioned above, which are thus not visible externally—hence the reference to their constituting the "internal" upper tip of the snout.

THE SKELETON

The limb part of the skeleton consists of a pelvic (hip) and pectoral (chest) girdle, and associated bones that support the pelvic or ventral fins and the pectoral fins. However, since fish also have other appendages—such as anal (belly), caudal (tail), and dorsal (back) fins, plus, in some types, adipose (second dorsal) fins—they also possess additional supporting bones.

Running the length of the body, from the back of the skull to the caudal fin, lies the backbone or vertebral column. In the posterior half of the body, the individual

ANATOMY OF A FISH.

The principal external features of a fish

dorsal fin

lateral line

scale

gills

mout

caudal fin

anal fin

pelvic fin

pectoral fin

The internal organs of a fish

swim
bladder

kidney

liver

gills

heart

ovary

intestines

The skeleton of a fish

fin spine

fin ray support

neural spine

opercle

neurocranium

eye socket

upper jaw
(premaxilla
and maxilla)

tail bones

hemal spines

lower jaw
(dentary)

backbone

pelvic girdle

ribs

pectoral girdle

bones have two vertical spines, an upwardly directed one (the neural spine) and a ventrally directed one (the hemal spine). Further forward, in the region that lies above the abdominal cavity, the hemal spines are much reduced or absent, leaving space for the internal organs as well as acting as basal supports for the ribs.

The tail of a fish is a highly complicated and beautifully put together structure referred to as the caudal complex. The base itself consists of modified neural and hemal spines, the most modified of which are referred to as hypurals; these act as supports for the fin rays. Fish tails are superb examples of biological engineering. Their exceptional qualities can be fully appreciated only by close microscopic examination.

THE FINS

Fish usually possess two sets of paired fins (the pectorals and the pelvics), and two single ones (though they may be divided into finlets), the so-called median fins consisting of the dorsal and the anal, plus the single caudal complex. In addition, some fish—for example, characins such as piranhas and tetras—possess a "second" dorsal fin. This is called the adipose fin, and it can be a small, singular structure (as in characins) or a more elaborate one (as in some catfishes). Either way, the term "adipose fin" is misleading, since adipose suggests that these fins—the function of which is not clearly understood—are fat stores or fatty in composition, which, generally speaking, they are not. Some authorities regard the dorsal as two separate fins: an anterior one (the first dorsal, made up of one or more rigid, unbranched spines) and a posterior one (the second dorsal, made up largely or exclusively of soft, usually branched, rays, sometimes preceded by a spine-like structure composed of a bundle of fused rays).

While adhering to this basic format—which also includes an assortment of unbranched spines and branched soft rays—fins have undergone major modifications during the course of evolution. In some cases, these modifications have been so extreme that the resulting structures are difficult to recognize as fins at all. The pelvics of gouramis belonging to the genera *Trichogaster* and *Colisa* for example have evolved into long, hairlike feelers that are virtually useless for locomotion or balance. In other fish, such as the seahorses with their upright posture, some fins have actually disappeared altogether and the locomotory functions of the caudal fin have been assumed by the dorsal. In livebearers, the anal fin of males has been modified, through natural selection, into an intromittent sexual organ.

The possibility of transforming fins through selective breeding has been exploited by breeders of ornamental fish for many years (a few centuries in the case of goldfish), and has resulted in a plethora of commercial varieties much sought after within the hobby. The most frequently encountered variations occur in the most popular species such as guppies, swordtails, platies, angels, Siamese fighters and goldfish. In most cases, the modifications consist of enlarged fins, while in others, such as Ranchu and Lionhead (varieties of goldfish), these modifications include the total elimination of the dorsal fin and the doubling of both the anal and caudal fins.

THE SCALES

Scales can be categorized into four basic types: placoid, cosmoid, ganoid, and cycloid.

Placoid scales are usually found in sharks, rays and their relatives. The term "dermal denticles" often (but inadequately, in biological terms) applied to sharks refers to modified placoid scales.

Cosmoid scales are frequently encountered in fossil fishes. Modern-day lungfishes have scales that have evolved from the basic cosmoid design.

Ganoid scales are found in some of the more "primitive" aquarium fishes, such as gars, bowfins and birchirs. This type of scale is generally rhomboid-shaped with an articulated joint between each scale.

Cycloid—also known as ctenoid—scales are possessed by the vast majority of bony fishes. They overlap each other, rather like roof tiles. Also typical of these scales is a spinous posterior margin.

THE GILLS

Gills are remarkable structures that act as super-efficient gas exchangers. They are constructed of finely divided, thin, platelike structures or lamellae (filaments), with each of these being further divided into even finer lamellae. The lamellae are served by a rich blood supply. Oxygen from the water diffuses across the gill membrane into the bloodstream, whence it is taken to the heart and then around the fish's body. As it circulates, it supplies tissues with oxygen and picks up waste carbon dioxide. As the carbon dioxide-rich, deoxygenated blood is returned to the gill lamellae, the toxic carbon dioxide diffuses out and new oxygen diffuses in.

This mechanism works perfectly for most species. However, not all fish live in oxygen-rich waters. Some, including the well-known gouramis and fighters as well as many catfish, inhabit waters that are either permanently or seasonally deficient in oxygen. Were such species to rely exclusively on their gills for their oxygen supply, they would, quite simply, asphyxiate. Through time, these species have evolved a variety of mechanisms that assure them of an adequate oxygen supply and an efficient carbon dioxide elimination mechanism. In catfish, for example, part of the gut can be used for this purpose, while in gouramis and other anabantoids, some of the gills have actually been reduced and the resulting space in the gill chamber has become occupied by the labyrinth, a convoluted, blood-rich organ that allows these fish to inhale oxygen direct from the air and expel carbon dioxide in the form of a bubble.

In addition to "breathing," gills also perform another vitally important function. They are one of the two main organs (the other one being the kidneys) via which ammonia, a highly toxic metabolic waste product generated by fish, is expelled from the body.

THE LATERAL LINE OF THE COMMON GOLDFISH (CARRASIUS AURATUS VAR.) CAN BE SEEN RUNNING THE LENGTH OF ITS BODY.

THE SWIMBLADDER

The swimbladder is the main buoyancy mechanism used by bony fishes, although the actual composition of the body tissues may also play a part in maintaining buoyancy. In many books, the swimbladder is referred to as the air bladder. Strictly speaking, though, both terms are inaccurate, for the bladder is not used for swimming and, though it contains the three main atmospheric gases, i.e., oxygen, carbon dioxide and nitrogen, their relative percentages are different to those found in air. A more appropriate term would therefore be "gas bladder."

The gas bladder enables a fish to control its buoyancy by adjusting the amount of gas it contains. This movement of gas enables a fish to acquire neutral buoyancy—

it neither sinks nor floats—which is the least energy-costly state for any animal that lives in water.

However, for benthic (bottom-dwelling) species, the presence of gas in the bladder would present them with a metabolic disadvantage in that they would need to expend large amounts of energy just to remain on the bottom. Not surprisingly therefore, such species have either a reduced gas bladder or no bladder at all.

Besides using it as a buoyancy mechanism, certain fish can use the gas bladder either to produce sound, or as an organ to receive ("hear") sound.

THE LATERAL LINE SYSTEM

The lateral line system is a sensory apparatus that reacts to wave vibrations in the water. This helps a fish detect potential prey, predators, or any submerged objects. It is made up of two main components: the cephalic lateral line canals, located in the head, and the lateral line, which runs longitudinally along the body.

Of the two, the lateral line is more easily visible to the naked eye as a row of dots. These may extend the whole length of the body, either in a single, usually gently undulating or curved line, as an anterior (shorter and higher) section separated by several lines of scales from a posterior portion, or as a single line that may extend only partially down the body. Each "dot" is, in fact, a pore (a neuromast) containing a number of sensory hair cells, supporting cells, and nerve endings. It is these that are stimulated by vibrations, enabling a fish to be aware of changes in its environment.

TEMPERATURE CONTROL

Fish are usually referred to as poikilothermic or "cold-blooded." More accurately, they are "ectothermic." The term cold-blooded suggests that the temperature of a fish's blood is consistently cold, irrespective of external conditions, just as endothermic animals—humans, other mammals and birds—have "warm blood" irrespective of the ambient temperature. In reality, it means that the temperature of a fish's blood fluctuates to match that of its environment, so, in coldwater conditions, a fish's blood temperature is low; in tropical, warm-water environments, the blood temperature is warm.

While the vast majority of fish are ectotherms, a few—most notably, tuna and their closest relatives—are endotherms, conserving internal body heat generated by their constantly active swimming muscles.

Natural Habitats

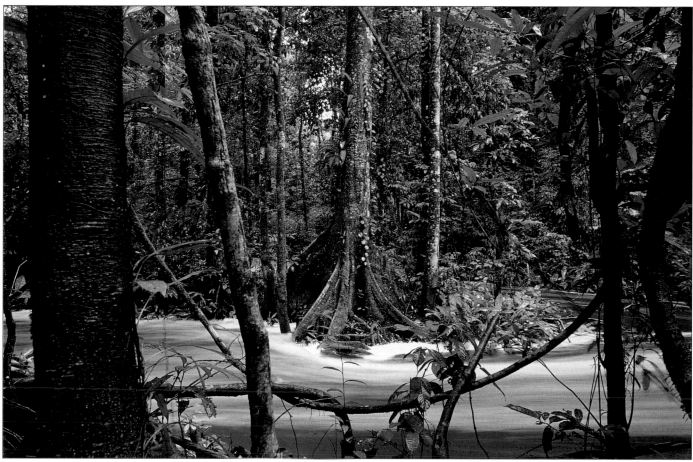

Fish occupy habitats as diverse as the so-called Arctic "wastes," tiny mudpools no bigger than an elephant's footprint, the coldest, darkest recesses of the midocean abysses, and the illuminated, warm, crystal-clear shallows of coral reefs.

A little over 70 percent of the planet's surface is covered by seas and oceans. Add to this the areas taken up by landmasses, and what is left—the freshwater areas—appears meager, especially given that four fifths of the world's freshwater is tied up in glaciers, polar ice sheets and ground water. However, the tiny fraction that remains still includes the vast expanses of the Amazon basin, the inland "seas" such as the African Rift Lakes and the Great Lakes, plus all the other countless rivers, lakes, streams, rivulets and ditches that help to make up an environment of untold richness and potential. Of the available freshwater—about 30,000 cubic miles (125,000 cubic km)—four

fifths is contained in some 40 lakes. The remaining one fifth is accounted for by all the other bodies of freshwater, including mighty rivers such as the Amazon, Yangtze and Mississippi.

THE AMAZON AND ITS TRIBUTARIES

One fifth may not sound like much, but it is estimated that the Amazon is fed by no fewer than 1,100 tributaries, together disgorging enough water into the Atlantic Ocean for it to be detectable some 100 miles (160km) from land. It takes a largish European river such as the Thames a whole year to match the volume of water that flows out of the Amazon in a single day. While the main Amazon river system is an awe-inspiring 4,000 miles (6,400km) or so long, even this pales into insignificance when compared with the approximate 50,000 miles (80,500km) of navigable waters spread out over the basin itself. If this isn't enough to convey the scale of this giant river, consider that the island of Marajó, which nestles between the banks of the Amazon's gaping mouth, is approximately the same size as Switzerland.

A closer look at the nature of Amazonian water itself reveals that the one thing it lacks is uniformity. It could be said that there are as many Amazons as there are tributaries. Nowhere is this more vividly illustrated than around the city of Manáus, in Brazil. Here, the two mighty tributaries of the Amazon proper—the Rio Negro and the Solimões—converge. The dark-stained, but clear, sediment-free, black waters of the Rio Negro meet the sediment-laden, milky-tea-col-

LAKE TANGANYIKA IN EAST AFRICA IS HOME TO MANY ENDEMIC CICHLIDS.

ored waters of the Solimões in a dramatic confluence known as the "Encontro das Aguas," or "Meeting of the Waters." Such is the awesome power of these two tributaries, that their distinct waters flow side by side for some 50 miles (80km) downriver, only gradually mixing until they form the uniformly brown waters of the lower Amazon.

The main channels of the Amazonian tributaries yield remarkably few aquarium fishes. The waters here are too open and fast-flowing for most of the small species adored by aquarists worldwide. Yet move away from these major arteries, and a spellbinding world unfolds. This is the world of creeks (agarapé), flooded

blackwater forests (igapó), and the floodplain lakes of the turbid tributaries (várzea). Differing in depth and expanse—and even in degree of permanence—the waters of these habitats show a range of properties from clear, almost uncolored, waters, through yellow-stained waters, to the true blackwaters for which the Rio Negro is famous, and the turbid, silty waters bordering the Solimões. The chemical composition also varies, not just from place to place, but from season to season.

Not surprisingly, such a diverse assortment of habitats supports an unknown, and perhaps unknowable, complement of species, each subtly tuned and in harmony with its environment. It is quite impossible to give an accurate figure for the number of fish species that the Amazon holds. New species are constantly being discovered, numerous others remain to be discovered, and there are some that may never be discovered—such is the immensity of the basin and the inaccessibility of some of its remotest backwaters. A rough estimate would place the number of fish species distributed throughout the Amazon at somewhere around 3,000.

THE AFRICAN RIFT LAKES

In sharp contrast to the soft, acid waters of the Amazon, those of the African Rift Lakes are hard and alkaline. Just as Amazonian tributaries are very different from each other, so are the African Rift Lakes. However, the range of species they contain, while being much wider than indicated in popular aquarium literature, is restricted when compared with that of the Amazon basin. Within the aquarium hobby, the African Rift Lakes are famous for their cichlids, most notably the mouthbrooding species, which include the rockdwellers or mbuna.

Of the three lakes making up the African Rift Lakes, Lake Tanganyika is, at 4,800 feet (1,470m), by far the deepest, followed by Lake Malawi at 2,300 feet (700m) and, finally, Lake Victoria at no more than 145 feet (45m). (Lake Tanganyika is in fact the second deepest lake in the world, the deepest being the Siberian Lake Baikal at 5,315 feet/1,620m.) Other statistics are equally impressive. Lake Tanganyika, for example, is about 420 miles (675km) long and around 85 miles (140km) wide, while Lake Malawi is around 360 miles (580km) long and 50 miles (80km) wide, and Lake Victoria is approximately 200 miles (320km) long and only slightly less (about 185 miles/300km) wide. In terms of surface area; Lake Victoria is the largest at around 26,540 sq. miles (68,800 sq. km)—making it the third largest in the world, behind the Caspian Sea and Lake Superior—followed by Lake Tanganyika at around 13,120 sq. miles (34,000 sq. km) and Lake Malawi at 11,570 sq. miles (30,000 sq. km). In practice, though not necessarily by strict definition, the African Rift Lakes can be considered inland seas.

Alkalinity—a feature all three lakes share—varies from lake to lake and between areas within each lake: approximate pH value 7.8–8.5 in Lake Malawi, pH 8.0–9.5 in Lake Tanganyika, and pH 7.1–9.0 in Lake Victoria. A further common characteristic is that the cichlid species of all three lakes are largely endemic, being found in these lakes and nowhere else. Each lake in turn has its own array of endemic cichlids. The world-famous *Pseudotropheus*, *Aulonocara* and *Melanochromis* species for example are endemic to Lake Malawi; the equally celebrated *Lamprologus*, *Neolamprologus* and *Julidochromis* species are restricted to Lake Tanganyika; and the very distinct *Haplochromis* species occur only in Lake Victoria.

OTHER HABITATS

While the Amazon and the African Rift Lakes may be the two best-known regions, there are others that aquarists should know about. Mexico, for example, is particularly rich in livebearing species, with the fascinating goodeids (family Goodeidae)—sometimes referred to as Mexican Livebearers—endemic to the country. Tropical far-eastern stillwater regions are particularly rich in labyrinth species, including all the *Trichogaster* gouramis and the numerous species of "fighters" (genus *Betta*), while Papua New Guinea, Irian Jaya, neighboring countries, and Australia, are home to the impressive rainbowfishes.

The Indian subcontinent is a relative newcomer in supplying fish for the international aquarium hobby (although it is the home of many barbs and the *Colisa* gouramis). However, its vastness encompasses a wide diversity of aquatic habitats, from torrential mountain streams to still, weed-choked waters. Not surprisingly, the range of species found in its waters is extremely varied. The habitats found in mainland China are equally varied, encompassing (as in India) everything from mountain streams to still, heavily vegetated waters, with the added variable of a larger temperature range: from cold, oxygen-rich waters at one end of the spectrum, to permanently warm waters at the other. As a result, China has a vast range of fish species, some of which began to reach the hobby market during the early 1990s. Similar in terms of habitat diversity (though

not in temperature or size) is Sri Lanka, whose tropical waters are home to numerous magnificent species of barb, such as the Ruby Barb (*Barbus nigrofasciatus*) and the Cherry Barb (*B. titteya*), along with some fascinating anabantoids such as the Combtail (*Belontia signata*) and *Malpulutta kretseri*.

In the United States, most of the aquarium fish natural habitats—while varying in water composition, levels of oxygenation and intensity of flow—are temperate, rather than tropical, with some subtropical areas in the extreme south, where species such as the Everglades Pygmy Sunfish (*Elassoma evergladei*) originate.

Although they may differ significantly in temperature, softness/hardness, acidity/alkalinity, level of oxygenation and a host of other parameters, the habitats mentioned so far are all strictly freshwater. So-called "freshwater" aquarium fish are, however, also found in waters whose salt content (mainly sodium chloride) varies from mere traces to almost fully marine levels. Such waters are found in estuaries and mangrove swamps and are referred to as "brackish." Perhaps the best-known freshwater aquarium species originating from such waters are the scats (*Scatophagus*), monos (*Monodactylus*), glassfish (*Parambassis* or *Chanda*) and archerfish (*Toxotes*), but there are others, many of which are featured in the Aquarium Fish section (pp.82–297).

Aquarium fish come from many (and diverse) corners of the globe, not all of which I have referred to. The result is that aquarists have an almost inexhaustible range of species from which they can stock their aquaria.

MANGROVES PROVIDE THE COASTLINE WITH VITAL NATURAL PROTECTION AGAINST HURRICANES, AS WELL AS OFFERING SUITABLE HABITATS FOR MANY SPECIES OF FISH.

FISH CONSERVATION

Fish conservation involves conserving habitats as diverse as coral reefs and rainforests. Without the survival of these habitats, species conservation can only, at best, achieve modest success. Sometimes species-centered conservation programs—in which species are conserved in aquaria rather than the wild—are the only option available. Where this is the case, as with the Gold Sawfin Goodeid (*Skiffia francesae*) from Mexico, such programs can make the difference between survival, albeit in captivity, and extinction.

INTERNATIONAL MEASURES

The International Union for the Conservation of Nature and Natural Resources (IUCN) publishes and updates the "Red List," which categorizes species according to the levels of threat that they are actually (or believed to be) under in the wild. The current Red List classifies animals and plants in the following categories: Extinct, Extinct in the Wild, Critically Endangered, Endangered, Vulnerable, Lower Risk (subdivided into Conservation Dependent, Near Threatened, and Least Concern), Data Deficient and Not Evaluated.

According to this list, there are just over 80 species of bony fishes that are either Extinct or Extinct in the Wild and just over 700 considered to fall within one or other of the higher categories of threat, i.e. Critically Endangered, Endangered and Vulnerable. Within the Lower Risk and Data Deficient categories, there are nearly 350 further species.

THE GOLD SAWFIN GOODEID (SKIFFIA FRANCESAE) BECAME EXTINCT IN THE WILD ONLY A DECADE AFTER ITS DISCOVERY IN 1978. IT CONTINUES TO SURVIVE IN CAPTIVITY, HOWEVER.

At the time of writing, the revised fish list details had not yet been determined. However, it is known from previous lists that several barbs (family Cyprinidae), livebearers (families Poeciliidae and Goodeidae), bony tongues (family Osteoglossidae), and lungfishes (family Ceratodontidae) are among freshwater species generally regarded as "aquarium" fish that are, and will be, officially classified under one or other of the IUCN Red List categories. These, however, represent only a small number of the grand total, which also includes marine species.

The IUCN Red List is compiled exclusively on scientific criteria and for scientific purposes. The Convention on International Trade in Endangered Species of Wild Fauna and Flora (CITES), on the other hand, is concerned with trade in threatened species. CITES compiles three Appendixes that list known (or perceived) levels of threat to wild populations as a result of trade. Species listed in Appendix I "are endangered … and commercial import, export and sale is normally prohibited." Some flexibility exists over prohibition in that specimens may be legally traded if they have been bred in captivity and are able to fulfil certain CITES criteria. There are currently only eight fish species listed in Appendix I. These are the famous Coelacanth (*Latimeria chalumnae*), the Dragon Fish (*Scleropages formosus*), two sturgeons, a cyprinid, a schilbeid catfish, a catostomid (sucker) and a scianid (croaker or drum).

The species included in Appendix II "are vulnerable but … may be traded commercially provided that import or export permits have been obtained." The controls imposed by Appendix II listing are designed to protect wild populations of the listed species so that they don't slip into the endangered (Appendix I) category. Currently, only five fish species are listed in Appendix II: the Australian Lungfish (*Neoceratodus forsteri*), the Atlantic Sturgeon (*Acipenser oxyrhynchus*), the Paddlefish (*Polyodon spathulae*), the Arapaima or Pirarucu (*Arapaima gigas*) and the African Blind Barb (*Caecobarbus geertsi*).

Appendix III lists species that are not deemed to be under major threat. Trade in Appendix III species is controlled on a domestic, rather than an international, basis. Nevertheless, countries can call upon collaboration from other countries should they feel that trade needs to be internationally controlled.

The CITES Appendixes are continuously evolving and should not be considered as permanent diktats. Species are proposed for inclusion, deletion or transfer according to the changing status of wild populations. The species referred to above are therefore those that were included at the time of writing. Major changes are not expected overnight, but some will occur over time.

Conservation efforts extend well beyond the IUCN and CITES lists. Even in cases where CITES permits the legal export of listed species, as occurs with a number of farms that breed the Dragon Fish, importing countries may impose their own controls if they feel that imports could endanger the status of their native fish populations. History has shown such measures to be occasionally essential and often desirable. For example, the widespread and unrestricted introduction of species such as the Mosquito Fish (*Gambusia holbrooki*) as a biological means of malaria control in the first half of the twentieth century not only failed to eradicate the disease but also drove some native species to the verge of extinction. Similarly, the introduction of the Nile Perch (*Lates niloticus*) into Lake Victoria has wreaked untold damage among the endemic haplochromine cichlid populations.

THE EMERALD-BACKED CICHLID (ABOVE) OF LAKE VICTORIA IS THREATENED IN THE WILD BY THE INTRODUCTION OF THE NILE PERCH (BELOW).

CAPTIVE BREEDING

While some countries impose bans on the collection and export of threatened species for aquaria, others adopt a different approach. Sri Lanka, for example, is very rich in both freshwater and marine fish species, many of the former being endemic to the island. Among the best known of these are several barbs, most notably the Ruby Barb (*Barbus nigrofasciatus*), the Cherry Barb (*B. titteya*), Cuming's Barb (*B. cumingi*) and (more obscure) the Bandula Barb (*B. bandula*). In the past (and despite the availability of commercially bred varieties of the first three species in other countries) demand for wild-caught Sri Lankan specimens, rather than commercial varieties with more intense coloration or longer fins, remained at a high level. This, allied to habitat destruction and pollution, raised concern within Sri Lanka for the longterm survival of these and other species in sufficient quantities for sustainable harvesting.

As a result, in the mid-1990s, captive breeding programs were set up by a number of exporters under the aegis of the Sri Lankan authorities. They were permitted to collect sufficient specimens of the first three species of barb to set up broodstock populations. Over a number of years, the exporters bred these species on their farms—monitored by a government agency—

until stocks were deemed to be sufficiently high to resume their exportation under a quota system. The Bandula Barb was apparently "rescued" from its only known, and very restricted, locality which appeared to be under environmental threat. Some of the collected specimens were placed in the hands of an experienced breeder/exporter who, over a period of time, was able to produce several thousand specimens. The species was saved from extinction, but, owing to the precarious state of its natural habitat, controlled reintroduction to the wild has only recently been possible.

In the case of another endangered Sri Lankan species, the beautiful anabantoid *Malpulutta kretseri* (Labyrinth Fish), it was the exporters themselves who proposed that no specimens be exported until a sufficient level of captive-bred stock had been achieved. This being a relatively slow-breeding species, the program was expected to take several years, so it may well be that the first exports of captive-bred *Malpulutta* will become available some time during the first decade of the new millennium.

In another fish-producing country, Singapore, as well as in other parts of the Far East, the legendary Dragon Fish (*Scleropages formosus*) is held in high esteem, since owning one is believed to bring the owner health and wealth. It is also a species that has long been listed under CITES Appendix I as endangered (although there does not appear to be conclusive proof that this is the case). As mentioned earlier, Appendix I species may be traded, but only if certain strict criteria are met, one of these being proof that the specimens in question have been bred in captivity for at least two generations. In order to document proof, the government of Singapore, through its then Primary Production Department (PPD)—now the Agri-food and Veterinary Authority (AVA)—set up a collaborative captive breeding project with a local breeder/exporter, which, over a number of years, resulted in the certified data required by CITES for legal exports of the species to recommence. As a result, legally certified captive-bred Singaporean Dragon Fish first became available for export on December 4, 1994. The first batch consisted of 300 Red Dragons, which were exported to Japan. Since then, many thousands have been exported worldwide. Each specimen is implanted with a uniquely coded microchip and is sold with a government-issued Certificate of Identity. This certificate carries the same 30-digit code that can be read by a scanner, authenticating the identity of the fish and its official source (see Bibliography). Since then, other farms in Singapore and elsewhere have applied for, and been granted, CITES approval for exports of this species.

A CAPTIVE-BRED DRAGON FISH (SCLEROPAGES FORMOSUS): AN ENDANGERED SPECIES CITED UNDER APPENDIX I OF CITES.

HOBBYIST PARTICIPATION

Captive breeding programs will, no doubt, continue to play a large part in the conservation of endangered species the world over. Aquarists have contributed, and continue to contribute, to these projects in several very important ways. For example, in the case of *Skiffia francesae*, it was (and is) the dedicated efforts of aquarists belonging to specialist livebearer societies in the U.S. and Europe that have ensured the continued survival of the species; repeated attempts at rediscovering this fish in the wild having failed.

In the case of *Malpulutta kretseri*, aquarists belonging to the Anabantoid Association of Great Britain played a very important role by providing the Sri Lankan exporter involved in the government-approved program with details of the maintenance and breeding techniques that they had successfully employed in their own aquaria.

Groups of aquarists that specialize in the breeding of threatened species exist in virtually all the leading fishkeeping countries. They form part of both national and international networks, sometimes working exclusively with other aquarists, sometimes in collaboration with scientific institutions, public aquaria and other official bodies. Without a doubt, today's aquarists have a very important part to play in fish conservation.

INDUSTRY PARTICIPATION

The modern-day ornamental aquatic industry also plays its part in fish, as well as habitat, conservation. As conservationists began embracing the concept of sustainable use of natural resources as vital to the conservation of species and their habitats, so did the ornamental aquatic industry, particularly from the mid-1990s. Today, the industry is actively involved in conservation and sustainable use projects as diverse as the successful Ocean Voice International and International Marinelife Alliance net-training programs in the Philippines (designed to replace cyanide collecting with net collecting), and the development of sustainable fisheries strategies in the Amazon. The closeness of the collaboration between the industry and Bio-Amazonia Conservation International is such that the conservation organization now uses the slogan: "Buy an ornamental fish; help save the rainforest."

In 1999 the Amazonian fish exporters set up a scheme under which each box of ornamental fish leaving Manáus was to carry a conservation "levy" or fee—half of which was to be paid by the exporters and half by the importers. This levy was designed to raise many thousands of U.S. dollars every year, all of which were to be invested in research on Amazonian fish species and their sustainable harvesting, as well as analysis of their fundamental importance to the economies of the human riverine communities.

COMMERCIAL BREEDING
OF AQUARIUM FISH

Over 90 percent of all freshwater aquarium and pond fish are bred in captivity. The figure for marines is the reverse, with considerably less than 10 percent (probably around 5 percent) being commercially bred for the hobby. At first sight, the relatively low percentage of captive-bred marines might appear worrying, but the marine hobby is only approximately one tenth the size of the freshwater one. It is estimated that world demand for marine aquarium fish species amounts to something like 70–100 tonnes per year. The food fish industry accounts for around 100 million tonnes annually. Even the bycatch—the "waste" fish that are thrown overboard by trawlers—accounts for some 17 million tonnes every year.

Wild-caught fish for the marine aquarium hobby are collected from reefs spread out over an area of some 150,000 sq. miles (400,000 sq.km), thus avoiding to a large extent excessive pressure on individual reefs. Many programs are also now in place—and more are being developed—either to ensure that reefs do not suffer overexploitation, or to reverse the effects of past overexploitation.

Some of the programs include fish captive breeding or invertebrate culture projects *in situ*, and these, allied to *ex situ* programs as well as improved knowledge and husbandry techniques, are resulting in successes with species that had hitherto been considered impossible or very difficult to breed in captivity, such as marine angelfishes (Pomacanthidae). These successes are certain to continue and will gradually raise the percentage of commercially captive-bred marine species well above the current, modest level.

On the freshwater side, while the vast majority of so-called coldwater species and varieties available to aquarists and pondkeepers are bred commercially, a small number are still collected from the wild. In the main these consist of a restricted selection of Asiatic temperate species that have become available in recent years and for which demand is likely to remain low at least for the foreseeable future.

Most tropical freshwater species and varieties are bred in captivity for the hobby. However, the majority of the 10 percent or so of all freshwater species that are wild-collected are tropical in origin; coldwater species probably account for only about 1–2 percent. In some cases, it is perfectly feasible to breed these wild-caught species in captivity, and in quite large numbers. However, costs and consequently sale prices can be high when compared with those of wild-caught specimens. Certain species are therefore still usually wild-caught. The Sucking Loach or Chinese Algae Eater (*Gyrinocheilus aymonieri*) is one such species. It occurs in great abundance in its native waters in Thailand (not China as the species name implies) and is therefore widely available at reasonable prices. While it can be bred in captivity, only the golden and mottled varieties are captive-bred on a commercial basis; wild-type, i.e. "wild-colored," specimens are still collected from Thai hill-streams. Similarly, the abundance of the strikingly colored Clown Loach (*Botia macracantha*) from Indonesia makes captive breeding pointless. Shortly after the spawning season, gigantic shoals of juveniles occur downstream from the spawning grounds, and it is from these that the existing world demand for the species can be met without, apparently, affecting total populations.

The Cardinal Tetra (*Paracheirodon axelrodi*) is another popular aquarium species that occurs in vast numbers, this time in the Rio Negro basin in Brazil. During the middle to late 1990s, severe droughts were caused by the Pacific climatic phenomenon known as El Niño, and Cardinals became unavailable although they were not wiped out. As their native waters receded, the fish

PART OF THE OUTDOOR HOLDING AREA IN A SINGAPOREAN FISH FARM.

▲ *Cardinal Tetra (Paracheirodon axelrodi), a species obtained from the wild in Brazil, but also bred successfully in captivity.*
A bank of cartridge filter canisters and ultra-violet sterilizers. ▶

retreated into areas that were difficult to get to or too far from the fishermen's bases to make the harvesting exercise economically viable. As numbers of wild-caught Cardinals gradually dried up, captive-bred stocks—primarily from the Czech Republic—took over. They were more expensive, but at least they were obtainable. Eventually, as the El Niño effects gradually disappeared and normal conditions returned in the Rio Negro, wild-caught Cardinals once more became the main source of supply.

As can be seen, when it comes to deciding whether or not to breed a particular species in captivity, it is not just the ease of breeding that needs to be taken into consideration. Economics and relative abundance in the wild are also important factors, alongside fecundity, speed of maturation and size. As a result, while highly prolific and abundant species like the three cited above are largely collected from the wild, other, less productive and sometimes more expensive, species are mainly bred in captivity. Captive breeding is also favored if the species in question shows inherent variability, as happens with the Angelfish (*Pterophyllum scalare*) and Discus (*Symphysodon discus* and *S. aequifasciatus*). All three, including the three main nominal subspecies of *S. aequifasciatus*, are still collected from the wild, but this accounts for only a small percentage of the total numbers available to hobbyists, the vast majority now being produced commercially by breeders in a number of countries, including Germany, the United States, Singapore, Thailand, Taiwan and Malaysia.

Where the wild-type of a species has been completely replaced by cultivated varieties—as has happened with many of the most popular aquarium fishes such as guppies, swordtails, platies, mollies, Siamese fighters, goldfish and numerous others—world demand for these fancy varieties is of course met exclusively by captive-bred stocks.

BREEDING ESTABLISHMENTS

Breeding aquarium and pond fish to meet aquarists' ever-growing demands is big business these days. Commercial ornamental fish breeding farms are now found in numerous temperate and tropical regions. In Japan, for example, Koi farms exist in many areas of the country, particularly Niigata, where the very best pedigree specimens are bred to be distributed the world over. This can be such a specialist activity that some families or breeding enterprises dedicate all their energies and expertise to the production of a single bloodline or variety such as, say, the Kohaku (a red and white variety of Koi). In China, some communities are equally dedicated to the production of a single variety of goldfish—the Oranda, for example.

Apart from these, there are less specific specialist breeders, concentrating on, say, a range of varieties of goldfish, or guppy, or Koi, or barbs. Even more wide-ranging are those breeders that specialize in, for instance, livebearers, or the "bread-and-butter" species and varieties, i.e. the most popular types.

The size of breeding establishment also varies widely. In the Czech Republic, for example, large numbers of tropical fish are bred in modestly sized premises, sometimes consisting of a single, medium-sized room. Such facilities dictate that careful thought be given to the types of fish chosen. These need to be either small—guppies, tetras, etc.—or types that can generate a reasonable return, such as discus or dwarf cichlids. Owing to the compact size of most of these breeding units, which can also be quite expensive to run, large or medium-sized inexpensive species are usually left for other, larger, breeding establishments to handle. This is where the major producers—Singapore, Malaysia, the United States, Sri Lanka and Israel—really excel, although they also breed small and high-revenue-generating species and varieties.

The largest share of the international demand for aquarium fish (around 30 percent) is met by Singapore, which is sometimes referred to as the "ornamental fish capital of the world." Other

THE TIGER BARB (BARBUS TETRAZONA)—SEE DESCRIPTION P.169—HAS BEEN BRED IN VAST NUMBERS BY AQUARISTS AND COMMERCIAL BREEDERS SINCE THE 1930S.

countries, such as Malaysia, also hold a large share of the market. Some of the apparently Singapore-bred fish that we keep in our tanks have, in fact, been bred in Singaporean-owned facilities in Malaysia.

Such is the global demand for freshwater ornamentals that some of the farms dedicated to captive breeding are huge. In Florida, some of the largest producers own not just a main farm, but "satellite" farms as well. Young fish, bred at the main farm, are regularly flown to these satellites for growing on and then reflown back to base once they attain sale size. Despite the vast numbers and varieties of fish bred and reared in this way, most Florida-produced tropicals are destined for the home (U.S.) market.

A number of countries employ a version of the satellite scheme operated by some Florida breeders. Whereas in Florida both the main farm and the satellites are owned by the same breeding establishment, in some countries the main breeder supplies juvenile fish to one or more independently owned satellite farms. They are contracted to grow the fish on to marketable size for the main breeder, who then buys back the fish prior to export. In this way, breeders that may have restricted facilities for rearing fish, but may be very good at breeding them, can greatly increase their production.

Another commercial breeding system is the community-based farm, as in some *kibbutzim* in Israel. A number of breeders contribute to a centralized breeding/exporting cooperative. Again, as with the satellite systems, this arrangement results in large numbers of fish being bred under controlled conditions, with each type being cultured by specialists.

A TYPICAL CAPTIVE-BRED SPECIES, THE BLUE VARIEGATED DELTA GUPPY (POECILIA RETICULATA).

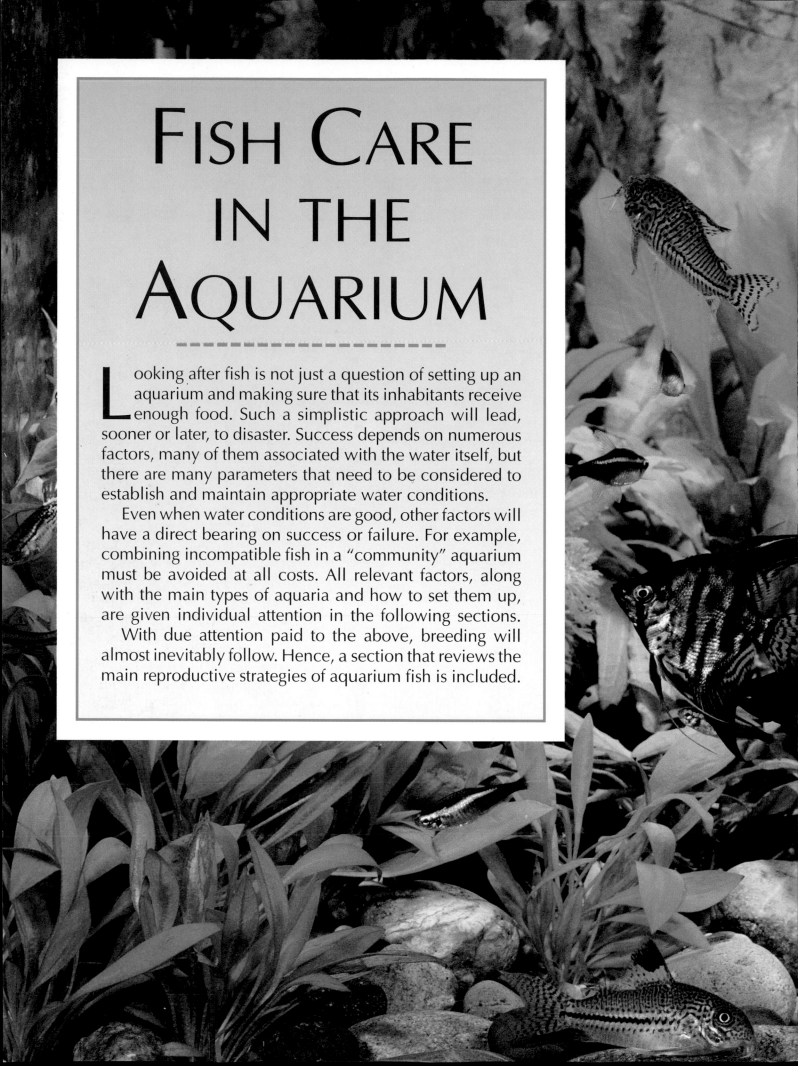

FISH CARE IN THE AQUARIUM

Looking after fish is not just a question of setting up an aquarium and making sure that its inhabitants receive enough food. Such a simplistic approach will lead, sooner or later, to disaster. Success depends on numerous factors, many of them associated with the water itself, but there are many parameters that need to be considered to establish and maintain appropriate water conditions.

Even when water conditions are good, other factors will have a direct bearing on success or failure. For example, combining incompatible fish in a "community" aquarium must be avoided at all costs. All relevant factors, along with the main types of aquaria and how to set them up, are given individual attention in the following sections.

With due attention paid to the above, breeding will almost inevitably follow. Hence, a section that reviews the main reproductive strategies of aquarium fish is included.

AQUARIUM SETUP AND MAINTENANCE

Today's freshwater aquarist has several thousand species and varieties to choose from. With such a diversity of shape, size, requirement and habit, it follows that there is no single, infallible aquarium setup that can cater for all aquarium fish. However, many species have broadly similar requirements and can be grouped together from the maintenance, if not always from the breeding, point of view.

This chapter deals with the main groupings and how to set up aquaria suited to each. For special requirements, refer to the individual entries in the Aquarium Fish section.

COLDWATER OR TROPICAL?

It is important to attempt to distinguish between coldwater fish on the one hand, and tropical fish on the other. The dividing line between one and the other is nowhere near as precise as the terms imply.

What, for example, constitutes cold water? There is no debate if the temperature is at one or other end of the scale: 50°F (10°C) is undoubtedly coldwater, just as 86°F (30°C) must be tropical. However, at what point does a coldwater environment cease to be so and become tropical in nature? Turning to the fish themselves, species and varieties such as koi and goldfish are universally referred to as coldwater fish: true enough of specimens kept in, say, northern Europe, but what of those kept in Singapore, or Fiji, or Hawaii, where the ambient temperature is firmly within the tropical part of the spectrum?

The survival of the traditional application of both terms to aquaria has to do with the origins of aquarium keeping as a leisure activity. For a long time the hobby was far more popular in western temperate regions than in the tropics. As a result, many of the terms that we use were coined from the temperate perspective. If a fish could be kept in an unheated aquarium in a temperate country, it could justifiably be regarded as "coldwater." Any species requiring additional heat would be regarded as "tropical."

As the hobby expanded, and imports of goldfish and koi from the temperate regions of China and from Japan became progressively more popular, the term coldwater could still be regarded as appropriate. Then, as large-scale breeding and export of these fish spread to the tropics, the coldwater label was retained, so that today goldfish and Koi bred in tropical countries are still referred to as coldwater fish.

In summary, the term "coldwater" is applied to those fish that may be kept in unheated aquaria in temperate zones. Those that require supplementary heat in these regions, either for routine maintenance or for breeding, are referred to as "tropical." Therefore, even in tropical countries, a goldfish is still regarded as a coldwater fish because it would require no heat if it were being kept in a temperate country. Similarly, angels are still universally regarded as tropical because they can only be kept in heated aquaria. Most of the time, this interpretation works perfectly well, but there are numerous exceptions, fish that are perfectly capable of surviving in unheated aquaria in many temperate zones but are traditionally regarded as tropical. The Paradise Fish (*Macropodus opercularis*), the Medaka (*Oryzias latipes*), the Mosquito Fish (*Gambusia affinis* and *G. holbrooki*) and the White Cloud Mountain Minnow (*Tanichthys albonubes*) are just a few of the many examples of fish that originate either in temperate zones with a relatively mild winter climate, or in the so-called subtropical regions.

COMMUNITY AND SPECIES AQUARIA

The term "community aquarium" is used for any setup that includes a range of species and/or varieties of fish and/or invertebrates that can live in harmony with each other. In its broadest sense, it can be applied to any type of community-containing aquarium, whether this is a coldwater one consisting of goldfish, Koi, shiners,

ALBINO PARADISE FISH (MACROPODUS OPERCULARIS VAR.)

minnows and the like, a tropical one consisting of guppies, Corydoras catfish, neons or cardinals, hatchetfish, and other peaceful species, or an equivalent marine system. Taking the definition a little further, it can also be applied to, say, an African Rift Lake cichlid community, an Amazonian species community, a brackish-water selection of compatible species, a reef fish community, a mixed collection of compatible marine fish and invertebrates, and so on.

To the hobbyist, the term "community aquarium" most usually denotes a setup containing a selection of compatible, modestly sized, hardy, freshwater tropical species. This is the type of aquarium that the majority of aquarists install when they first enter the hobby; it is also, globally, the most popular system, even among the more experienced hobbyists.

In contrast, a "species" aquarium is one set up, strictly speaking, to house specimens of a single species. In the case of species that have been developed into cultivated varieties, such as mollies or guppies, the tank often contains representatives of a number of varieties. However, if an attempt is being made to breed a specific species or variety then only representatives of the selected type are included. If, further, the type of fish being bred is a poeciliid livebearer, the selection of suitable female specimens is made very early on, that is, before they have been mated. The reason is that poeciliid livebearer females can store sperm and use these to fertilize a sequence of egg batches (as many as ten or more). Therefore, if mated by a male of the "wrong" type, an inseminated poeciliid female is virtually useless for line-breeding purposes. (This does not apply to all types of livebearer. Goodeids, for example, do not store sperm; and for egglayers of course, each spawning is a completely "new" and separate event.)

Sometimes, species tanks can look a little empty, especially if the fish in question is a surface or bottom dweller. Such aquaria are therefore often stocked with a second species, compatible in terms of behavior, but not breeding characteristics, which will occupy the "empty" level. Corydoras catfish, for example, are excellent "companion" choices for a wide range of other species.

BASIC AQUARIUM NEEDS

Every aquarium, irrespective of type or size, needs to provide a minimum number of essentials if fish and plants are going to thrive in it. The water needs to be of good quality and of the appropriate composition, the temperature must match the needs of the fish and plants, there must be sufficient oxygen for the aquarium inhabitants, and—where plants are being cultivated—the light must be of the right type, intensity and duration. Aquaria must also provide adequate shelter, especially for retiring species.

Water is, of course, at the very heart of aquarium keeping. In some ways aquarists are "water keepers" rather than fish keepers. New aquarists are sometimes surprised by this, seeing themselves in the first instance as fish guardians and doctors, but even a moment's consideration will indicate that looking after the fish is quite impossible without looking after the water. The water's importance is illustrated by an old—and perfectly valid—saying in the hobby: "Look after the water, and the water will look after your fish."

"Water keeping" involves the setting up and management of equipment designed to help us control the enclosed environment within our aquaria. The key pieces of essential equipment available for this purpose are filters, aerators, heaters, thermostats, and lighting systems.

Filters and Filtration

In the confined space of an aquarium, fish cannot swim away to a better, cleaner location—as they can in the wild—if water conditions deteriorate. Unless some way of treating their waste products is found, they will end up swimming in their own excreta (both liquid and solid). This is not only unpleasant; the highly toxic nature of some of the waste can actually kill the fish. In particular, fish and other aquatic creatures generate ammonia as one of their primary excretory products. Unfortunately, ammonia is highly toxic (although more so in hard, alkaline water than in soft, acid conditions). In fact, a concentration as low as 0.025 milligrams per liter (parts per million) can prove toxic to delicate fish, while a concentration of 0.2–0.5mg/l (parts per million) can kill many species in a relatively short time. Certain bacteria are capable of converting ammonia into nitrites, which, while being less toxic, can still cause problems at 0.1mg/l (parts per million). Other bacteria are able to oxidize nitrites into nitrates, which need to rise to around 50mg/l (parts per million) before they begin to become a serious threat to delicate species.

There is currently a degree of uncertainty concerning the actual identity of the bacteria responsible for this detoxification of wastes. Traditionally, bacteria belonging to the genus *Nitrosomas* have been regarded as the prime ammonia-to-nitrites converters, with *Nitrobacter* bacteria continuing the process from nitrites to nitrates. In the latter half of the 1990s, though, research results obtained in the United States threw this longheld belief into doubt, and while the matter has not yet been cleared up there is a distinct possibility that neither of these genera play key roles in the ammonia-nitrite-nitrate oxidation process.

Whatever the eventual answer turns out to be, there is no denying that there are some microorganisms universally present in aquarium water that are capable of detoxifying soluble fish wastes. The processes involved are aerobic and therefore require oxygen. The end products of the oxidation of ammonia are nitrates that, while being relatively nontoxic, can eventually become so if their concentration is allowed to rise indefinitely. Fortunately, there are also waterborne microorganisms that, through a series of biochemical reactions, have the effect of converting nitrates back into nitrogen which then diffuses back into the atmosphere. These processes—unlike the ones that convert ammonia to nitrites and nitrates—are anaerobic, and can therefore occur in the absence of oxygen.

Armed with this knowledge, aquarium equipment manufacturers have developed a wide range of filters that allow us to control waste treatment in our aquaria using similar principles to those employed in sewage treatment plants. Some filters are placed under the aquarium gravel, using the grains not just as mechanical sediment traps, but also as surfaces on which detoxifying bacteria and other micro-organisms can become established. Other filters use canisters, located either inside or outside the aquarium, to perform similar functions. In addition, many of these filters provide a third facility: highly porous media such as activated carbon or zeolite (clay-based granules) can adsorb (not absorb) certain chemicals, including ammonia, directly from the water.

Such media are said to perform "chemical filtration." Physical removal of solid wastes is termed "mechanical filtration," and bacteria-mediated detoxification is referred to as "biological filtration." Strictly speaking, only physical entrapment qualifies as filtration; the two other processes are more accurately categorized as purification or detoxification.

From the late 1980s onward, filter technology advanced enormously, as a result of which home aquaria can now be fitted not just with the long-established types of filter, such as undergravel, box or canister systems, but also with trickle, or wet/dry filters (both internal and external), high-speed sand filters, or even a system increasingly employed in commercial establishments (after a period of popularity with marine hobbyists)—fluidized bed filters. (Ultraviolet sterilizers, which are sometimes referred to as "filters," are not filters and will be discussed in the Health section, *see* p.62.)

Filter media, too, have undergone constant development and refinement to the extent that some of today's

MECHANICAL FILTRATION

water in — water out

mesh grid

module

filter floss

ceramic pieces or coarse pre-filter pad

CHEMICAL FILTRATION

pump and impeller housing

filter floss

activated carbon, resin, etc.

BIOLOGICAL FILTRATION

coarse biological medium—coral, gravel, sintered glass, etc.

THE THREE MAIN WAYS TO UTILIZE A CANISTER FILTER. THESE MODELS USE INTERNAL CLIP-TOGETHER MODULES, EACH HOLDING A DIFFERENT MEDIUM.

spray bar

filter wool or sand

filtered water returns
to main aquarium

plastic trays with
drainage holes

A KILLIFISH AQUARIUM INCORPORATING A FOAM SPONGE FILTER AND A COMBINED HEATER/THERMOSTAT UNIT.

▲ *A BASIC TRICKLER FILTER SYSTEM. UNITS SUCH AS THESE ARE SITED ABOVE THE MAIN TANK. THEY ARE SUPPLIED BY WATER PUMPED THROUGH A SPRAY BAR FROM A POWER FILTER. TRICKLE FILTERS HELP OXYGENATE THE WATER FLOWING THROUGH THEM AND SO INCREASE BACTERIAL ACTIVITY.*

▶ *A GRAVITY-FED RAPID SAND FILTER. THIS UNIT COMPRISES A SERIES OF COMPARTMENTS CONTAINING TRAYS, THROUGH WHICH THE TANK WATER IS PASSED. THE FILTER MEDIA INCLUDE COARSE, MEDIUM AND FINE FILTER SANDS.*

▼ *SMALL SINGLE-TRAY TRICKLE FILTERS SITED ABOVE THE TANK CAN BE USED EFFECTIVELY ON BREEDING AND REARING TANKS, OR WHERE IT IS IMPRACTICAL TO FIT A LARGE MULTI-TRAY UNIT.*

water flows by
gravity from
main aquarium

medium filter sand

fine filter sand

treated water
pumped out to
main aquarium

coarse filter sand

control valve

water in

media

water out

canister filter (positioned
below the tank) filled
with filter wool

super porous types can perform both nitrification (ammonia–nitrites–nitrates conversion) and denitrification (nitrates–nitrogen conversion) simultaneously. The old stalwart, filter floss or wool, is still around and still doing a great job as a mechanical medium. In between this and the latest "double-action" media, there is now a vast array of types and prices to choose from.

If a filter is well-matched with the job it needs to do, it will perform efficiently. However, push any system beyond its limits (commonly by overstocking or overfeeding), and not even the most efficient, sophisticated and expensive units will be able to cope. It is therefore vitally important to choose sensibly, seeking advice not just from manufacturers' literature but from experienced aquarists and professionals: speak to your dealer and explain your existing or proposed setup.

mains water in — →

nitrate-free water out →

filter pad   resin beads   filter pad

NITRATE FILTER. WHILE NITRATE IS NOWHERE NEAR AS TOXIC AS AMMONIA OR NITRITE, IT CAN STILL WEAKEN FISH AND LEAVE THEM VULNERABLE TO DISEASE. A RECHARGEABLE RESIN FILTER LIKE THIS ELIMINATES WHAT CAN BE UNDULY HIGH NITRATE LEVELS IN MAINS WATER IN SOME AREAS; AND ANY BUILDUP AS PART OF THE BIOLOGICAL FILTRATION CYCLE.

The accompanying diagrams will help you familiarize yourself with some of the most commonly encountered filtration systems. Although individual brands differ in details, the basic principles do not change. When choosing any system, it is advisable to opt for one that not only performs the mechanical/chemical/biological functions required (including, if at all possible, denitrification), but one that has capacity spare to cope with emergencies or increases in stocking levels.

Aeration

Aquarium aerators do not just supply oxygen to the water. They also eliminate toxic gases, such as carbon dioxide, into the air. It is not the actual bubbles of air produced by an aerating device that are the primary source of dissolved oxygen. Indeed, very little, if any, oxygen can dissolve out of a bubble in the few seconds that it takes to travel to the surface of the water. The finer the bubbles produced from an aerating unit, either via a diffuser or air stone or via a venturi built into a filter powerhead, the greater the likelihood of oxygen dissolving from these bubbles into the water. However, even in these cases, the primary role of the airstream is to cause disturbance of the water surface, thus facilitating the absorption of oxygen from the air above the aquarium into the water, and the diffusion of toxic gases (predominantly carbon dioxide) from the aquarium into the air.

An effective interchange between air and water also helps to oxidize some potentially harmful chemicals and render them safe. This is one of the reasons that stale or foul-smelling water (which has no place in an aquarium, of course!) will quickly improve under vigorous aeration. Another valuable function of aeration is that, by circulating water, it prevents "hotspots" and "coldspots," distributing the warm water generated by the heating unit evenly throughout the aquarium. This distribution is important, even in unheated aquaria: layering (stratification) of warm water above cooler water can occur in the absence of adequate circulation.

Since aeration depends to a large extent on the creation of water-surface turbulence, the mechanism by which this is achieved can vary. Air bubbles from an aerator or venturi can be replaced by some other form of "turbulence-generator," such as fine streams of water from a spraybar attached to the outflow of a power filter. Most modern-day power filters now come with detachable spraybars, thus offering the user maximum flexibility.

In the earlier days of aquarium keeping, undergravel filters were exclusively operated by introducing the air line from an aerator (with or without an attached air stone) down the filter uplift tube. Today, while this practice is still widespread, a powerhead is often fitted in the top (open) end of the filter uplift tube. The principle remains the same. A stream of air bubbles (in the case of an air-driven system) or water (in the case of a powerhead-driven one) rises within the uplift tube, and, in so doing, creates a negative pressure under the filter plate. Waste-laden water is drawn in from above the gravel, under the filter plate, whence it is eventually pulled up the filter tube and back into the aquarium.

Where powerheads are used instead of an air-operated system, it is possible to reverse the flow of water, down the uplift tube, into the space under the filter plate and upward through the gravel. One of the advantages claimed for this method (known as reverse

air in

airlift tube

gravel substrate

filter plate

A TANK FITTED WITH A CONVENTIONAL-FLOW UNDERGRAVEL FILTER. IN THIS SYSTEM, WATER IS DRAWN DOWN THROUGH THE FILTER BED (SUBSTRATE) AND RETURNED VIA THE AIRLIFT TUBE TO THE TOP OF THE AQUARIUM.

flow) is that solid matter is taken directly from the aquarium to the underplate space, thus reducing the degree of clogging of the gravel that inevitably occurs in normal flow filtration.

Aeration of aquaria can also be achieved, or enhanced, during the hours of daylight or under artificial illumination, with aquatic plants. In the presence of light, green plants perform a series of biochemical reactions collectively referred to as photosynthesis, one by-product of which is oxygen. This process (which is dealt with more fully in Aquarium Plants section), ceases at night. As a result, the oxygen level of a planted aquarium (even one that is not artificially aerated) will rise during the morning, reaching a peak in the early afternoon, and then gradually decrease during the hours of darkness, with the lowest concentration occurring during early morning. The actual quantities of oxygen dissolved in aquarium water depends on three main factors: the efficiency of the aerator, the surface area of the aquarium, and the temperature. A word of caution: some timid or retiring fish species do not welcome a turbulent environment, so this must be taken into account when planning the aeration system.

The cooler the water, the higher the level of oxygen that can be absorbed. The presence of pollutants and other compounds will also have an effect. In nature, many waters contain much less dissolved oxygen than the maximum (saturation) level possible, often as low as 2–5mg/l (parts per million)—a level that is too low for aquaria.

In aquaria, we should aim for levels close to saturation. We should also aim at keeping the dissolved-oxygen content as constant as possible. Both these criteria can be achieved with ease by employing an efficient aerating system, maintaining reasonable stocking levels, and following an adequate aquarium maintenance program. The table below gives approximate oxygen saturation levels for freshwater aquaria.

TEMPERATURE (°F/°C)	OXYGEN SATURATION LEVEL (mg/l—PARTS PER MILLION)
41/5	13.0–14.8
50/10	10.0–13.0
59/15	9.5–10.0
68/20	8.8–9.4
77/25	8.0–8.5
86/30	7.4–7.8

Although the highest levels of dissolved oxygen occur at the lowest temperatures, these are encountered only in home aquaria kept during winter in unheated rooms. Few aquaria experience such conditions. At the other end of the scale, aquaria designed for warmth-loving species such as Discus or mollies, are under threat of low oxygen saturation. Care with stocking such systems is therefore essential.

Temperature Control

Coldwater aquaria, as discussed earlier, do not require additional heat at any stage. Indeed, in warmer regions, particularly during the hottest periods of the year, they may even benefit from being kept cooler than the ambient temperature. In such cases, the use of an aquarium chilling unit may be found helpful, though not essential. There are some models available in a number of countries and professional advice from a specialist dealer should be sought before buying. Alternatively, switching the aquarium lights off during the hottest period of each day, ensuring that no direct sun hits the aquarium, vigorous aeration, and (even) floating a plastic bag with several ice cubes in it, may prove sufficient to lower the temperature by a few (and only a few) degrees.

In most homes, aquaria are kept in rooms that are either heated in winter—in those countries where this is necessary—or cooled by fans or air conditioners. Either way, the temperature of a coldwater aquarium will generally fall within acceptable limits without the need for additional heating or cooling. However, in the case of tropical setups, ambient (room) temperature is often several degrees below the optimum for fish, particularly in temperate zones (but the difference is rarely more than 15°F/8°C).

There are several ways in which an aquarium may be heated, and these methods may be direct or indirect. Space heating, where the room, rather than the aquarium, is heated to the required temperature, is an indirect method employed primarily by specialist hobbyists that have one or more rooms set aside exclusively for aquaria. Even in these cases, though, there is usually a backup direct system consisting of individual heater/thermostat units in each aquarium.

Submersible heater/thermostats—often referred to as heater/stats—are the most frequently used method of aquarium temperature control. So popular are they that there are units to match any size of aquarium, differing in heat output, sophistication, and price. They do not, however, differ in their essential function of heating the water up to a particular temperature and then switching off until the temperature drops once more to the level at which the unit has been set to reactivate.

1. ALCOHOL-FILLED THERMOMETER, WITH A GREEN "SAFETY ZONE" AND DUAL SCALE; 2. & 3. HEATERS WITH BUILT-IN THERMOSTATS; 4. HEATER ONLY, TO BE USED WITH 5., A TEMPERATURE CONTROLLER AND SENSOR PROBE; 6. LIQUID CRYSTAL DISPLAY (LCD) UNIT, ACCURATE AND EASY TO READ; 7. STANDARD ALCOHOL THERMOMETER; 8. COMBINED HYDROMETER/THERMOMETER; 9. STICK-ON LCD STRIP FOR BROAD-BASED READINGS.

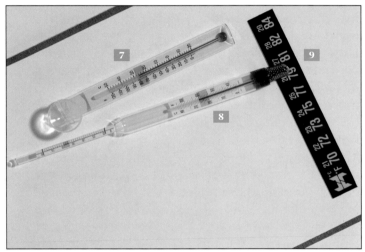

Other forms of heating include low-voltage undergravel cables and infilter heating units. Undergravel cables are very efficient and have the added advantage that they are never so hot that they can damage plant roots or gravel micro-organisms. Infilter heating units have the advantage that the heat source is removed from the aquarium and located inside a power filter instead, where it warms the water as it passes through the filter chamber. Another method, often employed in multichamber undertank filtration systems, uses this same principle: the heating unit is located in one of the filter compartments and is, thus, warmed within the filter, rather than within the aquarium.

Whichever method is employed (the choice depends on personal preference, budget and circumstances), one thing that needs to be determined is just how powerful a heating unit is required. Traditionally, the rule has been to allow about 4 watts per gal (4.5 watts per Imp. gal/1 watt per liter) of water. However, modern thinking has moved away toward lower figures, where (depending on the amount of heat estimated to be generated from aquarium lighting, etc.), we now recommend a maximum of just over 2 watts per gal (2 watts per Imp. gal/0.5 watts per liter)—or just under—but, preferably, around a little less than 1 watt per gal (around I watt per Imp. gal/0.2 watts per liter), depending on size of aquarium, ambient temperature, number and intensity of lights, and so on.

Using these figures, we can estimate the total approximate power (in watts) of the heating required for aquaria of different sizes kept in rooms whose temperatures differ from that of the aquarium water itself. The accompanying table shows some approximate figures for a range of aquarium capacities. (Note, though, that the figures are approximate and that the thermostatic unit of the heater will require adjustment to suit individual circumstances. The wattage/liter required increases relative to the temperature difference, as you would

TOTAL WATTAGE REQUIRED

AQUARIUM CAPACITY IN LITERS (APPROX. GAL/IMP GAL)	DIFFERENCE BETWEEN REQUIRED WATER AND ROOM TEMPERATURES IN °C				
	2	4	6	8	10
45 (12/10)	9W	19	29	39	48
60 (16/13)	11	23	34	45	57
80 (21/18)	14	27	41	55	69
100 (26/22)	16	32	48	64	80
150 (40/33)	21	42	56	76	95
200 (53/44)	25	51	76	101	127
250 (66/55)	29	57	86	114	143
300 (79/66)	33	66	99	133	166

expect. It also decreases as the tank capacity increases because larger volumes of water retain heat more effectively than smaller ones and, thus, require less input to maintain a constant temperature once the required level has been reached.

Comparing the figures in the capacity/temperature difference table above with the more widely published traditional heater recommendations below (which vary between books and manufacturers) it will immediately become evident that the former are considerably lower. Many aquarists therefore still believe that it is better to stick to the traditional values, since these appear to provide a wider safety margin in case of emergencies. During a power cut, it makes no difference, of course whether a heater is rated at 10 watts or 1,000 watts. However, where higher-wattage models can help is in the speed with which normal water temperature can be restored after the power is back on (always bearing in mind that rapid temperature changes are distressing or dangerous to most fish).

RANGE OF TRADITIONAL HEATER RECOMMENDATIONS

AQUARIUM CAPACITY IN LITERS (APPROX. GAL/IMP GAL)	APPROX. WATTAGE
45 (12/10)	50–70
60 (16/13)	70–100
80 (21/18)	100–125
100 (26/22)	125–150
150 (40/33)	150–175
200 (53/44)	175–200
250 (66/55)	200–250
300 (79/66)	Up to 300

Aquarium Lighting

There are two approaches to aquarium lighting. The first uses the type of lighting itself as the starting point: the lighting is chosen before everything else. For example, after seeing an aquarium setup incorporating spotlights, some may well be tempted to incorporate them in their own plans. This is fine, of course, but there are limits: a 24 × 12 × 12in (60 × 30 × 30cm) tank is far from ideal for spotlights, whereas a tastefully arranged 60 × 18 × 18in (150 × 45 × 45cm) one can be absolutely magnificent. This is especially so if the larger aquarium includes submerged light-loving plants, such as *Cabomba*, *Hygrophila*, *Vallisneria* and *Ludwigia*, with some *Riccia* or *Salvinia* on the surface.

The second approach uses the fish, invertebrates and plants as the starting point, which means establishing the requirements of the various species involved (details of which are given in the Fish and Plant sections respectively) and then choosing the most appropriate lighting, or combination lighting, for them.

For instance, if a species tank is being set up for Blind Cave Fish (*Astyanax mexicanus*) there really is no need for lighting of any sort. In fact, providing these fish with a brightly lit and well-planted tank, albeit harmless, rather misses the point. Nothing shows these fish up better than a dim, reddish spotlight strategically placed off-center in relation to the tank surface. This will not only enhance the appearance of the fish themselves, but can create a most attractive cave-like arrangement of light and shadow, particularly if the bottom of the tank is adorned with lengths of stalagmite.

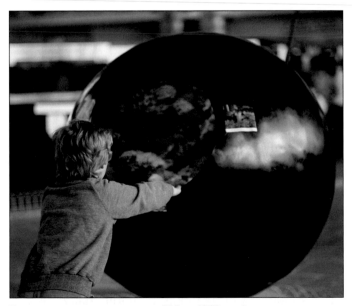

FOR AN UNUSUAL AQUARIUM LIKE THIS 100GAL (380 LITER) ONE, DESIGNED TO GIVE A FEELING OF LOOKING IN ON A SECRET UNDERWATER WORLD, GOOD LIGHTING IS AN ESSENTIAL PART OF THE EXPERIENCE.

For crepuscular (twilight) species, brightly lit tanks housing light-loving species of plant are, again, not the most appropriate setup. It is much better to tone down the light, choose shade-loving plants, such as various species of *Cryptocoryne* and Java Moss, *Vesicularia dubyana*, and provide a light/dark regime of approximately 10 hours on/14 hours off. (This, incidentally, also cuts down the risk of excessive algal growth.) Some species of fish that do well under these conditions (provided a vegetable/algal supplement is made available where necessary) are the Elephant-nose (*Gnathonemus petersii*), bristle-nosed catfish (*Ancistrus* spp.), spiny eels (*Mastacembelus* and *Macrognathus* spp.) and some knife fishes (e.g. *Notopterus* spp.).

Gouramis and closely related fishes, for their part, generally spawn at the water surface. Therefore, a tank housing these species should not be provided with high-heat-generating bulbs which will destroy the nest, the eggs and the newly hatched fry. Tungsten bulbs, spots and high-pressure bulbs are, therefore, best avoided. For these species, fluorescent lighting is more suitable.

Whatever the approach, one will still be faced with weighing up the pros and cons of the different types of lighting before making a final decision. For ease of reference, some of the main advantages and disadvantages are listed in the table (*left*).

Matching species and lighting is not the easiest of jobs, but with a thoughtful approach, paying due attention to the needs and characteristics of both the species and the various systems involved, most problems—including excessive algal growth—can be brought under control. If you have any doubts, consult your supplier or manufacturer, who will have literature in addition to the guidelines provided on the product packaging, which will prove invaluable in helping you to make a final decision.

The accompanying table (*below*) lists the approximate lighting requirements for a range of tank sizes. The figures shown apply broadly to well planted aquaria housing the more common species and varieties of

TYPE OF LIGHTING	SOME ADVANTAGES	SOME DISADVANTAGES
Daylight	The least expensive.	Unpredictable and difficult to control.
Tungsten (Incandescent) Bulbs and Tubes	Cheap to install. Reasonable lifespan. Can stimulate good plant growth.	Relatively expensive to run. Risk of implosion. Generate a great deal of heat. Unsuitable for most surface nesting species of fish. Bulky—may not fit inside some modern hoods.
Fluorescent Tubes	Cheap to run. Variety of light available to suit different needs, including "daylight" and "moonlight" tubes. Fit inside most aquarium hoods. Emit light at relatively low temperature.	Require starter unit. Expensive to install. Relatively expensive to replace.
Spotlights	Penetrate deeply—therefore good for large aquaria. "Cool" spots emit light at moderate temperatures compared to "normal" spotlights. Reasonably priced.	Bulky—do not fit inside conventional hoods. Generate a great deal of heat. Expensive to run.
High-pressure Mercury/ Metal Halide Bulbs	Brilliant penetrating light, suitable for deep tanks. Inexpensive to run. Long-lasting.	Bulky—do not fit inside conventional hoods. Generate a great deal of heat. Expensive to install. Require starter unit. Expensive to replace.

APPROXIMATE LIGHTING REQUIREMENTS

LENGTH OF TANK (in/cm)	TUNGSTEN BULBS	SPOTLIGHTS	FLUORESCENT TUBES	HIGH-PRESSURE MERCURY BULBS*
18/45	1 × 40W	Not suitable	1 × 8W	Not suitable
24/60	2 × 40W	Not suitable	1 × 15W	Not suitable
30/75	2 × 60W	2 × 60W	1 × 20W	Not suitable
35/90	3 × 40W	3 × 60W	2 × 20W	1 × 80W
47/120	3 × 60W	4 × 60W	2 × 30W	1 × 80W
59/150	5 × 40W	5 × 60W	2 × 40W	1 or 2 × 80W
71/180	5 × 60W	6 × 60W	2 × 50W	2 × 80W
NOTE				

*Wattages for metal halides are a little lower than those recommended for mercury bulbs

plants and fish available. What this chart, like all others, cannot show are some of the hidden snags.

For example, spotlights, metal halide, and high-pressure mercury bulbs, have bright, penetrating light and can, therefore, be a better choice for deep tanks than some of the other types of lighting. However, hand-in-hand with this tremendous advantage are several significant disadvantages, such as the intense heat generated by the bulbs and their large size, which makes their installation under standard aquarium hoods impossible, and requires that a space of 12in (30cm) or more be left between the bulbs and the water surface. In the case of high-pressure mercury and metal halide bulbs, it is also difficult to calculate the exact number required because of the spread of the light (approx. 24in/60cm at a height of around 8in/20cm) and its intensity (an 80W mercury bulb is assumed to equal two 150W spotlights in terms of output). Clearly, these parameters will vary according to how the bulbs are placed above the tank.

Water Chemistry

Good water quality is not just a matter of cleanliness, adequate oxygenation, and appropriate temperature, and lighting control. It also involves water chemistry. In particular, as aquarists, we need to concern ourselves primarily with three aspects of water chemistry (though the more aspects one becomes familiar with, the better this will be for both fish and plants):

a) tapwater chemistry
b) acidity/alkalinity
c) hardness.

Water that comes out of a faucet (tap) is a very different compound from that found in a tropical stream. Tropical waters are often heavily loaded with iron taken from iron-rich soils (laterite) over (and through) which water flows on its course downstream. Tapwater, on the other hand, often has little or no iron. Conversely, tropical stream water contains no chlorine or chloramine, disinfecting substances used to render tapwater safe to drink. Other compounds added to water during its treatment can also affect acidity/alkalinity, as well as hardness. In nature, these attributes tend to be constant in any area, unless a major external factor such as pollution dictates otherwise. We therefore find, for example, that the majority of tropical jungle streams in South America and the Far East are soft and acid. In fact, some Amazonian waters where *Discus* are found can have a pH value as low as 4.0, which is extremely acidic. The African Rift

A MULTIPLE WATER-TESTING KIT: pH, AMMONIA, NITRATE LEVELS, ETC.

Lakes, on the other hand, contain hard water with pH values that can exceed 9.0, remarkably alkaline. There are other differences between tapwater and natural water, such as oxygen and carbon dioxide content.

CHLORINE AND CHLORAMINE

In making tapwater safe for humans to drink, not only do we lose some "natural" components (or find them in reduced quantities), but we also "gain" substances—such as chlorine and chloramine—which can actually kill fish (and not just in high concentrations). A chlorine concentration as low as 0.5mg/l (parts per million) can be harmful to some fish species.

When chlorine is bubbled through water, the two react to form hydrogen chloride, or hydrochloric acid (HCl) and hypochlorous acid (HOCl). It is the latter that is believed to be the main killer. Matters become more complicated when chlorine is bubbled through water containing ammonia: another compound, chloramine, is formed and, while chloramine itself may not pose a direct threat to fish health, the hypochlorous acid that it forms when it "breaks down" (dissociates) certainly does.

Chloramine takes a long time to break down. Chlorine is quite volatile and will dissipate within a few hours if the water is adequately aerated. Chloramine, however, can take up to a week to dissociate completely. Therefore, if an aquarium is not adequately filtered, with the result that there is a permanent background level of ammonia in the water, the addition of chlorinated tapwater can result in an equivalent background level of chloramine and, hence, toxic hypochlorous acid. By making tapwater safe for us, we render it quite unsuitable for aquatic life.

The actual amount of hypochlorous acid present in water is not determined just by the amount of chlorine added, but by temperature and pH. At lower temperatures, a lower percentage of the added chlorine ends up as hypochlorous acid than at higher temperatures, although the differences are relatively slight. With regard to pH, however, the differences are quite dramatic. For example, at pH 5.0, nearly 100 percent of the available chlorine occurs as hypochlorous acid, while at pH 7.0 (i.e. neutral water), the percentage is around 70 percent. At pH 8.0, only about 26 percent of the chlorine occurs as hypochlorous acid, reducing further at pH 9.0 where the concentration is only 3 percent.

The obvious conclusion is that the higher the pH, the lower the risk of chlorine toxicity, owing to the reduced levels of hypochlorous acid produced. In terms of actual levels of toxicity, 0.004mg/l (parts per million) of hypochlorous acid has been recommended as the maximum long-term level for sensitive fish like salmon. For short exposure, levels as high as 0.1mg/l (parts per million) can be tolerated by most fish species. However, even a concentration as low as 1.0mg/l (parts per million) can prove fatal after a short exposure. Fortunately, chlorine is easy to remove from aquarium water and, while chloramine is more resistant, it, too, can be neutralized. Traditionally, activated carbon placed within a filter has been used to reduce chlorine and chloramine concentrations. Chlorine can also (as mentioned earlier) be eliminated within a few hours under vigorous aeration; chloramine can take up to a week. Recently, the efficiency of activated filter carbon has been questioned but it still appears to do quite a good job. An alternative, probably more effective and certainly more expensive technique uses ultraviolet irradiation (via a UV sterilizer—see Fish Health).

There are also commercially available dechlorinating and dechloraminating agents and these should be used in all cases where major water changes or additions are made, especially in the absence of other control methods. Where minor water changes or topping up is concerned, amounting to around 10 percent or less of the total volume, it is generally safe to proceed without the aid of detoxifying agents or UV, but, even so, safety measures—such as aeration—should be adopted. Test kits are now available for measuring chlorine and chloramines, and these should be deemed essential by every aquarist.

ACIDITY AND ALKALINITY

We are all familiar with acid substances (from lemons and vinegar to battery acid) and alkaline, or basic, ones (such as caustic soda). But there are countless substances that do not have a neutral pH value. If any of these substances are dissolved in water, they will convey their acidic or alkalinic properties to the resulting solution.

Aquarium water, being a complex solution consisting not just of pure water but a whole host of dissolved substances, will have acidic/alkalinic (basic) properties, and these need to be matched with those of the natural water from which our fish originate and in which they have evolved. Thus fish from the Amazon will have evolved in acid waters, while those from the African Rift Lakes or many Mexican waters will come from alkalinic environments. Most aquarium fish come from waters ranging in pH values from 6 to 8 (with notable exceptions) and most will exhibit greater or lesser tolerance to conditions other than their native ones. However, for longterm peak health, every effort should be made to match aquarium water conditions with those that the fish in question experience in their natural habitat.

Acidity/alkalinity is measured in terms of pH (from 0 to 14), which is an indication of the hydrogen ion concentration of the solution being measured. The abbreviation pH actually stands for pondus hydrogenii, i.e. the "weight" or concentration of hydrogen. Hydrogen ions are positively charged hydrogen atoms that react readily with other substances. Therefore, the higher the number of such ions, the higher the reactivity of the solution. At first sight, this might suggest that the higher the pH of a water sample, the higher the concentration of hydrogen ions and therefore the more reactive it will be. However, the exact opposite is the case, because the pH scale actually represents the "negative log10 hydrogen ion concentration" of the solution being measured. This may sound complicated, but it can be "translated" into everyday language.

MARBLED HATCHETFISH (CARNEGIELLA STRIGATA) PREFER SOFT, ACID WATER—SEE PAGE 218.

Avoid hard water for the Diamond Tetra (Moenkhausia pittieri)—see page 206.

A "log10" scale is one in which each unit represents a tenfold increase or decrease. Therefore, a pH value of 8 represents a level of alkalinity that is ten times as high as a neutral solution with a pH value of 7. Equally, a solution with a pH value of 6 is ten times more acid than one with a pH value of 7 and 100 times more acid than one with a pH value of 8. In terms of hydrogen ion concentration, since the scale is a "negative log10" one, a solution with a pH value of 8 actually has 10 times fewer hydrogen ions than one with a pH value of 7 and 100 times fewer hydrogen ion than one with a pH value of 6.

This helps explain why, for instance, ammonia is less toxic in acid aquaria than in alkaline ones. There are many more highly reactive hydrogen ions available in acid-water aquaria to "bind up" toxic ammonia and render it safer. The reverse, of course, applies in alkaline-water systems.

The tenfold increases per pH unit explain why what appears to be a modest change on that 0–14 scale can be stressful, or even fatal, to fish. All pH changes must therefore be carried out gradually in order to ease fish from one set of chemical conditions to another.

Nowadays, there are numerous pH test kits available, ranging from electronic ones to color-chart types. Prices and levels of sophistication and accuracy vary, but all reputable makes are reliable. A pH test kit is absolutely essential, especially where the more delicate and challenging species of fish are concerned.

Hard and Soft Water

Everyone can tell whether water is soft or hard. If it quickly forms a good lather, it is soft; if it doesn't, it is hard. We need to be rather more accurate when it comes to aquarium keeping. Without a more thorough understanding it is quite impossible to match fish with appropriate water conditions and, although many species and varieties will be able to adapt, others will not. Even those species that adapt quite readily to inappropriate hardness conditions may fail to breed. Cardinal Tetras (*Paracheirodon axelrodi*), and barbs such as the Tiger Barb (*Barbus tetrazona*), for example, can be acclimatized (gradually!) to survive perfectly adequately in water that is as hard as 300mg/l (parts per million). Under these conditions, though, egg fertilization is almost impossible.

Despite the importance of water hardness, some aquarists choose to ignore it, or pretend that it doesn't exist. The confusing terminology may well play a part in this: labels such as General, Total, Carbonate, Permanent, and Temporary Hardness do not help matters. Neither does the existence of different scales and units of measurement. Aquarium books, particularly some of the earlier works, are littered with terms such as Clark or English degrees of hardness, or American, or German degrees, which cannot easily or directly be compared.

Modern literature (thankfully) tends to adopt a more standardized or international approach that bases hardness on milligrams per liter (mg/l), which works out the same as parts per million (ppm). However, in order to make sense of any "nonstandard" units that may be encountered, the following are suitable conversion factors:

1 Clark or English Degree × 0.8 = 1 German Degree
1 Clark or English Degree × 0.84 = 1 American Degree

To convert these to mg/l or ppm, multiply:

1 Clark or English Degree × 14.3
1 German Degree × 17.9
1 American Degree × 17.1

It may be worth noting how the various degrees are calculated. Clark or English degrees of hardness are based on the number of grains—a grain = 64.7989mg, or 1/7000lb—of calcium carbonate ($CaCO_3$) per Imperial Gallon, while American degrees are an indication of grains of $CaCO_3$ per 1 million parts of water. German degrees represent parts of calcium oxide (CaO) per 100,000 parts of water.

Moving on to the terms used, Total Hardness refers, as its name implies, to the sum total of the hardness created by the various salts of calcium and magnesium present. Total Hardness includes:

1. General or Permanent Hardness produced by calcium and magnesium salts, primarily sulphates, nitrates and chlorides. This type of hardness is usually indicated as GH. Confusingly, "GH" is also used in many books to indicate Total Hardness.

THE FAIRY CICHLID (NEOLAMPROLOGUS BRICHARDI), "STAR" OF THE AFRICAN RIFT LAKES CICHLIDS, NEEDS MEDIUM-HARD, ALKALINE WATER—SEE PAGE 108.

2. Carbonate, Bicarbonate or Temporary Hardness produced by calcium and magnesium bicarbonates. This type of hardness is usually indicated as KH.

As the terms "Permanent" and "Temporary" indicate, the latter can be eliminated (by boiling, which results in an insoluble substance, the "fur" of kettles and other heating appliances) while the former will not be affected.

Both types are relevant to fishkeepers. A certain amount of Temporary/Carbonate/Bicarbonate Hardness (KH), for instance, helps to buffer or "cushion" water against abrupt fluctuations in pH. Bearing in mind the logarithmic nature of the pH scale (see previous section) and the potentially fatal consequences of abrupt changes, the importance of an appropriate KH becomes self-evident. General/Permanent Hardness (GH), on the other hand, needs to be low for some delicate species such as *Discus* and other fish from nutrient-poor, soft and acid waters, and high for fish from the other end of the spectrum, such as African Rift Lake cichlids.

If water is hard in any way, it may be softened through dilution either with rainwater or distilled water. Alternatively, proprietary products or ion-exchange units can achieve the same results. Temporary Hardness may be raised by gradually adding sodium bicarbonate ($NaHCO_3$) to water, while Permanent Hardness may be increased gradually through the use of limestone or other calcareous rocks as aquarium decorations, or through the use of coral sand or gravel, or limestone or marble pebbles, either as a substrate or enclosed in fine mesh within a filter. Alternatively, special salt mixes may be used.

When the hardness of a water sample is quoted, this usually refers to the Total Hardness, i.e. Temporary/ Bicarbonate/Carbonate Hardness, plus Permanent/ General Hardness. Water can be classified from very soft to very hard, depending on its total content of magnesium and calcium salts. Interpretation of where to draw the dividing line between one level of hardness and the next varies between books, so classifications must be regarded as guidelines only. Bearing in mind that most fish have a degree of hardness tolerance and that the crucial factor is the actual level of dissolved salts (and not how one splits them into categories) a workable hardness chart can be provided (see table p.41).

Although there is general agreement between the accompanying chart and most others at the "soft" end

WATER HARDNESS

WATER TYPE/CATEGORY	APPROX. TOTAL HARDNESS (mg/l—ppm)
Very soft	0–50
Moderately soft	50–100
Slightly hard	100–150
Moderately hard	150–200
Hard	200–300
Very hard	300+

ANUBIAS NANA *PLANTS BEING PLANTED INTO POCKETS OF A BOGWOOD DECOR PIECE. TANNINS THAT INITIALLY LEACH FROM BOGWOOD ARE ACTUALLY BENEFICIAL TO SOFT, ACIDIC WATER SYSTEMS.*

of the spectrum, some charts tend to have progressively higher values the further up the scale one moves toward the "hard" end of the range. I find the accompanying version particularly valuable in that it is a little "safer" than some other scales. The reason for this is that, while hardwater species can generally cope quite adequately with softer conditions, the more delicate softwater species can find hard conditions more challenging. By classifying the "harder" categories at lower values, the accompanying scale therefore tends to encourage the use of softer water. Three further points are worth considering before leaving the subject of water hardness:

1. It is important to know what type of hardness a test kit is actually designed to measure.
2. When measuring Temporary/Carbonate/ Bicarbonate Hardness, it is also important to appreciate that test kits designed to measure carbonate concentration do not always distinguish between calcium and magnesium salts and,

say, sodium carbonate (this last compound is particularly abundant in some African Lakes). As a result, Temporary Hardness readings can appear to be excessively high in such instances.
3. The term Total Dissolved Solids/Salts (T.D.S.) is sometimes used when referring to water hardness. In practical terms, it can be regarded as being equivalent to Total Hardness.

SETTING UP AN AQUARIUM

Aquaria can be set up to meet some very specific needs of fish: still or gently flowing, dimly lit, tannin-stained, soft, acid, brightly lit, clear, rockstrewn, hard or alkaline environments, according to species. Yet, despite specific differences, all aquaria share a number of basic characteristics. It is therefore possible to provide some general guidelines on setting up aquaria to suit a wide range of species, but which can be adapted accordingly to cater for more specialized requirements.

What follows is a series of easy-to-follow steps for setting up a general tropical community aquarium. Several versions of this setting up procedure exist, but all—in the end—achieve the same purpose.

1. Choose a site for the aquarium that is away from direct sunlight, drafts, banging doors, areas of high activity and other disturbances, making sure that the furniture or shelving on which the tank is to rest is capable of supporting the weight (water weighs about 10lb/gal (1kg/liter). Alternatively, buy a professional aquarium cabinet or stand.
2. Ensure that the chosen site has a sound, strong floor and—very importantly—that it is absolutely level.
3. Cushion the surface on which the base of the aquarium is to rest with appropriate material, e.g. strips or sheets of styrofoam.
4. Having rinsed the aquarium with clean water, *not* with detergents, to eliminate dust and other impurities, lay it on the styrofoam.
5. If an undergravel filter is being used, assemble it and rest the filter plate directly on the base of the aquarium.
6. To prevent the undergravel plate from becoming clogged with substrate, it is worth considering the use of a "gravel tidy." This is a meshlike sheet that can be laid on top of filter plates and prevents substrate grains being in direct physical contact with the slits or openings in the plate. This accessory is particularly useful when using fine-grained substrates.

7. Wash the gravel or other chosen substrate thoroughly in clean tapwater. Do *not* use detergents—they are highly toxic to all forms of aquatic life.

8. Add the substrate and arrange terracing or "integrated" decorations to give an attractive (preferably nonsymmetrical) effect. If undergravel filters are being used, it is important to provide a sufficiently thick layer of substrate for optimal biological filter activity; a thickness of some 2–3in (5–8cm) should be regarded as the minimum.

9. If the terracing being installed is commercially produced, then simply rinse it thoroughly prior to installation. If rocks and/or bogwood are being used, these may be glued together with silicone sealant, which must be allowed to set and "cure" before installation. To prevent bogwood or cork from floating, it is a good idea to stick the chosen pieces to slate, which can then be covered up with substrate. Make sure that rocks and/or bogwood or cork pieces are safely bedded into the substrate, avoiding the risk of their toppling over. This is particularly important in aquaria that will house bottom-rooting or burrowing/nesting species.

10. Position heaters, thermostats, internal filters (if these are being used) and air stone (and air line) strategically and, preferably, hidden from view. It is particularly important to ensure that there is no direct contact between the heater and either the decor or the substrate, since this will cause "hotspots." There are special mesh-type heater protectors (which, in reality, should be called fish protectors) and these may be used to eliminate the risk of causing burns to fish that like to rest close to the warmest spot in the aquarium. For optimal positioning the heater should be horizontal (or nearly so), approximately halfway along the back pane of the aquarium and as close to the substrate as possible. Do not plug in any electrical appliances at this stage! Whenever possible, air pumps should be positioned above water level (external to the aquarium, of course!). This minimizes the power needed in order to pump air along the air line and through the air or diffuser stone. It also eliminates the risk of water being siphoned into the pump when it is switched off. If it is not possible to locate the air pump as suggested, fit a non-return valve somewhere along the air line.

Yellow sandstone is used to good effect in this setup, providing lightness and height.

11. To fill the aquarium with water, pour gently from a bucket or other suitable container, onto a plate or saucer, or into a jar stood on the plate or saucer, allowing the water to overflow gently onto the substrate, thus preventing any unnecessary disruption to the substrate or decor. If desired, the water can be warmed slightly before adding, speeding up the tank-warming process and protecting the plants against cold-temperature shock.

12. Once the aquarium is half-full, the plants can be installed or this can be delayed until the filling process has been completed. Both approaches have their advantages. The former makes the plants easier to position, while the latter provides a better idea of the overall effect from the outset.

13. The condensation tray—a clear plastic or glass cover designed to prevent excessive evaporation of aquarium water, as well as a means of protecting electrical connections from getting wet—can now be installed.

14. The lighting unit, starters, etc. can now also be fitted into the hood and the wiring appropriately arranged and connected. A cable tidy—a box that allows several pieces of electrical equipment to be wired centrally, with a single lead extending from the connection block to the mains—will help keep wiring neat and easy to manage. The one drawback of these devices is that every piece of equipment connected to them is then dependent on a single line of supply, with a single fuse (in those countries that use a fused plug/socket arrangement). The installation of a circuit breaker—a safety device that will cut off the electrical supply in case of

malfunction—is essential. If in any doubt whatsoever, consult a qualified electrician.

15. Put the thermometer in place and carry out water tests for pH and (if necessary) hardness. If these are outside the range required for the species that will be maintained, adjust accordingly. At this initial stage, proprietary adjusters (since they will produce results quickly) will be found particularly helpful.

16. Switch all the electrical equipment on and check that everything is working properly. Adjust the air flow, filter flow, temperature, etc., over the next few days while the aquarium is settling down.

17. Run the system on a 12–15 hours/day illumination period for about a week. Some aquarists do not deem this necessary, since proprietary water maturation products will speed up this initial settling-in phase. However, this first week is also valuable as a "training period" for the new aquarist.

18. The water may turn cloudy during this initial phase. However, resist the temptation to carry out a major water change. The cloudiness is caused by a bacterial bloom, which is characteristic of new aquatic systems. It will clear up of its own accord after a few days.

OTHER TYPES OF AQUARIA

While the guidelines given in the previous section will result in a well-setup freshwater tropical community aquarium, it will not (and cannot) cater for the needs of all types of freshwater aquarium fish. The basic principles will need modification in order to match the environmental and behavioral characteristics of the species in question. The following paragraphs provide a few pointers that should prove helpful in the design of some of these other types of systems.

Goldfish and Related Species

The most obvious difference between goldfish and fish that would qualify as tropical community species—in the general sense of the term—is that goldfish do not require the provision of supplementary heat. Therefore, when setting up an aquarium for goldfish, this stage does not apply. Among several other factors relating to goldfish aquaria, the following deserve special consideration:

1. Goldfish spend a great deal of time rooting among the gravel for morsels of food. In so doing, they very soon uncover the plates of an undergravel filter or, if this is protected by a gravel tidy, the mesh of the "tidy" itself. It is therefore sensible to avoid both undergravel filters and gravel tidies when designing goldfish aquaria.

2. Because of their almost incessant rooting, goldfish will mouth not just the substrate, but the surfaces of any submerged objects as well, including, of course, the rockwork. It is therefore particularly important to avoid the use of sharp-edged rocks or synthetic decorations in goldfish aquaria. (In any case, sharp-edged decor should be avoided in all types of aquaria).

3. Again, owing to their digging, bottom-feeding activities, goldfish will uproot most aquarium plants sooner or later. To prevent this, arrange plants in plastic pots or other suitable non-toxic containers and bury these in the substrate or hide them with rocks or other decorations. A layer of pebbles that are too large to be removed by the fish should be laid on the surface of the planting medium. Alternatively, surround any plants that are bedded directly into the substrate with large smooth pebbles to prevent direct access by the fish.

4. Goldfish and many related cyprinids are largely herbivorous in eating habits. They will therefore devour any delicate, succulent plants included in the aquarium decor. Only tough plants should therefore be used in such systems. Alternatively (or additionally), consider some of the excellent artificial plants currently available.

5. Continuing with the "artificial" theme, goldfish aquaria—particularly those housing the more fancy varieties—can be very effectively decorated

RED ORANDA (CARASSIUS AURATUS VAR.) NEED SPECIAL CONSIDERATION WHEN DESIGNING AN AQUARIUM.

counterparts. However, such shops possess staff with the expertise to monitor and maintain good water quality. They also enjoy the benefits of large, efficient water management systems, often incorporating such features as ultraviolet sterilization, fluid bed filtration, protein skimmers, substantial water reservoirs connected to centralized circulation/filtration, and facilities for isolating individual aquaria when necessary.

Few aquarists, if any, can boast such facilities at home. Nevertheless, the same principle of water quality as the key factor in determining stocking density should be applied. With this approach, the starting point is not the traditional one of using a guidance chart (like the accompanying one) for determining stocking levels, but the water itself. The great advantage using this method is that (always allowing for specific factors, such as temperament and compatibility), stocking levels are always kept within the tolerance limits of the aquarium support system. The potential disadvantage is that, in order not to exceed this limit, initial stocking can be a relatively slow process. This is a good thing, but new aquarists can find it difficult to keep to the longer stocking-time schedule, which involves regular testing of the water for the key environmental parameters discussed earlier. For coldwater and tropical freshwater fish, the recommended values for four key chemical parameters are given below. Specific requirements for delicate species may fall outside these limits.

MALE BETTA (BETTA SPLENDENS VAR.) DISPLAYING TO A FEMALE. MALE BETTAS WILL NOT LIVE PEACEFULLY TOGETHER.

The more traditional method of calculating stocking levels is based on unit lengths of fish (minus tail) in relation to surface area. For freshwater tropical species, this works out at around 12.5 sq. in (80 sq. cm) per 1–2in (2.5–5cm) fish, just over 17 sq. in (110 sq. cm) per 5–7.5cm (2–3in) fish and nearly 20 sq. in (130 sq. cm) per 3–4in (7.5–10cm) fish. For coldwater species, such as goldfish, the figures work out (again, very approximately) at 55 sq. in (360 sq. cm) per 2–3in (5–7.5cm) fish, and 93 sq. in (600 sq. cm) for fish measuring 3–4in (7.5–10cm). Using these formulae, we can arrive at approximately safe stocking levels (see chart below).

It must be stressed that the figures are rough guidelines only. They represent total stocking levels and relate to fish that are fully grown and are neither over-aggressive nor excessively territorial.

When stocking an aquarium, it is advisable to begin with at most 50 percent of the eventual stocks. Although even this relatively light stocking density will place some stress on the aquarium's raw filtration

DISSOLVED OXYGEN:	6mg/l (ppm)	MINIMUM
FREE AMMONIA:	0.02mg/l (ppm)	MAXIMUM
NITRITE:	0–0.2mg/l (ppm)	MAXIMUM
NITRATE:	50mg/l (ppm)	MAXIMUM

APPROXIMATE AQUARIUM STOCKING LEVELS

	NUMBER OF FISH				
SURFACE DIMENSIONS OF AQUARIUM (in/cm)	COLDWATER SPECIES/VARIETIES		TROPICAL SPECIES/VARIETIES		
	2–3in (5–7.5cm)	3–4in (7.5–10cm)	Up to 2in (5cm)	2–3in (5–7.5cm)	3–4in (7.5–10cm)
18 × 10 (45 × 25)	3	2	14	10	Not advisable
24 × 12 (60 × 30)	5	3	22	16	14
36 × 12 (90 × 30)	7	5	33	24	21
48 × 12 (120 × 30)	10	7	44	32	29
60 × 18 (150 × 45)	18	13	83	80	54

NOTE:

For African Rift Lake cichlids, the minimum size of aquarium recommended is one having surface dimensions of 90 × 30cm. In addition, stocking levels approximately 50% above those quoted in the chart are recommended (see earlier section for details)

system, it should be able to cope, as long as other parameters are satisfactory and the fish are not of the more delicate and demanding types. Once the fish have been introduced (*see* Safe Introductions below), water chemistry parameters should be monitored regularly and no further fish added until favorable conditions are being maintained without any significant fluctuations. Subsequent stocking can then be undertaken, with eventual numbers being reached gradually over a period of at least several weeks.

Selecting Fish

No one can give you a cast-iron guarantee that any fish you buy—however healthy they may look—are 100 percent disease/parasite-free. Indeed, as every living thing carries a natural safe "load" of parasites, it could be said that if a fish is completely free of parasites, it is dead! The reason why pathogenic (disease-causing) organisms don't normally cause epidemics is that if the fish carrying the load is strong, the microorganisms just can't secure a good enough foothold, or hookhold, or whatever, to multiply in sufficient numbers to cause disease. Despite the fact that it is quite impossible to give 100 percent health guarantees, there are a few signs that one can look for when buying fish. If, for example, several fish in a shop aquarium look decidedly unhealthy, it is best to forget buying any of the other fish, however healthy they may appear, from the same batch. It is not worth taking the risk.

A COCKATOO DWARF CICHLID (APISTOGRAMMA CACATUOIDES) WITH GOOD STRONG ERECT FINS AND CLEARLY IN GOOD HEALTH.

Look for raised scales (dropsy), swollen abdomens (possibly fluid retention), protruding eyes (pop-eye or exophthalmia, but in certain varieties of goldfish, such as telescope-eye moors, protruding eyes are quite normal), ulcers (bacterial lesions), "overlarge" heads (possibly a sign of what is usually referred to as "consump-

WHAT TO LOOK FOR IN A HEALTHY FISH

1. ERECT FINS. A lively fish will tend to carry its fins well extended. The dorsal (back) fin is often flicked open and shut, usually as the fish hovers or changes direction, and is generally held down as a fish allows a flick of the caudal fin (tail) to propel it over short distances. If, however, you are buying a long-tailed variety such as Sarassa Comet or a Fancy Guppy or Betta, the caudal will not be carried by such fish in as fully extended a state as in shorter-finned varieties.

2. LIVELY DISPOSITION. Fish that "hang" in midwater, or float on the surface, or lie on the bottom with little visible movement, are best avoided (unless, of course, you are buying a bottom dweller, like a Tench, or a surface swimmer, like a Halfbeak, which just happens to be resting). These exceptions aside, healthy fish are constantly on the move and exhibit quick reactions.

3. BRIGHT EYES. These are not always easy to spot, particularly from above, or where small and/or bottom-hugging fish are concerned. Take your time nevertheless and look out for signs of cloudiness. Healthy eyes are clear, injured or unhealthy ones tend to be "milky" in appearance.

4. BRIGHT COLORS. This can be a little difficult for the untrained or inexperienced buyer. What is meant by "bright" is the absence of a milky or cloudy covering of excess mucus on the body. Excess mucus creates a dull overall effect that, once recognized—and that presupposes knowledge of the "true" color—is unmistakable.

5. BALANCED SWIMMING. Healthy fish don't normally "roll around" or lose their balance when swimming; neither do they float or sink. However, immediately after a meal perfectly healthy fish, particularly larger types, will often hover and can sometimes rock gently as they chew their food. It is important to bear this in mind.

6. FULL BODY. This must not be taken to mean a full-looking belly. It is the flesh or muscle that we are talking about here. A healthy fish will look "solid." With the exception of naturally large-headed fish—fancy goldfish varieties such as Orandas, for example—healthy fish don't have oversize heads. In particular, look immediately behind the head; it should not look pinched. In other words, the "neck" area should either be about as wide as, or (in some species and varieties) even slightly wider than the head itself.

7. GOOD APPETITE. Tread carefully with this one! Without a doubt, healthy fish have healthy appetites. Consequently, aquarists are sometimes advised to ask to see the fish they want to buy actually feeding. Simple enough? Well, not quite. For a start, if the fish have already been fed, they may not be as voraciously hungry as you might wish them to be. You are going to have to time your visit. Then, suppose they are hungry and devour the food offered. Happy that you are buying healthy fish, you ask for your chosen specimens to be netted and bagged up for the journey home. The stress of being netted—especially immediately after a meal—soon results in the fish excreting in the bag water during the journey home. This is hardly the ideal way to undertake a journey, particularly a long one. Perhaps, therefore, it's best to forget about asking for a demonstration of healthy appetite and concentrate on the other factors, as well as relying on your dealer or an experienced aquarist for advice.

GENERAL AQUARIUM MAINTENANCE

Once an aquarium has been set up and stocked—even at its initial, reduced level—it needs regular maintenance to keep it operating smoothly. This is one of those instances where prevention is certainly better than cure. By establishing and adhering to a good maintenance program, most problems can be prevented and, even those that can arise quickly—like pollution from an accidental overfeed—can be corrected before they develop into crises.

One of the many major pluses of regular maintenance is that it keeps water quality on an even keel. Without this, some conditions would change at such a slow rate that they may go undetected until it's too late, or until the change needed to redress the anomaly is too large to be undertaken safely in a single step. Maintenance jobs range from those that need to be carried out on a daily basis, to those that only need attention once or twice a year. They are all, however, equally important in their own ways.

Daily Maintenance

1. Switch aquarium lights on either after daybreak, or after the room lights have been on for a little while, thus avoiding an abrupt (and stressful) dark-to-light change.
2. Check health status of all fish and take appropriate action if necessary (see Health Management, p.62).
3. Feed fish. For community fish and most other types, two feeds, one in the morning and one in the evening should suffice, but fish with specialist needs or behavior, such as crepuscular or nocturnal feeders, need their own feeding schedule and diet.
4. Check for breeding activity and remove pair to a separate aquarium if required; some fish become over-aggressive at breeding time. Removal is also necessary if fry are to be reared subsequently. In the case of livebearers, it might be easier to remove the fry, although removing the female gently (not lifting her physically from the water, but guiding her into a bowl) is preferable.
5. Check the water temperature.
6. Check all equipment to ensure that it is working properly and replace or repair if necessary.
7. Toward evening, check the health status of crepuscular and/or nocturnal species which will have been resting under cover during the day.
8. At the end of the day, turn off the aquarium lights some minutes before the room lights, thus avoiding an abrupt light-to-dark change.

Weekly Maintenance

1. Check ammonia, nitrite and pH levels and adjust accordingly or take remedial action, e.g. a partial water change (see earlier sections on these topics for details). It is essential to carry out changes gradually. Remember, one unit of difference in pH value represents a tenfold increase or decrease in acidity or alkalinity.
2. Carry out a more thorough check on aquarium equipment than that carried out on a daily basis.
3. Except in those cases where fish are being conditioned for breeding, or fry are being reared, do not feed the fish for one whole day. This will help counteract the effects of small-scale overfeeding that can take place over the week.
4. Check on stocks of foods, medications, water treatments, test kit reagents, etc., and replace as necessary.

Two-weekly Maintenance

1. Switch off air pump or power filter.
2. Gently stir up the surface of the substratum, taking care not to disturb plant roots.
3. Scrape encrusting algae off the front pane of the aquarium and sides if necessary (if the sides are in full view, encrusting algae may look unsightly). If possible, leave the back pane untreated, thus providing a fresh food supply for algal feeders.
4. Trim plants as necessary, removing all dead or dying leaves.
5. Allow the algae and debris to settle on the bottom.
6. Siphon off about a quarter of the total aquarium water, taking in the accumulated debris. (Use a

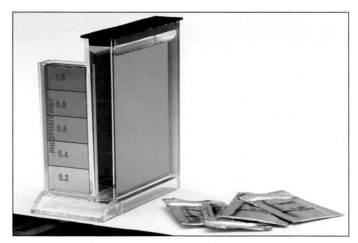

PHOSPHATE TEST KIT. PHOSPHATE LEVELS ARE INCREASING IN MANY DOMESTIC WATER SUPPLIES. DURING THE MATURATION OF THE AQUARIUM WATER IT IS ADVISABLE TO CHECK PHOSPHATE LEVELS FORTNIGHTLY. WHEN THE AQUARIUM IS ESTABLISHED THEY MAY OCCASIONALLY BE WORTH CHECKING, ESPECIALLY IF NUISANCE ALGAE ARE PREVAILING.

syphon bulb. NEVER suck water by mouth!) If weekly ammonia or nitrite readings are above safe levels, weekly partial water changes may be necessary until the underlying cause is remedied.

7. Replace removed water with tap or rainwater brought up to temperature (with boiled water) in a bucket or other suitable receptacle. Add dechlorinator or dechloraminator if the water change is larger than around 20–25 percent. Replacement water should match the aquarium water for hardness and pH.

8. Clean condensation tray or cover glass if necessary and reposition. Check and change activated carbon filter medium if necessary or as recommended by the manufacturer.

9. Switch on air pump or power filter.

Monthly Maintenance

1. Change or clean mechanical and chemical filter media.

2. Wash out biological filter media, in aquarium water if possible, to maintain full bacterial viability. Never use any form of detergent, despite thorough rinsing, since this will kill off the filter microfauna/flora and is toxic to fish, even in small concentrations. Boiling and sterilization of biological filter media will, likewise, kill off the microorganisms and must also be avoided.

3. In the case of undergravel filters, insert a siphon tube down the airlift and suck out (not by mouth!) a small amount of the debris accumulation from under the filter plates.

4. Check all lighting equipment terminals and connections.

5. Clean out all filter pipes and spray bar attachments.

6. Check air pump diaphragm and replace if necessary.

7. Clean air (diffuser) stones.

8. Clean condensation tray and cover glass if this was not necessary at the two-weekly check.

9. Replace poor plant specimens and generally tidy up the aquascape.

Biannual/Occasional Maintenance

1. If a UV sterilizer is being employed, replace the radiation-emitting tube after six months.

2. Check fluorescent lighting levels and replace tube if necessary, or if plant growth is suffering. If several tubes are being used, replace one or more, and the remaining ones on a six-month rotation.

ACTIVATED CARBON MADE FROM COCONUT SHELLS HAS NOW REPLACED CHARCOAL AS A METHOD OF EXTRACTION OF DISSOLVED ORGANIC MATTER AND SOME METALS. IT SHOULD BE REPLACED—ACCORDING TO AQUARIUM SIZE AND STOCKING LEVELS—EVERY TWO TO THREE WEEKS.

3. Replace the air filter in the air pump, which, by now, will be partly blocked with trapped airborne particles.

4. Service power filter or powerhead motors. If you do not possess the necessary skills, your local shop, or an experienced aquarist, may be able to do this for you. Either way, use a replacement filter if the job is going to take longer than a day or so. Otherwise, ensure that aeration is strong enough to help counterbalance the temporary absence of the filter.

Pre-vacation Maintenance

1. A properly maintained aquarium should not present any significant problems to family vacations. Leading up to the vacation, though, check that all equipment is operating as it should and replace any for which there is some doubt. It is very important not to leave these checks, cleanouts and replacements until the last minute. Allow yourself 10–14 days to ensure that serviced or new equipment is functioning properly and has had ample opportunity to "settle down."

2. Lighting should be controlled by a timer. Alternatively, if friends are looking after things, brief them on the light/dark regime you operate, so that your plants don't suffer during your absence.

3. Feeding may be carried out via an automatic feeder that dispenses pre-determined amounts of dry food (flake or pellets) at set times. Most people, though, place this responsibility in the hands of friends. Ideally, these should be versed in aquarium keeping, but if they are not, take them through your feeding routine, as well as through the operation of your equipment. Leave food prepared in daily "doses," suitably labeled with the date, thus ensuring that the fish are not overfed, a real danger with temporary foster parents! There are also commercially produced vacation blocks that contain food in a slow-release matrix, and these may be worth considering. Finally, if fish have been fed properly throughout the rest of the year, and particularly if the aquarium is well planted, they will have built up adequate reserves to take them through several weeks without any undue hardship.

TREATMENTS Acriflavine, Chloramphenicol and other antibiotics (*see* Note 1). Furan, Nifurpyrinol and related compounds are also effective, but may be dangerous to humans if use is prolonged (check with your vet, both for dosage levels of antibiotics and correct use of Furan and related products). Some proprietary remedies are available. Follow instructions to the letter.

MOUTH FUNGUS, CAUSATIVE AGENT: *Flexibacter columnaris* and, possibly, other bacteria (a misleading name because this is clearly not a fungus)

SYMPTOMS Whitish growths around the mouth, gradually progressing into the jaw bones and anterior cheek area, resulting in erosion of tissues.

TREATMENTS As for fin rot.

BACTEREMIA (milder form), Septicemia (more acute form), CAUSATIVE AGENT: *Aeromonas hydrophila*

SYMPTOMS Frayed fins, blood spots, ulcers, exophthalmia (pop-eye), individually or in combination.

TREATMENTS Chloramphenicol, Tetracycline, Oxolinic Acid (available in medicated flake or granule form). Some proprietary remedies are available. Chances of a cure are

▲ MOUTH FUNGUS
HOLE-IN-THE-HEAD ▶
▼ DROPSY

variable, depending on severity of infection. If treatment is being administered by injection (as antibiotics often are in the case of large fish), ask a vet to carry this out.

HOLE-IN-THE-HEAD/BODY; ULCER DISEASE or FURUNCOLOSIS, CAUSATIVE AGENT: primarily *Aeromonas salmoncida*, but *A. hydrophila* may act as a secondary agent

SYMPTOMS Ulcers (often circular) in head region and/or body.

TREATMENTS Chloramphenicol, Tetracycline, Sulphonamides, e.g. Furan-based remedy (*see* fin rot). Some proprietary remedies are available. After treatment, dress large ulcers with an oil-based antiseptic cream to protect the wound and prevent excessive intake of water through the lesions. Adding salt to the aquarium water to give a 3 percent solution will also help affected fish to control their water intake.

FISH TB, PRIMARY CAUSATIVE AGENT: *Mycobacterium* spp.

SYMPTOMS Any one or combination of: loss of color/condition, raised scales, exophthalmia, loss of appetite, emaciation, ulceration, frayed fins.

TREATMENTS No reliably effective treatment. Some antibiotics, e.g. Terramycin, may effect a cure when infection is not too severe. Fish TB can cause painful localized infected areas in humans, which can prove slow to cure. Always observe good personal hygiene procedures: wear rubber gloves, and avoid immersing your hands in water or handling fish if you have open or fresh cuts (*see* Risks to Humans, p.67).

DROPSY (BACTERIAL HEMORRHAGIC SEPTICEMIA), CAUSATIVE AGENT: *Aeromonas liquefaciens* (*ascitae* and/or *typica*) and, possibly, other bacteria

SYMPTOMS Swollen abdomen and raised scales, giving the body a "pine-cone" appearance.

TREATMENTS Usually no cure, but Chloramphenicol (see vet for instructions) may help. Humane destruction of affected specimens, plus good hygiene, are the most effective methods of eradicating the disease and preventing its recurrence.

FUNGAL INFECTIONS

COTTONWOOL DISEASE OR FUNGUS, CAUSATIVE AGENT: *Saprolegnia* and *Achyla* species; usually occurs on fish that are already weakened in some way, or on damaged tissues

SYMPTOMS White or cream-colored fluffy patches on fins and/or body.

TREATMENTS Proprietary remedies are widely available, usually based on Phenoxethol, Malachite Green (*see* Note 2), Copper Sulfate, Potassium Permanganate or Methylene Blue. Salt bath: 2–5 percent solution for 10–15 minutes.

▲ WHITE SPOT   ▼ FUNGAL INFECTION

PROTOZOAN INFECTIONS

WHITE SPOT (ICHTHYOPHTHIRIASIS, OR "ICH"), CAUSATIVE AGENT: *Ichthyophthirius multifiliis*; often occurs in fish that are already weakened or are subjected to chilling

SYMPTOMS   Body and fins covered in small white spots; in severe infestations, the spots may appear to join up; fins carried close to the body; violent swimming action or shimmying; scratching against stones, plants and pond equipment.

TREATMENTS Numerous proprietary remedies are available, many based on Malachite Green (*see* Note 2), Methylene Blue or Copper Sulfate. Repeat treatment is often necessary to attack free-swimming stages of the parasite.

COSTIASIS (infectious turbidity of gills and skin), CAUSATIVE AGENT: *Ichthyobodo (Costia) necatrix*

SYMPTOMS   Slimy, bluish-white coloration of the skin and gills; badly affected areas may show blood spots; awkward swimming movements with fins carried closed to body; scratching, as in white spot.

TREATMENTS Acriflavine (10ml of 0.001 percent stock solution/5 liters of water); salt (approx. 5g/liter): Formalin (approx. 15ml of 10 percent stock solution/5 liters for 15–20 minutes). Since free-swimming stages can survive only for

about one hour away from a host, affected aquaria can be disinfected by removing fish and treating them elsewhere.

CHILODONELLIASIS, CAUSATIVE AGENT: *Chilodonella cyprini*

SYMPTOMS   Similar to costiasis; in addition, the skin in the neck to dorsal fin region may develop a lumpy texture; respiration may be impaired.

TREATMENTS A combination of Acriflavine (1g/100ml of water) at a temperature of 82°F (28°C) for 10 hours is normally effective; Malachite Green, *see* Note 2 (0.15mg/liter) for an indefinite period. Salt (25g/liter for 10–15 minutes or 10–15g/liter for 20 minutes); Potassium Permanganate (1g/100 liters) for 90 minutes; Methylene Blue (30ml of 1 percent solution/100 liters) for an indefinite period.

TRICHODINIASIS, CAUSATIVE AGENT: *Trichodina* spp.

SYMPTOMS   Similar to costiasis, but usually less severe. Microscopic examination is necessary for definite diagnosis.

TREATMENTS   As for *Ichthyobodo (Costia)* and *Chilodonella*.

WORM INFECTIONS

GILL FLUKE INFECTION by *Dactylogyrus* spp.—monogenetic trematodes

SYMPTOMS   Inflamed gills; excessive secretion of mucus on gills; accelerated respiration; gill covers may be held open; scratching of gill covers on aquarium sides, bottom and equipment.

TREATMENTS Some proprietary remedies are available. These are based on a range of compounds, e.g. Copper Sulfate; salt bath (10–15g/liter for 20 minutes or 25g/liter for 10–15 minutes); Formalin (20ml commercial formalin/100 liters) for 30–35 minutes; Methylene Blue (30ml of 1 percent stock solution/100 liters) indefinitely.

SKIN FLUKE INFECTION (may also affect the gills) by *Gyrodactylus* spp.—monogenetic trematodes

SYMPTOMS   Inflamed patches on the skin and fins; erratic swimming; excessive secretion of body slime; accelerated respiration (if gills are affected); some loss of color; scratching on aquarium sides, bottom and equipment.

TREATMENTS   As for *Dactylogyrus*.

CRUSTACEAN INFECTIONS

FISH LOUSE INFECTION, CAUSATIVE AGENT: *Argulus*—usually *A. foliaceus*

SYMPTOMS   Nervous swimming and jumpiness, frequent, vigorous scratching, often resulting in loss of scales; heavy infestations are accompanied by anaemia and loss of color; the almost-transparent parasites can be seen attached to the body, mainly along the fin bases (adult parasites can be nearly ⅖in/1cm long).

TREATMENTS Organophosphate (Dichlorvos) bath (*see* Note 3). This treatment is recommended only for large fish: 1ppm for less than 1 hour, accompanied by very vigorous aeration, as Dichlorvos reduces oxygen levels; Potassium Permanganate (1g/liter for 30–45 seconds or 1g/10 liters for 5–10 minutes); physical removal of individual parasites with forceps followed by disinfection with a proprietary disinfectant, e.g. an Acriflavine-based compound.

ANCHOR WORM INFECTION, CAUSATIVE AGENT: *Lernaea* spp.

SYMPTOMS Long, thin, white, wormlike parasites (up to ¾in/2cm in length) attached to the body and/or fins; two white egg-sacs at the posterior end are usually visible.

TREATMENTS Some proprietary remedies are available, e.g. based on Copper Sulfate; Potassium Permanganate—as for *Argulus*. Salt bath (10–15g/liter for 20 minutes or 25g/liter for 10–15 minutes); Trichlorphon has been used (but *see* Note 3) at 1mg/liter as an indefinite bath, during which the parasite may become dislodged.

Several important questions that arise quite regularly in discussions regarding fish health management include the dangers of over/underdosing fish, how to dispose of terminally sick fish humanely, possible effects of medications on filters, and health implications for humans. These are briefly addressed in this section.

In addition to consulting some of the specialized texts recommended in the Bibliography, check aquarium magazines and the worldwide web for features on health management, as well as for information about short courses at academic institutions and (as happens from time to time) those sponsored by some of the leading aquatic industry manufacturers.

NOTES

1. Whenever antibiotics are being considered, it is wise to check with a vet for accurate dosage levels, even in countries where such products are legally available without prescription.
2. Malachite Green is currently widely available, but this situation may change owing to its possessing carcinogenic properties (although, at the levels used to treat ornamental fish, there appears to be no evidence that it poses any danger either to humans or fish).
3. It is vitally important to check on the legality of using organophosphates. For instance, the only such product that is licensed for use on fish in the U.K. (and even then,

◄ FISH LOUSE ▼ ANCHOR WORM

not on ornamentals) is Dichlorvos. It is now illegal to sell, or even give away, Trichlorphon products in Britain. (Trichlorphon breaks down into Dichlorvos, the active ingredient, after a longer or shorter time, depending on ambient conditions). However, it is legal to import it for use on one's own animals.

ADMINISTERING MEDICATION

When administering medications, it may prove necessary or desirable to treat an individual fish rather than a whole community. In such cases, the affected fish must be removed, either to a temporary bowl or bucket (if the treatment is designed to last for only a few minutes), or to a separate aquarium (quarantine tanks are particularly useful for this). Either way, the transfer should be carried out with as little stress to the fish as possible. Remember that the fish is already stressed as a result of its problems. Sick fish should be coaxed into a bowl or jar for transfer, rather than lifted physically from the water in a net. In any case, large fish, such as Koi, Dragon Fish, Arapaima or Pacus, should never be lifted in a net as their considerable weight means that—in the absence of supporting water—delicate internal organs can become damaged. Nets and receptacles used during transfer and treatment must be disinfected thoroughly after use.

Incorrect Dosage

Overdosing can kill not just the pathogens but the patient as well. It is therefore essential to know the exact capacity of the aquarium into which a medication is being introduced and to follow the recommended dosage levels to the letter. It is also vitally important to take the characteristics of the fish into consideration, since some types—scaleless species and varieties, such as some loaches, for example—

can be oversensitive to certain medications. Where relevant, such risks are normally pointed out by the medication's manufacturers.

Underdosing can be doubly injurious. In the short term, an inadequate dose will not kill the pathogenic organism, thus prolonging the treatment period and making it necessary to administer additional medication. In the long term, repeated use, particularly of antibiotics in low doses, can lead to a buildup of resistance.

If a fish exhibits any signs of distress while being subjected to medication, treatment must be stopped and the fish allowed to recover sufficiently before a revised dosage level is administered.

Filters, UV Sterilizers and Medications

Some filter media, such as ammonia-adsorbers, have only minor effects on medications. Other adsorbing media, such as activated carbon, can, however, remove at least some of the dosage. It is therefore advisable to switch off the aquarium filter during treatment or, alternatively, remove such media from the filter until treatment has been completed. Antibiotics do not generally distinguish between "good" and "bad" bacteria: they destroy both. As a result, filter bacteria will suffer if a biological filter is left in operation during antibiotic treatment.

Ultraviolet sterilizers can also neutralize or reduce the effects of certain medications, so they too should be switched off while the fish in an aquarium are undergoing treatment.

HUMANE DISPOSAL

This is a subject that causes great distress to many aquarists. However, it is one that must be faced, since some fish will become so ill that recovery is highly unlikely or out of the question. Several methods have been recommended over the years and, while some may be especially efficient in that death is virtually immediate, the mere fact that they involve inflicting physical damage on the fish rules them out for some. Two of the gentler forms of euthanasia appear not to cause undue distress and are therefore generally found to be acceptable.

Gradual Chilling

The fish is placed in a bag or bowl containing water with several tablespoonfuls of salt dissolved in it (this appears to calm the fish down). The bag or bowl is then placed in a freezer and allowed to cool gradually for several hours or overnight. As the temperature

drops, the metabolism of the fish slows down until it eventually ceases.

Anesthesia

Fish anesthetics, when used at higher than normal concentrations, will take fish beyond anesthesia to the point at which their metabolism stops (some time after they slip into unconsciousness). Anesthetics may be available with or without a vet's prescription, but, either way, professional advice should be sought when using this method of euthanasia.

RISKS TO HUMANS

Despite the occasional alarming headlines and distressing incidents of humans picking up disease organisms from aquatic animals (zoonoses), the risks are, in reality, very low and can be reduced even further with suitable precautions. Personal hygiene and protection measures adopted during aquarium maintenance should ensure that—barring an unforeseen circumstance—no contamination of any kind will occur.

ALWAYS ENSURE THAT YOU:

Use surgical gloves while carrying out maintenance or handling fish; particularly unhealthy specimens.

Avoid consuming food and drink while carrying out aquarium maintenance or handling sick fish.

Avoid exposing cuts or abrasions to aquarium water.

Wash hands thoroughly after carrying out aquarium maintenance or handling sick fish.

Never—but *never*—suck water via a siphon tube out of an aquarium by mouth.

The two pathogenic organisms that are associated with aquaria and, from time to time, cited as potentially harmful to humans are Salmonella (which can be contracted from many other sources, such as family pets, probably more easily than from aquarium water) and fish TB. Although the fish TB bacteria (at least two species of mycobacterium) are not ideally suited to survival within mammalian tissues, they can, on occasion, infect humans (usually via cuts or abrasions) and can cause localized and sometimes painful skin lesions that may require antibiotic treatment or chemotherapy and may prove slow to clear. Should any form of infection be suspected, medical advice should be sought promptly.

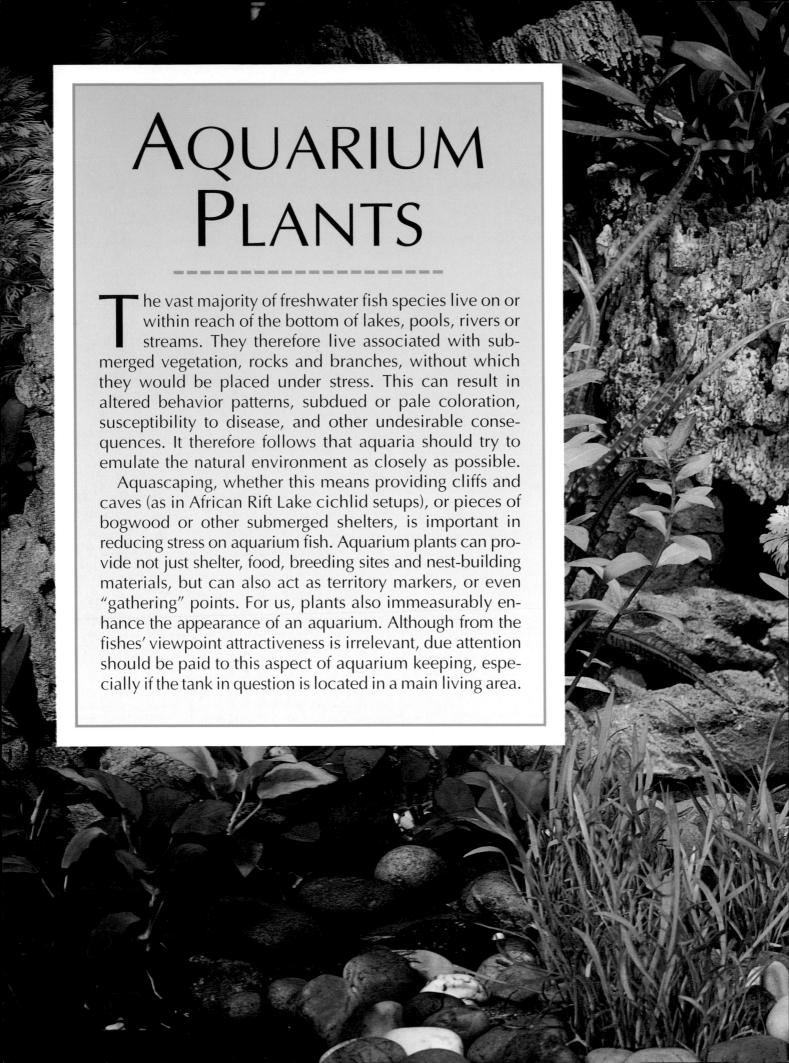

AQUARIUM PLANTS

The vast majority of freshwater fish species live on or within reach of the bottom of lakes, pools, rivers or streams. They therefore live associated with submerged vegetation, rocks and branches, without which they would be placed under stress. This can result in altered behavior patterns, subdued or pale coloration, susceptibility to disease, and other undesirable consequences. It therefore follows that aquaria should try to emulate the natural environment as closely as possible.

Aquascaping, whether this means providing cliffs and caves (as in African Rift Lake cichlid setups), or pieces of bogwood or other submerged shelters, is important in reducing stress on aquarium fish. Aquarium plants can provide not just shelter, food, breeding sites and nest-building materials, but can also act as territory markers, or even "gathering" points. For us, plants also immeasurably enhance the appearance of an aquarium. Although from the fishes' viewpoint attractiveness is irrelevant, due attention should be paid to this aspect of aquarium keeping, especially if the tank in question is located in a main living area.

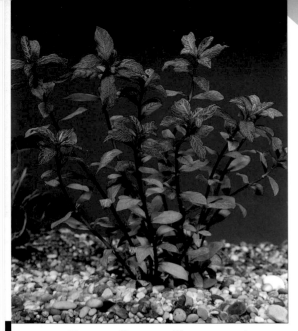

Variegated Hygrophila (Hygrophila spp.)

SPADE LEAF PLANT

Gymnocoronis spp. ■

WATER PREFERENCES: *Not critical*

LIGHTING: *Medium to very high*

TEMPERATURE RANGE: *Coldwater/tropical*

HEMIANTHUS MICRANTHEMOIDES ■

WATER PREFERENCES: *Not critical*

LIGHTING: *Medium to very high*

TEMPERATURE RANGE: *Coldwater/tropical*

HEMIGRAPHIS SPP. ▲

WATER PREFERENCES: *Not critical*

LIGHTING: *Medium to high*

TEMPERATURE RANGE: *Coldwater/tropical*

WATER STARGRASS

Heteranthera zosterifolia

WATER PREFERENCES: *Not critical*

LIGHTING: *High to very high*

TEMPERATURE RANGE: *Coldwater/tropical*

WATER VIOLET

Hottonia inflata and *H. palustris*

WATER PREFERENCES: *Soft to medium hard*

LIGHTING: *High to very high*

TEMPERATURE RANGE: *Coldwater/tropical (lower end)*

HYDRILLA

Hydrilla verticillata

WATER PREFERENCES: *Not critical*

LIGHTING: *High*

TEMPERATURE RANGE: *Tropical*

NUMEROUS TYPES, e.g. HYGROPHILA, WATER WISTERIA, WATER STAR

Hygrophila spp. and varieties ■
(*H. polysperma* ●)

WATER PREFERENCES: *Not critical*

LIGHTING: *Low to high, depending on type*

TEMPERATURE RANGE: *Coldwater (upper end)/ tropical*

CRISPA

Lagarosiphon major

WATER PREFERENCES: *Not critical*

LIGHTING: *High*

TEMPERATURE RANGE: *Coldwater*

FALSE TENELLUS

Lilaeopsis brasiliensis, L. novaezelandiae

WATER PREFERENCES: *Not critical*

LIGHTING: *Medium to very high*

TEMPERATURE RANGE: *Coldwater/tropical (lower end)*

AMBULIA

Limnophila spp.

WATER PREFERENCES: *Soft to medium hard*

LIGHTING: *Medium to very high*

TEMPERATURE RANGE: *Tropical (L. aquatica tolerant of slightly lower temperatures)*

LOBELIA

Lobelia cardinalis ■

WATER PREFERENCES: *Not critical*

LIGHTING: *Medium to very high*

TEMPERATURE RANGE: *Coldwater/tropical (lower end)*

LUDWIGIA

Ludwigia spp. ■

WATER PREFERENCES: *Not critical for most species (notable exception: L. inclinata—soft to medium)*

LIGHTING: *Medium to high*

Java Fern (Microsorum pteropus) ▶

TEMPERATURE RANGE: *Coldwater/tropical for most species. Notable exceptions: L. arcuata and L. glandulosa ("perennis")—only upper end of coldwater range; L. inclinata—only tropical*

MONEYWORT, CREEPING JENNY

Lysmachia nummularia ■

WATER PREFERENCES: *Not critical*

LIGHTING: *High to very high*

TEMPERATURE RANGE: *Coldwater/tropical (lower end)*

False Tenellus (Lilaeopsis brasiliensis)

MARCH TREFOIL, CLOVER

Marsilea crenata

WATER PREFERENCES: *Soft to medium*

LIGHTING: *Medium to high*

TEMPERATURE RANGE: *Coldwater*

JAVA FERN

Microsorum pteropus and varieties ● ■

WATER PREFERENCES: *Not critical*

LIGHTING: *Not critical*

TEMPERATURE RANGE: *Coldwater/tropical*

MILFOIL

Myriophyllum spp. ■ *some species*

WATER PREFERENCES: *Not critical*

LIGHTING: *High to very high*

TEMPERATURE RANGE: *Coldwater/tropical*

INDIAN NAJAD

Najas indica ●

WATER PREFERENCES: *Soft to medium hard*

LIGHTING: *Medium to high*

TEMPERATURE RANGE: *Tropical*

GIANT HYGROPHILA

Nomaphila stricta ● ■

WATER PREFERENCES: *Not critical*

LIGHTING: *High*

TEMPERATURE RANGE: *Coldwater (upper end)/ tropical*

JAPANESE SPATTERDOCK

Nuphar japonica

WATER PREFERENCES: *Not critical*

LIGHTING: *Not critical*

TEMPERATURE RANGE: *Coldwater/tropical*

AFRICAN TIGER LOTUS

Nymphaea maculata

WATER PREFERENCES: *Not critical*

LIGHTING: *High*

TEMPERATURE RANGE: *Coldwater (upper end)/ tropical*

BANANA PLANT

Nymphoides aquatica

WATER PREFERENCES: *Not critical*

LIGHTING: *High*

TEMPERATURE RANGE: *Coldwater (upper end)/ tropical*

JAPANESE FOUNTAIN PLANT

Ophiopogon japonicus ▲

WATER PREFERENCES: *Not critical*

LIGHTING: *Medium to very high*

TEMPERATURE RANGE: *Coldwater/tropical*

ALUMINUM PLANT

Pilea cadieri ▲

WATER PREFERENCES: *Not critical*

LIGHTING: *Not critical*

TEMPERATURE RANGE: *Coldwater/tropical*

FLORIDA CRYPTO

Physostegia leptophylla ■

WATER PREFERENCES: *Not critical*

LIGHTING: *Medium to high*

TEMPERATURE RANGE: *Coldwater (upper end)/ tropical*

CURLED PONDWEED

Potamogeton crispus

WATER PREFERENCES: *Not critical*

LIGHTING: *High*

TEMPERATURE RANGE: *Coldwater*

ROTALA

Rotala spp. and varieties ■

WATER PREFERENCES: *Not critical, but some exceptions, e.g. R. wallichii—soft to medium hard*

LIGHTING: *High to very high*

TEMPERATURE RANGE: *Coldwater/tropical, but some exceptions, e.g. R. macrandra—tropical*

SAG or SAGITTARIA

Sagittaria spp. ● (some species) and ■

WATER PREFERENCES: *Not critical*

LIGHTING: *Not critical*

TEMPERATURE RANGE: *Coldwater/tropical*

WATER CABBAGE, WATER ROSE

Samolus spp. ■ (*S. parviflorus* ●)

WATER PREFERENCES: *Not critical*

LIGHTING: *High to very high*

TEMPERATURE RANGE: *Coldwater/tropical*

LIZARD'S TAIL

Saururus cernuus ■

WATER PREFERENCES: *Not critical*

LIGHTING: *High to very high*

TEMPERATURE RANGE: *Coldwater/tropical*

MEXICAN OAK LEAF

Shinnersia rivularis ■

WATER PREFERENCES: *Not critical*

LIGHTING: *Medium to high*

TEMPERATURE RANGE: *Coldwater/tropical*

STRAIGHT VALLIS (VALLISNERIA SPP.) ▶

SPATHIPHYLLUM

Spathiphyllum wallisii ■

WATER PREFERENCES: *Soft to medium hard*

LIGHTING: *Not critical*

TEMPERATURE RANGE: *Tropical*

SYNGONIUM, IVY LEAF

Syngonium podophyllum ▲

WATER PREFERENCES: *Not critical*

LIGHTING: *Not critical*

TEMPERATURE RANGE: *Coldwater/tropical*

BLADDERWORT

Utricularia spp.

WATER PREFERENCES: *Not critical*

LIGHTING: *Medium to high*

TEMPERATURE RANGE: *Coldwater/tropical*

VALLIS, TAPE GRASS

Vallisneria spp. and varieties ●

WATER PREFERENCES: *Not critical*

LIGHTING: *Not critical*

TEMPERATURE RANGE: *Coldwater/tropical*

JAVA MOSS

Vesicularia dubyana ● ■

WATER PREFERENCES: *Not critical*

LIGHTING: *Not critical*

TEMPERATURE RANGE: *Coldwater/tropical*

AQUARIUM FISH

T HE SECTION THAT FOLLOWS CONTAINS AN EXTENSIVE selection of species and varieties of fish that are available for aquaria. As both popularity and availability vary from country to country, the selection includes species that may be virtually unknown, or which might only be occasionally encountered, in some regions. Every attempt has been made to use the latest scientific names for all species. However, level of acceptance or frequency of use of scientific names also vary between countries and alternatives have been indicated where they might help identification: *Barbus conchonius*, for example, the Rosy Barb, is also frequently referred to as *Puntius conchonius*. Hopefully, this double reference will help aquarists in different countries identify the fish in question without any difficulty.

All the major fish families carry an introductory section highlighting their main characteristics. However, space limitations dictate that this is not possible for every family. The Bibliography lists works that will allow interested readers to obtain such information.

unrelated, reasons. It was one of the first cichlids to be imported into Europe (1902), and it is the northernmost cichlid species known. A similar-looking species, the Blue or Green Texas Cichlid (*H. carpinte*), from Mexico (not Texas!) is sometimes confused with *H. cyanoguttatus*. Other *Herichthys* species are only infrequently encountered in the hobby.

DISTRIBUTION: *Texas and northern Mexico*

SIZE: *Up to 12in (30cm), but usually smaller*

BEHAVIOR: *Aggressive and territorial burrower that will uproot plants*

DIET: *Wide range of large foods accepted*

AQUARIUM: *Only stout, protected plants are suitable (see Aquarium Plants). Large open spaces with shelters should be provided. Water chemistry not critical but well-filtered water important. Temperature range: 59–77°F (15–25°C)*

BREEDING: *Eggs are laid on a precleaned site. Parental care is not as pronounced in this species as in most other cichlids*

SEVERUM CICHLID
EYESPOT, or BANDED, CICHLID
Heros severus

THE SEVERUM IS ANOTHER OLD FAVORITE (FIRST imported in 1909) that has held its own against strong competition from other species. Undoubtedly, the cultivated golden form of the species has played a large part in this.

DISTRIBUTION: *Northern South America, down to the Amazon basin*

SIZE: *Some wild-caught specimens reported up to 12in (30cm), but usually smaller*

BEHAVIOR: *Territorial but not overaggressive toward other medium-size or large tankmates, except during breeding*

DIET: *Wide range of foods accepted*

AQUARIUM: *Spacious, with substantial plants, shelters, and at least one flat-topped or smoothly rounded rock. Water chemistry not critical, but soft, acid, well-filtered water recommended. Temperature range: 73–77°F (23–25°C); slightly higher for breeding*

BREEDING: *Eggs are laid on a precleaned site and are defended—as are the fry—by both parents. This species is sometimes reported as showing some signs of mouthbrooding*

PARROT CICHLID

Hoplarchus psittacus

DESPITE ITS COMMON NAME, THIS SPECIES IS quite distinct from the Red Parrot Cichlid

TEXAS CICHLID (HERICHTHYS CYANOGUTTATUS)

featured elsewhere (*see* "*Cichlasoma*" Red Parrot, p.93). It is a large species in which fully adult males have a well-rounded head.

DISTRIBUTION: *Rio Negro and Rio Orinoco*

SIZE: *Fully mature males reported up to 16in (40cm); usually smaller*

BEHAVIOR: *Territorial, but can be kept with other large species in roomy aquaria*

DIET: *All large foods accepted; vegetable component recommended*

AQUARIUM: *Large tank with stout vegetation and sizable rocks (without sharp edges!) and/or bogwood. Water chemistry not critical, but soft, acid, well-filtered water is best. Temperature range: 75–81°F (24–27°C); slightly higher for breeding*

BREEDING: *Infrequent in aquaria. Eggs are laid on a precleaned site (often vertically oriented) and protected by both parents*

CHOCOLATE CICHLID
Hypselacara coryphaenoides

SYNONYM: *Hypselacara temporalis*

THE COMMON NAME CHOCOLATE CICHLID IS sometimes used for *Hypselacara temporalis* as well as for *H. coryphaenoides*. This has

led to frequent confusion and the misuse of the scientific names for the two "Chocolate Cichlids." It is for this reason that *H. temporalis*, which originates in the Brazilian and Peruvian Amazon, is listed above.

DISTRIBUTION: *Rio Orinoco basin*

SIZE: *Males up to 12in (30cm), but usually smaller*

BEHAVIOR: *Territorial, particularly during breeding*

DIET: *All large foods*

AQUARIUM: *Large, deep, with numerous shelters and stout plants. Water chemistry not critical, but soft, slightly acid, well-filtered water preferred. Temperature range: 75–82°F (24–28°C)*

BREEDING: *Eggs are laid on a precleaned site and protected by both parents*

RUSTY CICHLID
PETROTILAPIA TRIDENTIGER
Iodotropheus sprengerae

ALTHOUGH SOME COLOR MORPHS OF THIS SPECIES undoubtedly have a "rusty" element to their body coloration, *I. sprengerae* is, nevertheless, more colorful and variable than its name suggests. This is one of the easier species of African Rift Lake cichlids to keep and breed, and it is therefore often recommended for those entering this branch of the hobby for the first time. A few other *Iodotropheus* species are available but, generally, not as widely as the Rusty Cichlid.

DISTRIBUTION: *Southeastern arm of Lake Malawi*

SIZE: *Around 4in (10cm)*

BEHAVIOR: *Relatively tolerant, even of its own species (in a sufficiently roomy aquarium)*

DIET: *Wide range of foods accepted*

AQUARIUM: *Typical African Rift Lake layout (see Aquarium Set-up). Medium-hard, alkaline, well-filtered water important. Temperature range: 72–77°F (22–25°C); slightly higher for breeding*

BREEDING: *Typical maternal mouthbrooder; will breed even when quite small and relatively young (at around three-and-a-half months)*

DICKFELD'S JULIE
BROWN JULIE

Julidochromis dickfeldi

UNUSUALLY FOR AN AFRICAN RIFT LAKE SPECIES, the various Julies, including *J. dickfeldi*, are not mouthbrooders. This species, the Yellow

or Ornate Julie (*J. ornatus*), and the Masked or Black-and-white Julie (*J. transcriptus*), are often referred to as the "dwarf" Julies, although the size difference between them and the other two species is not always as large as their "labels" might suggest.

DISTRIBUTION: *Southwestern part of Lake Tanganyika*

SIZE: *Up to 4in (10cm), but often smaller*

BEHAVIOR: *Intolerant toward its own species*

DIET: *Wide range of foods accepted*

AQUARIUM: *African Rift Lake layout (see Aquarium Set-up) with numerous rock shelters and open sandy areas. Medium-hard, alkaline, well-filtered water important. Temperature range: 72–77°F (22–25°C); slightly higher for breeding*

BREEDING: *Eggs are laid in a cave, and they and the fry are cared for by both parents*

MARLIER'S JULIE

Julidochromis marlieri

ALONG WITH THE STRIPED OR REGAN'S JULIE (*J. regani*), this variably patterned species is regarded as one of the "large" Julies. Some authors believe that the two groups

should be regarded as separate subgenera, but the majority opinion still favors the current status quo.

DISTRIBUTION: *Discontinuous, occurring both in the northern and southeastern parts of Lake Tanganyika*

SIZE: *Up to 6in (15cm) reported, but usually smaller*

BEHAVIOR: *As for J. dickfeldi*

DIET: *As for J. dickfeldi*

AQUARIUM: *As for J. dickfeldi*

BREEDING: *As in J. dickfeldi, but may hybridize with J. ornatus. Egg care may be undertaken more by female than by male*

FUELLEBORN'S CICHLID

Labeotropheus fuelleborni

VIRTUALLY INDISTINGUISHABLE PHYSICALLY FROM *L. trewavassae* (*see* p.102), this exceptionally variable species is restricted to shallow, wave-washed habitats. Many morphs are available, both wild-caught and captive-bred ones.

DISTRIBUTION: *Throughout Lake Malawi*

RUSTY CICHLID (IODOTROPHEUS SPRENGERAE)

DICKFELD'S JULIE (JULIDOCHROMIS DICKFELDI)

SIZE: *Male, wild-caught specimens reported up to 7in (18cm), but usually smaller; females smaller*

BEHAVIOR: *Males are territorial and aggressive toward both sexes, particularly other males*

DIET: *Wide range of foods accepted*

AQUARIUM: *Roomy African Rift Lake layout (see Aquarium Set-up) with numerous caves and shelters. Robust plants may be added, as well as at least one flat-topped rock. Medium-hard, alkaline, well-filtered water important. Temperature range: 70–77°F (21–25°C); slightly higher for breeding*

BREEDING: *Eggs are laid on a flat surface or inside a cave and are incubated orally by female*

FUELLEBORN'S CICHLID
(LABEOTROPHEUS FUELLEBORNI)

▲ *Flag Cichlid* (Mesonauta festivus)   ▼ *Zebra Cichlid* (Metriaclima zebra)

doubt regarding the true identity of the species, with a school of thought leaning toward the "festivus" from the Río Negro being renamed *M. insignis* and those from other areas being regarded as the "true" *M. festivus*.

DISTRIBUTION: *Amazon basin, but may exist elsewhere, e.g. Guyana*

SIZE: *Up to 8in (20cm) reported, but usually smaller*

BEHAVIOR: *Territorial at breeding time, but otherwise can be timid*

DIET: *All foods accepted*

AQUARIUM: *Spacious and well planted, with adequate shelter and at least one flat-topped or smooth, rounded rock. Water chemistry not critical, but soft, slightly acid conditions preferred. Temperature range: 72–77°F (22–25°C); slightly higher for breeding*

BREEDING: *Eggs are laid on a precleaned site, which can be a broadleaved plant or a rock. Eggs and fry are protected by both parents*

ZEBRA CICHLID
NYASA BLUE CICHLID
Metriaclima zebra

SYNONYM: *Pseudotropheus zebra*

THIS IS ONE OF THE "KEYSTONE" SPECIES OF THE African Rift Lake cichlid hobby. Numerous morphs occur in the wild, and male coloration is very different to that of the female. Some of the types are incapable of interbreeding, and this has given rise to the belief that they may constitute separate species, rather than morphs. As a result, the collection of all these intimately related species/morphs are referred to as the "zebra complex." The new name, *Metriaclima*, was erected in 1997 and now includes several new species that would formerly have been regarded as *Pseudotropheus*.

DISTRIBUTION: *Widely distributed in Lake Malawi*

SIZE: *Up to 6in (15cm) reported, but usually smaller*

BEHAVIOR: *Territorial and aggressive, particularly toward its own kind*

DIET: *Wide range of foods accepted*

AQUARIUM: *Typical African Rift Lake layout (see Aquarium Set-up). Medium-hard to hard, alkaline, well-filtered water important. Temperature range: 72–82°F (22–28°C)*

BREEDING: *Typical maternal mouthbrooder*

ALTISPINOSA BUTTERFLY CICHLID
BOLIVIAN BUTTERFLY CICHLID
Microgeophagus altispinosus

SYNONYM: *Papiliochromis altispinosus*

SLIGHTLY LARGER THAN ITS BETTER-KNOWN closest relative, the Ram (*M. ramirezi, see* below), this beautiful and variable species also has a particularly striking dorsal fin when it is fully extended. Males have extended top and bottom caudal fin rays and, generally speaking, brilliantly colored pelvic and anal fins.

DISTRIBUTION: *Eastern Bolivia and Mato Grosso, Brazil*

SIZE: *Males around 3in (8cm); females slightly smaller*

BEHAVIOR: *Peaceful and tolerant of other tankmates; territorial during breeding*

DIET: *Wide range of foods accepted, but livefoods preferred*

AQUARIUM: *Well planted, with adequate shelter, fine-grained substratum, and a flat-topped or rounded rock. Soft, slightly acid to slightly alkaline water recommended. Raw water should be avoided. Temperature range: 72–77°F (22–25°C); slightly higher for breeding*

BREEDING: *Eggs are laid on a precleaned site and are protected primarily by female. Care of fry (which are often transferred between pits dug by male) is undertaken by both parents*

RAM
BUTTERFLY, or RAMIREZ'S, DWARF CICHLID
Microgeophagus ramirezi

SYNONYM: *Papiliochromis ramirezi*

THIS SPECTACULAR DWARF CICHLID HAS BEEN popular in the hobby for over 50 years, and with good reason. The wild type, in particular, is one of the "jewels" of the aquarium, although many of the cultivated forms, especially the gold, are also extremely attractive. In the late 1990s, a "Jumbo" form of the Ram was introduced. Whether it ever replaces its smaller counterparts, though, only time will tell.

▲ RAM *(MICROGEOPHAGUS RAMIREZI)*
FRIEDRICHSTHAL'S CICHLID *(NANDOPSIS FRIEDRICHSTHALII)* ▶

DISTRIBUTION: *Colombia and Venezuela*

SIZE: *Wild-caught specimens and most cultivated forms up to 2¾in (7cm), but usually smaller; Jumbos somewhat larger*

BEHAVIOR: *As for* M. altispinosus

DIET: *As for* M. altispinosus

AQUARIUM: *As for* M. altispinosus

BREEDING: *Eggs are laid on a precleaned site or in a depression in the substratum, and they and the fry are cared for by both parents*

RED TERROR
FESTA'S, OR TIGER, CICHLID
Nandopsis festae

SYNONYMS: *Cichlasoma festae, Herichthys festae*

SOME OF THE COLOR FORMS OF THIS LARGE SPECIES are truly stunning, particularly during breeding. Orange-bodied, black- or blue-banded types with iridescent scales are especially striking.

DISTRIBUTION: *Ecuador*

SIZE: *Fully mature males reported up to 20in (50cm), but usually somewhat smaller; females smaller*

BEHAVIOR: *Aggressive and territorial; should be kept only with equally large, robust tankmates*

DIET: *Large commercial formulations and livefoods accepted*

AQUARIUM: *Spacious, with open spaces and substantial shelters. Rocks and other decor should be well bedded. Plants need to be protected (see Aquarium Plants). Water chemistry not critical, but well-filtered, soft, neutral water recommended. Temperature range: 77–82°F (25–28°C)*

BREEDING: *Eggs are laid on a precleaned site (usually a rock). Female guards eggs while male defends territory. Fry are initially moved between predug pits by both parents*

FRIEDRICHSTHAL'S CICHLID
Nandopsis friedrichsthalii

SYNONYMS: *Cichlasoma friedrichsthalii, Herichthys friedrichsthalii, Parachromis friedrichsthalii*

A LITTLE SMALLER BUT SOMEWHAT MORE ELONGATE than *N. festae*, This is another well-marked species whose beauty is best appreciated in fully mature specimens.

DISTRIBUTION: *Widely distributed in Central America*

SIZE: *Up to 13¾in (35cm), but usually smaller; females smaller than males*

BEHAVIOR: *As for* N. festae

DIET: *As for* N. festae

AQUARIUM: *As for* N. festae, *but temperature range: 72–81°F (22–27°C)*

BREEDING: *As for* N. festae

MANAGUA CICHLID
JAGUAR CICHLID
Nandopsis managuense

SYNONYMS: *Cichlasoma managuense, Heros managuense, Herichthys managuensis, Parachromis managuense*

THE SECOND COMMON NAME OF THIS SPECIES APTLY describes both the coloration and patterning

MANAGUA CICHLID (NANDOPSIS MANAGUENSE)

of this impressive cichlid which, like other widely distributed species, occurs in several forms, depending on locality.

DISTRIBUTION: *Central America*

SIZE: *Some fully mature males reported over ca.18in (45cm), but usually smaller; females smaller than males*

BEHAVIOR: *As for N. festae*

DIET: *As for N. festae*

AQUARIUM: *As for N. festae, but temperature range: 73–77°F (23–25°C)*

BREEDING: *Basically, as for N. festae, but female often takes on the major share of fry care*

JACK DEMPSEY

Nandopsis octofasciatus

SYNONYMS: *Cichlasoma octofasciatum, Cichlasoma biocellatum, Heros octofasciatus*

NAMED AFTER LEGENDARY BOXER, JACK DEMPSEY, this pugnacious cichlid lives up to its name. However, it is a most attractively marked species that despite its temperament is still much sought after.

DISTRIBUTION: *Belize, Guatemala, Honduras and southern Mexico*

SIZE: *Males to over 8in (20cm); females smaller*

BEHAVIOR: *Territorial, aggressive burrower; will damage plants*

DIET: *As for N. festae*

AQUARIUM: *As for N. festae, but temperature range: 72–77°F (22–25°C)*

BREEDING: *As for N. festae*

SALVIN'S CICHLID

TRICOLOR CICHLID

Nandopsis salvini

SYNONYMS: *Cichlasoma salvini, Heros salvini, Herichthys salvini*

THIS IS ANOTHER SPECTACULARLY COLORED MEMber of the genus. Although it is a substantial fish, the adult coloration begins to develop (particularly in males) while the fish are still modestly sized (i.e. about half the full size).

DISTRIBUTION: *Guatemala, Honduras and southern Mexico*

SIZE: *Fully mature males reported over 8in (20cm), but usually smaller; females smaller*

BEHAVIOR: *Territorial and intolerant of rivals, but may be kept with similar-sized fish. Unlike other members of the genus, does not uproot plants*

DIET: *As for N. festae*

AQUARIUM: *As for N. festae, but temperature range: 72–79°F (22–26°C)*

BREEDING: *As for N. festae*

GOLDEN DWARF ACARA

GOLDEN-EYED DWARF CICHLID

Nannacara anomala

THIS IS A HIGHLY VARIABLE SPECIES whose coloration and patterning both differ between localities. This has led to some doubt regarding its possible presence in French Guiana, with some authorities believing that the fish that are found in this region belong to a separate species, the Goldhead Nannacara (*N. aureocephalus*). A third species, the Adok Nannacara (*N. adoketa*) from the Río Negro in Brazil is also sometimes available to aquarists.

DISTRIBUTION: *Northern South America and, possibly, French Guiana (see above)*

SIZE: *Males up to 3½in (9cm); females much smaller*

BEHAVIOR: *A peaceful, tolerant species, except during breeding*

DIET: *Most commercial formulations accepted, but livefoods preferred*

AQUARIUM: *Heavily planted, with ample shelter and fine-grained substratum recommended. Soft to moderately hard, slightly acid water is best. Temperature range: 72–77°F (22–25°C); slightly higher for breeding*

BREEDING: *Eggs are laid in a cave, and both they and the fry are guarded by female, which develops distinctive coloration at this time*

CONGO DWARF CICHLID

NUDICEPS

Nanochromis parilus

SYNONYMS: *Nanochromis parilius, N. nudiceps*

THIS SPECIES, ALONG WITH TWO OF ITS CLOSEST relatives, *N. dimidiatus* and *N. transvestitus*, is one of the relatively few dwarf cichlids from Africa (excluding the Rift Lake dwarves) that is fairly widely available in the hobby. Both sexes are beautifully, though differently, colored. Females appear to be full of eggs all the time and possess a pinkish belly flush,

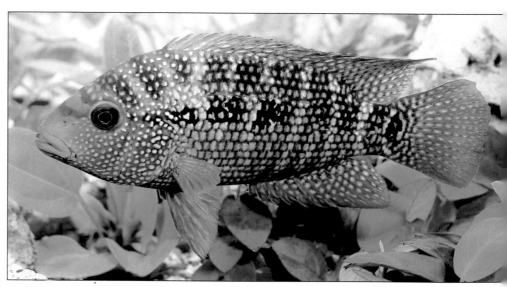

▲ JACK DEMPSEY (NANDOPSIS OCTOFASCIATUS)　　▼ SALVIN'S CICHLID (NANDOPSIS SALVINI)

OTHER *NANDOPSIS* SPECIES

Despite the obvious drawbacks that their large size and generally territorial and aggressive behavior pose, *Nandopsis* species are quite popular. In addition to the featured species, the following are also available with varying regularity. The sizes given below are for fully mature males; females are smaller.

SCIENTIFIC NAME	COMMON NAME(S)	SIZE
N. bartoni	Barton's Cichlid	8¾in (22cm)
N. beani	Bean's Cichlid	10in (25cm)
N. dovii	Dow's, or Wolf, Cichlid	20in (50cm)
N. facetum	Chancito Cichlid	10in (25cm)
N. grammodes	Sieve, or Many-pointed, Cichlid	10in (25cm)
N. haitiensis	Haiti Cichlid	10in (25cm)
N. istlanum	Rio Ixtla Cichlid or Istlanum	12in (30cm)
N. labridens	Tooth-lipped Cichlid	10in (25cm)
N. loisellei	Loiselle's Cichlid	12in (30cm)
N. motaguense	Motagua Cichlid	12in (30cm)
N. ornatus	Ornament Cichlid	10in (25cm)
N. ramsdeni	Ramsden's Cichlid	13¾in (35cm)
N. steindachneri	Steindachner's Cichlid	10in (25cm)
N. tetracanthus	Cuban Cichlid	13¾in (35cm)
N. umbriferus	Dark, or Blue-speckled, Cichlid	24in (60cm)
N. urophthalmus	Tail-spot Tiger, or Eight-barred, Cichlid	16in (40cm)
N. vombergae	Mia's Cichlid	8in (20cm)

DOW'S CICHLID (N. DOVII)

GOLDEN DWARF ACARA (NANNACARA ANOMALA)

CONGO DWARF CICHLID (NANOCHROMIS PARILUS)

which reveals the relationship of this species with the other African dwarves commonly referred to as Kribs (*see Pelvicachromis pulcher*, p.111).

DISTRIBUTION: *Zaire basin, particularly Stanley Pool*

SIZE: *Males up to 3in (8cm); females a little smaller*

BEHAVIOR: *Males are aggressive toward rivals and often toward unreceptive females as well*

DIET: *Commercial formulations accepted but livefoods preferred*

AQUARIUM: *Well planted, with numerous shelters and caves. Soft, slightly acid water (preferably filtered through peat or containing a "blackwater"* commercial additive) is best. Temperature range: 72–77°F (22–25°C); slightly higher for breeding

BREEDING: *Eggs are laid in a cave, and both they and the fry are guarded by female while male generally defends territory*

LITTLE LAKE CICHLID
PYGMY GREEN-EYED CICHLID
Neetroplus nematopus

SYNONYMS: *Neetroplus fluviatilis, N. nematopus*

THIS MODESTLY SIZED SPECIES IS NOT SEEN AS often as it should be. One particularly interesting feature is that a breeding pair will reverse their color pattern once spawning is over. The female is first to change, with her body darkening and the dark body bar lightening; the male follows once the eggs hatch and fry care begins. An even more geographically variable species, *N. panamensis* (from Panama), is also available.

DISTRIBUTION: *Costa Rica and Nicaragua*

SIZE: *Up to 5½in (14cm)*

BEHAVIOR: *Can become very aggressive and territorial, particularly during breeding*

DIET: *All foods accepted; vegetable component recommended*

BEHAVIOR: *Aggressive toward its own species; only one pair should be kept*

DIET: *Livefoods preferred*

AQUARIUM: *Typical African Rift Lake layout (see Aquarium Set-up). Well-filtered, medium-hard, alkaline water important. Temperature range: 73–79°F (23–26°C)*

BREEDING: *Eggs are laid inside a cave and are protected*

LIVINGSTONI

Nimbochromis livingstonii

SYNONYMS: *Haplochromis livingstonii, Cyrtocara livingstonii*

THIS RELATIVELY LARGE CICHLID SPECIES IS exceptionally marked. In particular, the brown body patches on a light-colored base, coupled with the red tinge of the anal fin of males, make it a striking fish even among more spectacularly colored species.

DISTRIBUTION: *Throughout Lake Malawi*

SIZE: *Up to 10in (25cm)*

BEHAVIOR: *Predatory; lies on the bottom feigning death, and lunges at any swallowable fish that swims up to investigate*

DIET: *Large commercial formulations accepted, but prefers livefood*

AQUARIUM: *Well-filtered, African Rift Lake layout (see Aquarium Set-up), with sandy areas. Medium-hard, alkaline water required. Temperature range: 73–79°F (23–26°C)*

BREEDING: *Maternal mouthbrooder*

VENUSTUS

Nimbochromis venustus

SYNONYMS: *Haplochromis venustus, Cyrtocara venusta*

WHILE VENUSTUS POSSESSES SOME DARK BODY patches, they are usually less pronounced than in *N. livingstonii*. The head is blue with or without yellow on the top. There is also yellow on the top of the caudal peduncle and elsewhere on the body.

DISTRIBUTION: *Throughout Lake Malawi*

SIZE: *Up to 9in (22.5cm) recorded in the wild*

BEHAVIOR: *Territorial and intolerant burrower*

DIET: *Commercial diets accepted, but livefoods preferred*

AQUARIUM: *As for N. livingstonii*

BREEDING: *As for N. livingstonii*

VENTRALIS CICHLID

BLUE GOLD-TIP CICHLID
Ophthalmotilapia ventralis

SYNONYM: *Ophthalmochromis ventralis*

THE MOST IMMEDIATELY DISTINGUISHABLE CHARacteristic of the four available *Opthalmotilapia* species are the extremely long pelvic fins of the males, each with a distinctively marked thickening of the tip. These act in the same way as the eggspots on the anal fin of other Rift Lake cichlids.

DISTRIBUTION: *Most of Lake Tanganyika, but not north of the Ubwari Peninsula*

SIZE: *About 6in (15cm)*

BEHAVIOR: *Territorial during breeding; may burrow while spawning; males aggressive toward each other*

DIET: *Wide range of foods accepted, but livefoods preferred; vegetable component recommended*

AQUARIUM: *African Rift Lake layout (see Aquarium Set-up), with sandy areas. Medium-hard, alkaline water required. Temperature range: 73–79°F (23–26°C)*

BREEDING: *Maternal mouthbrooder*

OTHER *NIMBOCHROMIS* SPECIES

Three other *Nimbochromis* are regularly available. All are predatory and have the same basic requirements as the two featured species.

SCIENTIFIC NAME	COMMON NAME(S)	SIZE
N. fuscotaeniatus	Fuscotaeniatus	10in (25cm)
N. linni	Elephant-nosed Cichlid	10in+ (25cm+)
N. polystigma	Polystigma	9in (23cm)

◀ LIVINGSTONI (NIMBOCHROMIS LIVINGSTONII)
▼ VENUSTUS (NIMBOCHROMIS VENUSTUS)

OTHER *OPHTHALMOTILAPIA* SPECIES

In addition to *O. ventralis*, the three following species, which have similar requirements, are often available.

SCIENTIFIC NAME	COMMON NAME(S)	SIZE
O. boops	Dusty Gold-tip Cichlid	6in (15cm)
O. heterodonta	Gold-tip Cichlid	5½in (14cm)
O. nasuta	Nasutus, or Long-nosed, Cichlid	8in (20cm)

MOZAMBIQUE MOUTHBROODER

Oreochromis mossambicus

SYNONYMS: *Sarotherodon mossambicus, Tilapia mossambica*

THIS IS A LARGE, TOUGH FISH THAT IS ABLE TO tolerate a wide range of conditions (even fully marine ones) and will reproduce with great facility and regularity in aquaria. A "red" variety, which is more pink than red, plus several mottled ones, are available. It hybridizes with its close relatives and is widely used as a food fish, as are the two other *Oreochromis* species that are occasionally encountered in the hobby: *O. (Sarotherodon) galileus* and *O. niloticus*.

DISTRIBUTION: *Eastern Africa, but widely introduced elsewhere*

SIZE: *Fully mature males up to 16in (40cm); females much smaller*

BEHAVIOR: *Aggressive burrower that destroys (and eats) plants; highly territorial during breeding*

DIET: *All large foods accepted; vegetable supplement recommended*

AQUARIUM: *Large, with well-bedded decor or rocks. Well-filtered water. Water chemistry not critical and can range from soft to brackish. Temperature range: 68–74°F (20–24°C); slightly higher for breeding*

BREEDING: *Male excavates large pit to which he attracts females. After spawning, female incubates the eggs orally and subsequently cares for the fry*

POLLENI
MARAKELY

Paratilapia polleni

THIS IS AN IMPRESSIVE DARK-BROWN SPECIES with numerous, small, white, or cream-colored spots. During breeding, males turn almost blue-black, making them even more attractive. Being a large fish, the Marakely is primarily regarded as a food fish in wild.

DISTRIBUTION: *Madagascar*

SIZE: *Up to 12in (30cm)*

BEHAVIOR: *Territorial; should only be housed with similar-sized fish*

DIET: *Wide range of foods accepted, but livefoods preferred*

AQUARIUM: *Spacious, with appropriately large shelters. Plants need protection (see Aquarium Plants). Well-filtered water, avoiding extremes of pH and hardness, is recommended, as is*

YELLOW KRIB (PELVICACHROMIS HUMILIS)

the addition of a little salt (one teaspoonful per 1 Imp gal/4.5 liters). Temperature range: 77–82°F (25–28°C); slightly higher for breeding

BREEDING: *Male excavates a simple nest to which he attracts the female. Egg care is usually undertaken by female; fry are protected by both parents*

YELLOW KRIB

Pelvicachromis humilis

SYNONYM: *Pelmatochromis humilis*

THE YELLOW PIGMENTATION INDICATED IN the common name is restricted to the cheek, chest, or belly in males. Females lack this distinctive coloration, but have violet or reddish bellies. At least three naturally occurring color morphs exist.

DISTRIBUTION: *Guinea, Liberia and Sierra Leone*

SIZE: *Males reported up to 5in (13cm), but usually smaller; females smaller*

BEHAVIOR: *Generally peaceful, but territorial during breeding*

DIET: *Wide range of foods accepted*

AQUARIUM: *Well matured and well planted, with shelters (caves). Soft, acid water recommended. Temperature range: 75–79°F (24–26°C); slightly higher for breeding*

BREEDING: *Eggs are laid in a cave, and both they and the fry are protected*

KRIB

KRIBENSIS, or PURPLE, CICHLID

Pelvicachromis pulcher

SYNONYM: *Pelmatochromis pulcher*

THIS OLD FAVORITE IS PERHAPS THE MOST POPULAR of all the African cichlids, with the possible exception of some of the Rift Lake species. It is a colorful, though variable, species in which the females always appear to be full of eggs and exhibit a particularly striking, reddish belly patch (not so pronounced in males). A well-matched pair make excellent parents. A large morph (possibly a separate species) usually referred to as *Pelvicachromis* cf. *pulcher* (Giant), is also available.

DISTRIBUTION: *Nigeria, often in brackish water*

SIZE: *Males up to 4in (10cm), but usually smaller; females smaller*

KRIB (PELVICACHROMIS PULCHER)

BEHAVIOR: *Territorial at breeding time, but usually peaceful toward other species*

DIET: *Wide range of foods accepted*

AQUARIUM: *Well planted, with adequate shelters (caves) and an open swimming area. Good-quality water important; medium-hard, slightly acid water recommended. Temperature range: 75–79°F (24–26°C); slightly higher for breeding*

BREEDING: *Eggs are laid on the roof of a cave, and both they and the fry are guarded by female; male defends territory, though he will also participate in fry care*

ROLOFF'S KRIB

Pelvicachromis roloffi

SYNONYM: *Pelmatochromis roloffi*

THIS IS ANOTHER BEAUTIFUL AND NATURALLY variable Krib in which females are particularly well patterned and colored.

DISTRIBUTION: *Guinea, Liberia and Sierra Leone*

SIZE: *Up to 3½in (9cm), but usually smaller; females smaller than males*

BEHAVIOR: *As for P. humilis*

DIET: *As for P. humilis*

AQUARIUM: *As for P. humilis*

BREEDING: *As for P. humilis*

EYESPOT KRIB

Pelvicachromis subocellatus

SYNONYM: *Pelmatochromis subocellatus*

THIS SPECIES IS HIGHLY VARIABLE, DEPENDING on locality, and it is found in a range of

naturally occurring conditions, including brackish water. Despite the "ocellatus" part of its name, some specimens—particularly males—may lack ocelli ("eyespots") altogether.

DISTRIBUTION: *Widely distributed in western Africa*

SIZE: *Males up to 4in (10cm); females smaller*

BEHAVIOR: *As for P. pulcher*

DIET: *As for P. pulcher*

AQUARIUM: *As for P. pulcher*

BREEDING: *As for P. pulcher*

STRIPED DWARF CICHLID

STRIPED KRIB

Pelvicachromis taeniatus

SYNONYM: *Pelmatochromis taeniatus*

DESPITE BEING IMPORTED INTO EUROPE AS EARLY as 1911, and despite appearing in numerous aquarium books, this species is relatively rare in the hobby in comparison with, say, *P. pulcher*. Like the other members of the genus, it is a variable species with numerous naturally existing morphs.

DISTRIBUTION: *Widely distributed within southern Nigeria, Liberia and Cameroon*

SIZE: *Males up to 3½in (9cm); females smaller*

BEHAVIOR: *As for P. pulcher*

DIET: *As for P. pulcher*

AQUARIUM: *As for P. pulcher*

BREEDING: *As for P. pulcher*

PETEN CICHLID

GIANT CICHLID, or BAY/RED SNOOK

Petenia splendida

JUVENILES OF THIS SPECIES, WHICH IS ONE OF THE larger cichlids, are occasionally available in the hobby. While these specimens may appear attractive, the real beauty of the Peten Cichlid is fully appreciated only in mature fish.

DISTRIBUTION: *Belize, Guatemala, Nicaragua and southern Mexico*

SIZE: *Up to 20in (50cm) reported, usually smaller; females smaller than males*

BEHAVIOR: *Adults territorial and aggressive; should be kept only with similar species*

Diet: *Large commercial formulations accepted, but livefoods preferred*

AQUARIUM: *Spacious, with robust, well-bedded decor, caves and large rocks. Well-filtered, medium-hard, slightly alkaline water advisable. Temperature range: 71–77°F (22–25°C); slightly higher for breeding*

BREEDING: *Large numbers of eggs are laid on a precleaned site, and both they and the fry are protected by the parents*

LAVENDER MBUNA

Petrotilapia tridentiger

THERE IS CONSIDERABLE DEBATE REGARDING THE classification of *Petrotilapia* species, with many still awaiting scientific description. In the end, it may be that the fish available as

P. tridentiger belong to an, as yet, undescribed species, *P.* sp. "Yellow Chin" from a relatively wide area extending from Makanjila Point to Metangula, and around the Maleri, Mbenji and Namalenje islands. If so, it is also possible that the "true" *P. tridentiger* is the fish found around Boadzulu Island and Chia Lagoon.

DISTRIBUTION: *If the above applies, the species occurs in the southernmost area of Lake Malawi. Otherwise, the distribution area extends further northward along the east coast of the lake*

SIZE: *Up to 10in (25cm) reported, but usually smaller*

BEHAVIOR: *Intolerant and territorial*

DIET: *Wide range of foods accepted, but livefoods preferred; vegetable component recommended*

AQUARIUM: *African Rift Lake layout (see Aquarium Set-up). Well-filtered, medium-hard, alkaline water important. Temperature range: 75–81°F (24–27°C)*

BREEDING: *Typical maternal mouthbrooder*

DEEPWATER HAP

Placidochromis electra

SYNONYMS: *Haplochromis electra, H. jahni*

THIS SPECIES IS RELATIVELY EASY TO DISTINGUISH from other blue Rift Lake cichlid species by its two dark patches, one extending from the eye down to the throat area, and the other located on the "shoulder."

DISTRIBUTION: *Eastern coast of Lake Malawi, from Hai Reef southward to Makanjila Point, taking in Likoma Island*

SIZE: *Around 6¾in (17cm)*

BEHAVIOR: *More peaceful and less territorial than many of its closest relatives*

DIET: *Wide range of commercial formulations*

AQUARIUM: *Typical African Rift Lake layout (see Aquarium Set-up), with sandy areas. Medium-hard, alkaline water important. Temperature range: 75–79°F (24–26°C)*

BREEDING: *Spawning tubes, i.e. lengths of plastic piping, placed either on sand or on a rock, with female subsequently picking up eggs and incubating them orally*

FENESTRATUS

Protomelas fenestratus

SYNONYM: *Haplochromis fenestratus*

ALSO KNOWN IN THE TRADE AS *HAPLOCHROMIS steveni* "Thick Bars," this is one of several *Protomelas* species available, some of which are still awaiting scientific description.

DISTRIBUTION: *Throughout Lake Malawi*

SIZE: *Around 6in (15cm)*

PETEN CICHLID (PETENIA SPLENDIDA)

▲ DEEPWATER HAP (PLACIDOCHROMIS ELECTRA)   ▼ FENESTRATUS (PROTOMELAS FENESTRATUS)

BEHAVIOR: *Territorial but not overaggressive*

DIET: *Wide range of foods accepted, but livefoods preferred*

AQUARIUM: *Typical African Rift Lake layout (see Aquarium Set-up), with sandy areas. Well-filtered, medium-hard, alkaline water important. Temperature range: 75–79°F (24–26°C)*

OTHER *PROTOMELAS* SPECIES

Several other *Protomelas* species are available. Those listed below are among the most commonly encountered. All have the same basic requirements, although the degree of territorial behavior varies.

SCIENTIFIC NAME	COMMON NAME(S)	SIZE
P. annectens	Chunky Hap	8in (20cm)
P. ornatus	Ornate Hap	10in (25cm)
P. similis	Gorgeous Hap or Haplochromis Sunset	7in (18cm)
P. spilonotus	Two-bar Hap	8in (20cm)
P. taeniolatus	Spindle Hap, Haplochromis Fire Blue or Red Empress	7½in (19cm)

*EGYPTIAN MOUTHBROODER
(PSEUDOCRENILABRUS MULTICOLOR)*

BREEDING: *Males construct sand nests to which they attract females; female incubates eggs orally*

EGYPTIAN MOUTHBROODER

Pseudocrenilabrus multicolor

SYNONYMS: *Haplochromis multicolor, Hemihaplochromis multicolor*

THIS INTERESTING SPECIES WAS FIRST IMPORTED into Europe as far back as 1902. It once enjoyed enormous popularity owing to its breeding habits, but has since been overtaken by more colorful species, particularly from the African Rift Lakes.

DISTRIBUTION: *From Lower Nile basin southward to Uganda and Tanzania (as far as Lake Victoria)*

SIZE: *Up to 3in (8cm); females smaller than males*

BEHAVIOR: *Generally (but not invariably) peaceful and tolerant; territorial during breeding*

DIET: *All foods accepted*

AQUARIUM: *Well planted, with sandy bottom, swimming areas, and adequate shelter (caves). Turbulent water conditions should be avoided. Floating plants recommended to provide subdued lighting conditions underwater. Water chemistry not critical as long as extremes are avoided. Temperature range: 68–79°F (20–26°C)*

BREEDING: *Eggs are laid either in a depression dug by male, or on a rock, and are picked up by female; female incubates eggs orally and subsequently protects the fry*

SOUTH AFRICAN MOUTHBROODER
DWARF COPPER MOUTHBROODER
Pseudocrenilabrus philander

SYNONYM: *Hemihaplochromis philander*

THREE SUBSPECIES OF *P. PHILANDER* ARE GENERALLY recognized, with two—*P. p. dispersus* and *P. p. philander*—being more regularly available than the third, *P. p. luebberti*. All require the same aquarium conditions, and all are well worth keeping. However, to avoid crossbreeding, the three subspecies should not be kept not together.

DISTRIBUTION: *From southern Africa northward to Mozambique*

SIZE: *Up to 4¼in (11cm)*

BEHAVIOR: *Territorial and aggressive, particularly toward its own kind during breeding, when burrowing activities increase*

DIET: *As for P. multicolor*

AQUARIUM: *As for P. multicolor*

BREEDING: *As for P. multicolor*

AURORA CICHLID
Pseudoctropheus aurora

SYNONYMS: *Maylandia aurora, Metriaclima aurora*

AT THE PRESENT TIME, ALL THREE SCIENTIFIC names above are in use for species that, like the impressive Aurora Cichlid, form part of the so-called zebra complex (*see Metriaclima zebra*, p.104). Until the matter is resolved, and for some time subsequent to this, both the Aurora Cichlid and the other members of the complex will therefore appear under a variety of names in aquarium literature.

DISTRIBUTION: *Lake Malawi: originally around Likoma Island and a short stretch of the eastern coast (between Mara Point and Tumbi Point). Subsequently introduced around Thumbi West Island and Otter Point*

SIZE: *Around 4¼in (11cm)*

BEHAVIOR: *Territorial and aggressive*

DIET: *Wide range of foods accepted*

AQUARIUM: *Typical African Rift Lake layout (see Aquarium Set-up). Medium-hard, alkaline water important. Temperature range: 75–79°F (24–26°C)*

BREEDING: *Maternal mouthbrooder*

HORNET CICHLID
Pseudotropheus crabro

THIS SPECIES, BEAUTIFULLY MARKED IN BROWN and yellow, is not a member of the zebra complex and is thus not included in the *Pseudotropheus/Maylandia/Metriaclima* debate.

DISTRIBUTION: *Most of Lake Malawi*

SIZE: *Wild specimens reported up to 4¾in (12cm); aquarium specimens may be larger*

BEHAVIOR: *In the wild, this species is usually associated with the large catfish, Bagrus meridionalis, which it "serves" as a cleaner. P. crabro also feeds on catfish eggs and fry. In the aquarium, males are territorial, but not overaggressive*

DIET: *As for P. aurora*

AQUARIUM: *As for P. aurora*

BREEDING: *As for P. aurora*

KENNYI MBUNA
Pseudotropheus lombardoi

SYNONYMS: *Maylandia lombardoi, Metriaclima lombardoi*

IN THIS ZEBRA COMPLEX SPECIES, MALES, WHILE varying in coloration, are orangy/yellow, with or without vertical dark bands. Females are pale metallic blue with dark vertical bands.

DISTRIBUTION: *Mbenji Island and Nkhomo Reef in Lake Malawi*

SIZE: *Around 4¼in (11cm)*

BEHAVIOR: *As for P. aurora*

DIET: *As for P. aurora*

AQUARIUM: *As for P. aurora*

BREEDING: *As for P. aurora*

South African Mouthbrooder (Pseudocrenilabrus philander)

Aurora Cichlid (Pseudoctropheus aurora)

Hornet Cichlid (Pseudotropheus crabro)

Kennyi Mbuna (Pseudotropheus lombardoi)

TROPHEOPS BRIGHT YELLOW

Pseudotropheus macrophthalmus

SYNONYM: *Tropheops macrophthalmus*

THIS IS YET ANOTHER SPECIES FOR WHICH scientific names are not fully standardized or agreed. As the common name indicates, it is a stunningly colored fish, particularly the males

DISTRIBUTION: *The eastern coastline of Lake Malawi*

SIZE: *Wild-caught specimens reach about 4¾in (12cm) in length; aquarium specimens may attain 6in (15cm)*

BEHAVIOR: *Territorial,but less aggressive than its closest relatives*

DIET: *As for P. aurora*

AQUARIUM: *As for P. aurora*

BREEDING: *As for P. aurora*

Different morph of Pseudotropheus macrophthalmus but just as attractive, Orange Cheek Cichlid

MINUTUS

Pseudotropheus minutus

THIS IS ONE OF THE SMALLER SPECIES IN THE genus. Superficially, it looks like a smaller version of a blue/black morph of *Metriaclima zebra*.

DISTRIBUTION: *Mainly found in Nkata Bay in Lake Malawi*

SIZE: *Up to 3½in (9cm)*

BEHAVIOR: *Territorial males aggressive, particularly toward rivals*

DIET: *As for P. aurora*

AQUARIUM: *As for P. aurora*

BREEDING: *As for P. aurora*

EDUARD'S MBUNA

Pseudotropheus socolofi

THIS IS ONE OF THE VERY FEW SPECIES THAT ARE named after someone, in this case Ross

EDUARD'S MBUNA
(PSEUDOTROPHEUS SOCOLOFI)

LEOPOLD'S ANGEL

Pterophyllum leopoldi

THIS SPECIES, WHICH IS CONSIDERABLY SHORTER from dorsal to anal fin than *P. altum* and more closely resembles *P. scalare*, is only rarely seen in the hobby. It is generally smaller all round than its two other relatives, and the body often carries rusty-reddish spots.

DISTRIBUTION: *Believed to be restricted to an area extending about 56 miles (90km) upriver from Manacapurú (Colombia)*

SIZE: *Around 6in (15cm)*

BEHAVIOR: *As for P. altum*

DIET: *As for P. altum*

AQUARIUM: *As for P. altum*

BREEDING: *No reports of aquarium breeding available*

ANGEL
SCALARE

Pterophyllum scalare

THIS IS, BY FAR, THE BEST KNOWN OF THE ANGEL species. It is also one of the most popular of all aquarium fish. It was first imported into Europe in 1909 and, since then, has been bred extensively in captivity, which has led to the development of numerous fin and color varieties. The vast majority of specimens available in shops come from this source, with wild-caught specimens catering primarily for the specialist market.

DISTRIBUTION: *Widely distributed in the Amazon basin, from Peru down to the mouth of the River Amazon at Belem. Also found in many tributaries and in northeast South America*

SIZE: *Around 6in (15cm); usually smaller, but occasionally larger*

BEHAVIOR: *Territorial, but not aggressive, though very small fish may be regarded as food*

DIET: *Wide range of foods accepted, but livefoods preferred; vegetable supplement recommended*

AQUARIUM: *As for P. altum, but temperature range: 75–82°F (24–28°C)*

BREEDING: *Easy. Eggs are usually laid on a vertical surface, e.g. on an Amazon Swordplant (Echinodorus sp.) and are protected, as are fry, by both parents. After hatching, the fry feed on body mucus ("milk") secreted by the parents*

OTHER *PSEUDOTROPHEUS* SPECIES

Owing to the debate surrounding the genus *Pseudotropheus*, with some species being variously transferred to *Maylandia*, *Metriaclima*, and *Tropheops*, it is difficult to state with any certainty how many *Pseudotropheus* species and/or morphs are currently available in the hobby, although they are certainly numerous. This situation is likely to remain somewhat "fluid" for several years at least. For a review of the main issues, along with the assignations of the various species and morphs to the different genera, readers are advised to consult specialist literature. *African Cichlids I, Malawi Mbuna* (see Bibliography) will prove particularly useful in this respect. Specialist cichlid societies and dealers are also valuable sources of up-to-date information.

Socolof. However, some writers believe that the species itself is not valid and that the specimens collected from the wild are crosses between an undescribed species from Mozambique that was introduced into the area where "socolofi" is now found and one or more of the resident species.

DISTRIBUTION: *Central eastern coast of Lake Malawi from Tumbi Point to Cobue; fish reported from elsewhere, e.g. Thumbi West Island in the extreme southwest of the lake, are likely to be the result of the introductions that give rise to the doubt regarding the validity of the species*

SIZE: *Aquarium specimens up to 4¾in (12cm); wild-caught fish usually smaller*

BEHAVIOR: *Territorial, but one of the more peaceful Mbunas*

DIET: *As for P. aurora*

AQUARIUM: *As for P. aurora*

BREEDING: *As for P. aurora*

ALTUM ANGEL
DEEP-FINNED, or LONG-FINNED, ANGEL

Pterophyllum altum

WHILE THE SCALARE (*PTEROPHYLLUM SCALARE*) has been known for well over 100 years,

the Altum was imported into Europe for the first time only in 1950. Despite its overall similarity to its better-known relative, the Altum is easily distinguished by its much deeper (taller) size, especially when its dorsal and anal fins are extended. A further difference is that while *P. scalare* breeds with great ease in aquaria, *P. altum* is extremely challenging in this respect.

DISTRIBUTION: *Central Rio Orinoco, partly in Colombia and partly in Venezuela*

SIZE: *Up to ca.10in (25cm) reported, but usually smaller*

BEHAVIOR: *Territorial, but generally peaceful; will nevertheless consume very small fishes*

DIET: *A wide selection of foods accepted, but livefoods preferred; vegetable supplement recommended*

AQUARIUM: *Deep, with tall plants and non-calcareous rock decorations or, preferably, bogwood; subdued lighting advisable. Excellent water quality essential, but filtration should not cause excessive turbulence. Soft, acid water important. Temperature range: 75–84°F (24–29°C)*

BREEDING: *Challenging and only occasionally achieved in aquaria. Eggs are usually laid on a vertical service, e.g. on Amazon Swordplant (Echinodorus sp.), and both they and the fry are cared for by the pair .*

◀ ALTUM ANGEL (PTEROPHYLLUM ALTUM)
▲ HALF-BLACK ANGEL (PTEROPHYLLUM SCALARE VAR.)

ALBINO GOLDEN DIAMOND ANGEL
(PTEROPHYLLUM SCALARE VAR.) ▶
▼ BLUE BLUSHING ANGEL (PTEROPHYLLUM SCALARE VAR.)

number of dorsal-fin rays. *Brochis* have 11 or more rays (Giant Brochis possesses 15–18), while, in *Corydoras*, the number rarely exceeds seven. The Giant Brochis is a relatively new addition to the hobby, first making its appearance in significant numbers during the last decade and a half of the 20th century.

DISTRIBUTION: *Mainly Mato Grosso, Brazil*

SIZE: *Up to 5in (13cm) reported, but usually a little smaller*

BEHAVIOR: *Peaceful shoaler that, despite its size, can be kept with small tankmates*

DIET: *Wide range of foods accepted*

AQUARIUM: *Roomy, well-planted, with open areas, as well as hiding places. Substratum fine-grained, with no sharp edges on which the fish could damage their mouths and/or barbels. Water chemistry not critical, but quality must be good. Temperature range: 72–77°F (22–25°C)*

BREEDING: *No documented accounts currently available, but probably as for* Corydoras

HOG-NOSED BROCHIS
LONG-FINNED BROCHIS
Brochis multiradiatus

FAMILY: Callichthyidae
SUBFAMILY: Corydoradinae

AS ITS SCIENTIFIC NAME IMPLIES, HOG-NOSED Brochis has many dorsal-fin rays (around 17). Although it is slightly outdone in this department by *B. britskii* (*see* previous entry), the latter had not yet been discovered when Hog-nosed Brochis was first described. Both species are similar-looking

overall, but this one lacks the bony plate that covers the underside of the head in its close relative. It also possesses a much longer snout and is a little smaller.

DISTRIBUTION: *Madeira River region (Brazil); Rio Lagarto/Upper Napo (Ecuador), and Ucayali and Nanay (Peru)*

SIZE: *Up to 4in (10cm)*

BEHAVIOR: *As for* B. britskii

DIET: *As for* B. britskii

AQUARIUM: *As for* B. britskii

BREEDING: *As for* B. britskii

COMMON BROCHIS
EMERALD, SHORT-BODIED or SAIL-FIN, BROCHIS/CORYDORAS/CATFISH
Brochis splendens

SYNONYM: *Brochis coeruleus*
FAMILY: Callichthyidae
SUBFAMILY: Corydoradinae

OF ALL ITS COMMON NAMES, THE ONE THAT FITS this species best is Emerald Brochis. It is a truly beautiful species, which can be found in, at least, two (named) naturally occurring color forms—spotted and

▲ HOG-NOSED BROCHIS (BROCHIS MULTIRADIATUS)
◄ COMMON BROCHIS (BROCHIS SPLENDENS)

black—in addition to the more usual emerald one. Of the three *Brochis* species, this is the one that has been in the hobby longest, having first been imported in the late 1930s.

DISTRIBUTION: *Brazil, Ecuador and Peru*

SIZE: *Up to 3in (8cm)*

BEHAVIOR: *As for* B. britskii

DIET: *As for* B. britskii

AQUARIUM: *As for* B. britskii. *Temperature range: 70–82°F (21–28°C)*

BREEDING: *Challenging in aquaria. Eggs are deposited on the underside of broadleaved plants (egg deposition among floating plants has also been reported). No parental care is exhibited, and hatching takes about four days*

ARMORED CATFISH

Callichthys callichthys

FAMILY: Callichthyidae
SUBFAMILY: Callichthyinae

THE FEATURE THAT BEST DISTINGUISHES THIS subfamily from that containing *Corydoras* and its relatives (Corydoradinae) is the snout. In the Callichthyinae, it is depressed, i.e. "flattened" to a certain extent, while in the Corydoradinae it is considerably more rounded. The Armored Catfish—after which the family was named—has been known in the hobby for over a century, having first been imported into Europe in 1897.

DISTRIBUTION: *Widely distributed in tropical regions of South America*

SIZE: *Up to 8in (20cm) reported, but usually smaller*

BEHAVIOR: *Relatively inactive during daylight hours. May consume very small tankmates, but generally peaceful. Surfaces periodically to gulp in air, which it passes down into its hindgut, where oxygen is absorbed into the bloodstream*

DIET: *Wide range of chunky foods accepted, particularly sinking formulations like granules and tablets. Food should be administered during the evening, i.e. shortly before tank lights are switched off*

AQUARIUM: *Thickly planted, with numerous shelters. Water chemistry not critical. Temperature range: 64–82°F (18–28°C)*

BREEDING: *A cover of floating plants must be provided. The male will build a nest of mucus-covered bubbles among the floating plants. Spawning takes place beneath this raft and the eggs are deposited among the bubbles. The male will then vigorously defend the nest against all comers*

BRONZE CORYDORAS

BRONZE CATFISH

Corydoras aeneus

FAMILY: Callichthyidae
SUBFAMILY: Corydoradinae

CORYDORAS SPECIES ARE, BY FAR, THE MOST popular of all the catfish kept in aquaria, and justifiably so. Most are hardy, adaptable, peaceful shoalers, and they have a habit that humans find particularly appealing: they "wink" at their owners. In reality, of course, they don't wink at all; rather, it is an effect created when a fish rotates its eyes quickly—as *Corydoras* species can do. As the eye is rotated downward, the pupil and iris disappear briefly from view, with the surrounding reflective tissues becoming momentarily visible. As the eye rotates back into its more normal orientation, the illusion of a wink is created. Of all the *Corydoras* species, Bronze Corydoras is the best known and still one of the most popular. Several naturally occurring color forms are known, e.g. Belem, Peru Gold Shoulder Red, Gold Shoulder Green, Peru Green Stripe, Peru Gold Stripe and even Aeneus Black. In addition, a cultivated albino form is regularly available.

DISTRIBUTION: *Bolivia, Brazil, Colombia, Ecuador, Peru, Suriname, Trinidad and Venezuela*

SIZE: *Around 2¾in (7cm); occasionally a little larger*

BEHAVIOR: *Peaceful shoaler that looks impressive in a group*

DIET: *Wide range of foods accepted, particularly bottom-dwelling livefoods and sinking commercial formulations*

AQUARIUM: *Well-planted, with open swimming areas, and fine-grained substratum. Water*

BRONZE CORYDORAS (CORYDORAS AENEUS)

ones) are generally held out horizontally and pointing forward. The relatively light body armor helps distinguish the two *Dianema* species from their closest relatives in the subfamily, *Callichthys* and *Hoplosternum*.

DISTRIBUTION: *Ambyiac and Pacaya rivers (Peru)*

SIZE: *Up to 4in (10cm)*

BEHAVIOR: *Peaceful shoaler; can be kept with smaller tankmates except, perhaps, very small fry. Becomes progressively more active as evening falls*

DIET: *Wide range of foods accepted*

AQUARIUM: *Spacious, containing clumps of vegetation, open swimming areas, and resting and hiding places (e.g. pieces of bogwood). Water chemistry not critical, but softish, slightly acid conditions preferred. Temperature range: 72–79℉ (22–26℃)*

BREEDING: *Challenging in aquaria. Males build bubble nests into which the eggs are deposited. Shallow water and raised temperature (82℉/28℃) recommended*

FLAG-TAILED CATFISH
STRIPE-TAILED CATFISH

Dianema urostriata

FAMILY: Callichthyidae
SUBFAMILY: Callichthyinae

THIS SPECIES IS VERY SIMILAR TO *D. LONGIBARBIS* (*see* previous entry). However, it can be immediately distinguished by its boldly striped caudal fin (in D. longibarbis, the tail is plain). Occasionally, specimens without any body speckling appear in shipments of this attractive species.

DISTRIBUTION: *Manáus area of the Rio Negro (Brazil)*

SIZE: *Females reported up to 4¾in (12cm); males about ¾in (2cm) shorter*

BEHAVIOR: *As for* D. longibarbis

DIET: *As for* D. longibarbis

AQUARIUM: *As for* D. longibarbis

BREEDING: *As for* D. longibarbis

CASCUDO HOPLO

Hoplosternum littorale

FAMILY: Callichthyidae
SUBFAMILY: Callichthyinae

THIS IS ONE OF THREE SIMILAR-LOOKING SPECIES that have traditionally been regarded as members of the genus *Hoplosternum*. In 1997, a review of these resulted in their being split into three distinct genera (*see Lethoplosternum* and *Megalechis*). Of the three, Cascudo Hoplo was the only species left within its original genus. It is the largest of the three species and may also be distinguished by its lightly forked caudal fin. Owing to its wide distribution, a number of variants are known, but whether these are morphs or separate species remains to be decided.

DISTRIBUTION: *Widely distributed in tropical South America*

SIZE: *Up to 8¾in (22cm)*

BEHAVIOR: *Generally peaceful except at spawning time*

DIET: *Wide range of foods accepted*

AQUARIUM: *Roomy, well-covered, with plenty of resting and hiding places, and subdued lighting. Water chemistry not critical. Temperature range: 70–79℉ (21–26℃); slightly higher for breeding*

BREEDING: *Male builds bubble nest at the water surface. Eggs are deposited among the bubbles and are guarded by male. Hatching takes three to four days*

DWARF HOPLO
SPOTTED HOPLO

Lethoplosternum pectorale

SYNONYM: *Hoplosternum pectorale*
FAMILY: Callichthyidae
SUBFAMILY: Callichthyinae

AS ONE OF ITS COMMON NAME IMPLIES, THIS IS THE smallest of the three *Hoplo* species featured.

▲ *FLAG-TAILED CATFISH (DIANEMA UROSTRIATA)*

▼ *PORTHOLE CATFISH (DIANEMA LONGIBARBIS)*

PORT HOPLO (MEGALECHIS THORACATA)

Its base color is yellowish brown (though this can vary), liberally covered in small dark spots (hence its other common name). A further distinguishing characteristic is that the caudal fin is gently rounded (it is slightly forked in *Hoplosternum littorale* and truncated in *Megalechis thoracata*). A naturally occurring "dwarf" of this species—attaining only 3½in (9cm)—is occasionally seen. A fourth Hoplo, referred to as *Hoplosternum magdalenae*, may turn out to be *L. pectorale*, but differences of opinion exist. A long-barbeled form of unknown origin is also known to exist, but is only rarely imported.

DISTRIBUTION: *H. (Lethoplosternum) pectorale (magdalenae?) is reported from the Magdalena River in Brazil; the fish definitely identified as L. pectorale is found mainly in Paraguay*

SIZE: *Up to 6in (15cm) reported, but usually smaller*

BEHAVIOR: *As for* Hoplosternum littorale

DIET: *As for* Hoplosternum littorale

AQUARIUM: *As for* Hoplosternum littorale

BREEDING: *As for* Hoplosternum littorale

PORT HOPLO

Megalechis thoracata

SYNONYM: *Hoplosternum thoracatum*
FAMILY: Callichthyidae
SUBFAMILY: Callichthyinae

THIS IS THE MOST VARIABLE OF THE THREE HOPlos, so much so that some of the naturally occurring morphs may eventually turn out to be valid species in their own right. The one easily discernible feature that all possess—and that distinguishes them from the other hoplos—is the sharply truncated caudal fin (*see Lethoplosternum pectorale*, p.142). Port Hoplo males can also be distinguished from their *H. littorale* counterparts in that Port Hoplo's main pectoral fin spine does not turn up at the tip with advancing age (as it does in *H. littorale*). Further, during the breeding sea-

son, this ray turns orange in Port Hoplo and deep-red to maroon in *H. littorale*.

DISTRIBUTION: *Widely distributed in northern South America*

SIZE: *Up to 7in (18cm)*

BEHAVIOR: *As for* Hoplosternum littorale

DIET: *As for* Hoplosternum littorale

AQUARIUM: *As for* Hoplosternum littorale. *Temperature range: 64–82°F (18–28°C)*

BREEDING: *As for* Hoplosternum littorale, *but Port Hoplo is perhaps the easiest of the three hoplos to breed in aquaria*

FROGMOUTH CATFISH

ANGLER CATFISH

Chaca chaca

FAMILY: Chacidae

THE FROGMOUTH IS INACTIVE DURING THE DAY, lying perfectly camouflaged among the leaf litter that accumulates on the bottom of its native streams. In this position, it both rests and waits for suitable prey to come its way. When this happens, it wiggles its short, upper-jaw barbels to lure the potential victim into range of its cavernous mouth. Most feeding and higher levels of activity are, however, reserved for the hours of darkness. A very similar species, *C. bankanensis* (Chocolate Frogmouth Catfish), from peninsular Malaysia and Indonesia, is also available.

DISTRIBUTION: *Reported from Bangladesh, India, Myanmar (Burma), Borneo and Sumatra*

SIZE: *Up to 8in (20cm)*

BEHAVIOR: *Lone, predominantly nocturnal predator; should not be housed with tankmates that may be small enough to be swallowed*

DIET: *Live fish and crustacea preferred (a factor that needs to be considered prior to purchase). May be weaned off these and on to chunky foods, such as tablets*

AQUARIUM: *Appropriate hiding places (e.g. bogwood, rocks) and subdued lighting recommended. Water chemistry not critical. Temperature range: 72–75°F (22–24°C)*

BREEDING: *No documented accounts currently available*

WALKING CATFISH
CLARIAS CATFISH
Clarias batrachus

FAMILY: Clariidae

SO CALLED BECAUSE OF ITS REPORTED ABILITY TO "walk" out of water (e.g. during storms or humid weather), the Walking Catfish is, first and foremost, a food fish. The main reason that it has become known in the hobby is that albinos, which are produced primarily for human consumption, are particularly attractive and are therefore of interest to some aquarists. However, owing to the large size that specimens can attain, the species is suitable only for the specialist who can cater adequately for its needs.

DISTRIBUTION: *Widespread in tropical regions of Asia*

SIZE: *Up to ca20in (50cm) reported*

BEHAVIOR: *Predatory species; must not be kept with tankmates that are small enough to be swallowed*

DIET: *Wide range of live and chunky commercial foods accepted*

AQUARIUM: *Large, well-covered, and well-filtered. Decoration and shelters should consist of large pieces of bogwood, smooth rocks or equivalent. Large, robust (or artificial) plants may be provided. Water chemistry not critical. Temperature range: 68–77°F (20–25°C) adequate, but wider range tolerated*

BREEDING: *Not reported in aquaria. In the wild (or commercial farms), eggs are laid in burrows excavated in the banks of rivers and ponds*

PAINTED TALKING CATFISH
Acanthodoras cataphractus

FAMILY: Doradidae

OF THE THREE SPECIES IN THE GENUS, TWO— Painted Talking Catfish and *A. spinosissimus* (Talking Catfish) from Ecuador or eastern Peru—are frequently encountered in the hobby, while the third, *A. calderonensis*, is only rarely available. Both talking catfish species are often confused. However, the "granules" on the skull are much sharper in *A. spinosissimus*; and the

gill cover in Painted Talking Catfish has fine grooves, while in *A. spinosissimus* it is granular in texture.

DISTRIBUTION: *Lower Amazon*

SIZE: *4in (10cm)*

BEHAVIOR: *Peaceful species that becomes more active during the night and likes to rest partly buried or in hollows during the day. Avoid keeping with small tankmates*

DIET: *Wide range of foods accepted. Feed just before aquarium lights are switched off in the evening*

AQUARIUM: *Adequate shelters, ample planting and soft substratum required. Water chemistry not critical. Temperature range: 72–80°F (22–27°C)*

BREEDING: *Challenging in aquaria. Eggs are laid in a depression and guarded by both parents. Hatching take four to five days*

SPOTTED DORADID
WHITE-SPOTTED DORADID or SPOTTED TALKING CATFISH
Agamyxis pectinifrons

FAMILY: Doradidae

AS IN THE OTHER TALKING CATFISHES (*SEE* introduction to catfishes), Spotted Doradid is able to produce sounds by rotating its pectoral-fin spines and amplifying this via its swimbladder. The overall color is

▲ *WALKING CATFISH (CLARIAS BATRACHUS)*
◀ *SPOTTED DORADID (AGAMYXIS PECTINIFRONS)*

Hancock's Catfish (Amblydoras hancocki)

almost black, overlaid with numerous white or cream spots.

DISTRIBUTION: *Ecuador*

SIZE: *Up to 5½in (14cm) reported*

BEHAVIOR: *As for* Acanthodoras cataphractus

DIET: *As for* Acanthodoras cataphractus

AQUARIUM: *As for* Acanthodoras cataphractus. *Temperature range: 70–79°F (21–26°C)*

BREEDING: *No documented accounts currently available*

HANCOCK'S CATFISH
TALKING CATFISH
Amblydoras hancocki

FAMILY: Doradidae

THIS IS, PERHAPS, THE MOST WIDELY AVAILABLE of all the talking catfishes. It is an attractively marked species that tends to "talk" more than most other members of the family (*see* previous entry, as well as introduction to catfishes).

DISTRIBUTION: *Widely distributed from Brazil and Colombia to Guyana*

SIZE: *Up to 6in (15cm) reported, but usually smaller*

BEHAVIOR: *May be more active than some of its relatives during the day*

DIET: *As for* Acanthodoras cataphractus

AQUARIUM: *As for* Acanthodoras cataphractus. *Temperature range: 70–82°F (21–28°C)*

BREEDING: *No accounts of aquarium spawnings available. In the wild, it is reported that eggs are laid on the bottom, covered up with leaves, and guarded by both parents*

STAR-GAZING DORADID
STARRY GROWLER
Astrodoras asterifrons

FAMILY: Doradidae

SIMILARLY COLORED TO *AMBLYDORAS HANCOCKI*, Star-gazing Doradid is the only species in its genus. It can be distinguished from its

---

closest relatives, such as *Acanthodoras* and *Amblydoras* in that its dorsal-fin spine is serrated only along the front edge and not along the sides and back as well.

DISTRIBUTION: *Reported from Bolivia and the Brazilian Amazon*

SIZE: *Up to 4¾in (12cm), but usually smaller*

BEHAVIOR: *As for* Acanthodoras cataphractus

DIET: *As for* Acanthodoras cataphractus

AQUARIUM: *As for* Acanthodoras cataphractus. *Temperature range: 70–77°F (21–25°C)*

BREEDING: *No documented accounts currently available*

JAGUAR CATFISH
Liosomadoras oncinus

FAMILY: Doradidae (but *see* below)

THIS IS A BOLDLY MARKED SPECIES THAT LIVES UP to its name of Jaguar Catfish. It has been (and still is) the subject of some controversy with regard to its classification, since it possesses characteristics of two distinct families. Following Nelson (1994—*see* Bibliography), it is listed as a doradid here, but it frequently appears as a member of the Auchenipteridae (the driftwood catfish family) in some other publications.

DISTRIBUTION: *Reported from Brazil and Peru, but may also occur elsewhere*

SIZE: *Up to 8in (20cm)*

BEHAVIOR: *Mostly sedentary during daylight hours, hiding in caves or holes in bogwood*

Star-gazing Doradid (Astrodoras asterifrons)

DIET: *Large livefoods preferred, but chunky meat- or fish-based foods will also be accepted. It may also be accustomed to granular and tablet formulations*

AQUARIUM: *Spacious, well-filtered, with ample supply of shelters important. Soft, slightly acid water. Temperature range: 70–77°F (21–25°C)*

BREEDING: *Not reported in aquaria, but known to be as in driftwood catfishes, i.e. eggs are fertilized internally and subsequently released*

SNAIL-EATING DORADID

Megalodoras irwini

FAMILY: Doradidae

THIS IS ONE OF THE LARGEST SPECIES IN THE genus—a factor that requires careful consideration before purchase, although growth in aquaria is slow. Due care must also be taken with regard to the numerous spines that develop on the tough body plates, as well as to the serrations on the dorsal- and pectoral-fin spines.

DISTRIBUTION: *Reported from the Brazilian Amazon and northeast South America*

SIZE: *Up to 24in (60cm), or even slightly larger*

BEHAVIOR: *Mostly sedentary during daylight hours*

DIET: *Chunky meat- and fish-based diets accepted. Once acclimatized, granular and tablet formulations are also taken*

AQUARIUM: *Large, well-filtered, with roomy hiding places, essential. Water chemistry not critical, but extremes must be avoided. Temperature range: 72–79°F (22–26°C)*

BREEDING: *No documented accounts currently available*

CHOCOLATE DORADID

HUMBUG CATFISH

Platydoras costatus

FAMILY: Doradidae

THIS IS A BEAUTIFULLY MARKED SPECIES IN WHICH the base chocolate (or almost black) color of the body contrasts sharply with the white or creamy bands. Its only significant drawback for many aquaria is its eventual size.

DISTRIBUTION: *Widespread in the Brazilian Amazon and Peru*

SIZE: *Up to 8¾in (22cm)*

BEHAVIOR: *Sedentary and peaceful toward other species, but territorial toward its own. Likes to burrow*

DIET: *Wide range of foods accepted*

AQUARIUM: *Spacious, with adequate shelter and fine substratum. Protect plants against burrowing (see Aquarium Plants). Water chemistry not critical, but extremes must be avoided. Temperature range: 74–86°F (24–30°C)*

BREEDING: *No documented accounts currently available*

BLACK DORADID

Pseudodoras niger

FAMILY: Doradidae

THIS IS A VERY LARGE SPECIES, WHICH SHOULD BE purchased only by aquarists who can provide it with appropriate accommodations. The strong thorny spines on its body plates and powerful fin spines also mean that it must be handled with care.

DISTRIBUTION: *Widely distributed in the Amazon basin*

SIZE: *Up to 39in (100cm) reported*

BEHAVIOR: *Peaceful despite its size. Likes the company of its own species*

▼ CHOCOLATE DORADID (PLATYDORAS COSTATUS)
▼▼ BLACK DORADID (PSEUDODORAS NIGER)

DIET: *Wide range of chunky foods accepted*

AQUARIUM: *Large, well-filtered, with fine- or medium-grained substratum. Water chemistry not critical. Temperature range: 70–75°F (21–24°C)*

BREEDING: *No documented accounts currently available*

ASIAN STINGING CATFISH
LIVER CATFISH
Heteropneustes fossilis

FAMILY: Heteropneustidae

THIS IS ONE OF THE MOST POTENTIALLY DANGEROUS catfish species. Its venomous spines have, reportedly, caused deaths among rice-paddy workers. It is also said to be aggressive, actively seeking out and attacking victims. While reports of this behavior may be exaggerated, careful consideration must be given to this prior to purchase.

DISTRIBUTION: *Widely distributed in tropical Asia*

SIZE: *Up to 20in (50cm) reported, but usually smaller*

BEHAVIOR: *Can be aggressive; potentially very dangerous*

DIET: *Wide range of chunky foods accepted*

AQUARIUM: *Large, well-covered and with bogwood or rocks. Water chemistry not critical. Temperature range: 72–80°F (22–27°C)*

BREEDING: *Eggs are laid in a depression and guarded by both parents, as are the fry for a short time after hatching*

BLACK BULLHEAD
Ictalurus melas

SYNONYM: *Ameiurus melas*
FAMILY: Ictaluridae

MANY OF THE BULLHEAD CATFISHES, INCLUDING this one, are considered primarily as food or bait fishes, although several species—again, including the Black Bullhead—are also popular in the hobby among catfish specialists. Small or moderate-sized specimens may be housed in unheated aquaria, although its wide temperature tolerance also makes it suitable for appropriately large tropical setups.

DISTRIBUTION: *Widely distributed in North America and introduced into many locations outside its range*

SIZE: *Up to 24¼in (62cm), but usually much smaller*

BEHAVIOR: *Predatory; must not be housed with tankmates that are small enough to be swallowed*

DIET: *Live fish preferred (a factor that requires consideration prior to purchase), but other chunky livefoods and commercial diets may be accepted*

AQUARIUM: *Large, well-filtered, with substantial decor, e.g. bogwood, must be provided. Water chemistry not critical. Temperature range: from 50–86°F (10–30°C)*

BREEDING: *Challenging. Eggs are laid in a depression and guarded by the spawners, which also care for the fry for a short time after hatching*

BROWN BULLHEAD
Ictalurus nebulosus

SYNONYM: *Ameiurus nebulosus*
FAMILY: Ictaluridae

THIS IS A SLIGHTLY SMALLER SPECIES THAN *I. melas*, but it is even hardier in terms of water-quality tolerance. In the wild, it can even, reportedly, survive in wet mud when its pond dries up.

DISTRIBUTION: *Widely distributed in North America, and introduced into a large number of other countries*

SIZE: *Around 20in (50cm)*

BEHAVIOR: *As for I. melas*

DIET: *As for I. melas*

AQUARIUM: *As for I. melas*

BREEDING: *As for I. melas. Eggs may be guarded by just one parent, or both*

GRACEFUL CATFISH
STINGING, SPOTTED, or CHANNEL, CATFISH
Ictalurus punctatus

FAMILY: Ictaluridae

THIS IS THE MOST COMMONLY SEEN SPECIES OF ITS genus, probably as a result of the production of albino specimens (primarily for the food fish industry).

DISTRIBUTION: *Widely distributed in North America, and introduced elsewhere*

SIZE: *Up to 47¼in (120cm), but usually considerably smaller*

BEHAVIOR: *As for I. melas*

DIET: *As for I. melas*

AQUARIUM: *As for I. melas*

BREEDING: *As for I. melas. Eggs may be laid in caves or under rocks and are guarded by male*

ADONIS CATFISH
Acanthicus adonis

FAMILY: Loricariidae
SUBFAMILY: Ancistrinae

THIS SPECIES IS A RELATIVE NEWCOMER TO THE hobby, having been described as recently as 1988. In most features, it is very similar to *A. hystrix* (*see* next entry). However, the Adonis Catfish has white or cream-colored spots on its body.

DISTRIBUTION: *Tocantins river (Brazil)*

SIZE: *Up to 15¾in (40cm) reported, but usually smaller*

BEHAVIOR: *Generally sedentary, although territorial toward its own species and with a distinct appetite for plants*

DIET: *Almost exclusively vegetarian. Slices of potato or cucumber, plus lettuce leaves, may be provided on a regular basis*

AQUARIUM: *Spacious, well-filtered, with shelters and unpalatable/robust plants. A water current (created by, e.g., the outflow from a powerhead) recommended. Softish, slightly acid to neutral water preferred. Temperature range: 70–75°F (21–24°C)*

BREEDING: *No documented accounts available*

▲ ADONIS CATFISH (ACANTHICUS ADONIS)

BLACK ADONIS CATFISH

Acanthicus hystrix

FAMILY: Loricariidae
SUBFAMILY: Ancistrinae

FOR NEARLY 150 YEARS, THIS SPECIES WAS believed to be the sole representative of its genus until *A. adonis* was discovered and described (*see* previous entry). Black Adonis Catfish can be distinguished from its relative by its black body coloration and the absence of spots.

DISTRIBUTION: *Amazon and (possibly) Guyana*

SIZE: *Around 18in (45cm)*

BEHAVIOR: *As for* A. adonis

DIET: *As for* A. adonis

AQUARIUM: *As for* A. adonis

BREEDING: *As for* A. adonis

BIG-FINNED BRISTLENOSE

BLUE CHIN ANCISTRUS

Ancistrus dolichopterus

FAMILY: Loricariidae
SUBFAMILY: Ancistrinae

THERE ARE AROUND 50 DESCRIBED SPECIES OF *Ancistrus*, plus an almost equal number of undescribed ones referred to by their "L" number, or their "Loricariid Number," e.g. *Ancistrus* sp. Orange Spot (L110). For detailed information on this genus, it is therefore advisable to consult specialist literature (*see* Bibliography). In all species, mature males exhibit the characteristic, filament-like outgrowths of the snout— the "bristlenose"—from which one of its common names is derived.

DISTRIBUTION: *Widespread in tropical South America*

SIZE: *Around 5in (13cm)*

BEHAVIOR: *Peaceful toward other tankmates, but males territorial and aggressive toward other Ancistrus. Exhibits distinct appetite for succulent plants*

DIET: *Predominantly vegetarian, but commercial formulations accepted. A slice of potato or cucumber, or lettuce leaves will be appreciated*

AQUARIUM: *Spacious, with ample bogwood shelters. Water well-filtered and flowing (such as produced by powerhead outlet). Water chemistry not critical. Temperature range: 73–81°F (23–27°C)*

BREEDING: *Eggs are laid in hollows in bogwood or roots, and they and the fry are guarded by male. Soft, acid water appears to enhance chances of success. Hatching takes about five days*

SPOTTED BRISTLENOSE

SNOWFLAKE BRISTLENOSE

Ancistrus hoplogenys

FAMILY: Loricariidae
SUBFAMILY: Ancistrinae

VARIOUS WHITE-SPOTTED, BLACK-BASED SPECIES are available under the *A. hoplogenys* label. Some are, undoubtedly, correctly identified as this species; some of the others either belong to closely related species, such as *A. cirrhosus*, or are, as yet, undescribed and belong to species that at the moment can be referred to only by their "L" numbers, e.g. L107, L125 and others.

DISTRIBUTION: *Amazon basin*

SIZE: *Around 6in (15cm)*

FEMALE BIG-FINNED BRISTLENOSE (ANCISTRUS DOLICHOPTERUS); SEE MALE PHOTO P. 5

White-spotted chaetostoma (Chaetostoma sp.); see text, below

Behavior: *As for A. dolichopterus*

Diet: *As for A. dolichopterus*

Aquarium: *As for A. dolichopterus*

Breeding: *As for A. dolichopterus*

"REAL/TRUE" THOMASI

Chaetostoma thomasi

Family: Loricariidae
Subfamily: Ancistrinae

THE FISH NORMALLY AVAILABLE AS *C. THOMASI* has a tan or brownish base color with white spots, and is referred to as the White-Spotted Chaetostoma (*Chaetostoma* sp., probably L188). However, according to some authorities, the "Real" or "True" Thomasi has a tan or brownish base color with black spots. Considerable confusion therefore exists about the identity of this species.

Distribution: *Both types occur in Colombia*

Size: *"Real/True" Thomasi: around 4¾in (12cm); White-Spotted Chaetostoma: up to 6in (15cm)*

Behavior: *Generally peaceful toward other species, but territorial toward conspecifics*

Diet: *Will accept a variety of (particularly) sinking formulations and livefoods*

Aquarium: *Well-planted, with numerous bogwood and other shelters. A water current (as produced by powerhead outlet) recommended. Slightly acid or neutral, soft to medium-hard water preferred. Temperature range: 68–75°F (20–24°C)*

Breeding: *No documented accounts currently available*

STICK CATFISH

TWIG CATFISH

Farlowella acus

Family: Loricariidae
Subfamily: Loricariinae

TRUE TO ITS NAME, THIS SLENDER SPECIES LOOKS like a stick or twig, both in shape and coloration. Owing to its vegetarian habits, it is not the easiest of loricariids to keep and is better suited to experienced aquarists than to newcomers to the hobby. *F. gracilis* (also Twig Catfish), from Colombia, which has long, slender extensions to the caudal fin, is also regularly available.

Distribution: *Venezuela and southern tributaries of the Amazon*

Size: *Around 6in (15cm)*

Behavior: *Peaceful, generally retiring; should not be kept with boisterous tankmates*

Diet: *Largely herbivorous; vegetable dietary component, such as peas, lettuce, vegetable flake, etc., is therefore essential*

Aquarium: *Well-planted, with hiding places and clean, well-oxygenated, flowing, soft, slightly acid water recommended. Temperature range: 70–79°F (21–26°C)*

Breeding: *Adhesive eggs are laid, often in flowing water, and are guarded by male or by both parents*

Stick Catfish (Farlowella acus)

SPOTTED PLECO

SAILFIN SUCKERMOUTH CATFISH

Glyptoperichthys gibbiceps

SYNONYM: *Pterygoplichthys gibbiceps*
FAMILY: Loricariidae
SUBFAMILY: Hypostominae

THIS SPECIES STILL APPEARS UNDER ITS FORMER name in many aquarium books. However, the genus *Pterygoplichthys* is no longer valid, having been replaced by two genera, *Glyptoperichthys* and *Liposarcus* (*see* p.151). The common name of Pleco is also applied to species of the genus *Hypostomus* (*see* below), from which *Glyptoperichthys* is easily distinguished by its dorsal fin, which has more than ten rays; *Hypostomus* has only seven.

DISTRIBUTION: *Peru*

SIZE: *Up to 24in (60cm), but usually smaller*

BEHAVIOR: *Predominantly nocturnal and peaceful, even toward smaller tankmates*

DIET: *Almost exclusively vegetarian; offer plant-based sinking formulations, slices of potato or cucumber, lettuce, spinach or peas*

AQUARIUM: *Large, well-planted, well-filtered, with numerous shelters. Water chemistry not critical. A "moonlight" fluorescent tube to facilitate night viewing is advisable. Temperature range: 68–81°F (22–27°C)*

*SPOTTED PLECO
(GLYPTOPERICHTHYS GIBBICEPS)*

BREEDING: *No documented accounts of aquarium breeding currently available*

ZEBRA PECKOLTIA

ZEBRA PLECO

Hypancistrus zebra

FAMILY: Loricariidae
SUBFAMILY: Ancistrinae

THIS SPECIES, SPECTACULARLY PATTERNED IN BLACK and white (as indicated by its name) is a relatively recent introduction into the hobby. For a time, it was known only by its "L" number (L46) until it was officially described and named in 1991. Although rare at first, the Zebra Peckoltia is now quite readily available.

DISTRIBUTION: *Reported upriver of Altamira on the Xingu River (Brazil)*

SIZE: *Up to 4¾in (12cm) reported, but usually smaller*

BEHAVIOR: *Peaceful and sometimes retiring*

DIET: *Considerably less herbivorous than many of its relatives; will accept a range of (primarily) sinking formulations*

AQUARIUM: *Well-planted, with hiding places and subdued lighting recommended. Softish, slightly acid water preferred. Temperature range: 72–77°F (22–25°C)*

BREEDING: *No documented accounts of aquarium breeding currently available*

DWARF SUCKER CATFISH

Hypoptopoma thoracatum

FAMILY: Loricariidae
SUBFAMILY: Hypoptopomatinae

THE 12 OR SO SPECIES OF THIS GENUS ARE ALL referred to as dwarf sucker catfish. However, the real dwarves are the members of the genera *Parotocinclus* and *Otocinclus* (*see* pp.152). All *Hypoptopoma* species are distinguished by a long snout, large, laterally placed eyes, and a much reduced adipose fin (represented by a single spine in some species); in some cases, even this single spine is missing.

DISTRIBUTION: *Amazon up to the mouth of the Rio Negro (Brazil); also reported from the Mato Grosso*

SIZE: *3in (8cm)*

BEHAVIOR: *A peaceful loner; generally more active at dusk and during the night*

DIET: *Predominantly herbivorous (algae, vegetable flakes/pellets/tablets)*

AQUARIUM: *Well-planted, with hiding places and subdued lighting recommended. Softish, acid to slightly alkaline water preferred. Temperature range: 73–81°F (23–27°C)*

BREEDING: *No documented accounts currently available*

PLECO

PLEC

Hypostomus plecostomus

SYNONYM: *Plecostomus plecostomus*
FAMILY: Loricariidae
SUBFAMILY: Hypostominae

EVEN TODAY, OVER 240 YEARS AFTER THIS SPECIES was first described (as *Plecostomus*, rather than *Hypostomus*), confusion still exists about its name, or even the correct identity of plecos available to aquarists under the name *Hypostomus plecostomus*. The generic name *Hypostomus* did not appear until 1803, yet—for reasons that are unclear— it replaced *Plecostomus*. Despite this, aquarists around the world have traditionally referred to *H. plecostomus* and the other *Hypostomus* species as plecos or plecs, thus heightening the confusion. *Hypostomus* species—of which there are more than 100—are distinguished from their closest relatives in the genera *Glyptoperichthys* and *Liposarcus* in several ways. The most distinguishable feature is the small number of dorsal fin rays (seven) possessed by *Hypostomus* (cf *Glyptoperichthys gibbiceps*, above). Of the numerous species in the genus, very few are ever available within the hobby; *H. plecostomus* is one of these. At least two commercially produced varieties—an albino and a piebald— are occasionally available.

DISTRIBUTION: *Suriname*

SIZE: *Up to 24in (60cm) reported*

BEHAVIOR: *Peaceful despite its large size; most active at dusk and during the night*

DIET: *Herbivorous (algae, vegetable flakes/pellets/tablets, lettuce, spinach, peas, potato, cucumber slices, etc.)*

AQUARIUM: *Large, well-planted, with numerous sizable shelters. Water chemistry not critical, but quality must be good. Temperature range: 72–82°F (22–28°C)*

BREEDING: *No documented accounts of aquarium breeding currently available. In the wild and in commercial ornamental fisheries, the species breeds in deep burrows excavated in riverbanks.*

The male guards the eggs, and the fry feed off the body mucus—as in Symphysodon spp. *(Discus), see pp.119–20*

SPOTTED HYPOSTOMUS

SPOTTED PLECO

Hypostomus punctatus

SYNONYM: *Plecostomus punctatus*
FAMILY: Loricariidae
SUBFAMILY: Hypostominae

THIS BEAUTIFULLY SPOTTED SPECIES IS ONE OF THE few species of *Hypostomus* (other than *H. plecostomus*—*see* previous entry) regularly available in shops. It is somewhat smaller than *H. plecostomus* making it a little easier to accommodate.

DISTRIBUTION: *Southern and southeastern Brazil*

SIZE: *Around 12in (30cm)*

BEHAVIOR: *As for* H. plecostomus

DIET: *As for* H. plecostomus

AQUARIUM: *As for* H. plecostomus

BREEDING: *As for* H. plecostomus

SNOW KING PLEC

SNOW KING PLECO

Liposarcus anisisti

SYNONYMS: *Pterygoplichthys anisisti, Glyptoperichthys anisisti*
FAMILY: Loricariidae
SUBFAMILY: Hypostominae

ALONG WITH THE BLACK-SPOTTED *LIPOSARCUS multiradiatus* from the Amazon basin, Bolivia, Paraguay and Peru, the white-spotted Snow King Plec is the most widely available species in the genus. This is largely as a result of large-scale breeding

▲ ZEBRA PECKOLTIA (HYPANCISTRUS ZEBRA)   ▼ SPOTTED HYPOSTOMUS (HYPOSTOMUS PUNCTATUS)

▼ PLECO (HYPOSTOMUS PLECOSTOMUS)   ▼ SNOW KING PLEC (LIPOSARCUS ANISISTI)

of the species (predominantly in Florida ornamental fish farms).

DISTRIBUTION: *Brazil and Paraguay*

SIZE: *Over 15¾in (40cm)*

BEHAVIOR: *As for* Hypostomus plecostomus

DIET: *As for* Hypostomus plecostomus

AQUARIUM: *As for* Hypostomus plecostomus

BREEDING: *As for* Hypostomus plecostomus

DWARF OTOCINCLUS

GOLDEN OTOCINCLUS or
MIDGET SUCKER CATFISH

Otocinclus affinis

FAMILY: Loricariidae
SUBFAMILY: Hypoptopomatinae

DESPITE ITS COMMON NAMES, DWARF OTOCINCLUS is only slightly smaller than its close relative, *O. vestitus* (Ampiyacu Dwarf Sucker Catfish), from Rio de Janeiro in Brazil. It is also about the same size as *O. paulinus* (Marbled Otocinclus) from São Paulo, Brazil. Of the 20 or so species in the genus, these three are the ones most frequently seen in the hobby. All have the same basic requirements.

DISTRIBUTION: *Southeastern Brazil*

SIZE: *Up to 2in (5cm) reported, but usually smaller*

BEHAVIOR: *Peaceful; should not be housed with boisterous tankmates*

DIET: *Predominantly herbivorous: algae and vegetable flakes, plus lettuce or spinach leaves, peas, etc.*

AQUARIUM: *Well-planted, with numerous hiding and resting places. Good filtration and fine-grained substratum recommended. At first, the water should be soft and acid; both values can be raised gradually once fish are acclimatized. Temperature range: 68–79°F (20–26°C)*

BREEDING: *Adhesive eggs are deposited on broad leaves. Hatching takes about three days*

EMPEROR PANAQUE

PIN-STRIPED, or ROYAL, PANAQUE

Panaque nigrolineatus

FAMILY: Loricariidae
SUBFAMILY: Ancistrinae

THERE ARE ONLY SOME HALF-A-DOZEN SPECIES IN the genus *Panaque*, of which two—Emperor Panaque and the black-bodied *P. suttoni* (Blue-Eyed Plec, Pleco or Panaque) from northern South America—are regularly available. Distinguished by their large heads, sloping foreheads and beautiful eyes, panaques make interesting additions to appropriately furnished and maintained aquaria.

DISTRIBUTION: *Southern Colombia*

SIZE: *Up to 12in (30cm) reported, but usually smaller*

BEHAVIOR: *Generally peaceful toward other tankmates, but strongly territorial toward its own species*

DIET: *Predominantly herbivorous: sinking plant-based formulations (e.g. vegetable tablets/ granules/flakes), lettuce or spinach leaves, peas, etc.*

AQUARIUM: *Spacious, well-filtered, with flowing water (as produced by powerhead outlet), along with adequate plant and bogwood or rock cover. Softish, slightly acid water preferred, though some deviation tolerated. Temperature range: 72–79°F (22–26°C)*

BREEDING: *No documented accounts currently available*

REDFIN OTOCINCLUS

Parotocinclus maculicauda

FAMILY: Loricariidae
SUBFAMILY: Hypoptopomatinae

THIS LIBERALLY SPOTTED SPECIES HAS RED EDGES on its dorsal, pectoral and caudal fins (*see* photo p.1). The genus itself can be distinguished from its close relative, *Otocinclus*, by the adipose fin (absent in *Otocinclus*). Of the 13 or so other species, only *P. amazonensis* (False Sucker), from coastal areas of southern Brazil, is seen with any regularity.

DISTRIBUTION: *Southern Brazil*

SIZE: *Around 1¾in (4.5cm)*

EMPEROR PANAQUE (PANAQUE NIGROLINEATUS)

Spiny Plec (Pseudacanthicus spinosus)

BEHAVIOR: *As for* Otocinclus affinis

DIET: *As for* Otocinclus affinis

AQUARIUM: *As for* Otocinclus affinis. *Temperature range: 72–77°F (22–25°C)*

BREEDING: *No documented accounts currently available*

PRETTY PECKOLTIA

Peckoltia pulcher

SYNONYM: *Hemiancistrus pulcher*
FAMILY: Loricariidae
SUBFAMILY: Ancistrinae

ALTHOUGH, AS ITS NAME IMPLIES, THIS SPECIES IS pretty, the same could be said of the 18 or so other species in the genus. Of these, *P. arenaria* (Clown Plec) from Peru and *P. vittata* (Broad-Banded Peckoltia) from the Amazon are, perhaps, the two most frequently encountered species, other than Pretty Peckoltia. All have the same basic requirements.

DISTRIBUTION: *Rio Negro (Brazil)*

SIZE: *Around 2½in (6cm)*

BEHAVIOR: *Peaceful toward other tankmates, but territorial toward its own species*

DIET: *Predominantly herbivorous (algae, vegetable tablet/granules/flakes, lettuce, peas, etc.), but may also accept some livefoods*

AQUARIUM: *Well-planted, well-filtered, with adequate bogwood or rock cover. Softish, slightly acid to neutral water recommended. Temperature range: 75–82°F (24–28°C)*

BREEDING: *No documented accounts currently available*

SPINY PLEC
SPINY PLECO

Pseudacanthicus spinosus

FAMILY: Loricariidae
SUBFAMILY: Ancistrinae

AS THE NAME IMPLIES, THIS IS A SPINY FISH, BUT it also possesses serrations on the scales. All members of this genus are spiny by nature, making them difficult to handle. There are probably about 12 species in the genus (the number is unclear, as some have not been described and are currently referred to only by their "L" numbers). Of the described species, *P. leopardus* (Leopard Plec), from the Rio Negro area in Brazil, is one of the few other *Pseudacanthicus* that are fairly regularly available.

DISTRIBUTION: *Brazilian Amazon basin*

SIZE: *Around 9¾in (25cm)*

BEHAVIOR: *Highly territorial, particularly toward its own species*

DIET: *Wide range of sinking foods accepted*

AQUARIUM: *Large, well-filtered, with flowing water (as produced by powerhead outlet), recommended. Provide large bogwood or rock shelters. Softish, slightly acid to slightly alkaline water advisable. Temperature range: 72–79°F (22–26°C)*

BREEDING: *No documented accounts currently available*

DELICATE WHIPTAIL LORICARIA

Rineloricaria fallax

SYNONYMS: *Rineloricaria parva, Loricaria parva*
FAMILY: Loricariidae
SUBFAMILY: Loricariinae

OF THE 40 OR SO SPECIES IN THIS GENUS (SOME OF which are difficult to distinguish from one another), few clearly identified species are imported regularly. Delicate Whiptail Loricaria and *R. lanceolata* (Lanceolate Whiptail Catfish) are notable exceptions. Both have similar requirements, although the latter has a more restricted temperature range (70–77°F/21–25°C).

DISTRIBUTION: *Rio de la Plata region (Paraguay)*

SIZE: *Around 4¾in (12cm)*

BEHAVIOR: *Peaceful; most active at dusk and at night*

DIET: *Predominantly herbivorous, but will accept a range of commercial formulations and livefoods*

AQUARIUM: *Well-planted, well-filtered, well-oxygenated, with fine substratum and adequate shelters. Slow-flowing water (as produced by suitably adjusted powerhead outlet) also* recommended. Soft, acid water preferred. Temperature range: 59–77°F (15–25°C)

BREEDING: *Soft, acid conditions, and slightly higher temperature, recommended. Adhesive eggs are laid in caves or hollows and are protected by male. Hatching takes 9 to 12 days, depending on temperature*

HI-FIN WHIPTAIL

ROYAL WHIPTAIL, ROYAL FAR-LOWELLA, or STURGEON CATFISH

Sturisoma panamense

FAMILY: Loricariidae
SUBFAMILY: Loricariinae

OF THE 15 OR SO SPECIES IN THIS GENUS, ONLY TWO (or possibly three) are imported regularly. Of these, Hi-Fin Whiptail is, perhaps, the one most frequently seen, followed by *S. aureum* (Giant Whiptail, from Colombia, synonymized with Hi-Fin Whiptail by

this species more easily observable. Soft to medium hard, slightly acid to neutral water preferred. Temperature range: 72–81°F (22–27°C)

BREEDING: *Adhesive eggs are guarded by male. Hatching takes eight to ten days, depending on temperature*

ELECTRIC CATFISH

Melapterurus electricus

FAMILY: Malapteruridae

A FISH THAT CAN GENERATE AN ELECTRICAL current of up to 400 volts is most certainly one for the specialist who knows and respects its amazing qualities. High-voltage discharges are emitted only by the largest specimens, but even modest-sized individuals pack quite a punch. In addition to this species, one other electric catfish is known: *M. microstoma* (Smallmouth Electric Catfish) from the Congo basin. Of the two, Elec-

BREEDING: *No documented accounts of aquarium breeding currently available*

MOUSTACHE SYNODONTIS

Hemisynodontis membranaceus

FAMILY: Mochokidae

THE MOUSTACHE SYNODONTIS—THE ONLY SPECIES in its genus—has the typical Mochokidae pointed head and bony headshield (bony plate) sloping up to a dorsal fin with a prominent front spine and a large, well-developed adipose fin. Its mouth barbels are also well-developed, with one pair carrying the characteristic membrane responsible for its name. Some authors believe this genus to be synonymous with *Synodontis*.

DISTRIBUTION: *Widely distributed from west Africa to the Nile*

ELECTRIC CATFISH (MELAPTERURUS ELECTRICUS)

some authors), and *S. barbatum* (Long-Nosed Whiptail) from Cujaba-Fluss. The male Hi-fin Whiptail is distinguished from the female by his cheek bristles.

DISTRIBUTION: *Panama*

SIZE: *Up to 9¾in (25cm) reported, but often smaller*

BEHAVIOR: *Peaceful and tolerant despite its size; most active at dusk and during the night*

DIET: *Predominantly herbivorous, but will accept other foods*

AQUARIUM: *Spacious, well-planted, well-filtered, and with flowing water (as produced by powerhead outlet); numerous shelters and hiding places, and subdued lighting, recommended. A "moonlight" fluorescent tube makes the nighttime forages of*

tric Catfish is the one more commonly encountered, and it is seen both in its wild type and in its mottled or albino form.

DISTRIBUTION: *Widely distributed in central Africa*

SIZE: *Up to 39in (1m) reported, but usually much smaller*

BEHAVIOR: *Lone, nocturnal predator that stuns its prey*

DIET: *Chunks of meat, large livefoods, e.g. earthworms and live fish (a factor that demands consideration prior to purchase)*

AQUARIUM: *Large, well-filtered, with large shelters. Use only robust plants. Water chemistry not critical. Temperature range: 72–86°F (22–30°C)*

SIZE: *Up to approximately 20in (50cm), but usually smaller*

BEHAVIOR: *Relatively peaceful despite its size; prefers to be kept in groups. Tends to feed in an upside-down position, as the common name for the family (upside-down catfish) implies (although few species actually exhibit this behavior)*

DIET: *Floating livefoods and other formulations (including pellets) preferred*

AQUARIUM: *Large, with substantial shelters. Use only robust, well-protected plants. Water chemistry not critical. Temperature range: 72–77°F (22–25°C)*

BREEDING: *No documented accounts currently available*

PAYNE'S SYNODONTIS

Mochokiella paynei

FAMILY: Mochokidae

PAYNE'S SYNODONTIS IS ONE OF THE SMALLER species and the only representative of its genus. Atypically for a mochokid catfish, it has a somewhat blunt snout. Its attractive mottled patterning and its small size make it more suitable for community aquaria than the majority of its relatives.

DISTRIBUTION: *Sierra Leone*

SIZE: *Around 2in (5cm), but often smaller*

BEHAVIOR: *A peaceful species; most active at dusk and during the night*

DIET: *Livefoods preferred, but other formulations also accepted*

AQUARIUM: *Well-planted, with adequate shelter and some open swimming areas. Softish, slightly acid to slightly alkaline water preferred. Temperature range: 72–77°F (22–25°C)*

BREEDING: *No documented accounts currently available*

PAYNE'S SYNODONTIS (MOCHOKIELLA PAYNEI)

ANGEL CATFISH

ANGEL or POLKA DOT SYNODONTIS

Synodontis angelicus

FAMILY: Mochokidae

THIS IS A DARK, CHOCOLATE-BROWN FISH WITH numerous cream-colored spots. The intensity of the dark coloration, as well as the number, color and size of the spots, can vary considerably, but all variants are impressively patterned.

DISTRIBUTION: *Stanley Pool (Zaire) and Cameroon*

SIZE: *Up to 7in (20cm) reported, but usually smaller*

BEHAVIOR: *Territorial toward its own species, with open aggression sometimes displayed in confined spaces. Swims upside-down only occasionally; most activity occurs at dusk and during the night*

DIET: *Livefoods are preferred, but some commercial formulations also accepted*

AQUARIUM: *Spacious, well-planted, with adequate shelter, fine-grained substratum and subdued lighting. A "moonlight" fluorescent tube will make nighttime activity of the species easily observable. Soft to moderately hard, slightly acid to slightly alkaline water preferred. Temperature range: 72–82°F (22–28°C),*

BREEDING: *No documented accounts currently available*

BRICHARD'S SYNODONTIS

BANDED SYNODONTIS

Synodontis brichardi

FAMILY: Mochokidae

THIS IS A SLIM-BODIED SPECIES, ATTRACTIVELY marked with dark, vertical body bands separated by light-colored stripes.

DISTRIBUTION: *Congo River*

SIZE: *Up to 7in (18cm) reported, but usually smaller*

ANGEL CATFISH (SYNODONTIS ANGELICUS)

FEATHERFIN SYNODONTIS (SYNODONTIS EUPTERUS)

BEHAVIOR: *Generally peaceful, but may prey on very small fish; will occasionally swim upside-down*

DIET: *As for* S. angelicus

AQUARIUM: *As for* S. angelicus *but requires vigorous water flow (as produced by powerhead outlet). Temperature range: 72–77°F (22–25°C)*

BREEDING: *As for* S. angelicus

DECORATED SYNODONTIS

CLOWN SYNODONTIS

Synodontis decorus

FAMILY: Mochokidae

THIS IS A SPECTACULAR SPECIES, NOTABLE NOT just for its large, black blotches on a pinky-white base, but especially for the long, delicate extension of the dorsal fin in adult specimens.

DISTRIBUTION: *Upper Zaire and Cameroon*

SIZE: *Up to 12in (30cm) reported, but usually smaller*

BEHAVIOR: *Peaceful; swims upside-down only occasionally*

DIET: *As for* S. angelicus

AQUARIUM: *As for* S. angelicus. *Temperature range: 73–81°F (23–27°C)*

BREEDING: *As for* S. angelicus

FEATHERFIN SYNODONTIS

Synodontis eupterus

FAMILY: Mochokidae

AS ITS COMMON NAME SUGGESTS, THIS SPECIES—like *S. decorus*—develops a dorsal fin extension. This, and its numerous, small, dark body spots, make it a much-sought-after *Synodontis*.

DISTRIBUTION: *Widely distributed from west Africa to the White Nile*

SIZE: *Around 6in (15cm)*

BEHAVIOR: *Peaceful, even toward smaller tankmates. Swims upside-down only occasionally*

DIET: *As for* S. angelicus

AQUARIUM: *Basically, as for* S. angelicus. *Temperature range: 72–79°F (22–26°C)*

BREEDING: *As for* S. angelicus

STRIPED SYNODONTIS

PYJAMA SYNODONTIS

Synodontis flavitaeniatus

FAMILY: Mochokidae

THIS IS ONE OF THE MOST BEAUTIFUL OF ALL *Synodontis*. Its unusual body patterning includes narrow, yellowish to orange, longitudinal stripes on a dark background. It

is not, however, seen as frequently as some of its relatives.

DISTRIBUTION: *Stanley Pool region (Zaire)*

SIZE: *Up to 8in (20cm)*

BEHAVIOR: *As for* S. brichardi

DIET: *As for* S. angelicus

AQUARIUM: *Basically, as for* S. angelicus. *Temperature range: 73–79°F (23–26°C)*

BREEDING: *As for* S. angelicus

CUCKOO SYNODONTIS

MANY-SPOTTED SYNODONTIS

Synodontis multipunctatus

FAMILY: Mochokidae

THIS SPECIES IS OFTEN CONFUSED WITH OTHER similarly patterned species. Its white base color is overlaid with black spots that increase in size from the head to the tail. The Cuckoo Synodontis is of special interest because of its breeding habits.

DISTRIBUTION: *Lake Tanganyika*

SIZE: *Reported up to 12in (30cm), but almost always considerably smaller*

BEHAVIOR: *Can be territorial toward its own species; breeding behavior unusual (see below)*

DIET: *As for* S. angelicus

Aquarium: Typical African Rift Lake cichlid layout suits this species well (see Aquarium Set-up). Neutral to alkaline water preferred. Temperature range: 70–77°F (21–25°C)

BREEDING: *Pairs spawn among mouthbrooding cichlids that are, themselves, spawning. The female cichlids therefore pick up the Cuckoo's eggs along with their own and incubate them orally. They will also protect the catfish fry as if they were their own offspring*

BLACK-SPOTTED UPSIDE-DOWN CATFISH

COMMON UPSIDE-DOWN CATFISH

Synodontis nigriventris

FAMILY: Mochokidae

OF ALL THE *SYNODONTIS* KNOWN IN THE HOBBY, this is the species that spends most time in an inverted swimming position. The habit is so highly developed in this fish that it has actually evolved reversed body shading, i.e. in some species, the belly is darker than the back—the complete opposite to the shading pattern exhibited by other fishes, including other members of the Mochokidae. Despite its upside-down habit, the Black-Spotted Upside-Down Catfish is perfectly capable of swimming the "right way up," and occasionally does so. Interestingly, young fish do not adopt the upside-down orientation until they are about two months old.

DISTRIBUTION: *Congo basin*

SIZE: *Up to 4in (10cm) or larger reported, but often smaller*

BEHAVIOR: *A peaceful fish that can be kept in groups; spends most of its time in an upside-down position; most activity occurs at dusk and during the night*

DIET: *Floating livefoods, freeze-dried or deep-frozen diets are preferred; other foods accepted more reluctantly*

AQUARIUM: *As for* S. angelicus

BREEDING: *Challenging, but achievable, in aquaria. Eggs are laid in a depression, hollow or on the roof of a cave. There may be some degree of parental care. Hatching takes about seven days*

ONE-SPOT SYNODONTIS

Synodontis notatus

FAMILY: Mochokidae

THIS IS ONE OF THE MOST FREQUENTLY SEEN species of *Synodontis*. It is easily identified by its single central body spot (although some specimens may exhibit more than one) on a pinkish, grayish or silvery background.

DISTRIBUTION: *Zaire*

SIZE: *Up to 8in (20cm) reported, but usually smaller*

BEHAVIOR: *Peaceful toward tankmates, but adults can be boisterous*

DIET: *As for* S. angelicus

AQUARIUM: *As for* S. angelicus. *Temperature range: 72–79°F (22–26°C)*

BREEDING: *As for* S. angelicus

ASIAN SHARK CATFISH
SIAMESE or IRIDESCENT SHARK

Pangasius sutchi

FAMILY: Pangasiidae

THE PANGASIIDAE CONTAINS *PANGASIANODON GIGAS* (Giant Catfish), which can grow to over 6½ft (2m) and weigh over 240lb (110kg). The genus *Pangasius* is the only one of the pangasiids encountered with any frequency in the hobby, with the Asian Shark Catfish being the species most often seen, either in its wild type or albino forms. Most specimens offered are juveniles, but these will soon grow into large fish. This is therefore a species that is suitable only for aquarists who can provide appropriate accommodations. It is widely bred commercially as a food fish as well as an ornamental.

DISTRIBUTION: *Around Bangkok, Thailand*

BLACK-SPOTTED UPSIDE-DOWN CATFISH (SYNODONTIS NIGRIVENTRIS)

OTHER *SYNODONTIS* SPECIES

There are more than 100 species in the genus *Synodontis*. Although not all are available within the hobby, a wide selection, in addition to the ones featured in the previous pages, may be found with varying degrees of regularity. Of these, most are capable of swimming upside down from time to time, but relatively few habitually exhibit this behavior. Sizes within the genus can vary between some 2½in (6cm) and 28in (70cm). Most species offered for home aquaria, however, are 12in (30cm) or less. Even so, these are sizable catfish, so adequate accommodations must be provided (see, for example, S. angelicus). Although temperature requirements may vary a little between species, most are happy between 72°F (22°C) and 79°F (26°C). The following are some of the most frequently available species. The sizes quoted are indicative of approximate maximum lengths; most individuals are somewhat smaller.

SCIENTIFIC NAME	COMMON NAME(S)	SIZE
S. alberti	Albert's or Congo Hi-Fin Synodontis	8in (20cm)
S. batesii	Bate's Synodontis	6in (15cm)
S. budgeti	Brown Synodontis	8¾in (22cm)
S. camelopardalis	Ruki Synodontis	6in (15cm)
S. congicus	Congo Synodontis	6in (15cm)
S. longirostris	Long-Nosed Synodontis	24in (60cm)
S. nigrita	Dark-Spotted or False Upside-Down Synodontis	8in (20cm)
S. njassae	Nyassa Synodontis	8in (20cm)
S. ornatipinnis	White-Barred Synodontis	12in (30cm)
S. petricola	Pygmy Leopard or Even-Spotted Synodontis	5½in (14cm)
S. pleurops	Big-Eyed Synodontis	8in (20cm)
S. schoutedeni	Vermiculated Synodontis	5½in (14cm)
S. victoriae	Victoria Synodontis	12in (30cm)

SIZE: *Up to 39in (1m) reported, but usually smaller*

BEHAVIOR: *Large shoals are encountered in the wild; in aquaria, however, only single specimens should be kept, except during the juvenile phase; a nervous, predatory species that can disrupt aquarium decor*

DIET: *Substantial, chunky livefoods and commercial preparations accepted*

AQUARIUM: *Spacious, well-covered, with ample swimming space, efficient filtration, and water current (as produced by power filter or powerhead outlet). Neutral, soft to medium-hard water preferred. Temperature range: 72–79°F (22–26°C)*

BREEDING: *No documented accounts currently available*

BANDED SHOVELNOSED CATFISH

DOURADA, or GOLDEN, ZEBRA

Brachyplatystoma juruense

FAMILY: Pimelodidae

THIS PREDATORY SPECIES IS USUALLY AVAILABLE in its boldly patterned juvenile phase. It will eventually grow into a large fish with an equally large appetite and exacting demands. It is undoubtedly a species best reserved for the specialist, as are the few other species of this genus that are occasionally encountered.

DISTRIBUTION: *Juruá Rivèr (Brazil)*

SIZE: *Up to 31½in (80cm)*

BEHAVIOR: *Highly predatory*

DIET: *Large livefoods—including fish—accepted (a factor that demands consideration prior to purchase)*

AQUARIUM: *Large, well-covered, well-filtered, with water current (as produced by power filter or powerhead outlet) essential. Provide large shelters. Water chemistry not critical, but extremes must be avoided. Temperature range: 72–81°F (22–27°C)*

BREEDING: *No documented accounts currently available*

SPOTTED SHOVEL-NOSED CATFISH

PORTHOLE, or FLAT-NOSED, ANTENNA CATFISH

Hemisorubim platyrhynchos

FAMILY: Pimelodidae

THIS ATTRACTIVELY SPOTTED CATFISH IS considerably more manageable than *Brachyplatystoma juruense* in home aquaria. It is smaller and more flexible in its dietary habits than *B. juruense*, although it is still a substantial fish.

DISTRIBUTION: *Northern and eastern South America*

SIZE: *Up to 20in (50cm), but usually smaller*

BEHAVIOR: *Predatory*

DIET: *Chunky livefoods and meat-based diets accepted, as well as tablets and granules*

AQUARIUM: *As for* Brachyplatystoma juruense, *but subdued lighting and soft substratum also recommended*

BREEDING: *Unknown in aquaria*

SAILFIN MARBLED CATFISH

SAILFIN PIM

Leiarius pictus

FAMILY: Pimelodidae

THIS SPECTACULAR SPECIES IS DISTINGUISHED BY its large, sail-like dorsal fin and bold chocolate-brown and creamy-pink body patterning. Its most obvious disadvantages as an aquarium fish are its large size and feeding habit, which make it suitable only for those specialist hobbyists who can cater for its needs. A mottled species, *L.*

▲ *SPOTTED SHOVELNOSED CATFISH (HEMISORUBIM PLATYRHYNCHOS)*
◄ *SAILFIN MARBLED CATFISH (LEIARIUS PICTUS)*

marmoratus (False Perrunichthys), from the Brazilian and Peruvian Amazon, is also occasionally available.

DISTRIBUTION: *Amazon basin*

SIZE: *Up to 24in (60cm)*

BEHAVIOR: *As for* Brachyplatystoma juruense

DIET: *As for* Brachyplatystoma juruense

AQUARIUM: *As for* Brachyplatystoma juruense

RED-TAILED CATFISH (*PHRACTOCEPHALUS HEMIOLIOPTERUS*)

BREEDING: *As for* Brachyplatystoma juruense

BUMBLEBEE CATFISH

Microglanis iheringi

FAMILY: Pimelodidae

OF THE EIGHT OR SO SPECIES IN THIS GENUS, ONLY two are encountered on a regular basis: this one and the smaller, equally beautifully marked *M. poecilus* (Dwarf Marbled Catfish) from Suriname.

DISTRIBUTION: *Widely distributed in northern South America*

SIZE: *Up to 4in (10cm) reported, but usually about half this size*

BEHAVIOR: *Sedentary; nocturnal; peaceful toward tankmates of a similar size; small fish may be treated as prey*

DIET: *Livefoods preferred, but commercial formulations also accepted*

AQUARIUM: *Well-planted, with adequate shelter, fine-grained substratum, and some water movement (as produced by powerhead outlet) recommended. A "moonlight" fluorescent tube will facilitate nighttime viewing. Water chemistry not critical, but extremes should be avoided. Temperature range: 70–79°F (21–26°C)*

BREEDING: *No documented accounts currently available*

RED-TAILED CATFISH

Phractocephalus hemioliopterus

FAMILY: Pimelodidae

THIS CATFISH IS EXCEPTIONAL IN THAT ITS coloration remains bright and distinct, even in large specimens. It is, undoubtedly, one of the most attractive of all large catfish, and offers the extra advantage that it can become very tame. On the downside is its eventual large size—an important factor that needs careful consideration. The small, commercially bred juveniles that are generally available will, in appropriate conditions, grow into giants in a relatively short period of time.

DISTRIBUTION: *Widely distributed in the Amazon basin*

SIZE: *Up to 4ft (1.2m)*

BEHAVIOR: *Highly predatory*

DIET: *Large livefoods, including fish, preferred (a factor that requires consideration prior to purchase). Chunky meat-/fish-based foods and commercial formulations may also be accepted*

AQUARIUM: *Large, well-covered, well-filtered, with some large pieces of decor. Water chemistry not critical, but quality must be good. Temperature range: 70–81°F (21–27°C)*

BREEDING: *No documented accounts of aquarium breeding currently available, although the species has been bred commercially*

GRACEFUL PIM

Pimelodella gracilis

SYNONYMS: *Pimelodella cristata, P. geryi*
FAMILY: Pimelodidae

THE CURRENT STATE OF *PIMELODELLA* AND *Pimelodus* classification is highly confused. The main difference between the two is based, largely, on the shape of one of the skull bones (the postoccipital process). This variable factor, plus the close similarity between species, makes correct identification extremely difficult. It also means that a particular fish may appear as a *Pimelodella* in one book and as a *Pimelodus* in another. Graceful Pim—as its name suggests—is a graceful species, with scattered body spots on a silvery base color and a black longitudinal band running the whole length of the body. Note that this, and other pimelodids, possess powerful dorsal- and pectoral-fin spines that can inflict painful injuries and cause allergic reactions in some people.

DISTRIBUTION: *Widely distributed in tropical South America*

SIZE: *Up to 12in (30cm) reported, but usually considerably smaller*

BEHAVIOR: *May prey on small tankmates, but generally peaceful toward similarly sized fish; most active in the evening and during the night*

DIET: *Livefoods preferred, but will accept some commercial formulations*

AQUARIUM: *Sufficiently large to accommodate a group, and with open swimming spaces and adequate shelter. Well-filtered, soft, slightly acid water preferred. Temperature range: 72–77°F (22–25°C)*

BREEDING: *No documented accounts available*

ORNATE PIM

Pimelodus ornatus

FAMILY: Pimelodidae

THIS UNUSUALLY MARKED SPECIES HAS A GREY, broad, vertical band in the "shoulder" region, behind which are two similarly colored, but longitudinal, bands that run all along the body and into the caudal fin. The whitish dorsal fin has a distinct black spot.

DISTRIBUTION: *Tropical South America*

SIZE: *Around 9¾in (25cm)*

BEHAVIOR: *As for* Pimelodella gracilis

DIET: *As for* Pimelodella gracilis

AQUARIUM: *As for* Pimelodella gracilis

BREEDING: *As for* Pimelodella gracilis

ANGELICUS PIM

Pimelodus pictus

SYNONYM: *Pimelodella pictus*
FAMILY: Pimelodidae

THIS STRIKING FISH IS ONE OF THE MOST frequently seen pims in the hobby. It is also one of the most peaceful, though care must be taken not to house it with small tankmates.

DISTRIBUTION: *Colombia and Peru*

SIZE: *Up to 6in (15cm) reported, but usually smaller*

BEHAVIOR: *As for* Pimelodella gracilis

DIET: *As for* Pimelodella gracilis

AQUARIUM: *As for* Pimelodella gracilis

BREEDING: *As for* Pimelodella gracilis

STURGEON CATFISH

Platystomatichthys sturio

FAMILY: Pimelodidae

THE COMMON NAME OF THIS SPECIES DERIVES FROM the long snout, which may be upturned at the tip and thus look very similar to the snout possessed by many *Acipenser* (sturgeon) species. Another notable feature of

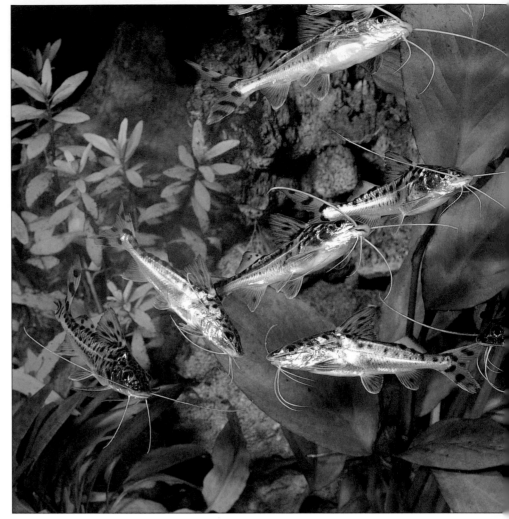

ANGELICUS PIM (PIMELODUS PICTUS)

OTHER *PIMELODID* SPECIES

Owing to the considerable confusion that exists between the genera *Pimelodella* and *Pimelodus*, as well as the difficulties with the correct identification of many of the similar-looking species, pims are found under a variety of names, some accurate, some less so. In general, *Pimelodella* is regarded as containing more than 60 species, while *Pimelodus* may contain around 20. Of these, it is unclear just how many are actually available on a regular basis. In addition to the featured species, though, the following are, at least, reasonably well known in the hobby.

SCIENTIFIC NAME	COMMON NAME(S)	SIZE
Pimelodella dorseyi	Dorsey's Pim	8¾in (22cm)
Pimelodella laticeps	Flat-Headed Pim	6in (15cm)
Pimelodella linami	Linam's Pim Pim	4¾in (12cm)
Pimelodus albofasciatus	White-Spotted, or White-Striped, Pim	9¾in (25cm)
Pimelodus blochi	Dusky Pim	9¾in (25cm)
Pimelodus maculatus	Spotted Pim	9¾in (25cm)

this species is the extremely long maxillary barbels, which can extend beyond the tip of the caudal fin.

DISTRIBUTION: *Amazon basin*

SIZE: *Up to 24in (60cm) reported*

BEHAVIOR: *As for* Brachyplatystoma juruense

DIET: *As for* Brachyplatystoma juruense

AQUARIUM: *As for* Brachyplatystoma juruense, *although Sturgeon Catfish may be somewhat more difficult to acclimatize to aquarium conditions*

BREEDING: *As for* Brachyplatystoma juruense

TIGER SHOVELNOSED CATFISH

Pseudoplatystoma fasciatum

FAMILY: Pimelodidae

SEVERAL SIMILAR SHOVELNOSES ARE KNOWN, giving rise to the possibility that at least two—Tiger Shovelnosed Catfish and *P. tigrinum*—are either closely related species or subspecies, or even variants of one species. As many as five subspecies of Tiger Shovelnosed Catfish are generally recognized.

DISTRIBUTION: *Eastern South America, from east of the Andes to the Panamá/Rio de la Plata basin*

SIZE: *Up to 39in (1m) reported*

BEHAVIOUR: *As for* Brachyplatystoma juruense

DIET: *As for* Brachyplatystoma juruense

AQUARIUM: *As for* Brachyplatystoma juruense

BREEDING: *As for* Brachyplatystoma juruense

DUCKBEAK SHOVEL-NOSED CATFISH

Sorubim lima

FAMILY: Pimelodidae

THIS SPECIES IS EASILY DISTINGUISHED FROM ITS relatives by the broad, black band that runs from the snout to the caudal fin, dipping "down" into the lower lobe of the fin. The area of the body below the band is silvery white.

DISTRIBUTION: *Amazon basin*

SIZE: *Up to 24in (60cm) reported*

BEHAVIOR: *As for* Brachyplatystoma juruense

DIET: *As for* Brachyplatystoma juruense

AQUARIUM: *As for* Brachyplatystoma juruense. *Temperature range: 73–86°F (23–30°C)*

BREEDING: *As for* Brachyplatystoma juruense

AFRICAN GLASS CATFISH

Eutropiellus debauwi

FAMILY: Schilbeidae

AFRICAN GLASS CATFISH IS AN UNUSUALLY patterned species that likes to swim in midwater. It is often confused with *E. van-derweyeri* from the Niger River system.

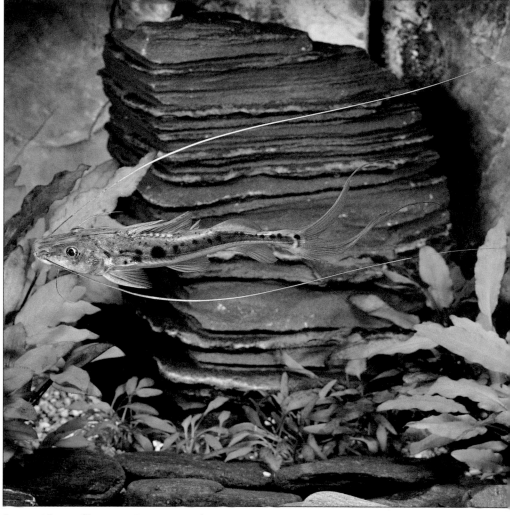

STURGEON CATFISH (PLATYSTOMATICHTHYS STURIO)

However, the latter has black streaks on both lobes of the caudal fin.

DISTRIBUTION: *Congo and Gabon*

SIZE: *Around 3in (8cm)*

BEHAVIOR: *A peaceful shoaler, active during the day*

DIET: *Will accept a range of commercial diets*

AQUARIUM: *Ample swimming areas should be provided, along with some shelter, surface cover*

EUTROPIELLUS VANDERWEYERI; *SEE TEXT, ABOVE*

(floating plants) and a water current (as produced by powerhead outlet). A dark substratum and peat filtration (or tannin-stained water, see Aquarium Set-up) also desirable. Soft to medium-hard, acid to slightly alkaline water suitable. Temperature range: 75–81°F (24–27°C)

BREEDING: *No documented accounts currently available*

STRIPED SCHILBE

BUTTER CATFISH

Schilbe mystus

FAMILY: Schilbeidae

GENERALLY AVAILABLE AS SMALL SPECIMENS, THIS active species can grow to a relatively large size, making it unsuitable for community aquaria (other than those housing equally sized tankmates). At slightly less than half the size, *S. marmoratus* (African Shoulder-Spot Catfish) is easier to accommodate but is not seen as frequently.

DISTRIBUTION: *From west Africa to the Nile Lakes; Chad and Victoria*

SIZE: *Up to 13¾in (35cm)*

BEHAVIOR: *Active shoaler; may eat small fish*

DIET: *Larger livefoods, although chunky commercial preparations also accepted*

AQUARIUM: *Large, well-filtered, with soft, dark substratum and ample swimming space recommended. Water chemistry not critical. Temperature range: 73–81°F (23–27°C)*

BREEDING: *No documented accounts available*

GLASS CATFISH

GHOST CATFISH

Kryptopterus bicirrhis

FAMILY: Siluridae

THE GLASS CATFISH BELONGS TO THE SAME family as the gigantic *Silurus glanis* (Wels Catfish), which can attain lengths of around 10ft (3m), and *Wallago attu*, which can grow to over 6½ft (2m); both are most unsuitable aquarium fish despite being occasionally available. Unusually for a catfish, the Glass Catfish is a midwater swimmer that looks absolutely stunning when kept—as it should be—in a shoal. A second, less transparent, species, from the same general area—*K. macrocephalus* (the so-called Poor Man's Glass Catfish)—is also available, along with a smaller, highly transparent species, *K. minor*, and a species from Borneo, *K. cryptopterus*. All have the same basic requirements.

DISTRIBUTION: *Eastern India and southeast Asia*

SIZE: *Up to 6in (15cm), but usually smaller*

BEHAVIOR: *Peaceful, midwater shoaler; must be kept in a group*

DIET: *Swimming livefoods preferred, but deep-frozen, freeze-dried and other formulations may be accepted, especially if distributed via a current (as produced by a powerhead)*

AQUARIUM: *Well-planted, with ample open swimming areas. Water chemistry not critical, but soft, slightly acid water preferred. Temperature*

range: 70–79°F (21–26°C)

BREEDING: *No documented accounts currently available*

GLASS CATFISH

Ompok bimaculatus

FAMILY: Siluridae

DESPITE ITS COMMON NAME, THIS GLASS CATFISH is nowhere as transparent as its better-known, smaller relative, *Kryptopterus bicirrhis* (the "true" glass catfish)—*see* previous entry. This species is characterized by two spots, one behind the gill cover and the other on the caudal peduncle. Another species, *O. eugeniatus* (Vaillant's Butter Catfish), which is smaller, is also occasionally available.

DISTRIBUTION: *Widely distributed in tropical Asia*

SIZE: *Up to 18in (45cm), but usually about half this size*

BEHAVIOR: *Relatively peaceful shoaler, which is active during the day; adults may become quarrelsome*

DIET: *Chunky meat-/fish-based foods and commercial formulations accepted*

AQUARIUM: *Well-lit, well-planted, well-filtered, with ample open swimming space for a group, recommended. Water chemistry not critical. Temperature range: 68–79°F (20–26°C)*

BREEDING: *Aquarium spawnings have not been reported, but spawning in tropical ponds has occurred*

GLASS CATFISH (KRYPTOPTERUS BICIRRHIS)

VAILLANT'S BUTTER CATFISH (OMPOK EUGENIATUS)

CLOWN CATFISH

Gagata cenia

FAMILY: Sisoridae

SO CALLED (LIKE MANY OTHER SIMILARLY PAT-
terned species) because of its black spots
on a light background, the Clown Catfish
has been known since 1822—although it
did not begin to appear with much frequency until the 1990s. An albino form is
occasionally available.

DISTRIBUTION: *Mainly from north and northeast
India*

SIZE: *Around 6in (15cm)*

BEHAVIOR: *Generally peaceful, active shoaler*

DIET: *Livefoods preferred, but other foods also
accepted*

AQUARIUM: *Plants not vital, but well-lit, well-planted
aquarium with gravelly bottom and some flat or
smoothly rounded resting places recommended.
Provide a water current (as produced by power
filter or powerhead outlet). Hard alkaline water
preferred. Temperature range: 64–72°F (18–22°C)*

BREEDING: *No documented accounts available*

BUTTERFLY CATFISH

Hara hara

FAMILY: Sisoridae

TWO SPECIES OF *HARA* ARE OCCASIONALLY AVAIL-
able—the Butterfly Catfish and its smaller
relative, *H. jerdoni* (Dwarf Anchor Catfish). The two other species in the genus
are only rarely seen in aquaria. All species
have the same basic requirements.

DISTRIBUTION: *Indian subcontinent*

▲ CLOWN CATFISH (GAGATA CENIA)   ▼ BUTTERFLY CATFISH (HARA HARA)

SIZE: *Up to 1½in (4cm)*

BEHAVIOR: *Peaceful, retiring; may be kept in
groups*

DIET: *Sinking livefoods preferred, but commercial
formulations also accepted*

AQUARIUM: *Well-filtered, with numerous shelters
and subdued lighting recommended. Soft, acid
water preferred. Temperature range: 64–72°F
(18–22°C)*

BREEDING: *No documented accounts available*

CYPRINIDS

THE FAMILY CYPRINIDAE IS THE LARGEST OF THE exclusively freshwater families of fishes and, with the possible exception of the freshwater/brackish/marine family, the Gobiidae, it is also the largest family of vertebrates. Indeed, the family as we currently recognize it is deemed by some authorities to be artificially large.

Not surprisingly, therefore, opinions vary as to how the family should be subdivided. The following listing of subfamilies follows that of Nelson (1994)—*see* Bibliography.

Cyprininae (about 700 species). These fish usually (but not invariably) possess anterior and posterior barbels. The three *Carassius* species (including the Goldfish—*C. auratus*), for instance, don't possess barbels, while the Common Carp and, therefore, Koi (*Cyprinus carpio*), *Barbus* and relatives, *Labeo* and *Epalzeorhynchus* ("Sharks" and Flying Foxes) and numerous other species, have barbels.

Gobioninae, which includes the European Gudgeon (*Gobio gobio*).

Rasborinae (= Danioninae), which—as the name implies—includes all the popular tropical aquarium rasboras and danios.

Acheilognathinae, which includes the amazing bitterlings (*Rhodeus* and *Tanakia*).

Leuciscinae, the intra-subfamilial relationships of which are, perhaps, debatable, but that—as things stand—includes the minnows (*Phoxinus*), the Ide or Orfe (*Leuciscus*), the Roach (*Rutilus*), the Rudd (*Scardinius*) and the Tench (*Tinca*).

Cultrinae, consisting of Eastern Asian genera like *Parabramis*.

Alburninae, including the Bleak (*Alburnus*).

Psilorhynchinae, with only two genera from Nepal, India and parts of Myanmar (Burma): *Psilorhynchoides* and *Psilorhynchus*.

There are about 2,010 species in the family spread among some 210–220 genera in Eurasia, North America and Africa. With such a high number of species and such wide distribution, it is to be expected that cyprinids will exhibit great diversity of shape, size and characteristics.

There are giant species, such as *Catlocarpio siamensis* from Thailand and *Tor putitora*, the Large-scaled Barb or Mahseer, from the Bhramaputra, in Eastern India, both of which are known to grow to lengths in excess of 8ft (2.5m). In contrast, the largest specimen of *Danionella translucida*, from Burma so far found is a mere ½in (1.2cm) in length. It is hardly surprising, therefore, that the debate regarding the actual composition of the family and its subdivision into subfamilies is so complex and still apparently so far from being resolved. Even selecting characteristics that are shared by all members of the family and which distinguish them from other families is fraught with difficulty. Cyprinids have a protrusile, or extendible, mouth and jaws without teeth. However, they possess pharyngeal ("throat") bones with teeth. They also exhibit a number of skull bone and muscle modifications, along with two pairs of mouth barbels (but not in all species) and a scaleless head. They lack an adipose ("second dorsal") fin.

The difficulty with using these features to identify a fish as belonging to the family Cyprinidae is that none of these characteristics is unique to cyprinids. Furthermore, all of them, plus others, are shared with the other families which together constitute the order Cypriniformes.

Yet, despite this sharing of characteristics with fish belonging to related families, there is a general consensus as to what constitutes a cyprinid. The selection of species that follows can be safely regarded as consisting of noncontroversial, universally accepted members of the family Cyprinidae.

SILVER SHARK
BALA, MALAYSIAN or
TRI-COLOR SHARK
Balantiocheilos melanopterus

SYNONYM: *Balantiocheilus melanopterus*
SUBFAMILY: Cyprininae

SHARK IN NAME AND, SUPERFICIALLY, IN OVERALL shape—but certainly not in demeanour—the Silver Shark is a predominantly herbivorous species which has been popular for many years. This is, perhaps, a little surprising, since this species can attain a substantial size (*see* details below) and can outgrow most home aquaria. However, with the improvements in aquarium technology that are being seen in recent times, and as the keeping of larger setups becomes more feasible, the Silver Shark is likely to continue enjoying popularity among aquarists. It may even be possible to breed this attractive and active fish in aquaria before long.

The Silver Shark is a shoaling species and should therefore be kept in groups. However, the average home aquarium will only be able to house a shoal of juveniles, which, provided with an appropriate diet, will soon outgrow their quarters. In the past, Silver Sharks used to be collected in large numbers from the wild. Today, this species is bred commercially in the Far East and it is these captive-bred stocks that meet most of the demand.

DISTRIBUTION: *Southeast Asia; Kalimantan (Borneo), Thailand, Sumatra and Peninsular Malaysia*

SIZE: *Usually sold as juveniles measuring 4in (10cm) or less, but can grow to around 14in (35cm) in roomy aquaria with good water quality and an appropriate diet*

BEHAVIOR: *Nonaggressive, even toward smaller fishes, despite its size; active shoaler*

DIET: *Will accept a wide range of livefoods and commercial diets, which should include vegetable matter. Delicate plants are likely to suffer in an aquarium housing this species*

AQUARIUM: *Roomy with ample swimming space and a well-fitting cover to prevent specimens from jumping out. Will tolerate a wide range of hardness and pH—although the latter should, ideally, be kept between slightly acid and neutral. Temperature range: 72–82°F (22–28°C)*

BREEDING: *This has not been reported in home aquaria. However, the species is commercially bred in large numbers*

ARULIUS BARB
FOUR-SPOT or LONGFIN BARB
Barbus arulius

SYNONYMS: *Puntius arulius, Capoeta arulius*
SUBFAMILY: Cyprininae

ACCORDING TO SOME AUTHORS, THE GENERIC name *Barbus* should only be used in connection with African and European species of barb. If this recommendation is accepted, the Arulius Barb, which originates in India, should be known as *Puntius arulius*, rather than *Barbus arulius*. However, difficulties in barb taxonomy, which embraces not just variations between species, but even within individual species, has—so far—meant that the recommendation has not found universal acceptance. In this book, therefore, for the sake of simplicity, all the barbs will be referred to as *Barbus*, with alternative names indicated as in this entry.

The Arulius Barb is an active shoaler in which males are slow to develop their full adult characteristics, consisting of extended dorsal ray fins. This relative slowness (it can take over a year) is one of the main reasons why this species has not become more popular. Although mature males can grow quite large (*see* below) for a community fish, this barb is relatively peaceful and can be kept with tankmates smaller than itself. In reflected light, the white/silvery areas between the black body bands have an iridescent sheen—particularly attractive in mature males.

DISTRIBUTION: *Southern and southeast India*

SIZE: *Up to 4¾in (12cm)*

BEHAVIOR: *Sociable fish which is tolerant of other species and should be kept in a shoal*

DIET: *Wide range of foods accepted; vegetable matter should be included*

AQUARIUM: *Roomy with plenty of swimming space and clumps of vegetation. Although tolerant of a range of conditions, soft, slightly acid water is recommended. Temperature range: 66–77°F (19–25°C)*

BREEDING: *This is an egg-scattering species which releases its spawn among vegetation. Relatively few eggs are laid*

TWO-SPOT BARB
REDSIDE BARB
Barbus bimaculatus

SYNONYM: *Puntius bimaculatus*
SUBFAMILY: Cyprininae

THIS IS A SLIM-BODIED BARB IN WHICH MATURE specimens sport a red line running the length of the body, originating in the top half of the eye and ending at the posterior edge of the fork in the caudal fin. In some wild populations, such as the one from Ginigathena in Sri Lanka, this line is either missing or very faint. The dorsal fin in all types is reddish and carries a black spot halfway along its base. The second spot responsible for one of the common names for this species is located on the caudal peduncle. Albino specimens are

SILVER SHARK (BALANTIOCHEILOS MELANOPTERUS)

ARULIUS BARB (BARBUS ARULIUS)

Rosy Barb (Barbus conchonius)

occasionally encountered. It is a hardy species suitable for beginners.

DISTRIBUTION: *Sri Lanka and Mysore (southern India)*

SIZE: *Up to 2¾in (7cm), but usually smaller*

BEHAVIOR: *This is a shoaling species that prefers to stay close to the bottom; it is tolerant of other fish*

DIET: *Accepts most aquarium foods, but should receive a vegetable supplement*

AQUARIUM: *A medium-sized aquarium will prove adequate for a small shoal which should be provided with both open swimming spaces and shelter. Although the species does not have strict water chemistry requirements, extremes of both acidity/alkalinity and hardness should be avoided. Temperature range: 72–77°F (22–25°C)*

BREEDING: *Typical egg-scattering species that can produce several batches of eggs in a single season. Hatching takes about 48 hours.*

ROSY BARB

Barbus conchonius

SYNONYM: *Puntius conchonius*
SUBFAMILY: Cyprininae

THIS IS ONE OF THE MOST FAMOUS AND POPULAR species in the aquarium hobby. As the name implies, the basic body color is rosy—but only really pronounced in males, particularly during the breeding season. Over the years, many varieties of this attractive fish have been produced by commercial breeders, most notably long-finned, red and copper/bronze types in which the females are also more deeply pigmented than their wild or basic counterparts. The Rosy Barb can tolerate relatively low temperatures (*see* below), making them suitable for some

coldwater aquaria—but not in areas that experience severe winter weather.

DISTRIBUTION: *Northern India*

SIZE: *Up to 6in (15cm) reported, but usually much smaller*

BEHAVIOR: *An active shoaling species which is tolerant of others*

DIET: *All livefoods and commercial diets are accepted*

AQUARIUM: *Open swimming areas, along with plant thickets should be provided. Although a wide range of water chemistry conditions are tolerated, extremes of pH and hardness should be avoided. Temperature range: as low as 59°F (15°C) can be tolerated during the winter season*

without trouble (I have kept this species in outdoor ponds in Southern Spain for many years without the slightest difficulty). At other times of the year, 64–77°F (18–25°C)

BREEDING: *A typical egg scatterer among fine-leaved vegetation. As with all other scatterers, the parents will consume their eggs, given the opportunity. Hatching takes about 30 hours at the higher end of the temperature range*

CUMING'S BARB

Barbus cumingi

SYNONYM: *Puntius cumingii*
SUBFAMILY: Cyprininae

CUMING'S BARB SHOULD REALLY BE FAR MORE popular than it is, for it is a delightful little fish that does well in aquaria. A possible reason for its relatively low demand among aquarists could be the deeper colors and longer finnage found in cultivated varieties of *B. nigrofasciatus* (*see* p.168) (with which it shares certain physical characteristics) and *B. conchonius*.

Two different color variants are found in the species' native waters in Sri Lanka: a red-finned variety from the Kelani River catchment and northward from there, and a yellow-finned variety from the Kalu River and the areas to the south. Speckled red and speckled yellow specimens are also encountered in the wild.

While in the past all the Cuming's Barbs available were wild-caught, recent years have seen the development of very successful captive breeding programmes. Today, all

CUMING'S BARB, RED FINNED (BARBUS CUMINGI)

Cuming's Barbs exported from Sri Lanka are bred in farms.

The close similarity between Cuming's Barb and its closest relatives, particularly *B. bandula* and *B. nigrofasciatus*, allied to the possibility of hybridization occurring between all three, means that the status of the species is a little debatable. Cuming's Barb has also been considered as a possible "parental" species of the Odessa Barb (*Barbus "odessa"*)—*see* p.168.

DISTRIBUTION: *Mountain streams in southwest Sri Lanka*

SIZE: *Up to 2in (5cm)*

BEHAVIOR: *Peaceful shoaling species*

DIET: *Wide range of natural and commercial foods accepted*

AQUARIUM: *Medium-sized aquarium with open swimming spaces and shaded areas. Neutral, slightly soft water suits this species best. Temperature range: 72–81°F (22–27°C)*

BREEDING: *Typical egg-scattering barb. Not one of the easiest species to breed. Hatching takes just over 1 day at the higher end of the temperature range*

CLOWN BARB

Barbus everetti

SYNONYM: *Puntius everetti*
SUBFAMILY: Cyprininae

FISH THAT HAVE EITHER BLACK BANDS OR SPOTS separated by golden/orange patches, are often given the name "Clown" and this species is no exception. When fully colored, this is a truly beautiful fish. It is not always as widely available as some other species but when it is—and when it is displayed as a sizable shoal of fully mature fish—it almost sells itself. Unfortunately, males can take up to 18 months to mature and show their full colors, so the majority of specimens that are offered for sale are not quite as attractive as they will eventually become. It is therefore worth bearing this in mind when on the lookout for fish to buy and investing in the future by obtaining a small shoal of specimens, whatever their size.

DISTRIBUTION: *Southeast Asia: Singapore, Kalimantan, Sarawak*

SIZE: *Up to 5in (13cm) reported, but generally smaller than this*

BEHAVIOR: *Peaceful shoaler, but older (and larger) specimens may be a little aggressive toward small fish. This species prefers the lower reaches of the aquarium and has a tendency to nibble tender plants*

DIET: *A wide range of livefoods and commercial diets is accepted; a vegetable supplement should be provided*

CLOWN BARB (BARBUS EVERETTI)

AQUARIUM: *Roomy with open swimming spaces and heavily planted areas. Soft, slightly acid water is preferred, with regular partial water changes. Temperature range: 75–86°F (24–30°C)*

BREEDING: *Not an easy egg-scattering species to breed. Chances of success are improved if the potential, fully mature breeders are kept apart for several weeks and conditioned well with both livefoods and vegetable matter. Positioning the roomy breeding tank where it will catch the rays of the morning sun also seems to help*

BLACK-SPOT BARB
FILAMENT BARB

Barbus filamentosus

SYNONYM: *Puntius filamentosus*
SUBFAMILY: Cyprininae

THE BLACK-SPOT BARB IS ANOTHER SPECIES THAT only exhibits its full characteristics once it matures fully. Even then, it is only the males that develop the extended dorsal fin rays responsible for one of the common names, the Filament Barb. Immature specimens, which account for the majority of those offered for sale, are very attractive in their own right but do not give a true indication of the full beauty and elegance of this fish. This, allied to the fact that some specimens can reportedly grow to a substantial size (*see* below) means that the Black-spot Barb is not always widely available.

DISTRIBUTION: *Sri Lanka and southern India*

SIZE: *Up to 6in (15cm) reported, but usually remains considerably smaller, rarely exceeding 4–4¾in (10–12cm)*

BEHAVIOR: *A lively, sociable species which should be kept in a shoal*

DIET: *Wide range of foods accepted; vegetable supplement recommended*

AQUARIUM: *Owing to its relatively large size, a spacious aquarium is required, with ample swimming space. Subdued lighting shows off its iridescence to good effect. Soft, slightly acid water is recommended. Temperature range: 68–75°F (20–24°C)—slightly higher for breeding purposes*

BREEDING: *Large numbers of eggs (up to 1,000) are laid by this egg-scattering, egg-eating species. Hatching takes 36 hours at the top end of the temperature range*

GOLDEN DWARF BARB

Barbus gelius

SYNONYM: *Puntius gelius*
SUBFAMILY: Cyprininae

DESPITE ITS SMALL SIZE AND APPARENTLY DELICATE appearance, the Golden Dwarf Barb is quite hardy and easy to keep. It should, however, only be kept with other small species. Markings vary between individuals, but all specimens are attractive, particularly under lighting conditions that allow the golden body sheen to glisten.

DISTRIBUTION: *Widely reported as from central India, but Tekriwal and Rao (see Bibliography) report it from eastern and northeastern India*

SIZE: *Up to 1½in (4cm), but often smaller*

BEHAVIOR: *A sociable shoaling species which should never be kept either as single specimens or pairs (males are slimmer)*

CHERRY BARB (BARBUS TITTEYA)

unless conditions are soft and slightly acid.
Temperature range: 68–79°F (20–26°C); a little
higher for breeding

BREEDING: *Typical egg scatterer, egg eater.
Hatching takes about 36 hours. Mated pairs are
recommended for optimal results*

CHERRY BARB
Barbus titteya

SYNONYM: *Puntius titteya*
SUBFAMILY: Cyprininae

THIS IS A STUNNINGLY BEAUTIFUL FISH WHEN IN
peak condition. In particular, fully mature
males exhibit the cherry coloration to
perfection. Wild-caught specimens are
variable in their coloration, with at least
three varieties known from different
localities. Virtually all aquarium specimens are now commercially bred, in Sri

OTHER BARB SPECIES

The genus *Barbus sensu lato*—in the broadest sense, including those fish variously referred to as
Capoeta and *Puntius*—contains more than 100 species. Of these, a considerable number over and
above those featured here are available. Generally, all do well under the same basic conditions,
but check individual requirements elsewhere if in doubt, beginning with experienced aquarists
and your local dealer. The following is a selection of some of the species that are most commonly
encountered.

SCIENTIFIC NAME	COMMON NAME	SIZE	TEMPERATURE
B. bariloides	Orange Barb	2in (5cm)	73–79°F (23–26°C)
B. binotatus	Spotted Barb	4¾in (12cm) but 7in (18cm) reported	75–79°F (24–26°C)
B. callipterus	Clipper Barb	3½in (9cm)	72–77°F (22–25°C)
B. denisoni (umangii)	Red Line Torpedo Fish	6in (15cm)	72–77°F (22–25°C)
B. fasciatus*	Striped, Banded or Melon Barb	c.2½in (6cm)	72–77°F (22–25°C)
B. holotaenia	—	4¾in (12cm)	75–86°F (24–30°C)
B. hulstaerti	Butterfly Barb	1½in (3.5cm)	75°F (c.24°C)
B. lineatus	Striped Barb	4¾in (12cm)	70–75°F (21–24°C)
B. oligolepis	Checkered or Island Barb	6in (15cm)	68–75°F (20–24°C)
B. pentazona**	Five-banded Barb	2in (5cm)	68–79°F (20–26°C)
B. rhomboocellatus	Round-banded Barb	2in (5cm)	73–82°F (23–28°C)
B. stoliczkanus (B. ticto stoliczkanus)	Stoliczk's or Stoliczka's Barb	c.2½in (6cm)	72–75°F (22–24°C)
B. ticto (B. ticto ticto)	Ticto or Tic-Tac-Toe Barb	2in (5cm) but 4in (10cm) reported	57–72°F (14–22°C)
B. viviparus***	Livebearing Barb	2½in (6.5cm)	72–75°F (22–24°C)

NOTES:

* Two different species are variously referred to as *B. fasciatus*: the Striped or Banded Barb, from Malaysia,
Sumatra and Borneo, and the Melon Barb from India

** *B. pentazona* is often divided into subspecies: *B. pentazona pentazona*, *B. p. tetrazona* and *B. p. hexazona*

*** *B. viviparus* is not a livebearer, despite its name

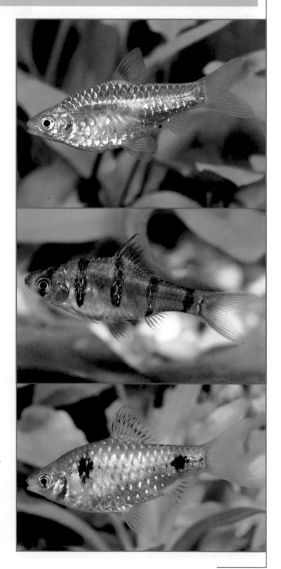

SPOTTED BARB (BARBUS BINOTATUS) ▲▲▲
FIVE-BANDED BARB (BARBUS PENTAZONA) ▲▲
TICTO BARB (BARBUS TICTO) ▲

◄ DWARF RASBORA (BORARUS MACULATA)   ▼ PEARL DANIO (BRACHYDANIO ALBOLINEATUS)

Lanka or elsewhere. An albino variety is occasionally available.

DISTRIBUTION: *Southwest Sri Lanka*

SIZE: *Up to 2in (5cm) widely reported; usually smaller*

BEHAVIOR: *Not as active or as prone to shoaling as many other species. It is nevertheless a peaceful fish which should be kept in groups*

DIET: *Most small foods are accepted; vegetable component recommended*

AQUARIUM: *This species is a little more retiring than most other barbs. Therefore, large open areas should be avoided. Some swimming space should, nevertheless, be provided, with ample shelter around. Soft, slightly acid water is best. Temperature range: 72–75°F (22–24°C) is adequate for normal maintenance, but should be raised to around 79°F (26°C) for breeding*

BREEDING: *Typical egg-scattering, egg-eating species. Hatching takes about 1 day*

DWARF RASBORA
PYGMY OR SPOTTED RASBORA

Borarus maculata

SYNONYMS: *Rasbora maculata. Microrasbora maculata*
SUBFAMILY: Rasborinae (Danioninae)

AT ONE TIME, ADULT DWARF RASBORA WERE thought to be juvenile *Rasbora kalochroma*, being similar but smaller. However, *B. maculata* is a species in its own right, and a particularly striking one at that. It is also one of the smallest fish kept in aquaria.

DISTRIBUTION: *Western Malaysia, Singapore, Sumatra*

SIZE: *Up to 1in (2.5cm), but often smaller*

BEHAVIOR: *A peaceful shoaler*

DIET: *Wide range of small-sized foods accepted*

AQUARIUM: *As for R. heteromorpha (see p. 184) but slightly lower temperature*

BREEDING: *Small breeding tank with soft, slightly acid, shallow water. Eggs are scattered among plants. Hatching takes about 1-1½ days*

PEARL DANIO
Brachydanio albolineatus

SUBFAMILY: Rasborinae (Danioninae)

THE DANIOS (*BRACHYDANIO* AND *DANIO* SPECIES) are all active shoalers and have been part of the hobby for many years. The Pearl Danio was first imported into Europe in 1911 and is still very popular today. This is despite the fact that it is not often displayed to maximum effect and therefore does not always show off its best colors. Two forms of the Pearl Danio are generally available (though several more exist): the wild type and, more infrequently, a yellow morph usually referred to as the Yellow Danio.

DISTRIBUTION: *Southeast Asia*

SIZE: *Up to 2⅜in (6cm); usually smaller*

BEHAVIOR: *Very active shoaler that prefers the upper layers of the water column, but will swim at all levels*

DIET: *Most livefoods and commercial diets are accepted*

AQUARIUM: *A well-covered aquarium with ample swimming areas should be provided, with no tall plants obstructing this space (tall plants are best arranged around the sides and back of the aquarium). Water chemistry is not critical, but*

overall quality must be good. Temperature range: *68–77°F (20–25°C); a little higher for breeding*

BREEDING: *Chances of success are enhanced if two males and a female are introduced into the breeding tank placed in a sunny position. This is an egg-scattering, egg-eating species. Hatching takes in about 36-48 hours*

KERR'S DANIO
BLUE DANIO

Brachydanio kerri

SUBFAMILY: Rasborinae (Danioninae)

THIS IS A MUCH MORE RECENT INTRODUCTION THAN the Pearl Danio, first making its appearance in the mid-1950s. Although quite widely available, this danio is not kept as often as some of its nearest relatives. Like them, it is a beautiful, active jumper.

DISTRIBUTION: *Restricted to two islands in Thailand*

SIZE: *Up to 2in (5cm)*

BEHAVIOR: *Active shoaler; excellent jumper*

DIET: *Most foods accepted*

AQUARIUM: *As for B. albolineatus. Temperature range: 72–77°F (22–25°C)*

BREEDING: *Eggs are scattered, primarily, over the substratum. Hatching can take up to 4 days. Will hybridize with its closest relatives*

SPOTTED DANIO
Brachydanio nigrofasciatus

SUBFAMILY: Rasborinae (Danioninae)

LIKE *B. ALBOLINEATUS*, THE SPOTTED DANIO HAS been around since 1911 and, while it is not now kept by as many aquarists as it

▲ SPOTTED DANIO (BRACHYDANIO NIGROFASCIATUS)

ZEBRA DANIO
LEOPARD DANIO
Brachydanio rerio

SYNONYMS: *Brachydanio frankei, B. "frankei"*

THIS IS BY FAR THE MOST POPULAR OF ALL THE danios. It is widely available in several forms, including wild, golden and long-finned types in different combinations. Of these, the wild type is the most robust. The Leopard Danio—also available as a long-finned variant—has traditionally been regarded as a separate species: *B. frankei*. However, genetic analysis of crosses between Leopards and Zebras have now confirmed that the Leopard is a Zebra morph and therefore belongs to the same species.

DISTRIBUTION: *Zebra—from Eastern India; Leopard—not encountered in the wild*

SIZE: *2⅓in (6cm) including extended fins; short-finned varieties generally only attain around 1¾in (4.5cm)*

BEHAVIOR: *Extremely active shoaler which may nip fin extensions of fancy varieties of Guppies, Swordtails, Angels, etc.*

DIET: *Most foods accepted*

AQUARIUM: *Open spaces surrounded by plant thickets. Water chemistry is not critical, but soft, slightly acid water is preferred. Temperature range: 64–75°F (18–24°C)—short-finned wild-type specimens can tolerate slightly lower temperatures in winter*

BREEDING: *Egg-scattering, egg-eating species. Eggs may be released over the substratum, as well as among plants. Best results are obtained with pairs that select themselves from a shoal; these will tend to stay together. Hatching takes about 2 days*

INDIAN GLASS BARB
INDIAN GLASS HATCHET, or BLUE LAUBUCA
Chela laubuca

SUBFAMILY: Rasborinae (Danioninae)

THERE ARE SEVERAL SPECIES OF *CHELA* occasionally available: *C. laubuca* (the most common), *C. cachuis* (Neon Hatchet), *C. dadyburjori* (Burjor's Brilliance or Orange Chela), *C. fasciata* (Striped Chela) and—perhaps the most colorful of all—*C. auropurpurens* (Orange False Barilius).

All are small, with the exception of the last species which is reported to attain 4in (10cm) in length. Despite two of its common names, *C. laubuca* is neither a barb nor a hatchet fish. Chelas can prove delicate during the initial phases of acclimatisation.

DISTRIBUTION: *Southeast Asia (widely distributed)*

▲▲ ZEBRA DANIO (BRACHYDANIO RERIO)   ▲ GOLDEN ZEBRA DANIO (BRACHYDANIO RERIO VAR.)

once was, it remains a firm favorite, especially among experienced hobbyists who appreciate its beauty, despite its small size.

DISTRIBUTION: *Myanmar (Burma)*

SIZE: *Around 1½in (4cm)*

BEHAVIOR: *A peaceful shoaler which is not quite as active as some of its closest relatives*

DIET: *Most foods accepted*

AQUARIUM: *As for other Brachydanio species. Temperature range: 74–82°F (24–28°C)*

BREEDING: *As for B. albolineatus, but at around 77–82°F (25–28°C). B. nigrofasciatus can hybridize with, at least, B. albolineatus, possibly other danios*

GOLDFISH

Carassius auratus

SYNONYM: *Carassius auratus auratus*
SUBFAMILY: Cyprininae

THE GOLDFISH IS BELIEVED TO BE NOT JUST THE MOST WIDELY KEPT ornamental fish in the world, but the most popular of all pets. Virtually every aquarist and pondkeeper in the world has kept a goldfish at one time or other. Although there is documentary evidence of the goldfish having been kept as a pet in ponds in China as far back as the Sung Dynasty (AD 960–1279), there are indications that its history could stretch back to the Western Jin Dynasty (AD 262–315), which would make the goldfish–human association at least 1,700 years old. Over the centuries, countless varieties of the goldfish have been developed in numerous countries. Today, there are over 100 officially recognized varieties, and an unknown number of "unofficial" ones.

A few of the best-known varieties are listed here. However, as variants are continually combined to select color or fin features, the rate at which new goldfish varieties become available shows no sign of slowing down. While some of the old favorites will remain so well into the future, every few years will most likely see the establishment of new favorites.

The alternative scientific name cited, *Carassius auratus auratus*, indicates that the goldfish was until quite recently regarded as a subspecies of the species *C. auratus*, the other one being *C. auratus gibelius*, the Gibel or Prussian Carp. Today though, both are regarded as valid species in their own right.

DISTRIBUTION: *China and parts of Siberia. However, widely introduced in numerous tropical, subtropical and temperate regions worldwide*

SIZE: *Up to around 12in (30cm) for slim-bodied types; round-bodied varieties tend to be considerably smaller, but some types of Orandas, for example, can also grow to substantial sizes*

BEHAVIOR: *Generally peaceful, although some specimens—and in particular mature males during the breeding season—can harass other fish. All varieties will eat soft, succulent plants and will constantly root around the bottom of the tank*

DIET: *All foods accepted; vegetable component important*

AQUARIUM: *This should be roomy with wide open areas that allow full view of the fish. Robust and/or unpalatable plants should be used, perhaps supplemented with artificial types. Roots should be protected (see Aquarium Plants). Water chemistry is not critical, but quality must be good. Efficient filtration and aeration are essential. Temperature range: from well below 50°F (10°C) to above 86°F (30°C); higher temperatures should not be maintained on a long-term basis*

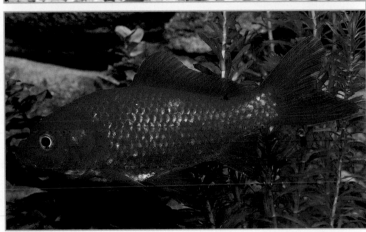

COMMON GOLDFISH *THE "CLASSIC" SHORT-FINNED VARIETY, USUALLY ORANGE-COLORED (TOP), BUT ALSO AVAILABLE IN OTHER SINGLE COLORS AND COMBINATIONS (ABOVE: BLOOD-RED VARIETY).*

COMET *SLIMMER THAN A BRISTOL SHUBUNKIN AND WITH A LONGER TAIL, PREFERABLY POINTED. THE MOST POPULAR TYPE IS RED AND WHITE IS KNOWN AS THE SARASA (LEFT).*

FANTAIL *OVAL-BODIED, DOUBLE-TAILED VARIETY WITH RELATIVELY SHORT FINS (BELOW: CALICO).*

BREEDING: *Persistent chasing (driving) by the male—which develops white pimple-like tubercles on its snout and gill covers during the breeding season—will eventually result in the pair (or a shoal) spawning among fine-leaved vegetation. Goldfish are egg scatterers/eaters, so, either they, or the eggs, should be removed after spawning (which tends to occur at temperatures above 68°F (20°C)). Hatching can take up to 1 week, but generally takes less*

RYUKIN *SUPERFICIALLY SIMILAR TO THE FANTAIL BUT WITH HIGH DORSAL (BACK) FIN AND VERY DEEP BODY.*

VEILTAIL *SIMILAR TO THE FANTAIL, BUT WITH LONG FLOWING FINS (ABOVE: CALICO; RIGHT: RED AND WHITE—ORIENTAL STYLE; BLOOD STREAKS IN TAIL SUGGEST POOR CONDITION).*

ORANDA *SIMILAR TO VEILTAIL, BUT WITH RASPBERRY-LIKE GROWTH (KNOWN AS A HOOD) ON THE HEAD (ABOVE LEFT: RED POM-POM; ABOVE: BICOLOR—CHOCOLATE AND SILVER; LEFT: BRONZE POM-POM AND RED CAP).*

MOOR *DOUBLE-TAILED, BUT WITHOUT A HOOD. THE EYE MAY PROTRUDE. BODY COLOR: BLACK.*

BUTTERFLY MOOR *LIKE THE MOOR, BUT WITH A SHORTER DOUBLE TAIL WHICH IS OFTEN SPLAYED OUT AND HAS THE APPEARANCE OF A BUTTERFLY (ABOVE: BLUE BUTTERFLY MOOR).*

HAMANISHIKI *OVAL-BODIED, SHORT-FINNED, DOUBLE-TAILED VARIETY WITH DOMED SCALES THAT LOOK LIKE PEARLS. TWO "BUBBLES" ON TOP OF THE HEAD. ALSO KNOWN AS THE HIGH-HEAD PEARLSCALE (ABOVE).*

LIONHEAD *SIMILAR TO AN ORANDA, BUT WITHOUT A DORSAL (BACK) FIN. THE DORSAL PROFILE IS RELATIVELY STRAIGHT (FAR LEFT: BLUE LIONHEAD; LEFT: RED-EYED LIONHEAD).*

RANCHU *LIKE THE LIONHEAD, BUT WITH A CURVED BACK PROFILE (BELOW LEFT: RED AND WHITE RANCHU; BELOW: BLACK RANCHU).*

CELESTIAL *SIMILAR BODY SHAPE CHARACTERISTICS TO THE LIONHEAD, BUT WITHOUT A HOOD AND WITH UPWARD-LOOKING EYES.*

BUBBLE-EYE *SIMILAR TO THE CELESTIAL BUT, WITH LARGE FLUID-FILLED EYE SACS (ABOVE: RED BUBBLE-EYE).*

SIZE: *Up to 2½in (6cm)*

BEHAVIOR: *A peaceful shoaler which has a strong preference for the surface layers of the aquarium*

DIET: *Wide range of (predominantly) floating foods accepted; will not feed off the bottom*

AQUARIUM: *Open swimming areas surrounded by vegetation. Frequent partial water changes recommended, as well as soft, slightly acid water. Temperature range: 75–79°F (24–26°C)*

BREEDING: *Eggs laid among fine-leaved vegetation. Hatching takes about 1 day*

SIAMESE FLYING FOX
SIAMESE ALGAE EATER
Crossocheilus siamensis

SUBFAMILY: Cyprininae (classified as Garrinae by some authors)

WHAT THE SIAMESE FLYING FOX MAY LACK IN brilliant coloration, it more than makes up for with its other attributes. In particular, it is one of the few aquarium fish that actually eats thread algae. Its only potential drawback for many home aquaria is that it can grow to a substantial size.

DISTRIBUTION: *Thailand, Peninsular Malaysia*

SIZE: *Up to 6in (15cm) reported, but usually smaller*

BEHAVIOR: *Tolerant of other species, but less so of its own*

DIET: *Wide range of foods accepted; vegetable component essential. Reported to eat planarian worms (flatworms) which are sometimes introduced accidentally with some livefoods*

AQUARIUM: *Roomy tank with thickets of vegetation (Siamese Flying Foxes will eat algae, but do not generally harm other plants). Hiding places should be provided. Well-oxygenated, soft, slightly acid water is recommended, though harder, more alkaline conditions are also tolerated. Temperature range: 73–79°F (23–26°C)*

BREEDING: *No details are available*

RED SHINER
SANDPAPER SHINER, RED HORSE MINNOW, or RAINBOW DACE
Cyprinella lutrensis

SYNONYM: *Notropis lutrensis*
SUBFAMILY: Leuciscinae

TWO OF THE COMMON NAMES REFER TO THE RED patches that mature males develop on top of and behind the head, as well as on all the fins. This contrasts beautifully with the grayish blue of the rest of the body,

making the Red Shiner a most attractive choice for the coldwater aquarium. While the Red Shiner (wild type or albino) is by far the most common shiner, other *Cyprinella* and *Notropis* species are beginning to appear with greater regularity.

DISTRIBUTION: *Mississippi River Basin (US) and Gulf drainages west of the Mississippi. Widely introduced elsewhere in the US; also in northern Mexico*

SIZE: *3½in (9cm)*

BEHAVIOR: *A very active shoaler*

DIET: *All foods accepted*

AQUARIUM: *Roomy with ample swimming space; well-filtered, well-oxygenated water and frequent partial water changes recommended. Water chemistry not critical. Temperature range: 50–77°F (10–25°C)*

BREEDING: *Eggs laid in a depression on a sandy/silty bottom. Hatching takes several days*

KOI
BROCADED CARP
Cyprinus carpio

SUBFAMILY: Cyprininae

IN THE PAST THESE HIGHLY DEVELOPED VARIETIES OF the Common Carp have only been kept in ponds but improvements in aquarium technology, along with the rise in interest in "companion pets", have led to some types of Koi being introduced into large aquaria.

Fairy or Butterfly (long-finned) Koi are the most popular of the "aquarium" varieties, but even the more traditional pond varieties are now being sought after by aquarists, many of whom also keep Koi in ponds.

The history of the Koi, though considerably shorter than that of the goldfish (the first recognized Koi being associated with developments during the early 19th century in Niigata Prefecture on the Japanese island of Honshu) is long enough to have produced numerous color and scale modifications. The result is a bewildering array of fish bred in vast quantities in Japan, Israel, Italy, the UK, the US, the Far East and virtually every other region with an interest in coldwater fishkeeping. However, Japan still leads the way in terms of pedigree fish production.

DISTRIBUTION: *Originally from the Danube and other freshwaters of the Black Sea Basin. Now found throughout Europe (except the extreme north) and numerous other regions*

SIZE: *Up to 40in (1m) for fully grown wild C. carpio; usually a little smaller for Koi, even "jumbo" specimens*

BEHAVIOR: *Generally peaceful, even toward smaller fish, but some males may become somewhat aggressive during the breeding season. All types will eat soft, succulent plants and will spend much of the time rooting around the bottom of the aquarium*

DIET: *All foods accepted; vegetable component important. Treats can include items like shrimp,*

KOI, HAND-FEEDING (CYPRINUS CARPIO)

SOME KOI VARIETIES

Nonmetallic Varieties

KOHAKU
White base color with red markings.

TANCHO SANKE (or SANKE)
White base color with superimposed red and black markings.

SHOWA SANSHOKU (usually referred to as SHOWA)
Black base color with red and white markings.

BEKKO
Black markings on a white, red or yellow base color.

UTSURIMONO
White, red or yellow markings on a black base.

ASAGI
Blue base with red on the belly, fins and sides of head; top of head is light grayish-blue.

TANCHO
Single, red marking on the top of the head; this classification is reserved for Kohaku, Sanke and Showa Koi that bear this very distinctive head spot.

Metallic Varieties

HIKARIMONO (or OGON)
Single-colored fish.

HIKARI-UTSURIMONO
Metallic versions of Utsuri and Showa.

HIKARIMONO-MONO
Term embracing all other types of metallic Koi.

Other Categories

KINGINRIN
Fish having 20 or more reflective/sparkling scales; previously, judging of this category at Koi shows embraced fish of any variety, provided they had the appropriate scalation. Nowadays, only Kohaku, Sanke and Showa are included.

▼ *SILVER OGON KOI (CYPRINUS CARPIO VAR.)*
▼▼ *BLUE MIRROR KOI (CYPRINUS CARPIO VAR.)*

*GOLD GHOST KOI
(CYPRINUS CARPIO VAR.)*

GOSHIKI
Five-colored Koi classified within the Kawarimono in countries other than Japan.

DOITSU
Doitsu-scaled fish (almost scale-less, but with a few rows of large, reflective scales, as found in the Mirror Carp) are generally classified under their color variety. However, in Japan, Doitsu fish of any variety are classified separately, except for Shusui.

HANA SHUSUI KOI (CYPRINUS CARPIO VAR.)

SHUSUI
Similar to the Asagi, but with dark blue coloration restricted to the large Doitsu scales (*see* OTHER CATEGORIES, below); naked areas are light blue, except for the head, which is light grayish-blue.

KOROMO
White base color with red markings that are overlaid with darker patterning.

KAWARIMONO
A catch-all term for all other types of nonmetallic Koi, including single-colored fish, e.g. Ki-goi (yellow fish), almost single-colored fish, e.g. Hajiro (black fish with white fin edges) and Goshiki (five-colored fish, but *see* OTHER CATEGORIES below).

peas, lettuce and brown bread, but not as major components of the diet

AQUARIUM: *Only large and deep aquaria which are efficiently filtered can be considered suitable. Use robust and unpalatable plants, perhaps combined with artificial types. Protect plant roots (see Aquarium Plants). Water chemistry not critical. Temperature range: from well below 50°F (10°C) to above 86°F (30°C); higher temperatures should not be maintained for long periods*

BREEDING: *This is difficult to achieve in most aquaria owing to the lack of space. Eggs are scattered among vegetation when the temperature rises above 63°F (17°C). Injuries may result during the vigorous chasing (driving) that occurs. Spawning brushes/mats are recommended, to be subsequently removed to another aquarium for hatching, which takes 3–4 days at 68–72°F (20–22°C).*

GIANT DANIO

Danio aequipinnatus

SYNONYM: *Danio malabaricus*
SUBFAMILY: Rasborinae (Danioninae)

THE GENUS *DANIO* IS VERY SIMILAR TO *BRACHY-danio*, differing only in details relating to fin ray and lateral line features. More obvious is the larger size attained by *Danio* species.

There is still considerable debate as to whether *D. aequipinnatus* and *D. malabaricus* are one and the same species or whether, at least in Sri Lanka, they constitute two very closely related species. Most authorities believe them to be the same fish. Several color varieties, including a golden one, are available.

DISTRIBUTION: *Southwest India and Sri Lanka*

SIZE: *Up to 6in (15cm) reported, but usually considerably smaller*

BEHAVIOR: *Very active, peaceful shoaler which prefers the upper layers of the water column*

DIET: *Wide range of foods accepted*

AQUARIUM: *Roomy with well-fitting cover, open swimming spaces and plant thickets. Water chemistry not critical but quality must be good. Temperature range: 72–75°F (22–24°C); slightly higher for breeding*

BREEDING: *Eggs are scattered among fine-leaved vegetation. Hatching takes about 1 day*

BENGAL DANIO
TURQUOISE DANIO

Danio devario

SUBFAMILY: Rasborinae (Danioninae)

THIS SPECIES IS THE LEAST STREAMLINED OF THE danios. The females in particular, have a relatively deep body. It is also the most subtly colored member of the genus, its colors

▲ *GIANT DANIO* (DANIO AEQUIPINNATUS)   ▼ *BARRED DANIO* (DANIO PATHIRANA)

best exhibited in reflected light and when kept as a shoal.

DISTRIBUTION: *Northern and eastern India, Bangladesh and Pakistan*

SIZE: *Up to 6in (15cm) reported, but generally significantly smaller*

BEHAVIOR: *An active shoaling species which can be a bit timid. It prefers the top layers*

DIET: *Wide range of foods accepted*

AQUARIUM: *A dark substratum helps to show off this species to good effect. Ample spaces surrounded by plant thickets should be provided. Water chemistry not critical. Temperature range: 59–79°F (15–26°C) considered by some*

to be adequate, but 68–79°F (20–26°C) is recommended

BREEDING: *This is a typical egg-scatterer. Hatching takes about 1 day*

BARRED DANIO

Danio pathirana

SUBFAMILY: Rasborinae (Danioninae)

THIS IS THE MOST RECENTLY DISCOVERED AND KEPT of the *Danio* species (officially described in 1990) and in the opinion of some, the most beautiful. Within its restricted range it has been found in both still and flowing waters.

Although bred in captivity, this species is not yet available in large numbers. It is, however, an adaptable fish which is likely to become progressively more popular.

DISTRIBUTION: *Southwest Sri Lanka*

SIZE: *About 2⅓in (6cm)*

BEHAVIOR: *Not as active as some of its closest relatives. Tends to form small groups, rather than large shoals, in the wild and exhibits fin-nipping behavior at times*

DIET: *Wide range of foods accepted*

AQUARIUM: *Basically as for D. aequipinnatus*

BREEDING: *Egg-scattering species, but details are unavailable*

RED-TAILED BLACK SHARK
RED-TAILED LABEO
Epalzeorhynchus bicolor

SYNONYM: *Labeo bicolor*
SUBFAMILY: Cyprininae (classified as Garrinae by some authors)

THIS IS BY FAR THE MOST STRIKINGLY COLORED OF all the aquarium "sharks"—which are only sharklike in their overall body shape and even then, only superficially. Unless water conditions are to its liking, this species will not show off its best colors, becoming darkish gray and faint red, rather than jet black and bright red. Due

attention must therefore be paid to aquarium layout and conditions.

DISTRIBUTION: *Thailand*

SIZE: *Up to 4¾in (12cm)*

BEHAVIOR: *A loner which stakes out its own territory and will become aggressive toward other members of its species. This intolerance can be extended to other species as well, particularly by older specimens*

DIET: *Wide range of foods accepted; sinking formulations and a vegetable component are recommended*

AQUARIUM: *Spacious, with shelters or caves provided. A fine-grained substratum is recommended, as is soft to medium-hard water. Temperature range: 72–79°F (22–26°C); higher for breeding*

BREEDING: *Infrequent in aquaria. Eggs are reported to be laid in a depression in the substratum. Hatching takes about 2 days*

RUBY SHARK
RAINBOW, or RED-FINNED, SHARK
Epalzeorhynchus frenatus

SYNONYMS: *Labeo frenatus, Labeo erythrurus*
SUBFAMILY: Cyprininae (classified as Garrinae by some authors)

THIS IS A SLIMMER SPECIES THAN *E. BICOLOR.* Specimens offered as *L. erythrurus* are generally believed to be either mature *E. frena-*

tus, or a local variety. A commercially produced albino morph is widely available.

DISTRIBUTION: *Thailand*

SIZE: *Up to 6in (15cm), but usually quite a bit smaller*

BEHAVIOR: *As for E. bicolor*

DIET: *As for E. bicolor*

AQUARIUM: *As for E. bicolor*

BREEDING: *Infrequent in aquaria; no documented accounts appear to be available*

FLYING FOX
Epalzeorhynchus kallopterus

SUBFAMILY: Cyprininae (classified as Garrinae by some authors)

THIS SPECIES IS SIMILAR IN APPEARANCE TO *Crossocheilus siamensis* (Siamese Flying Fox)—*see* p.176. At close quarters, the Flying Fox can be seen to possess two pairs of barbels on the upper lip, while *C. siamensis* only has one.

DISTRIBUTION: *Indonesia: Sumatra, Java, Kalimantan; also variously reported from Thailand and northern India*

SIZE: *Up to 6in (15cm) reported, but usually smaller*

BEHAVIOR: *Rests on the tips of its pectoral (chest) fins. Territorial, but otherwise generally peaceful*

DIET: *Grazes on algae; therefore wide-ranging diet must include a vegetable component*

AQUARIUM: *Hiding places and broad-leaved plants should be provided. Soft, slightly acid water and frequent partial changes recommended. Temperature range: 75–79°F (24–26°C), with some flexibility*

BREEDING: *No documented reports available*

FLYING BARB
Esomus thermoicos

SYNONYM: *Esomus danrica*
SUBFAMILY: Rasborinae (Danioninae)

MOST BOOKS WILL REFER TO THE FLYING BARB AS *E. danrica*, rather than *E. thermoicos*. However, comparative work carried out on Indian and Sri Lankan collections indicates that both nominal species are more closely related than first thought; they may be subspecies or even just normally varying populations. Further work is awaited. The most unusual feature of this attractive species is its very long, filament-like barbels responsible for its common name, although it is not a barb. It does, however, jump ("fly").

DISTRIBUTION: *India, Sri Lanka and Thailand*

SIZE: *Up to 6in (15cm) reported, but usually much smaller. About 2⅓in (6cm) common in wild-caught specimens*

RED-TAILED BLACK SHARK (EPALZEORHYNCHUS BICOLOR)

BEHAVIOR: *Very active fish with a tendency to leap out of the water. Prefers the top layers of the aquarium*

DIET: *Wide range of foods accepted*

AQUARIUM: *Roomy, well-covered tank with ample surface swimming space surrounded by plants. Water chemistry not critical but quality must be good. Temperature range: 72–75°F (22–24°C); higher (around 81°F—27°C) for breeding*

BREEDING: *Eggs are scattered among plants. Hatching takes 1–2 days, depending on temperature*

SIAMESE STONE-LAPPING SUCKER

Garra taeniatia

SUBFAMILY: Cyprininae

OVER RECENT YEARS, A NUMBER OF *GARRA* SPECIES have begun appearing in the hobby with increasing regularity. All are, basically, bottom-dwelling species from flowing-water habitats and are not difficult to keep. The Siamese Stone-lapping Sucker is the most commonly encountered species.

DISTRIBUTION: *Thailand*

SIZE: *Up to 6in (15cm)*

BEHAVIOR: *Generally tolerant of other species, but may disrupt the substratum, particularly when kept in groups*

DIET: *Most foods accepted, especially sinking formulations*

AQUARIUM: *Roomy, with ample resting/hiding places and robust plants, with roots protected (see Aquarium Plants). Water should be well*

SIAMESE STONE-LAPPING SUCKER (GARRA TAENIATIA)

aerated and filtered. Temperature range: 75–79°F (24–26°C)

BREEDING: *No details are available*

GUDGEON

Gobio gobio

SUBFAMILY: Gobioninae

THE GUDGEON IS PREDOMINANTLY A BOTTOM-dwelling species that has traditionally been regarded as a pondfish by (mostly) European hobbyists. However, as cold-water aquarium keeping has expanded, so has the gudgeon gained greater popularity.

DISTRIBUTION: *Europe, except most of Italy, northern Finland, Sweden and the Adriatic coast. Spanish, Scottish and Northern Irish populations are introduced, rather than native*

SIZE: *Up to 8in (20cm), but usually smaller*

BEHAVIOR: *Peaceful bottom-dweller that will learn to take food from the surface*

DIET: *Most foods accepted, particularly sinking formulations and livefoods*

GUDGEON (GOBIO GOBIO)

GOLDEN ORFE (LEUCISCUS IDUS)

AQUARIUM: *Well-filtered, well-oxygenated water essential (this species is sensitive to pollution). Substratum should be fine-grained and shelters should be provided. Neutral to slightly alkaline, medium-hard water is preferred. Temperature range: 50–68°F (10–20°C)*

BREEDING: *Infrequent in aquaria. Adhesive eggs laid on substratum in flowing water. Hatching takes 10-30 days, depending on temperature*

BLACK SHARK
BLACK LABEO
Labeo chrysophekadion
SUBFAMILY: Cyprininae

THIS IS THE LARGEST "SHARK" SPECIES KEPT IN aquaria. Most specimens offered are around 4in (10cm) or smaller, but will grow quickly and are therefore not suitable for average aquaria. However, if sufficiently spacious accommodation is available, a lone large specimen will prove a long-lived and impressive companion. Two other *Labeo* species (both smaller, but still substantial) are also available: *L. forskalli* (Plain Shark) and *L. variegatus* (Harlequin or Variegated Shark).

DISTRIBUTION: *Southwest Asia (widely distributed)*

SIZE: *Up to 24in (60cm) reported*

BEHAVIOR: *A loner which is aggressive toward members of its own species*

DIET: *All foods accepted; vegetable component important*

AQUARIUM: *Roomy, well-filtered, well-aerated aquarium with large shelters, e.g. caves or bogwood. Water chemistry not critical. Temperature range: 75–81°F (24–27°C)*

BREEDING: *No reports available*

MODERLIESCHEN
BELLICA or OPALINE
Leucaspius delineatus

SUBFAMILY: Leuciscinae (classified as Abraminae by some authors)

THIS PREDOMINANTLY SILVER-BODIED FISH, WITH a bluish line running from head to tail, gained considerable popularity, mainly in Europe, during the 1980s and early 1990s. Although it is still available, it is not so popular now and has not experienced a global demand.

DISTRIBUTION: *Mostly central and eastern Europe*

SIZE: *Up to 4¾in (12cm); usually smaller*

BEHAVIOR: *Active, peaceful shoaler*

DIET: *Wide range of diets accepted, but livefoods preferred*

AQUARIUM: *Roomy with ample swimming spaces and plant thickets. Water chemistry not critical, but medium-hard neutral water is recommended. Temperature range: 50–72°F (10–22°C)*

BREEDING: *Egg strips are looped around plants and are guarded by the male. Hatching takes several days*

GOLDEN ORFE
IDE
Leuciscus idus

SYNONYM: *Idus idus*
SUBFAMILY: Leuciscinae

LEUCISCUS IDUS IS USUALLY AVAILABLE AS A GOLD morph—known as the Golden Orfe—and is one of the most popular pondfish kept in Europe. However, growing numbers are now also kept in aquaria, either temporarily (for subsequent release into a garden pond) or on a permanent basis. In addition to the gold morph, there is the wild type (silver) morph and a blue variety which looks particularly attractive in aquaria.

DISTRIBUTION: *Most of Europe*

SIZE: *Up to 39in (1m) in the wild; cultivated varieties do not normally exceed 24in (60cm), even in large ponds*

BEHAVIOR: *Active shoaler that prefers the upper layers*

DIET: *All foods accepted, but livefoods preferred*

AQUARIUM: *Very spacious aquarium with open swimming areas and well-fitting cover. Well-oxygenated, well filtered water—very important. Water chemistry not critical. Temperature range: from near-freezing to over 86°F (30°C), but higher temperatures should be short-lived*

BREEDING: *Infrequent in aquaria. Egg-scattering species. Hatching may take up to 20 days at cool temperatures*

SOUTHERN RED-BELLY DACE
Phoxinus erythrogaster
SUBFAMILY: Leuciscinae

THIS DACE OR MINNOW STARTED GAINING IN popularity during the late 1980s and has become a great favorite among coldwater hobbyists. It is the spectacular red belly of mature

SOUTHERN RED-BELLY DACE (PHOXINUS ERYTHROGASTER)

males that is the most distinctive feature. The European Minnow (*P. phoxinus*) is also available, but is not as colorful. It has similar requirements.

DISTRIBUTION: *New York State and westward to Minnesota, including the Great Lakes and Mississippi River basins*

SIZE: *Up to 3½in (9cm)*

BEHAVIOR: *Peaceful shoaler*

DIET: *Most foods accepted, but livefoods preferred*

AQUARIUM: *Open swimming spaces, as well as adequate shelter. Water chemistry not critical, but quality must be good. Temperature range: 50–77°F (10–25°C)*

BREEDING: *Eggs scattered over the substratum. Hatching takes over 1 week at cooler temperatures*

FATHEAD MINNOW

GOLDEN MINNOW or ROSY RED

Pimephales promelas

SUBFAMILY: Leuciscinae

THE FATHEAD WAS ORIGINALLY CULTIVATED commercially in the United States as a bait fish. However, the attractive coloration of the golden morph, added to its interesting breeding habits, soon created a demand among aquarists. Today, virtually all the Fathead Minnows in the hobby are of the golden variety.

DISTRIBUTION: *Most of North America; introduced into many exotic locations as far south as Mexico*

SIZE: *Up to 4in (10cm); usually considerably smaller*

BEHAVIOR: *Active shoaler; males become territorial during breeding*

DIET: *All foods accepted*

AQUARIUM: *Caves and broad-leaved floating plants should be provided. Water chemistry not critical. Temperature range: 50–77°F (10–25°C)*

BREEDING: *Eggs are attached to the undersurface of floating plants or the roof of a cave and are guarded by the male. Hatching takes around a week*

HARD-LIPPED BARB

Osteochilus hasselti

SUBFAMILY: Cyprininae

THIS IS A SUBSTANTIAL FISH WHICH GROWS TOO large for many aquaria. However, juveniles, which are more brightly marked than adults, make good subjects for mixed collections, always assuming that larger accommodation can be provided in due course. In addition to the normally colored morph,

there is a pink-bodied, black-eyed variety which is occasionally available.

DISTRIBUTION: *Southeast Asia*

SIZE: *Up to 12½in (32cm) reported*

BEHAVIOR: *A peaceful shoaler which will, nevertheless, damage succulent plants and will also root around the bottom of the aquarium*

DIET: *All foods; vegetable component essential*

AQUARIUM: *Roomy, with stout and/or unpalatable plants, whose roots should be protected (see Aquarium Plants). Well-filtered water; chemistry is not critical, but soft, slightly acid water is recommended. Temperature range: 72–77°F (22–25°C)*

BREEDING: *Not recorded in home aquaria*

RED-TAILED RASBORA

Rasbora borapetensis

SUBFAMILY: Rasborinae (Danioninae)

THIS IS A SLENDER FISH WHICH ONLY LOOKS ITS best when water and tank conditions are right (*see* below). At other times, the red coloration responsible for the common name, and which makes a shoal of these rasboras an absolute delight, fades significantly.

DISTRIBUTION: *Thailand and western Malaysia*

SIZE: *2in (5cm)*

BEHAVIOR: *A peaceful shoaler*

DIET: *Most small foods accepted, but livefoods preferred*

AQUARIUM: *For best effect, lighting should not be too bright (floating plants will help diffuse it). Open swimming spaces and abundant vegetation should be provided. Soft, slightly acid water (perhaps filtered through peat) recommended. Temperature range: 72–79°F (22–26°C)*

BREEDING: *Egg-scattering/eating species. Shallow water recommended. Hatching takes about 1½ days*

GREATER SCISSORTAIL

GIANT, or SPOT-TAILED, SCISSORTAIL

Rasbora caudimaculata

SUBFAMILY: Rasborinae (Danioninae)

DESPITE TWO OF ITS COMMON NAMES, *R. caudimaculata* is no larger than its more widely available close relative *R. trilineata* (the Scissortail–*see* p.185). Both are very attractive fish when conditions are to their liking.

DISTRIBUTION: *Southeast Asia*

SIZE: *Up to 4¾in (12cm) reported, but usually smaller*

BEHAVIOR: *An active shoaler with excellent jumping ability*

DIET: *All foods accepted, particularly livefoods*

AQUARIUM: *Roomy, well-covered tank with ample swimming areas and plant thickets. Water chemistry not critical. Temperature range: 68–77°F (20–25°C); slightly higher for breeding*

BREEDING: *Egg-scattering species; breeding infrequent in aquaria*

EYE-SPOT RASBORA

HI-SPOT RASBORA

Rasbora dorsiocellata

SUBFAMILY: Rasborinae (Danioninae)

TWO SUBSPECIES OF *R. DORSIOCELLATA* ARE frequently referred to in aquarium literature: *R. d. dorsiocellata* and *R. d. macrophthalma*, in which the eyes (as the specific name indicates) are larger, although the fish itself is smaller. The former is more usually available and is generally referred to by its species, rather than subspecies, name.

DISTRIBUTION: *Southeast Asia: mainly Peninsular Malaysia and Sumatra*

SIZE: *Up to 2½in (6.5cm)*

RED-TAILED RASBORA (RASBORA BORAPETENSIS)

or one sometimes being almost diamond-shaped. The black line that runs along the base of the anal fin is also very distinctive.

DISTRIBUTION: *Southeast Asia*

SIZE: *Up to 8in (20cm) reported, but usually much smaller*

BEHAVIOR: *A peaceful shoaler despite its size*

DIET: *All foods accepted*

AQUARIUM: *Roomy with a well-fitting cover, ample swimming areas and plant thickets; a dark substratum is recommended. Soft, slightly acid water and regular partial changes preferred. Temperature range: 72–77°F (22–25°C)*

BREEDING: *As for R. dorsiocellata. Hatching takes about 1½ days*

SLIM HARLEQUIN
NARROW-WEDGED, GLOWLIGHT, or ESPE'S, RASBORA

Rasbora espei

SYNONYMS: *Rasbora heteromorpha espei, Trigonostigma espei*
SUBFAMILY: Rasboriniae (Danioninae)

(AS FROM 1999, THIS SPECIES, ALONG WITH R. hengeli and R. heteromorpha, was transferred to a new genus, *Trigonostigma*. While accepting this revision, all three species are included under *Rasbora* in this book for ease of access, until the new

BEHAVIOR: *A peaceful shoaler*

DIET: *All foods accepted*

AQUARIUM: *Ample swimming area and abundant plant thickets should be provided. Soft, slightly acid water is preferred. Temperature range: 68–77°F (20–25°C)*

BREEDING: *Low water level recommended for this egg-scattering/eating species. Introducing the female a day or so before the male may help. Hatching takes about 1 day*

ELEGANT RASBORA
TWO-SPOT RASBORA

Rasbora elegans

SUBFAMILY: Rasborinae (Danioninae)

WHILE THE ELEGANT RASBORA IS, UNDOUBTEDLY, an "elegant" fish, it is no more so than its close relatives. The most striking features about this attractive fish are its body spots which can vary in shape, the posteriname becomes more widely distributed in aquarium literature.)

The Slim Harlequin can be easily distinguished from its better-known relative *R. heteromorpha* (the Harlequin): the most distinctive feature of both, the dark body cone pattern, is much narrower in the Slim Harlequin. In this, it resembles the other closely related species, *R. hengeli*, the Glass or Hengel's Harlequin from Sumatra, which is rarely kept (most "*hengeli*" are probably *espei*). Further work is required to establish differences between the two.

DISTRIBUTION: *Thailand*

SIZE: *Up to 2in (5cm) reported, but usually smaller*

BEHAVIOR: *A peaceful shoaler*

DIET: *All small commercial and live foods*

AQUARIUM: *Subdued lighting and a dark substratum shows this species off to best effect. Soft, slightly acid water is recommended. Temperature range: 73–82°F (22–28°C)*

BREEDING: *Infrequent in aquaria. Shallow, mature water and trio (one female/two males) recommended. Eggs laid on underside of broad-leaved plants. Hatching takes about 1 day*

HARLEQUIN
RED RASBORA
Rasbora heteromorpha, Trigonostigma heteromorpha: see *Rasbora espei*

SUBFAMILY: Rasborinae (Danioninae)

THE HARLEQUIN IS ONE OF THE OLD AQUARIUM favorites, having first been imported into Europe way back in 1906. It is still very popular today, largely owing to its striking coloration and dark body cone. Of the three "harlequins", this species possesses the widest body cone, making it immediately identifiable. A dark or blue variety is now also widely available.

DISTRIBUTION: *Peninsular Malaysia, Singapore, Sumatra and probably Thailand*

SIZE: *Up to 1¾in (4.5cm)*

BEHAVIOR: *A peaceful shoaler*

DIET: *Most foods accepted*

AQUARIUM: *As for R. espei, but slightly lower top temperature recommended*

BREEDING: *As for R. espei*

CLOWN RASBORA
TWO-SPOT, or THREE-SPOT, RASBORA
Rasbora kalochroma

SUBFAMILY: Rasborinae (Danioninae)

THIS IS ONE OF THE LARGER RASBORAS (*SEE BELOW*) which is seen less often than it deserves, since it is a truly beautiful fish when in peak condition. It is a little more sensitive than some other species. Particular care should therefore be given to water chemistry and quality.

DISTRIBUTION: *Malaysia, Borneo and Sumatra*

SIZE: *Up to 4in (10cm)*

BEHAVIOR: *Although it should be kept as a group, this species does not exhibit the strong shoaling instincts of its close relatives*

DIET: *Most foods accepted, particularly livefoods*

AQUARIUM: *Ample swimming space, plus plant thickets should be provided. Mature, soft, slightly acid water is best. Subdued lighting and a dark substratum also recommended. Temperature range: 77–82°F (25–28°C)*

BREEDING: *No documented reports available, but almost certainly an egg-scattering/eating species*

GLOWLIGHT RASBORA
RED-STRIPED, or RED-LINE, RASBORA
Rasbora pauciperforata

SUBFAMILY: Rasborinae (Danioninae)

UNDER APPROPRIATE CONDITIONS THE GLOWLIGHT Rasbora really lives up to its name. Unlike other rasboras, though, this species can tolerate relatively low temperatures during the winter, something that may improve the chances of achieving breeding success, particularly if pairs are allowed to select themselves from a shoal.

DISTRIBUTION: *Western Malaysia, Sumatra*

SIZE: *Up to 2¾in (7cm) reported; usually smaller*

BEHAVIOR: *A rather timid species which prefers the lower reaches of the aquarium, especially among vegetation*

DIET: *Will take a range of commercial formulations, but prefers livefoods*

AQUARIUM: *Subdued illumination and ample vegetation recommended. Soft, slightly acid water with regular partial water changes and filtration through peat is preferred. Temperature range: 66–70°F (19–21°C) during winter, rising to 73–77°F (23–25°C) at other times and slightly higher for breeding*

BREEDING: *A challenging species which scatters eggs among fine-leaved vegetation. Hatching takes about 1–1½ days*

▲ *SLIM HARLEQUIN (RASBORA ESPEI VAR.)*

▼ *HARLEQUIN (RASBORA HETEROMORPHA)*

▲ *Glowlight Rasbora (Rasbora pauciperforata)*
Fire Rasbora (Rasbora vaterifloris) ▶

SCISSORTAIL
THREE-LINED RASBORA
Rasbora trilineata

SUBFAMILY: Rasborinae (Danioninae)

THIS IS ANOTHER OF THE LARGER RASBORAS (although the maximum size is rarely attained, either in aquaria or in the wild). It is a species that only looks at its best when kept in a shoal. It prefers the middle and upper reaches of the aquarium but will also venture farther down.

DISTRIBUTION: *Malaysia, Borneo and Sumatra*

SIZE: *Up to 6in (15cm) reported; almost always considerably smaller*

BEHAVIOR: *An active shoaling species*

DIET: *Wide range accepted, but livefoods preferred*

AQUARIUM: *Ample swimming areas surrounded by plant thickets. Dark substratum and soft, slightly acid water with regular partial changes recommended. Temperature range: 72–77°F (22–25°C); slightly higher for breeding*

BREEDING: *Shallow water required with plenty of fine-leaved vegetation. Challenging egg scattering/eating species. Hatching takes about 1 day.*

FIRE RASBORA
GOLDEN, or PEARLY RASBORA, FIRE or ORANGE-FINNED BARB
Rasbora vaterifloris

SUBFAMILY: Rasborinae (Danioninae)

WITHOUT BEING ONE OF THE MOST COLORFUL OF the rasboras, this species is one of the most beautiful when in peak condition and under appropriate lighting. It is a challenging fish best avoided by less-experienced aquarists.

DISTRIBUTION: *Sri Lanka*

SIZE: *Up to 1½in (4cm); usually a little smaller*

BEHAVIOR: *A shy, peaceful shoaler that avoids bright lights*

DIET: *Wide range of foods accepted, particularly livefoods; will not generally feed off the bottom*

AQUARIUM: *Subdued lighting and a dark substratum recommended. Sensitive to water*

OTHER *RASBORA* SPECIES

In addition to the *Rasbora* species featured, there are others which are available with greater or lesser regularity. Although individual requirements may need checking out, basic aquarium needs are generally similar for all: soft, slightly acid, good-quality water, swimming space/plant thickets, etc.

SCIENTIFIC NAME	COMMON NAME	SIZE	TEMPERATURE
R. argyrotaenia	Silver Rasbora	6¾in (17cm)	64–77°F (18–25°C)
R. cephalotaenia	—	5in (13cm)	68–75°F (20–24°C)
R. daniconius	Striped Rasbora	4in (10cm)	75–79°F (24–26°C)
R. einthovenii	Brilliant, or Long-banded, Rasbora	3½in (9cm)	72–77°F (22–25°C)
R. reticulata	Net Rasbora	2½in (6cm)	72–79°F (22–26°C)
R. somphongsi (Trigonostigma somphongsi)	—	1in (3cm)	73–77°F (23–25°C)
R. taeniata	Black-striped or Black-lined Rasbora	2¾in (7cm)	72–75°F (22–24°C)
R. urophthalma	—	1¼in (3.5cm)	73–77°F (23–25°C)

STRIPED RASBORA (R. DANICONIUS)   BRILLIANT, OR LONG-BANDED, RASBORA (R. EINTHOVENII)

conditions which should be mature, soft, slightly acid and well-filtered. Some swimming areas with ample planting should be provided. Temperature range: 75–82°F (24–28°C)

BREEDING: Challenging. Prolific in the wild, but not in aquaria. Shallow, mature, well-planted conditions recommended. Egg-scattering species. Hatching takes about 1½ days

BITTERLING

Rhodeus sericeus

SYNONYMS: *Rhodeus amarus, R. amarus sericeus, R. sericeus amarus*
SUBFAMILY: Acheilognathinae (sometimes classified as Rhodeinae)

DESPITE IT BEING A LONG-ESTABLISHED AQUARIUM fish, there is still debate regarding the correct scientific name of this species, with the weight of opinion tending toward *R. sericeus*. Males look particularly attractive during the breeding season (April to August) and when subjected to side lighting.

DISTRIBUTION: Most of Europe north of the Alps, but excluding Scandinavia and most of the British Isles (although there are introduced populations)

SIZE: 4in (10cm)

BEHAVIOR: An active fish which may be kept in pairs or small groups

DIET: All foods accepted, particularly livefoods; vegetable component recommended

AQUARIUM: Roomy and well planted. At least part of the substratum should be fine-grained to accommodate Freshwater Mussels (e.g. Anodonta or Unio) if breeding is required. Water chemistry not critical but quality must be good. Temperature range: 64–70°F (18–21°C); cold spell at around 50°F (10°C) during winter improves chances of breeding success

BREEDING: Egg are laid and fertilized inside breathing tube (inhalant siphon) of Mussel. Hatching can take up to 3 weeks

RUDD (SCARDINIUS ERYTHROPHTHALMUS)

RUDD
RED-EYE

Scardinius erythrophthalmus

SUBFAMILY: Leuciscinae

THE RUDD IS AVAILABLE IN TWO COLOR FORMS: the silvery wild type and a cultivated golden form. It is the latter which is kept, primarily by pondkeepers, but to an increasing extent by aquarists as well.

DISTRIBUTION: Europe, north of the Pyrenees, but absent from the extreme north; introduced into numerous exotic locations

SIZE: Up to 18in (45cm); usually considerably smaller

BEHAVIOR: An active peaceful shoaler which prefers the upper layers of the water column

DIET: Wide range of foods accepted

AQUARIUM: Roomy, well oxygenated and well filtered. Water chemistry not critical. Temperature range: from close to freezing up to tropical temperatures, but 50–68°F (10–20°C) recommended

BREEDING: Only feasible in large aquaria. Up to 200,000 eggs may be released by a large female. Hatching takes 8–15 days

WHITE CLOUD MOUNTAIN MINNOW

Tanichthys albonubes

SUBFAMILY: Rasborinae (Danioninae)

TWO COLOR TYPES OF THIS POPULAR FISH ARE available: one with light-colored anal and dorsal fin edges and one with red edges. A long-finned variety which almost disappeared during the early 1990s is now found with greater frequency once more.

DISTRIBUTION: White Cloud Mountain region near Canton, China (type with light-colored fin edges); "red" type found around Hong Kong, probably from aquarium-bred escapes

SIZE: 1¾in (4.5cm)

BEHAVIOR: A peaceful shoaler

DIET: All foods accepted

AQUARIUM: A dark substratum in a well-planted tank that offers some swimming spaces is recommended. Water chemistry not critical. Temperature range: 50°F (15°C) during winter to 64–77°F (18–25°C) at other times

BREEDING: Eggs are scattered among fine-leaved vegetation. Hatching takes about 1½ days

TENCH
DOCTOR FISH

Tinca tinca

SUBFAMILY: Leuciscinae (sometimes classified as Cyprininae)

THE TENCH IS ANOTHER TRADITIONAL PONDFISH that is gradually making a transition to (large) aquaria. To the mid-1990s, two color forms were available: the green (or wild type) and a golden (sometimes mottled)

WHITE CLOUD MOUNTAIN MINNOW (TANICHTHYS ALBONUBES)

variety. Since then, at least two other colors have become available: a deep orange (sometimes referred to as red) and an orange/red and white type.

DISTRIBUTION: *Widespread in Europe and stretching eastward to Russia; absent from northern Scandinavia, possibly Scotland, Ireland, Iberia and the Adriatic coastline; widely introduced into exotic locations, including the United States*

SIZE: *Up to 28in (70cm) reported in the wild; usually much smaller*

BEHAVIOR: *Bottom dweller that will rise to the surface for food. Juveniles may be kept as a shoal*

DIET: *All foods accepted*

AQUARIUM: *Large, well-filtered (for water clarity purposes) aquaria with robust vegetation. Water chemistry not critical. Temperature range: from near freezing to over 86°F (30°C), but 68–77°F (20–25°C) is perfectly adequate*

BREEDING: *Difficult in aquaria. Huge numbers of eggs (up to 900,000) laid among plants in late spring/early summer. Hatching takes 6–8 days*

▲ RED AND WHITE TENCH (TINCA TINCA VAR.)
▼ RED TENCH (TINCA TINCA VAR.)   ▼▼ GOLDEN TENCH (TINCA TINCA VAR.)

ZACCO
PALE CHUB
Zacco platypus

SUBFAMILY: Rasborinae (Danioninae)

THIS IS A BEAUTIFUL FISH WHICH SHOULD BE SEEN more often. In addition to their unusual and attractive body coloring and patterning, males also possess an interesting extension of the anal (belly) fin.

DISTRIBUTION: *Far East; mainly imported from Japan*

SIZE: *Up to 7in (18cm); usually smaller*

BEHAVIOR: *Undemanding; excellent jumping ability; not suitable for keeping with small tankmates*

DIET: *All foods accepted*

AQUARIUM: *Spacious and well-covered aquaria, with well-oxygenated, well-filtered water. Water chemistry not critical. Temperature range: wide tolerance, but 68–77°F (20–25°C) is adequate*

BREEDING: *No details available*

L. arcus (Lipstick Leporinus), which has three. Both have similar characteristics and requirements.

DISTRIBUTION: L. striatus: *widely distributed in northern South America;* L. arcus: *reportedly restricted to Venezuela*

SIZE: L. striatus: *reported up to 16in (40cm), but usually smaller;* L. fasciatus: *reported up to 12in (30cm), but usually remaining smaller*

BEHAVIOR: *Generally peaceful shoaler, with an appetite for succulent plants*

DIET: *As for* L. affinis

AQUARIUM: *As for* L. affinis, *but temperature range: 72–79°F (22–26°C)*

BREEDING: *As for* L. affinis

SPOTTED CACHORRO

Acestorhynchus falcatus

FAMILY: Characidae
SUBFAMILY: Characinae

PIKE-LIKE CHARACINS, INCLUDING THE SPOTTED Cachorro, are grouped together according to certain body characteristics—usually the depth of the body in relation to its length. The *A. falcatus* group or complex is distinguished by its body depth being 4.0 to 4.75 times shorter than its body length. Members of other groups are hardly ever encountered in the hobby, while the Spotted Cachorro itself is only occasionally imported.

DISTRIBUTION: *Guiana, Amazon and Orinoco basins*

SIZE: *Up to 12in (30cm)*

BEHAVIOR: *Highly aggressive and predatory*

DIET: *Feeds almost exclusively on other fishes, thus raising ethical questions about its maintenance in aquaria*

AQUARIUM: *Large, well-filtered, well-covered, and with open spaces. Soft, acid water preferred. Temperature range: 73–81°F (23–27°C)*

BREEDING: *Unknown in aquaria*

FALSE FLAME-TAILED TETRA

Aphyocharax alburnus

SYNONYM: *Aphyocharax erythrurus (but see below)*
FAMILY: Characidae
SUBFAMILY: Uncertain

THERE ARE ABOUT 20 SPECIES OF APHYOCHARAX known, but only a few are available to hobbyists. All are slender fish, most with varying degrees of red in their fins, particularly the pelvic and anal fins, and the lower lobe of the caudal fin. This has given rise to their common names of flamed-tailed tetras or bloodfins. The False Flame-tailed Tetra does not possess the intense coloration of some of its closest relatives but, nevertheless, makes an impressive sight when kept as a shoal. The almost-identical *A. erythrurus* (from the Guianas), is regarded as a separate species by some ichthyologists, and as a geographical variant of the False Flame-tailed Tetra by others.

OTHER *LEPORINUS* SPECIES *

Several other *Leporinus*** species are available from time to time. All require the same basic conditions described for the featured species. These elegant fish are usually sold as juveniles and will soon outgrow most home aquaria. Sizes given below are approximate only.

SCIENTIFIC NAME	COMMON NAME(S)	SIZE
L. agassizi	Half-striped Leporinus	4¾in (12cm)
L. desmotes	Black/Yellow Leporinus	8¾in (22cm)
L. friderici***	Frideric's Leporinus	8in (20cm)
L. granti	Grant's Leporinus	6in (15cm)
L. maculatus	Spotted Leporinus	8in (20cm)
L. megalepis	Big-scaled Leporinus	9¾in (25cm)
L. melanopleura	Spot-tailed Leporinus	10½in (27cm)
L. melanosticus	Silver Leporinus	4in (10cm)
L. moralesi	Faded Leporinus	5in (12.5cm)
L. nigrotaeniatus	Black-lined Leporinus	15¾in (40cm)
L. octofasciatus	Eight-banded Leporinus	6¼in (16cm)
L. pellegrini	Belted Leporinus	4¾in (12cm)
L. spp.****	Golden Leporinus	9¾in (25cm)
L. spp.****	Reticulated Leporinus	12in (30cm)

NOTES:

*The genus *Leporinus* is still one of the least known of the characoid genera. As a result, the names given in the chart are likely to vary between publications and are likely to change with time. There is doubt even regarding the validity of some of the listed species, e.g. the fish known in aquarium literature as *L. maculatus* may, in fact, be synonymous with *L. pellegrini*. The situation regarding *L. granti* and *L. megalepis* is similarly confused.

**Leporinus* translates as "young or little hare" and is used for this genus because of its snout, which bears a characteristic cleft in the center creating a "hare lip" type of mouth. Two prominent teeth help complete the hare lip effect.

***This species is also encountered in aquarium literature as *L. frederici* (Frederic's Leporinus).

****Several *Leporinus* species are awaiting scientific description.

SPOTTED LEPORINUS (LEPORINUS MACULATUS)

DISTRIBUTION: *Reported from southern Brazil, Bolivia, Argentina, Paraguay, Peru and, possibly, the Guianas*

SIZE: *Up to 2¾in (7cm), but often smaller*

BEHAVIOR: *Peaceful, shoaler*

DIET: *Wide range of commercial diets and livefoods accepted*

AQUARIUM: *Well-planted, with some open spaces recommended. A dark substratum helps show these fish to good effect. Water chemistry not critical, but pH values above 7.5 should be avoided. Temperature range: 68–82°F (20–28°C)*

BREEDING: *Soft, acid water recommended. Eggs are scattered, either in the open or among vegetation (usually in the morning), and may be eaten by the parents. Hatching takes about one-and-a-half days*

BLOODFIN
ARGENTINIAN BLOODFIN
Aphyocharax anisitsi

SYNONYM: *Aphyocharax rubripinnis*
FAMILY: Characidae
SUBFAMILY: Uncertain (classified as Aphyocharacinae by some authors)

THIS IS THE FISH GENERALLY REGARDED WITHIN THE hobby as the "true" Bloodfin, although *A. rathbuni* (*see* below) can exhibit even deeper red coloration. Coming from an area a little distance from the genuinely tropical zones of South America, this species can tolerate coldwater aquarium temperatures, as long as these are not allowed to drop excessively. However, best coloration is exhibited when kept within a tropical regime. The species is long-lived, with some specimens reportedly attaining an age of ten years.

DISTRIBUTION: *Mainly Paraná River (Argentina)*

SIZE: *Up to 3in (7.5cm) reported, but usually smaller*

BEHAVIOR: *As for A. alburnus*

DIET: *As for A. alburnus*

AQUARIUM: *As for A. alburnus, but more tolerant of slightly higher pH (up to 8). Temperature range: 64–82°F (18–28°C)*

BREEDING: *As for A. alburnus*

RATHBUN'S BLOODFIN
Aphyocharax rathbuni

FAMILY: Characidae
SUBFAMILY: Uncertain (classified as Aphyocharacinae by some authors)

WHEN IN PEAK CONDITION, RATHBUN'S BLOODFIN is the most colorful *Aphyocharax* species generally available for aquaria. In *A. alburnus*, there is no red on the lower side of the body, while in *A. anisitsi*, the red pigmentation extends a little way into the body from the anal fin base. In Rathbun's Bloodfin, this can extend from the front edge of the anal fin, up to almost half the body width, and then back toward the caudal fin, creating a most impressive cone-like patch.

DISTRIBUTION: *Paraguay River basin*

SIZE: *Up to 2in (5cm)*

BEHAVIOR: *As for A. alburnus*

DIET: *As for A. alburnus*

AQUARIUM: *As for A. alburnus*

BREEDING: *As for A. alburnus*

RED-EYED TETRA
AFRICAN RED-EYED CHARACIN
Arnoldichthys spilopterus

FAMILY: Characidae
SUBFAMILY: Alestiinae

THIS SPECIES IS THE ONLY REPRESENTATIVE OF ITS genus. It was first imported into Europe in 1907; since then it has always been available but has never achieved the "greatness" of some other tetras, despite its undoubted beauty.

DISTRIBUTION: *From the Niger delta to Lagos in west Africa*

SIZE: *Up to 4¾in (12cm) reported, but usually smaller*

BEHAVIOR: *Peaceful, but active; should be kept as a shoal*

▲ *BLOODFIN (APHYOCHARAX ANISITSI)*
◄ *RATHBUN'S BLOODFIN (APHYOCHARAX RATHBUNI)*

DIET: *Range of commercial formulations accepted, but livefoods preferred*

AQUARIUM: *Spacious, with large, open swimming spaces, plants around sides and back, and dark substratum. Tannin-stained water advisable (see Aquarium Set-up). Water chemistry not critical, but raw water* should be avoided. Temperature range: 73–82°F (23–28°C)

BREEDING: Soft, acid water required. Eggs are scattered and hatch in about one-and-a-half days

BLIND CAVEFISH

BLIND CAVE CHARACIN or MEXICAN TETRA

Astyanax mexicanus

SYNONYMS: *Astyanax fasciatus, Astyanax fasciatus mexicanus, Astyanax mexicanus jordani, Anoptichthys jordani*
FAMILY: Characidae
SUBFAMILY: Tetragonopterinae

THE BLIND CAVEFISH AND THE MEXICAN TETRA were once believed to belong not just to different species, but to different genera, as the former name of *Anoptichthys* shows. However, they were eventually shown to be very different-looking members of the same species, the Mexican Tetra being the form that inhabits above-ground watercourses, while the Blind Cavefish lives underground. There is still some debate as to whether the current name for the species is *A. fasciatus* or *A. mexicanus*. Not so long ago, *A. fasciatus* appeared to be the preferred name, but in recent years the balance has moved toward the latter.

DISTRIBUTION: *Blind Cavefish form: limestone caves in a 87-mile (140-km) area that includes Sierra del Abra, Sierra de Guatemala, and Sierra de Colmera, in the region of San Luis Potosi, Mexico; Mexican Tetra form: widely distributed through Texas, Mexico, and Central America, through to Panama*

SIZE: *Around 3½in (9cm)*

BEHAVIOR: *Active but peaceful shoaler that likes to nibble succulent plants. Blind Cavefish may be harassed by aggressive tankmates*

DIET: *All foods accepted; vegetable component advisable*

AQUARIUM: *May be kept in well-lit aquarium, with standard decor, but best effects are created in plantless, darkened aquarium, with calcareous gravel and pieces of stalagmites or stalactites. Illumination can be provided by a "night" fluorescent tube (widely available for use in marine aquaria). Water chemistry not critical, as long as the quality is good, but medium-hard, alkaline conditions preferred. Temperature range: from 59–64°F (15–18°C) at the lower end, to 82–86°F (28–30°C), with 77°F (25°C) being adequate, both for maintenance and breeding*

BREEDING: *Eggs are scattered and may be eaten by the parents. Hatching takes one to three days, depending on temperature. The cave morph will hybridize easily with the sighted, fully colored Mexican Tetra*

PEPPER TETRA

WHITE-STAR TETRA

Axelrodia stigmatias

FAMILY: Characidae
SUBFAMILY: Tetragonopterinae

THIS TINY, GLORIOUS LITTLE FISH IS NOT SEEN AS frequently as it deserves to be. Kept in a shoal under appropriate conditions, the red, white, and silver are shown off to excellent effect. Since the 1970s, a similar, but slightly deeper-bodied species, *A. riesei*

(Ruby Tetra) from the Meta River in Colombia, has also been available.

DISTRIBUTION: *Amazon basin*

SIZE: *Up to 2in (5cm) reported, but usually smaller*

BEHAVIOR: *Peaceful shoaler*

DIET: *A range of small commercial formulations accepted, but livefoods preferred*

AQUARIUM: *Well-planted, but with subdued lighting and floating plants recommended, as well as dark substratum. Soft, slightly acid water required, preferably peat- or tannin-stained (see Aquarium Set-up). Temperature range: 72–79°F (22–26°C)*

BREEDING: *No documented accounts currently available*

LONG-FINNED CHARACIN

Brycinus longipinnis

SYNONYM: *Alestes longipinnis*
FAMILY: Characidae
SUBFAMILY: Alestiinae

SO CALLED BECAUSE OF THE EXTENDED DORSAL FIN rays of mature males, this species should be kept as a group, despite its relatively large size, for best effect. It is the most frequently encountered species of its genus, all of which are predominantly silvery-bodied fish with black bands originating in the fork of the caudal fin and extending to varying lengths into the body. Yellow-gold, reddish or white coloration usually accompanies the bands.

DISTRIBUTION: *Tropical west Africa*

SIZE: *Up to 5in (13cm)*

BEHAVIOR: *Peaceful shoaler*

DIET: *Wide range of foods accepted*

AQUARIUM: *Roomy, well-covered, well-filtered, with ample swimming space, planted along sides*

and back; dark substratum recommended. Soft to medium-hard, slightly acid to slightly alkaline water preferred. Temperature range: 72–79°F (22–26°C)*

BREEDING: *Soft, slightly acid water should be provided. Eggs are scattered among vegetation and take up to six days to hatch*

TAIL-LIGHT TETRA

Bryconops melanurus

FAMILY: Characidae
SUBFAMILY: Tetragonopterinae

THIS SPECIES HAS A LARGE HEAD AND EYE, attractive black edging on its body scales, and a black blotch in the fork of its caudal fin with a reddish orange/golden patch directly above it. Although it is the most commonly available species of its genus, it is one of the less frequently seen tetras.

DISTRIBUTION: *Amazon and the Guianas*

SIZE: *Up to 4in (10cm) reported, but usually grows to around 2¼in (6cm)*

BEHAVIOR: *Peaceful when young, but progressively more intolerant with age*

DIET: *Wide range of commercial formulations accepted, but livefoods preferred*

AQUARIUM: *Spacious, well-filtered, well-oxygenated, well-planted, with ample swimming space recommended. Soft, acid water required. Temperature range: 73–79°F (23–26°C)*

BREEDING: *No documented accounts currently available, but likely to be an egg scatterer with an appetite for its own eggs*

PINK-TAILED CHARACIN
PINK-TAILED CHALCEUS

Chalceus macrolepidotus

FAMILY: Characidae
SUBFAMILY: Uncertain (*see* below)

THE GENUS *CHALCEUS* HAS A NUMBER OF characteristics that place it close to the

genus *Brycon*. In addition, it seems to resemble some *Brycinus* (*Alestes*) species. As mentioned in the introductory section to characoids, Nelson (whose classification is followed here) does not allocate *Brycon* to any subfamily of the Characidae, while *Brycinus* belongs to the subfamily Alestiinae. As a result, the taxonomic position of these large-scaled, silvery-bodied tetras must be considered uncertain at this stage. The Pink-tailed Characin has pink/red fins, while the closely related *C. erythrurus* (Yellow-finned Characin) from the Amazon basin (believed, by some, to be a color form rather than a separate species) has yellow fins, except for the caudal fin, which contains some red.

DISTRIBUTION: *Amazon basin and Guianas*

SIZE: *Up to 9¾in (25cm)*

BEHAVIOR: *Predatory species; should be kept only with similar-sized tankmates*

DIET: *Can be weaned off livefoods and on to substantial deep-frozen or freeze-dried diets and tablet food. Juveniles will accept other formulations*

AQUARIUM: *Large, well-covered, well-filtered, with ample swimming space and plants around sides and back. Water chemistry not critical. Temperature range: 73–82°F (23–28°C)*

BREEDING: *No documented accounts currently available*

BANDED CHARACIDIUM

Characidium fasciatum

FAMILY: Characidae
SUBFAMILY: Characidiinae

THIS SUBFAMILY IS GENERALLY KNOWN AS THE South American darters, indicating at least a passing similarity to the North American darters of the family Percidae. They share a generally elongated body shape and bottom-hugging habits, and are often found in flowing waters. Few

LONG-FINNED CHARACIN (BRYCINUS LONGIPINNIS)

PINK-TAILED CHARACIN (CHALCEUS MACROLEPIDOTUS)

AQUARIUM: *Well-planted, with open swimming spaces. Medium-hard, slightly acid to slightly alkaline water recommended. Temperature range: 72–79°F (22–26°C)*

BREEDING: *Spawning may be stimulated by high levels of illumination. Eggs are scattered over plants or the substratum. Hatching can take up to five or six days*

BRILLIANT RUMMY-NOSED TETRA

Hemigrammus bleheri

FAMILY: Characidae
SUBFAMILY: Tetragonopterinae

THIS SPECIES (LARGELY EXPORTED FROM THE RÍO Negro, in Brazil, and the Vaupés, in Colombia, and first imported into Europe in 1965) was originally known simply as the Rummy Nose or Rummy-nosed Tetra (*see* photo p.1). However, a very similar species, *H. rhodostomus*, which had been imported for many years prior to this from around the Belém region in Brazil, was already known as the Rummy Nose. This, invariably, led to considerable confusion, with the Rio Negro Rummy Nose being frequently named *H. rhodostomus*, instead of *H. bleheri*. The distinction between the two was not settled—at least, ichthyologically—until 1986, but exports of *H. bleheri* from the Rio Negro are still often referred to as *H. rhodostomus*. Skeletal differences exist between the two but these are impossible to determine in living specimens. Fortunately, there are several other, more easily identified, distinguishing

characteristics: in *H. bleheri*, the red coloration in the head region covers most of the head and extends some way into the body, while in *H. rhodostomus*—the "True" or Banded Rummy Nose—it is much more restricted; the tip of the snout is more rounded in *H. bleheri*; the black band that, in *H. rhodostomus*, extends along the base of the anal fin, is lacking in *H. bleheri*, as are any marks on the rays of the anal fin. A third species, *Petitella georgiae* (the False Rummy Nose) is similar to both these rummy noses but has a number of distinguishing features.

DISTRIBUTION: H. bleheri: *middle Rio Negro (Brazil); those from Colombia appear to be* H. bleheri *but formal confirmation of this is still awaited.* H. rhodostomus: *Belém region of Brazil; also reported from Venezuela*

SIZE: *Around 1¾in (4.5cm)*

BEHAVIOR: *Peaceful shoalers;* H. bleheri *is known to "parasitize" brooding pairs of* Uaru amphiacanthoides *by feeding on the "body milk" that the Uarus secrete and on which their fry feed during their early days*

DIET: *Most foods accepted*

AQUARIUM: *Well-planted, with swimming spaces. Soft, slightly acid, good-quality, tannin-stained water (see Aquarium Set-up) recommended. Temperature range: 72–79°F (22–26°C).* H. rhodostomus *is a little more tolerant of fluctuations*

BREEDING: *Very soft, acid water recommended. Eggs are scattered among vegetation or over the substratum. Hatching takes about one-and-a-half days*

BUENOS AIRES TETRA

Hemigrammus caudovittatus

FAMILY: Characidae
SUBFAMILY: Tetragonopterinae

THIS ACTIVE SPECIES HAS BEEN KNOWN IN THE hobby since 1922. It is often recommended as an ideal community fish, although its behavior does not always justify this (*see* below). Specimens in peak condition exhibit very attractive red coloration in the fins, except the pectoral fins. A variant, in which the caudal fin is predominantly yellow, is occasionally available.

DISTRIBUTION: *Argentina (mainly around Rio de la Plata), southeastern Brazil, and Paraguay*

SIZE: *Up to 4¾in (12cm) reported, but usually around 2¾–3in (7–8cm)*

BEHAVIOR: *Generally peaceful shoaler, but larger specimens can become progressively more aggressive with age. Has a distinct appetite for succulent plants*

DIET: *Wide variety of foods accepted*

AQUARIUM: *Plant thickets (not delicate succulent types) and open swimming spaces required. Water chemistry not critical, but quality must be good and oxygenation level high. Temperature range: 64–82°F (18–28°C)*

BREEDING: *Eggs are scattered among vegetation and may be eaten by the parents. Hatching takes about one day*

GLOWLIGHT TETRA

Hemigrammus erythrozonus

FAMILY: Characidae
SUBFAMILY: Tetragonopterinae

THE GLOWLIGHT IS ONE OF THE OLD FAVORITES OF the hobby and deservedly so. A shoal of these tiny fish kept under appropriate conditions makes a truly impressive sight. There is some doubt regarding the assignation of this species to the genus *Hemigrammus*, and studies may eventually result in its being assigned to the genus *Cheirodon*.

DISTRIBUTION: *Essequibo basin (Guyana)*

SIZE: *Around 1½in (4cm)*

BEHAVIOR: *Peaceful shoaler*

DIET: *Wide range of small foods accepted*

AQUARIUM: *Well-planted, with open swimming spaces, and tannin-stained water (see Aquarium Set-up). Soft, slightly acid water preferred, but some deviation accepted if adjustments are made gradually. Temperature range: 72–82°F (22–28°C)*

BUENOS AIRES TETRA (HEMIGRAMMUS CAUDOVITTATUS)

BREEDING: Spawning may be achieved using either pairs or a shoal. Eggs are scattered among vegetation in soft, acid water. Hatching takes about one day

HEAD-AND-TAIL LIGHT TETRA

BEACON FISH

Hemigrammus ocellifer

FAMILY: Characidae
SUBFAMILY: Tetragonopterinae

TWO SUBSPECIES ARE GENERALLY RECOGNIZED: *H. ocellifer falsus* (first imported into Europe in 1910, and the type most frequently encountered in aquaria); and *H. o. ocellifer* (introduced around 1960). Both are very similar, but *H. o. ocellifer* has a distinct, gold-bordered, black spot just behind the gill covers; in *H. o. falsus*, this feature is indistinct. In *H. o. ocellifer*, there are also two red patches on the top and bottom lobes of the caudal fin.

DISTRIBUTION: H. o. falsus: *the Amazon basin;* H. o. ocellifer: *the lower reaches of the Amazon and French Guiana*

SIZE: *Around 1¾in (4.5cm)*

BEHAVIOR: *Peaceful shoaler*

DIET: *Wide range of foods accepted*

AQUARIUM: *Basically, as for* H. erythrozonus. *Temperature range: 72–79°F (22–26°C) for* H. o. falsus, *75–82°F (24–28°C) for* H. o. ocellifer

BREEDING: *As for* H. erythrozonus

PRETTY TETRA

BLACK-WEDGE, OR GARNET, TETRA

Hemigrammus pulcher

FAMILY: Characidae
SUBFAMILY: Tetragonopterinae

THE PRETTY TETRA IS, INDEED, VERY PRETTY, BUT the second (less-often-used) common name is far more appropriate given the black, wedge-like patch that occupies the posterior lower section of the body. Two subspecies are generally recognized: *H. pulcher haraldi*, which is not frequently kept; and *H. p. pulcher*, the popular type.

DISTRIBUTION: H. p. haraldi: *the central Amazon around Manáus;* H. p. pulcher: *wider distribution, including the Peruvian Amazon*

SIZE: *Around 1¾in (4.5cm)*

BEHAVIOR: *As for* H. erythrozonus

DIET: *As for* H. erythrozonus

AQUARIUM: *Basically as for* H. erythrozonus. *Temperature range: 73–81°F (23–27°C)*

BREEDING: *Breeding is not difficult once a good pair has been established. Eggs are scattered*

▲ *PRETTY TETRA (HEMIGRAMMUS PULCHER)*　　　▼ *ULREY'S TETRA (HEMIGRAMMUS ULREYI)*

among vegetation and may be eaten by the parents. Hatching takes about one day

GOLDEN TETRA

Hemigrammus rodwayi

SYNONYM: *Hemigrammus armstrongi*
FAMILY: Characidae
SUBFAMILY: Tetragonopterinae

THE DEGREE OF GOLD COLORATION— KNOWN AS "gold dust"—varies between specimens. This variation may be related to the amount of guanin that is secreted as a protective measure against skin parasites. Specimens with little or no gold dust are occasionally available, but are not generally considered to be as attractive as their golden counterparts.

DISTRIBUTION: *Guyana*

SIZE: *Around 2¼in (5.5cm)*

BEHAVIOR: *Peaceful shoaler*

DIET: *Wide range of foods accepted*

AQUARIUM: *Basically, as for* H. erythrozonus. *Temperature range: 75–82°F (24–28°C)*

BREEDING: *As for* H. erythrozonus. *The gold sheen may disappear after one or more generations of aquarium breeding.*

ULREY'S TETRA

Hemigrammus ulreyi

FAMILY: Characidae
SUBFAMILY: Tetragonopterinae

THIS SPECIES, WHILE LACKING SOME OF THE MORE intense coloration of some other tetras is, nevertheless, every bit as beautiful when in good condition and kept in a shoal. In

EMPEROR TETRA (NEMATOBRYCON PALMERI)

BREEDING: *Can be challenging. Soft, acid water and darkened aquarium recommended. Eggs are laid singly among vegetation and may be eaten by the spawning pair. Hatching takes one to two days*

CARDINAL TETRA

Paracheirodon axelrodi

SYNONYMS: *Cheirodon axelrodi, Hyphesso-brycon cardinalis*
FAMILY: Characidae
SUBFAMILY: Tetragonopterinae

THE CARDINAL TETRA IS ONE OF THE MOST famous and popular species in the hobby. It is a truly magnificent fish, which forms the cornerstone of the Brazilian Amazon ornamental fishery. It is also bred commercially in several countries, most notably the Czech Republic. Several forms of the species are known within its natural range, and may represent several, rather than a single, species. A cultivated golden variety is occasionally available.

DISTRIBUTION: *From the Orinoco (Venezuela), through the northern tributaries of the Rio Negro (Brazil), on to western Colombia*

SIZE: *Up to 2in (5cm)*

BEHAVIOR: *Peaceful shoaler*

DIET: *Wide range of foods accepted*

AQUARIUM: *Well-planted, with some open spaces and subdued lighting (e.g. provided by floating plants), recommended. These fish are often, but not invariably, found in tannin-stained*

water (see Aquarium Set-up). Soft, acid water recommended, but harder, more alkaline conditions tolerated if adjustments carried out gradually. Temperature range: 73–81°F (23–27°C)

BREEDING: *Challenging in aquaria. Subdued lighting and very soft, acid, tannin-stained water will enhance chances of success. Eggs are scattered among vegetation and may be eaten by the parents. Hatching takes about one day*

NEON TETRA

Paracheirodon innesi

SYNONYM: *Hyphessobrycon innesi*
FAMILY: Characidae
SUBFAMILY: Tetragonopterinae

AT FIRST SIGHT, THIS SPECIES MAY BE CONFUSED with *P. axelrodi*. However, in the Neon Tetra, the red body coloration occupies only the posterior half of the body, while, in *P. axelrodi* it extends from head to tail. Traditionally, there have been two major sources of neons: wild-caught specimens from South America, and captive-bred stocks from Hong Kong. However, other sources of captive-bred fish are becoming established, particularly in Sri Lanka. Several cultivated varieties of neon are available in addition to the wild type, including Diamondhead, Gold, Albino, Brilliant, and "Mon Cheri" (yellow).

DISTRIBUTION: *Putumayo river, eastern Peru*

SIZE: *Around 1½in (4cm)*

BEHAVIOR: *As for P. axelrodi*

DIET: *As for P. axelrodi*

AQUARIUM: *As for P. axelrodi. Temperature range: 68–79°F (20–26°C)*

BREEDING: *As for P. axelrodi*

FALSE NEON TETRA
GREEN NEON TETRA

Paracheirodon simulans

SYNONYM: *Hyphessobrycon simulans*
FAMILY: Characidae
SUBFAMILY: Tetragonopterinae

THIS IS THE LEAST FREQUENTLY ENCOUNTERED OF the three *Paracheirodon* species featured. In overall coloration, it falls somewhere in between *P. innesi* and *P. axelrodi*. Despite its relative rarity, at least two varieties are known in addition to the wild type: a White Green (or False) Neon and a Gold Green (or False) Neon.

DISTRIBUTION: *Jufaris or Tupari rivers in the area of the Rio Negro (Brazil)*

SIZE: *Up to 1½in (4cm), but usually a little smaller*

BEHAVIOR: *As for P. axelrodi*

DIET: *As for P. axelrodi*

FALSE NEON TETRA (PARACHEIRODON SIMULANS)

CARDINAL TETRA
(PARACHEIRODON AXELRODI) ▼

▲ CARDINAL TETRA (PARACHEIRODON AXELRODI)

NEON TETRA (PARACHEIRODON INNESI) ▼ ▶

AQUARIUM: *As for* P. axelrodi. *Avoid alkaline, hardwater conditions*

BREEDING: *Challenging in aquaria; conditions similar to those for* P. axelrodi *recommended*

FALSE RED-NOSED TETRA

FALSE RUMMY-NOSED TETRA

Petitella georgia

FAMILY: Characidae
SUBFAMILY: Tetragonopterinae

THIS SPECIES IS SUPERFICIALLY SIMILAR TO THE other rummy-nosed tetras (*Hemigrammus bleheri* and *H. rhodostomus—see* p.198). However, in *Petitella*, the central black band in the caudal fin extends forward somewhat into the body, and the black band along the base of the anal fin is wider than in *H. rhodostomus*. False Red-nosed Tetra is also a larger fish.

DISTRIBUTION: *Upper Amazon basin*

SIZE: *Up to 3in (8cm) reported, but usually around 5cm (2in)*

BEHAVIOR: *Peaceful shoaler*

DIET: *Most foods accepted*

AQUARIUM: *As for* Hemigrammus bleheri

BREEDING: *No documented reports currently available*

CONGO TETRA

Phenacogrammus interruptus

SYNONYM: *Micralestes interruptus*
FAMILY: Characidae
SUBFAMILY: Alestiinae

THE SCIENTIFIC NAME OF THIS SPECIES IS ONE OF the most "fluid" among the tetras, apparently changing in acceptance and popularity with time. During the early part of the last decade of the 20th century, for example, *Micralestes* gained ground over the former choice, *Phenacogrammus*. As the new millennium approached, though, *Phenacogrammus* seemed to come back into fashion. The main contributing factor to this confusion is the considerable overlap in certain characteristics between the two genera. The main distinguishing feature between the two is that, in *Phenacogrammus*, the lateral line is incomplete, while in *Micralestes* it is complete (although this distinction is not infallible since, in some *Micralestes*, the lateral line can also be incomplete). Whatever its true identity, the species is an elegant fish that looks splendid when kept in appropriate conditions and in a small shoal.

DISTRIBUTION: *Zaire (Republic of Congo)*

CONGO TETRA (PHENACOGRAMMUS INTERRUPTUS)

SIZE: *Fully mature males up to 3½in (9cm); females somewhat smaller*

BEHAVIOR: *Peaceful and tolerant; may become timid in the presence of robust, hyperactive, or aggressive tankmates. May also nibble delicate or succulent plants*

DIET: *Wide range of foods accepted; vegetable component recommended*

AQUARIUM: *Spacious, well-planted, with ample swimming areas. Soft, slightly acid water, preferably tannin-stained (see* Aquarium Set-up*) recommended. Temperature range: 75–81°F (24–27°C)*

BREEDING: *Uncommon in aquaria. Bright illumination may act as a stimulus for well-matched pairs or shoals. Eggs are scattered over the substratum and take up to six days to hatch*

SAILFIN CHARACIN

SAILFIN TETRA

Crenuchus spilurus

FAMILY: Characidae
SUBFAMILY: Crenuchinae

THIS SPECIES HAS THE SAME CAVERNOUS MOUTH as its close relative, *Poecilocharax weitzmani* (Black Darter Tetra), *see* below. It is not quite as vividly colored but is, nonetheless, an impressive fish—the males, with their large expanded dorsal fins, more so than the females.

DISTRIBUTION: *Guyana and middle Amazon*

SIZE: *Up to 2½in (6cm)*

BEHAVIOR: *Large specimens may prey on small fish; otherwise peaceful, if sometimes timid*

DIET: *Livefoods and deep-frozen diets preferred, but acclimatized specimens will also accept some commercial formulations*

AQUARIUM: *Dense vegetation, ample shelters, and subdued lighting. Soft, acid, tannin-stained water (see* Aquarium Set-up*) preferred. Temperature range: 75–81°F (24–27°C)*

BREEDING: *Very challenging in aquaria. Eggs may be laid on a flat or smooth rock, and may receive some parental care*

BLACK DARTER TETRA

WEITZMAN'S PREDATOR TETRA

Poecilocharax weitzmani

FAMILY: Characidae
SUBFAMILY: Crenuchinae

FOR A SMALL FISH, THIS SPECIES CAN BE absolutely stunning. Males, in particular, have large (relatively speaking) dorsal and anal fins, which, during displays, they spread out while at the same time opening the cavernous mouth to its full extent, thus creating the impression that they are much larger than they really are. This is a challenging species best suited to the experienced aquarist.

DISTRIBUTION: *Upper Solimões, Upper Rio Negro and Orinoco basins*

SIZE: *Up to 1½in (4cm), but often smaller*

BEHAVIOR: *A shoaler; males display to each other but do not generally cause any damage*

DIET: *Livefoods preferred; deep-frozen, freeze-dried diets may be accepted*

AQUARIUM: *Well-planted, with some open spaces and subdued lighting recommended. Soft, acid water, preferably tannin-stained (see* Aquarium Set-up*). Temperature range: 75–82°F (24–28°C)*

BREEDING: *No documented reports of aquarium breeding currently available*

GLASS BLOODFIN

TRANSLUCENT BLOODFIN or GLASS BLOODFISH

Prionobrama filigera

SYNONYMS: *Aphyocharax filigerus*,
Prionobrama madeirae
FAMILY: Characidae
SUBFAMILY: Uncertain (classified as Paragoni-
atinae by some authors)

CLOSELY RELATED TO *APHYOCHARAX ANISITSI*
(Bloodfin), *see* p.193, this species is much
less frequently seen in the hobby. This is a
shame because it is an elegant, strikingly
patterned fish, with the added attraction
that the male's anal fin possesses a bril-
liant-white, curved extension along its
front edge.

DISTRIBUTION: *Reported from central and
southern Brazil, Madeira, Paraguay rivers, and
Argentina*

SIZE: *Around 2¼in (6cm)*

BEHAVIOR: *Peaceful shoaler*

DIET: *Wide range of foods accepted*

AQUARIUM: *Well-planted, with ample swimming
space, recommended. Surface cover in the form
of floating plants also advisable. Softish, slightly
acid water appears to be preferred, but higher
pH and hardness also tolerated. Temperature
range: 72–86°F (22 30°C)*

BREEDING: *Soft, acid, tannin-stained water (see
Aquarium Set-up) recommended. Sunlight will also
help. Eggs are scattered among fine-leaved
vegetation and hatch after about three days*

X-RAY TETRA

X-RAY FISH or WATER GOLDFINCH

Pristella maxillaris

SYNONYM: *Pristella riddlei*
FAMILY: Characidae
SUBFAMILY: Tetragonopterinae

THIS IS AN UNDEMANDING SPECIES THAT TOLER-
ATES a range of aquarium conditions.
However, for its colors to be seen to best
effect, the overall water quality must be
good. The somewhat intriguing common
name of Water Goldfinch probably derives
from the gold, white, black, and red coloration, which is shared with its feathered
namesake.

DISTRIBUTION: *Lower Amazon, Guyana, and
Venezuela*

SIZE: *Around 1¾in (4.5cm)*

BEHAVIOR: *Peaceful shoaler*

DIET: *Wide range of foods accepted*

AQUARIUM: *Well-planted, with ample swimming
space, a dark substratum, and subdued lighting
will show off a shoal to great effect. Water*
chemistry not critical (although soft, slightly acid
conditions preferred), but quality must be good.
Temperature range: 70–82°F (21–28°C)—low
temperatures should not be maintained on a
long-term basis*

BREEDING: *Sometimes difficult if pairs are not well
matched; otherwise spawning is easy. Eggs are
scattered and take about one day to hatch*

RED-BELLIED PIRANHA

Pygocentrus nattereri

SYNONYMS: *Serrasalmus nattereri, Pygocen-
trus altus*
FAMILY: Characidae
SUBFAMILY: Serrasalminae

AS IN THE CASE OF OTHER MEMBERS OF THE SUB-
family Serrasalminae, such as the silver dollars (e.g. *Metynnis, Myleus*—*see* pp.205 and
206 respectively), piranha taxonomy is
currently somewhat unsettled. The former
subgeneric name, *Pygocentrus*, for example,
is now becoming more widely accepted as a
full generic name for some types of piranha,
as indicated above. Despite its formidable
reputation, the Red-bellied Piranha is not
quite the indiscriminate killer it is made out
to be. It is, nevertheless, a potentially dangerous species and even small specimens
must be treated with due caution, particularly when cleaning their aquaria.

DISTRIBUTION: *Amazon and Orinoco basins*

SIZE: *Up to 12in (30cm)*

BEHAVIOR: *Aggressive, often toward subordinate
tankmates of their own species, but can be timid
when housed in bare, brightly lit aquaria*

DIET: *Meat/fish-based diet and large livefoods.
Live fish will also be eaten, but the ethics of this
practice need to be considered before providing
such a diet*

GLASS BLOODFIN (*PRIONOBRAMA FILIGERA*)

RED-BELLIED PIRANHA (*PYGOCENTRUS NATTERERI*)

SWORDTAIL CHARACIN (STEVARDIA RIISEI)

AQUARIUM: *Large, deep, well-filtered, and with large pieces of bogwood laid out for shelter. Only robust and/or artificial plants suitable. Lighting should not be too bright. Soft, slightly acid water preferred, but not essential. Temperature range: 73–81°F (23–27°C)*

BREEDING: *Infrequent in aquaria. Eggs have been laid among the feathery roots of large floating plants such as Water Hyacinth (Eichhornia crassipes), but usually they are laid inside a depression dug in the substratum. Both parents, or one (usually the male), will defend the eggs until they hatch about two to three days later*

BLACK PIRANHA

WHITE, or SPOTTED, PIRANHA

Pygocenrus rhombeus

SYNONYMS: *Serrasalmus rhombeus, S. niger,* and several others
FAMILY: Characidae
SUBFAMILY: Serrasalminae

LIKE *P. NATTERERI*, THIS LARGE, PREDATORY species is regularly available, albeit under a variety of names. Other members of the genus, as well as related ones, are only occasionally encountered, with the possible exception of *Serrasalmus hollandi* (Holland's Piranha), which is found south of the Amazon basin and known not to be as aggressive as *P. nattereri* and Black Piranha.

DISTRIBUTION: *Amazon basin and Guyana*

SIZE: *Up to c.15in (38cm)*

BEHAVIOR: *As for P. nattereri*

DIET: *As for P. nattereri*

AQUARIUM: *As for P. nattereri*

BREEDING: *As for P. nattereri*

SWORDTAIL CHARACIN

Stevardia riisei

SYNONYM: *Corynopoma riisei*
FAMILY: Characidae
SUBFAMILY: Glandulocaudinae

THIS BASICALLY SILVER-COLORED FISH HAS RATHER unusual, and distinguishing, physical and reproductive characteristics. Mature males possess a long extension of the lower rays of the caudal fin—the "sword" that gives the species its common name. In addition, they have a long, filament-like extension on each gill cover, with a fleshy structure at the tip; it is believed that this "paddle" is used as a lure to attract a female into the appropriate breeding position.

DISTRIBUTION: *Meta river in Colombia and (possibly) Trinidad*

SIZE: *Up to 2¾in (7cm)*

BEHAVIOR: *Peaceful shoaler; should not be housed with fin-nipping species such as Barbus tetrazona (Tiger Barb)*

DIET: *Wide range of foods accepted*

AQUARIUM: *Well-planted, with ample swimming areas recommended. Water chemistry can range from slightly acid to slightly alkaline and from soft to medium-hard. Temperature range: 72–82°F (22–28°C)*

BREEDING: *Unusually for a characin, the eggs are fertilized internally (hence the need for the female to adopt a precise position for mating). The eggs are subsequently released and hatch in one to one-and-a-half days*

BOEHLKE'S PENGUIN FISH

BLACK-LINE THAYERIA

Thayeria boehlkei

FAMILY: Characidae
SUBFAMILY: Tetragonopterinae

THIS SPECIES LOOKS BEST WHEN KEPT IN A SHOAL, as this emphasizes the bold, black, gold-bordered body band, as well as the unusual way in which this band extends into the lower part of the caudal fin. The species also adopts a characteristic angled posture when at rest, with the head pointed slightly upward, and often with all the fish in a shoal facing in the same direction.

DISTRIBUTION: *Peruvian Amazon, and Araguaia (Brazil)*

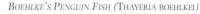

BOEHLKE'S PENGUIN FISH (THAYERIA BOEHLKEI)

SIZE: *Up to 3in (8cm) reported, but usually smaller*

BEHAVIOR: *Peaceful shoaler*

DIET: *Wide range of foods accepted*

AQUARIUM: *Thickly planted, with some (but not necessarily ample) swimming space, recommended. Soft, slightly acid, well-oxygenated water preferred, but some deviation is tolerated, as long as changes are carried out gradually. Frequent water changes (observing this rule) also advisable. Temperature range: 72–82°F (22–28°C)*

BREEDING: *Eggs are scattered freely among fine-leaved vegetation. Hatching takes about one day*

PENGUIN FISH
SHORT-STRIPED THAYERIA

Thayeria obliqua

FAMILY: Characidae
SUBFAMILY: Tetragonopterinae

AT FIRST SIGHT, THIS SPECIES CAN BE CONFUSED with *T. boehlkei* (*see* above). However, in the Penguin Fish the black band extends forward from the tip of the lower lobe of the caudal fin at an upwardly directed angle to a point on the back just posterior to the dorsal fin. In *T. boehlkei*, the band extends all the way along the center of the body right up to the gill cover.

DISTRIBUTION: *Amazon basin*

SIZE: *Up to 3in (8cm) reported, but usually smaller*

BEHAVIOR: *As for* T. boehlkei

DIET: *As for* T. boehlkei

AQUARIUM: *As for* T. boehlkei

BREEDING: *No documented reports appear to be available, but breeding strategy likely to be as in* T. boehlkei

NARROW HATCHETFISH (*TRIPORTHEUS ANGULATUS*)

NARROW HATCHETFISH

Triportheus angulatus

FAMILY: Characidae
SUBFAMILY: Uncertain (classified as Bryconinae by some authors)

MEMBERS OF THIS GENUS (OF WHICH THIS SPECIES is the most frequently encountered in the hobby) have a keel-like chest that resembles that found in the "true" hatchetfishes (family Gasteropelecidae—*see* pp.218–19). This forms the anchor for powerful chest muscles that allow the fish to jump out of the water and—with the aid of wing-like pectoral fins—glide for short distances, thus escaping predators.

DISTRIBUTION: *Amazon basin*

SIZE: *Up to 8in (20cm) reported, but usually smaller*

BEHAVIOR: *Generally peaceful, but may attack small tankmates*

DIET: *Livefoods preferred, but will accept a range of commercial diets*

AQUARIUM: *Large, well-covered, well-illuminated, with ample swimming areas, recommended. Well-oxygenated water important, but composition may vary from slightly acid to slightly alkaline, and from soft to medium-hard. Temperature range: 72–82°F (22–28°C)*

BREEDING: *No documented reports currently available*

LINED CITHARINID

Citharinus citharus

FAMILY: Citharinidae
SUBFAMILY: Citharininae

THIS LARGE, PREDOMINANTLY SILVERY FISH HAS dusky dorsal, caudal, and anal fins, clear pectoral fins, and reddish pelvic fins. Only juveniles are suitable for average-sized aquaria. This species is therefore best avoided unless adequate accommodation can be provided for adults.

DISTRIBUTION: *From Senegal to the Nile basin*

SIZE: *Up to 20in (50cm) reported, but usually much smaller*

BEHAVIOR: *Not aggressive; may be kept in shoals, space permitting. Likes to dig in the substrate in search of food*

DIET: *Wide range of foods accepted*

AQUARIUM: *Large, deep, with ample swimming space and fine-grained substratum recommended. Neutral to alkaline, soft to medium-hard water preferred. Temperature range: 72–82°F (22–28°C)*

BREEDING: *Believed to be an egg scatterer, but no documented accounts currently available*

LINED CITHARINID (*CITHARINUS CITHARUS*)

SILVER DISTICHODUS (DISTICHODUS AFFINIS)

SILVER DISTICHODUS

Distichodus affinis

FAMILY: Citharinidae
SUBFAMILY: Distichodontinae

THE SILVER DISTICHODUS WAS FIRST IMPORTED into Europe in 1911 and has been available ever since, despite its plant-eating habits. Overall, it is similar to *D. noboli* (Nobol's Distichodus) from Upper Congo (Zaire) with which it is sometimes confused. All *Distichodus* are specialist feeders and are best suited to experienced aquarists.

DISTRIBUTION: *Congo (Zaire) basin*

SIZE: *Up to 5in (13cm)*

BEHAVIOR: *Peaceful, with a distinct liking for succulent plants*

DIET: *Some commercial foods accepted, particularly vegetable flakes; lettuce, spinach, watercress, and other plants, should form an important part of the diet*

AQUARIUM: *Roomy, with rock and bogwood decor, recommended. Use only unpalatable or artificial plants, and provide swimming space. Slightly acid to neutral, soft to medium-hard water. Temperature range: 73–81°F (23–27°C)*

BREEDING: *No documented accounts currently available*

LONG-NOSED DISTICHODUS

Distichodus lusosso

FAMILY: Citharinidae
SUBFAMILY: Distichodontinae

OWING TO THE LARGE SIZE ATTAINED BY ADULTS, only juveniles of this species are suitable for most aquaria. A similar-looking species, *D. sexfasciatus* (Six-lined Distichodus)—also from the Congo (Zaire) basin—can be confused with this species, although, as its name implies, the Long-nosed Distichodus has a somewhat longer and more pointed snout than its close relative.

DISTRIBUTION: *Congo (Zaire) basin, Angola, Cameroon*

SIZE: *Up to 16in (40cm) reported, but usually smaller*

BEHAVIOR: *Peaceful, with a strong appetite for plants*

DIET: *As for D. affinis*

AQUARIUM: *As for D. affinis. Temperature range: 72–79°F (22–26°C)*

BREEDING: *As for D. affinis*

OTHER *DISTICHODUS* SPECIES

In addition to the two featured species and the two others mentioned, several other *Distichodus* are available. All are plant eaters and require the same basic care and feeding.

SCIENTIFIC NAME	COMMON NAME(S):	SIZE
D. antonii	Antoni's Distichodus	8¼in (21cm)
D. atroventralis	Gray Distichodus	6in (15cm)
D. decemmaculatus	Dwarf Distichodus	3in (8cm)
D. fasciolatus	Shark-tailed Distichodus	12in (30cm)
D. maculatus	Many-spotted Distichodus	8in (20cm)*
D. notospilus	Red-finned, or African, Straight Distichodus	6in (15cm)*

Note

*Sizes up to 12in (30cm) have been reported but are not encountered in aquaria.

RED-FINNED DISTICHODUS (DISTICHODUS NOTOSPILUS)

▲ LONG-NOSED DISTICHODUS (DISTICHODUS LUSOSSO)
ANSORGE'S NEOLEBIAS (NEOLEBIAS ANSORGII) ▶

ONE-STRIPED AFRICAN CHARACIN

Nannaethiops unitaeniatus

FAMILY: Citharinidae
SUBFAMILY: Distichodontinae

ALTHOUGH IT LOOKS QUITE DIFFERENT TO THE other members of the family featured in the foregoing entries, the One-striped Characin possesses fin ray, skeletal, and tooth characteristics that identify it as a citharinid. Despite the subtle coloration of this species, it nevertheless makes an impressive display when kept in appropriate conditions. A gold-striped variety is also occasionally available.

DISTRIBUTION: *Widely distributed in tropical regions of Africa*

SIZE: *Around 2¾in (7cm)*

BEHAVIOR: *Peaceful shoaler best kept in a species aquarium, i.e. one set up specifically for it*

DIET: *Wide range of foods accepted once specimens have been adequately acclimatized*

AQUARIUM: *Brightly lit, with ample swimming space and fine-grained substratum recommended. Tannin-stained water (see Aquarium Set-up) advisable. Neutral, softish water preferred, but a little deviation accepted. Temperature range: 73–79°F (23–26°C)*

BREEDING: *Morning sunlight appears to stimulate spawning. Eggs are scattered, and hatch in a little over one day*

ANSORGE'S NEOLEBIAS

Neolebias ansorgii

SYNONYM: *Neolebias ansorgei*
FAMILY: Citharinidae
SUBFAMILY: Distichodontinae

THIS COLORFUL SPECIES (THE MOST COLORFUL OF ITS genus) has been available since the 1920s without ever attaining the high levels of popularity it deserves. It is, nevertheless, the most widely available *Neolebias* species. Unusually for characoids, *Neolebias* species lack an adipose fin.

DISTRIBUTION: *Widely distributed from Cameroon to Congo (Zaire)*

SIZE: *Around 1½in (3.5cm)*

BEHAVIOR: *Peaceful, timid; best kept in a species aquarium, i.e. one set up specifically for it*

DIET: *Livefoods preferred, but other foods accepted*

AQUARIUM: *Subdued lighting, dark substratum, and ample planting recommended, as is relatively shallow water (around 8in/20cm). Raw water must be avoided (add a good conditioner when carrying out partial changes). Slightly acid, softish water preferred. Temperature range: 73–82°F (23–28°C)*

BREEDING: *Peat or moss base recommended. Eggs are scattered, and hatch in about one day*

OTHER *NEOLEBIAS* SPECIES

Four other species of *Neolebias*, in addition to the one featured, are occasionally available.

SCIENTIFIC NAME	COMMON NAME(S)	SIZE
N. axelrodi*	Axelrod's Neolebias	1¼in (3cm)
N. trewavasae*	Three-lined**, or Trewavas', Neolebias	2in (5cm)
N. trilineatus	Three-lined**, Goldband, or Goldenline, Neolebias	2in (5cm)
N. unifasciatus	Schwarzer, or Black, Neolebias, One-banded African Tetra	2in (5cm)

Notes

*These species are more colorful than the others.

**Confusingly, the common name Three-lined Neolebias is sometimes used for both these species. The name seems to be more appropriate for *N. trilineatus*.

AFRICAN PIKE CHARACIN (PHAGO MACULATUS)

AFRICAN PIKE CHARACIN

Phago maculatus

FAMILY: Citharinidae
SUBFAMILY: Distichodontinae

THE THREE MEMBERS OF THIS GENUS (OR FOUR members according to some literature) look quite different from the other citharinids featured above. The body is long and slim, and the mouth is armed with a fearsome set of cutting teeth. The snout itself is elongated into a "beak" whose top half actually lifts when the mouth is opened. Since *Phago* species are known for eating small fishes and biting the fins of larger specimens, they are often referred to as the "fin-eaters."

DISTRIBUTION: *Niger basin in West Africa*

SIZE: *Around 5½in (14cm)*

BEHAVIOR: *Unsociable and highly predatory; despite this, Phago can be very timid in aquaria*

DIET: *May eat larger invertebrate livefoods, but exhibits a clear preference for live fish. This species should therefore be kept only after serious consideration of its dietary requirements*

AQUARIUM: *Roomy, with ample swimming space, and suitable shelters of bogwood or caves. Water chemistry not critical. Temperature range: 73–82°F (23–28°C)*

BREEDING: *No accounts of successful aquarium breeding currently available*

SPOTTED PIKE CHARACIN

Boulengerella maculata

FAMILY: Ctenoluciidae

BUILT IN A WAY THAT CLEARLY INDICATES ITS predatory habits, the Spotted Pike Characin is the most frequently encountered member of its genus. It is demanding in its requirements and is a fish for the specialist.

DISTRIBUTION: *Amazon basin*

HUJETA (CTENOLUCIUS HUJETA)

SIZE: *Up to 13¾in (35cm)*

BEHAVIOR: *May be extremely nervous in exposed aquaria and may injure itself as it dashes about in panic. Group specimens less likely to exhibit this behavior than solitary ones*

DIET: *Juveniles may accept commercial diets, but adults prefer livefoods, particularly small fish—a factor that needs to be taken into consideration before acquiring this species*

AQUARIUM: *Spacious, with large open areas on surface, plus some plant and/or bogwood shelters. Slightly acid to slightly alkaline, soft to medium-hard, well-oxygenated water recommended. Temperature range: 73–81°F (23–27°C)*

BREEDING: *No documented accounts currently available*

HUJETA

PIKE CHARACIN or GAR

Ctenolucius hujeta

Family: Ctenoluciidae

LIKE ITS RELATIVES IN THE GENUS *BOULENGERELLA* (*see* above), the Hujeta is a slim-line fish with a pointed snout in which the lower jaw is slightly shorter than the upper one. It, too, is a fish for the specialist aquarist. Three subspecies are generally recognized: *C. h. beani* (Panama and Colombia); *P. h. insculpus* (Colombia); and *C. h. hujeta* (Venezuela).

DISTRIBUTION: *Central and northwest South America*

SIZE: *Up to 28in (70cm) reported, but usually less than half this size*

BEHAVIOR: *As for* Boulengerella maculata

DIET: *As for* B. maculata

AQUARIUM: *As for* B. maculata, *but surface cover in the form of floating plants may be provided. Temperature range: 72–77°F (22–25°C)*

BREEDING: *Challenging in aquaria, but has been achieved. Chances of success may be improved by using two males to a single female. Eggs may hatch in just under one day*

DIAMOND SPOT CURIMATA

Curimata spilura

FAMILY: Curimatidae
SUBFAMILY: Curimatinae

THE DIAMOND SPOT CURIMATA BELONGS TO A group of some 80 to 90 species, sometimes referred to as the "small curimatas." (The "large curimatas" are distinguished, partly, by their large number (48–110) of lateral line scales.) The small curimatas are subdivided into several groups, sometimes making positive identification difficult. Diamond Spot Curimata belongs to a species complex that carries a more or less conspicuous black spot in the caudal part of the body.

DISTRIBUTION: *Widely distributed in South America*

SIZE: *Around 3½in (9cm)*

BEHAVIOR: *Peaceful shoaler, with distinct appetite for succulent plants and algae*

DIET: *Wide range of foods accepted; vegetable component essential*

AQUARIUM: *Roomy, with good illumination, fine-grained substratum and tough or unpalatable plants (or artificial equivalents), recommended. Water chemistry not critical, but good filtration advisable. Temperature range: 70–81°F (21–27°C)*

BREEDING: *No documented accounts of aquarium breeding currently available*

SILVER PROCHILODUS

Semaprochilodus taeniurus

SYNONYM: *Prochilodus taeniurus*
FAMILY: Curimatidae
SUBFAMILY: Prochilodontinae

WHEN IN PEAK CONDITION, THE SILVER Prochilodus (one of only a few prochilodontids seen with any regularity) is an extremely attractive fish in which the black-and-white markings of the dorsal and caudal fins contrast beautifully with the silvery body and the bright-red pelvic fins. Its main drawbacks as an aquarium fish are its plant-eating and burrowing habits, plus its relatively large size.

DISTRIBUTION: *Brazil and western Colombia*

SIZE: *Up to 12in (30cm)*

BEHAVIOR: *Peaceful, despite its size*

DIET: *As for* Curimata spilura

AQUARIUM: *As for* C. spilura. *Temperature range: 72–79°F (22–26°C)*

BREEDING: *As for* C. spilura

GOLDEN TRAHIRA
BLACKBAND PREDATOR CHARACIN

Hoplerythrinus unitaeniatus

SYNONYMS: *Erythrinus unitaeniatus, E. gronovii, E. kessleri, E. salvus, E. vittatus*
FAMILY: Erythrinidae

THE LARGE NUMBER OF NAMES BY WHICH THIS species has been referred to in scientific and other literature indicates the difficulty encountered when dealing with a widely

distributed and variable species. It is unusual for a characoid in that it lacks an adipose fin. Other features include a thick layer of slippery body mucus and an ability to use its swimbladder as an auxiliary respiratory organ. The Golden Trahira is, most definitely, a fish for the specialist.

DISTRIBUTION: *Guyana, Paraguay, Trinidad and Venezuela*

SIZE: *Up to 40cm (16in)*

BEHAVIOR: *Solitary predator; can be kept with larger fish*

DIET: *Livefoods, including fish—a factor that needs to be considered prior to obtaining a specimen. May be weaned onto dead/frozen foods and some chunky commercial diets*

AQUARIUM: *Large, well-covered, well-filtered, with hiding places and robust plants, recommended. Water chemistry not critical. Temperature range: 72–81°F (22–27°C)*

BREEDING: *No documented accounts of aquarium breeding currently available*

WOLF FISH
SOUTH AMERICAN TIGER FISH

Hoplias malabaricus

FAMILY: Erythrinidae

THE WOLF FISH IS ONE OF THE BEST KNOWN OF all predatory characoids (other than the piranhas), although it is not seen with any great frequency. Like *Hoplerythrinus unitaeniatus* (*see* above), this species is widely distributed. One other species, *H. microlepis*, is very occasionally available: it is somewhat smaller and comes from southern Ecuador, Panama and Costa Rica.

DISTRIBUTION: *Widespread in Central America and northern South America*

SIZE: *Up to 20in (50cm)*

BEHAVIOR: *As for* Hoplerythrinus unitaeniatus

DIET: *As for* Hoplerythrinus unitaeniatus

AQUARIUM: *As for* Hoplerythrinus unitaeniatus

SILVER PROCHILODUS (SEMAPROCHILODUS TAENIURUS)

GOLDEN TRAHIRA (HOPLERYTHRINUS UNITAENIATUS)

WOLF FISH (HOPLIAS MALABARICUS)

BREEDING: *Has been achieved in aquaria, but details not currently available*

BLACK-WINGED HATCHETFISH

Carnegiella marthae

FAMILY: Gasteropelecidae

THIS IS ONE OF THREE *CARNEGIELLA* SPECIES, ALL of which are smaller than their closest relatives, *Gasteropelecus* (*see* below), from which they can also be distinguished by their lack of an adipose fin. The characteristic breast "keel" of hatchetfishes accommodates strong muscles that, allied to the wing-like pectoral fins, allow these fish to jump out of the water and glide (not fly!) for distances up to 50ft (15m), thus helping them escape from predators. All species are highly desirable aquarium fish. A former subspecies of Black-winged Hatchetfish, Scherer's Silver Hatchetfish (*C. m. schereri*) from Peru, is now generally regarded as a full species in its own right, *C. schereri*.

DISTRIBUTION: *Rio Negro area, Orinoco and Venezuela*

SIZE: *Up to 1½in (3.5cm)*

BEHAVIOR: *Peaceful shoaler; should not be kept with boisterous tankmates*

DIET: *Wide range of floating foods accepted; sinking foods usually ignored once they float down below top few centimeters of the water column*

AQUARIUM: *Well-covered and well-filtered, with some clear spaces on the surface, recommended. Plant thickets and some floating plants should be provided as shelter. Softish, slightly acid water*

preferred, as is a water current (produced via the outlet of a power filter or power head). *Temperature range: 73–81°F (23–27°C)*

BREEDING: *Challenging in aquaria. Spawning among the hanging roots of floating plants has been observed. The adhesive eggs stick to the feathery roots and hatch in one to one-and-a-half days*

MYER'S HATCHETFISH

PYGMY HATCHETFISH

Carnegiella myersi

FAMILY: Gasteropelecidae

THIS TINY HATCHETFISH IS NOT SEEN AS FREQUENTLY as its larger relatives although it is every bit as attractive. It should not be kept with larger, boisterous species.

DISTRIBUTION: *Peruvian Amazon, Ucayali river and Bolivia*

SIZE: *Around 1in (2.5cm)*

BEHAVIOR: *Very peaceful shoaler*

DIET: *As for C. marthae*

AQUARIUM: *As for C. marthae*

BREEDING: *No documented accounts currently available*

MARBLED HATCHETFISH

Carnegiella strigata

SYNONYM: *Carnegiella vesca*
FAMILY: Gasteropelecidae

TWO SUBSPECIES OF MARBLED HATCHETFISH (*SEE* photo p.38) are generally recognized: *C.*

strigata strigata, and *C. s. fasciata* (Dark Marbled Hatchetfish), which is found in the more southern regions of the range (although there is some overlap where "intermediate" specimens are known to occur). In *C. s. strigata*, the dark band that originates from the middle of the edge of the breast keel, and extends upward and backward through the body, is divided into two "sub-bands" almost from its point of origin. In *C. s. fasciata*, this dark band does not divide until it reaches the level of the pectoral fins. However, since this feature is variable, unequivocal identification can be difficult. A lutino morph of *C. s. strigata*, which lacks most of the body markings but (unlike albinos) possesses normal-colored eyes, is also occasionally available.

DISTRIBUTION: *Guianas and Amazon basin*

SIZE: *Around 1½in (4cm)*

BEHAVIOR: *As for C. marthae*

DIET: *As for C. marthae*

AQUARIUM: *As for C. marthae. Temperature range: 75–82°F (24–28°C)*

BREEDING: *Soft, acid, heavily tannin-stained water (see Aquarium Set-up) recommended, along with subdued lighting. Eggs are deposited among the feathery roots of floating plants, though not all will remain attached. Hatching takes just over one day*

SILVER HATCHETFISH

Gasteropelecus levis

FAMILY: Gasteropelecidae

THIS SPECIES IS VERY SIMILAR TO *G. STERNICLA* (Common Hatchetfish, *see* p.219), although its colors are somewhat more intense, particularly with regard to the black line that runs from behind the head to the base of the caudal fin.

DISTRIBUTION: *Lower Amazon*

SIZE: *Around 2¼in (6cm)*

BEHAVIOR: *Peaceful, though active, shoaler*

DIET: *As for Carnegiella marthae*

AQUARIUM: *As for C. marthae. Temperature range: 75–86°F (24–30°C)*

BREEDING: *No documented reports currently available*

SPOTTED HATCHETFISH

Gasteropelecus maculatus

SYNONYM: *Thoracocharax maculatus*
FAMILY: Gasteropelecidae

THE SPECKLING ON THE BODY OF THIS SPECIES makes it immediately distinguishable from its closest relatives. It is also the largest member of the genus.

DISTRIBUTION:	*Colombia, Panama, Suriname and Venezuela*
SIZE:	*Up to 3¼in (9cm) reported*
BEHAVIOR:	*As for* Carnegiella marthae
DIET:	*As for* C. marthae
AQUARIUM:	*Basically, as for* C. marthae. *Temperature range: 72–82°F (22–28°C)*
BREEDING:	*No documented reports available, but reproductive strategy assumed to be similar to that of* C. strigata

COMMON HATCHETFISH
BLACK-LINED, or BLACK-STROKE, HATCHETFISH

Gasteropelecus sternicla

FAMILY: Gasteropelecidae

WHILE SIMILAR TO *G. LEVIS* (SILVER HATCHET-fish, *see* p.218), the coloration in the Common Hatchetfish is somewhat less pronounced, a feature that also makes it appear similar to the other Silver Hatchetfish (*Thoracocharax securis, see below*).

DISTRIBUTION:	*Peruvian Amazon, Guianas, Suriname, Trinidad and Mato Grosso (Brazil)*
SIZE:	*Around 2½in (6.5cm)*
BEHAVIOR:	*As for* Carnegiella marthae
DIET:	*As for* C. marthae
AQUARIUM:	*Basically, as for* C. marthae. *Temperature range: 73–82°F (23–28°C)*
BREEDING:	*No documented accounts currently available*

SILVER HATCHETFISH
PECTOROSUS HATCHETFISH

Thoracocharax securis

SYNONYMS: *Gasteropelecus securis, Thoracocharax stellatus, T. pectorosus*
FAMILY: Gasteropelecidae

DEPENDING ON THE LITERATURE CONSULTED, there is either just one species in this genus (*T. securis*) or two, if *T. stellatus* is accepted as a valid species. Both appear almost identical, although *T. stellatus* has a black spot on the base of the dorsal fin and two or three rows of almost-microscopic scales along the base of the anal fin. *T. securis* lacks the spot and has five to six rows of tiny scales. *Thoracocharax* can be distinguished from *Gasteropelecus* by the more pronounced chest profile, whose anterior edge is almost vertical in *Thoracocharax* and more gently sloping in *Gasteropelecus*.

DISTRIBUTION:	*If* T. stellatus *is regarded as synonymous with* T. securis: *widespread in central South America; if not,* T. securis: *middle/upper parts of the Amazon basin*

COMMON HATCHETFISH (GASTEROPELECUS STERNICLA)

SIZE:	*Around 3½in (9cm)*
BEHAVIOR:	*As for* Carnegiella marthae
DIET:	*As for* C. marthae
AQUARIUM:	*Basically, as for* C. marthae. *Temperature range: 73–86°F (23–30°C)*
BREEDING:	*No documented accounts currently available*

SLENDER HEMIODUS

Hemiodopsis gracilis

SYNONYM: *Hemiodus gracilis*
FAMILY: Hemiodontidae (referred to as Hemiodidae by some authors)
SUBFAMILY: Hemiodontinae

THE SYNONYM (*HEMIODUS*), CURRENT GENERIC name (*Hemiodopsis*) and the common name, all reflect the uncertainty that still exists regarding the classification of these characoids. The main feature quoted as distinguishing *Hemiodus* are the scales on the back of adult and semi-adult specimens, which are quite distinctly smaller than those above the pelvic fins.

DISTRIBUTION:	*Amazon and Guyana*
SIZE:	*Around 6in (15cm)*
BEHAVIOR:	*Shoaler, with distinct appetite for succulent plants*
DIET:	*Most foods accepted; vegetable component recommended*
AQUARIUM:	*Spacious, with ample swimming space and robust, unpalatable, or artificial plants. Well-oxygenated water important; water chemistry not critical, but soft, acid conditions preferred. Temperature range: 73–81°F (23–27°C)*
BREEDING:	*No documented accounts currently available*

SLENDER HEMIODUS (HEMIODOPSIS GRACILIS)

HALF-LINED HEMIODUS

BLACK-AND-WHITE TAILED HEMIODUS or SILVER HEMIODUS

Hemiodopsis semitaeniatus

SYNONYMS: *Hemiodus semitaeniatus;* (possibly) *Hemiodopsis argenteus*
FAMILY: Hemiodontidae (referred to as Hemiodidae by some authors)
SUBFAMILY: Hemiodontinae

THE HALF-LINED HEMIODUS IS QUITE SIMILAR TO the previous species, but lacks some of the intensity of *H. gracilis*, particularly the red streak in the lower lobe of the caudal fin. It is also a little larger and possesses more lateral line scales (around 64, as opposed to around 42).

DISTRIBUTION: *Guaporé river*

SIZE: *Up to 8in (20cm) reported, but usually smaller*

BEHAVIOR: *As for* H. gracilis

DIET: *As for* H. gracilis

AQUARIUM: *As for* H. gracilis

BREEDING: *As for* H. gracilis

ONE-SPOT HEMIODUS

YELLOW-TAILED HEMIODUS

Hemiodus unimaculatus

Synonyms: *Anisitsia notata, Hemiodus microcephalus*
FAMILY: Hemiodontidae (referred to as Hemiodidae by some authors)
SUBFAMILY: Hemiodontinae

THE ONE-SPOT HEMIODUS IS SIMILAR IN OVERALL features to *Hemiodopsis microlepis* (Red-tailed, or Feather, Hemiodus), possessing a distinct black body spot and a black- or cream-streaked caudal fin. At full size, it is also slightly larger. In the southern parts of the range, around the Río Paraguay, there is yet another similar-looking species, *Hemiodus orthonops* (which has a greater number of lateral line scales). *Hemiodus rudolphoi* (Rudolph's Hemiodus), the only other species in the genus, is occasionally seen.

DISTRIBUTION: *Rio Negro (Brazil), the Guianas and the Orinoco system*

SIZE: *Up to 7½in (19cm)*

BEHAVIOR: *As for* Hemiodopsis gracilis

DIET: *As for* Hemiodopsis gracilis

AQUARIUM: *As for* Hemiodopsis gracilis

BREEDING: *As for* Hemiodopsis gracilis

ONE-SPOT HEMIODUS (HEMIODUS UNIMACULATUS)

OTHER *HEMIODOPSIS* SPECIES

While the two featured species are the most frequently seen species of *Hemiodopsis*, several others are also occasionally available. All have the same basic characteristics and requirements. The following are the ones most likely to be encountered.

SCIENTIFIC NAME	COMMON NAME(S)	SIZE
H. argenteus*	One-spotted Hemiodus/Hemiodopsis	6in (15cm)
H. goeldii	Goeld's Hemiodus/Hemiodopsis	4¾in (12cm)
H. immaculatus	Silver Hemiodus/Hemiodopsis	8¾in (22cm)
H. microlepis	Red-tailed or Feather Hemiodus/Hemiodopsis	6in (15cm)
H. quadrimaculatus quadrimaculatus	Four-banded Hemiodus/Hemiodopsis	4in (10cm)
H. quadrimaculatus vorderwinkleri	Vorderwinkler's Hemiodus/Hemiodopsis, Torpedo Fish, or Barred Hemiodus	4in (10cm)
H. sterni	Stern's Hemiodus/Hemiodopsis	4in (10cm)

NOTE

* This species may be synonymous with *H. semitaeniatus*

▼ FEATHER HEMIODUS/HEMIODOPSIS (HEMIODOPSIS MICROLEPIS)

AFRICAN PIKE CHARACIN

Hepsetus odoe

SYNONYM: *Sarcodaces odoe*
FAMILY: Hepsetidae

THIS SPECIES IS THE ONLY MEMBER OF ITS GENUS and family. It is built like a pike (*Esox* spp.), as indicated by its common name, and hunts using similar techniques of stealth followed by a lightning-fast strike. This is, most definitely, a species for the specialist.

DISTRIBUTION: *Widely distributed in tropical regions of Africa, except the Nile basin*

SIZE: *Up to 26–28in (65–70cm) reported in the wild, but usually around half this size*

BEHAVIOR: *Solitary predator; can only be kept with tankmates that are far too large to swallow. Can be timid and nervous in bare aquaria*

DIET: *Young specimens can be accustomed to chunky meat- and fish-based foods; adults are considerably more difficult, preferring live fish—a factor that needs to be considered before obtaining a specimen*

AQUARIUM: *Large, well-covered, well-filtered aquarium essential. Use bogwood and rounded rocks to construct shelters—avoid sharp objects as fish may injure themselves during "panic attacks." Water chemistry not critical, but extremes must be avoided. Temperature range: 79–82°F (26–28°C)*

BREEDING: *No documented accounts of aquarium breeding available. In nature, this species is known to build a bubble nest on the surface of the water, into which eggs are deposited; eggs guarded by one or both spawners*

RED-SPOTTED COPEINA

RED-SPOTTED CHARACIN

Copeina guttata

FAMILY: Libiasinidae
SUBFAMILY: Pyrrhulininae

PRIMARILY DISTINGUISHED FROM THE CLOSELY related members of the genus *Copella* (*see below*) by its jawbone characteristics, Red-spotted Copeina is popular for its striking coloration. Specimens in peak condition have a shiny light-blue body overlaid with numerous red spots. The pelvic, anal and lower lobe of the caudal fin all have red borders as well.

DISTRIBUTION: *Amazon basin*

SIZE: *Up to 6in (15cm) reported, but usually only about half this size*

BEHAVIOR: *Peaceful, except during breeding, when males may become aggressive*

DIET: *Wide range of foods accepted*

AQUARIUM: *Large aquarium usually recommended, with fine-grained substratum. Plants not eaten but may be uprooted during nestbuilding. Tannin-stained water (see Aquarium Set-up). Water chemistry not critical, but softish, acid to neutral conditions preferred. Temperature range: 73–82°F (23–28°C)*

BREEDING: *Male hollows out a shallow depression in the substratum, and the pair spawn in it. The eggs are guarded by male until they hatch one-and-a-half to two days later. Recommended breeding temperature: 82–86°F (28–30°C)*

SPLASHING TETRA/CHARACIN

JUMPING, or SPRAYING, TETRA/CHARACIN

Copella arnoldi

SYNONYM: *Copeina arnoldi*
FAMILY: Lebiasinidae
SUBFAMILY: Pyrrhulininae

SPLASHING TETRA OWES ITS COMMON NAMES TO its breeding habits, which are quite unusual. All other members of the genus breed in more "traditional" ways (*see C. metae*).

DISTRIBUTION: *Lower Amazon basin*

SIZE: *Males up to 3¼in (8cm); females somewhat smaller*

that some authorities identify as *Nannobrycon* characteristics. This species lacks an adipose fin.

DISTRIBUTION: *Rio Negro, western Colombia and Guyana*

SIZE: *Around 2in (5cm)*

BEHAVIOR: *As for* N. bifasciatus

DIET: *As for* N. bifasciatus

AQUARIUM: *As for* N. bifasciatus

Breeding: As for N. bifasciatus

ESPE'S PENCILFISH
BARRED PENCILFISH
Nannostomus espei

SYNONYM: *Poecilobrycon espei*
FAMILY: Lebiasinidae
SUBFAMILY: Pyrrhulininae

THIS IS AN ATTRACTIVELY MARKED (THOUGH small) pencilfish in which the body is adorned with a row of black blotches running from head to tail. This species possesses an adipose fin.

DISTRIBUTION: *Southwestern Guyana*

SIZE: *1¼in (3.5cm)*

BEHAVIOR: *As for* N. bifasciatus

DIET: *As for* N. bifasciatus

AQUARIUM: *As for* N. bifasciatus

BREEDING: *As for* N. bifasciatus

HARRISON'S PENCILFISH
Nannostomus harrisoni

SYNONYM: *Poecilobrycon harrisoni*
FAMILY: Lebiasinidae
SUBFAMILY: Pyrrhulininae

THIS PENCILFISH POSSESSES RED MARKINGS ON THE pelvic, anal and caudal fins. These, added to the snout-to-tail body band, make for an impressive show when the species is kept in a large shoal. This species possesses an adipose fin.

DISTRIBUTION: *Guyana*

SIZE: *Around 2½in (6cm)*

BEHAVIOR: *As for* N. bifasciatus

DIET: *As for* N. bifasciatus

AQUARIUM: *As for* N. bifasciatus

BREEDING: *As for* N. bifasciatus

DWARF PENCILFISH
Nannostomus marginatus

FAMILY: Lebiasinidae
SUBFAMILY: Pyrrhulininae

THIS IS A DELIGHTFUL SPECIES THAT, DESPITE ITS small size, creates a sparkling display. It has vivid red coloration on its fins (except the caudal fin), three prominent, dark-brown bands on its body, and a splash of several red scales along the midpoint of the central band. This species lacks an adipose fin.

DISTRIBUTION: *Guyana, Suriname and (possibly) lower reaches of the Amazon*

SIZE: *Around 1½in (3.5cm)*

BEHAVIOR: *As for* N. bifasciatus

DIET: *As for* N. bifasciatus

AQUARIUM: *As for* N. bifasciatus

BREEDING: *As for* N. bifasciatus

THREE-LINED PENCILFISH
Nannostomus trifasciatus

SYNONYMS: *Poecilobrycon trifasciatus, Nannostomus trilineatus*
FAMILY: Lebiasinidae
SUBFAMILY: Pyrrhulininae

THIS THREE-BANDED PENCILFISH CAN BE EASILY distinguished from *N. marginatus* by the two red patches at the base of its caudal fin. It is also a somewhat slimmer and longer species, and it possesses an adipose fin.

DISTRIBUTION: *Wide distribution in the Amazon basin*

SIZE: *Around 2¼in (5.5cm)*

BEHAVIOR: *As for* N. bifasciatus

DIET: *As for* N. bifasciatus

AQUARIUM: *As for* N. bifasciatus

BREEDING: *As for* N. bifasciatus

ONE-LINED PENCILFISH
Nannostomus unifasciatus

SYNONYM: *Nannobrycon unifasciatus*
FAMILY: Lebiasinidae
SUBFAMILY: Pyrrhulininae

THIS PENCILFISH IS ONE OF THE FEW THAT EXHIBIT the "head-up" orientation referred to under *N. beckfordi* (*see* p.223), as well as the enlarged lower caudal fin lobe—hence its synonym, *Nannobrycon*. The One-lined Pencilfish possesses an adipose fin.

DISTRIBUTION: *Middle and upper Amazon basin, Rio Negro, Upper Rio Orinoco and Guyana*

▲ *DWARF PENCILFISH (NANNOSTOMUS MARGINATUS)* ▼ *ONE-LINED PENCILFISH (NANNOSTOMUS UNIFASCIATUS)*

SIZE: *Around 2½in (6cm)*

BEHAVIOR: *As for* N. bifasciatus

DIET: *As for* N. bifasciatus

AQUARIUM: *As for* N. bifasciatus

BREEDING: *As for* N. bifasciatus

SHORT-LINED PYRRHULINA

SCALEBLOTCH PYRRHULINA

Pyrrhulina brevis

FAMILY: Lebiasinidae
SUBFAMILY: Pyrrhulininae

SUPERFICIALLY, MEMBERS OF THIS SPECIES ARE difficult to distinguish from *Copeina* and *Copella* species. There are, however, several cranial and dental characteristics that allow distinctions to be made on close examination of preserved specimens. In live specimens, perhaps the most easily detectable of these features is that, in *Pyrrhulina*, the nostrils are very close to each other. Within the genus *Pyrrhulina* (which—like its close relatives—lacks an adipose fin) confusion still exists regarding the exact number of species or, in some cases, even the full characteristics of single

SHORT-LINED PYRRHULINA (PYRRHULINA BREVIS)

species. The Short-lined Pyrrhulina is one of these, with some of the naturally existing variants possibly constituting subspecies, varieties or full species in their own right.

DISTRIBUTION: *Amazon basin, extending into Colombia (this applies to the Short-lined Pyrrhulina in its broadest sense)*

SIZE: *Up to 3¼in (8cm) reported, but usually around 2in (5cm)*

BEHAVIOR: *May react nervously to external disturbances; prefers to be kept in groups although it does not possess strong shoaling instincts*

DIET: *Predominantly livefoods, but may accept deep-frozen, freeze-dried, and other commercial formulations*

AQUARIUM: *Spacious, well-planted, with subdued lighting and dark substratum recommended. Slightly acid, medium-hard water preferred, particularly if tannin-stained (see Aquarium Set-up). Temperature range: 75–79°F (24–26°C)*

BREEDING: *No documented accounts currently available*

RED-SPOTTED RACHOW'S PYRRHULINA

EYESTROKE PYRRHULINA or FANNING CHARACIN

Pyrrhulina rachoviana

FAMILY: Lebiasinidae
SUBFAMILY: Pyrrhulininae

THIS ATTRACTIVELY MARKED SPECIES HAS A DARK band running from the tip of the snout to the base of the caudal fin and a golden band just above it. The dorsal fin carries a pronounced black blotch, and the body is covered in small red spots.

DISTRIBUTION: *Paraná and Río de la Plata basins*

SIZE: *Up to 2½in (6cm)*

BEHAVIOR: *As for* P. brevis. *Males become aggressive toward each other if kept in a single-sex group*

DIET: *As for* P. brevis

AQUARIUM: *As for* P. brevis

BREEDING: *Soft, acid water at 79–81°F (26–27°C) recommended. Adhesive eggs are laid on broadleaved plant and are subsequently fanned and guarded by male. Hatching takes about one day*

OTHER *PYRRHULINA* SPECIES

Several other *Pyrrhulina* species are available from time to time. They all have the same basic requirements. The sizes quoted are maximum sizes for fully mature males; females are generally smaller.

SCIENTIFIC NAME	COMMON NAME(S)	SIZE
P. eleanori	Elenor's Pyrrhulina	3¼in (8cm)
P. filamentosa	Longfin Pyrrhulina	4¾in (12cm)
P. laeta	Halfstroke or Half-striped Pyrrhulina	3¼in (8cm)
P. spilota	Blotched, or Whiteseam, Pyrrhulina	2½in (6cm)
P. vittata	Striped Pyrrhulina	2½in (6cm)
P. zigzag	Zig-zag or Black Pyrrhulina	3½in (9cm)

ZIG-ZAG PYRRHULINA VAR. "BLACK BLOTCHES" (PYRRHULINA ZIGZAG)

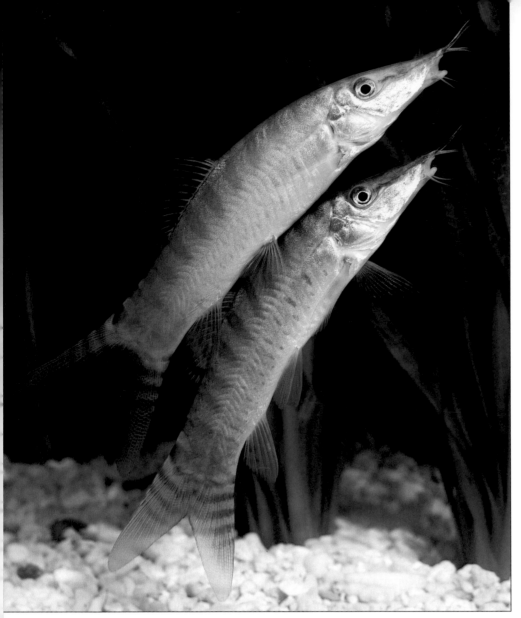

BANDED LOACH

Botia helodes

FAMILY: Cobitidae
SUBFAMILY: Botinae

THIS SPECIES IS SOMETIMES AVAILABLE AS *B. hymenophysa*, but the true *B. hymenophysa* has a different range (Borneo, southern Malaysia and Sumatra). Like some other *Botia* species, Banded Loach can produce clicking sounds when excited.

DISTRIBUTION: *Southeast Asia, but not overlapping B. hymenophysa*

SIZE: *Up to 8¾in (22cm), but usually smaller*

BEHAVIOR: *Very active and potentially aggressive, particularly toward conspecifics; most active in the evening and at night; likes to burrow*

DIET: *Wide range of foods accepted*

AQUARIUM: *A fine-grained substratum and shelters should be provided, but protect plants (see Aquarium Plants). Soft, slightly acid water and subdued lighting preferred. Temperature range: 75–86°F (24–30°C)*

BREEDING: *No documented accounts currently available*

PAKISTANI LOACH

Y-LOACH

Botia lohachata

FAMILY: Cobitidae
SUBFAMILY: Botinae

BOLDLY MARKED IN BLACK AND WHITE OR BLACK and cream (though the intensity of coloration can vary), this species can prove nervous and easily frightened during the initial stages of acclimatization to a new aquarium.

DISTRIBUTION: *Northern and northeastern India, and Bangladesh*

SIZE: *Up to 4¾in (12cm) reported, but usually much smaller*

BEHAVIOR: *As for B. helodes*

DIET: *As for B. helodes*

AQUARIUM: *As for B. helodes*

BREEDING: *As for B. helodes*

CLOWN LOACH

TIGER LOACH

Botia macracantha

SYNONYM: *Botia macracanthus*
FAMILY: Cobitidae
SUBFAMILY: Botinae

THIS IS THE BEST-KNOWN AND PROBABLY THE MOST attractive of the *Botia* loaches (*see* photo p.226). Owing to its relatively large size, it is considered a food fish in its native waters.

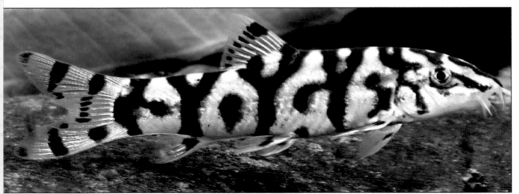

▲▲ *BANDED LOACH (*BOTIA HELODES*)*　　▲ *PAKISTANI LOACH (*BOTIA LOHACHATA*)*

attractive species totally unsuitable for most home aquaria.

DISTRIBUTION: *Yangtze River (China)*

SIZE: *Up to 39in (1m)*

BEHAVIOR: *A peaceful bottom dweller*

DIET: *Wide range of foods accepted, but diet must include vegetable component*

AQUARIUM: *Large, deep aquarium essential once specimens are approximating even one quarter of their eventual size. Efficient filtration, high oxygenation, and water current (as produced by a powerhead outlet), also recommended. Water chemistry not critical. Temperature range: below 59°F (15°C) to around 72°F (22°C)*

BREEDING: *No documented accounts currently available*

DISTRIBUTION: *Borneo, Sumatra and Indonesia*

SIZE: *Up to 12in (30cm) reported, but usually smaller*

BEHAVIOR: *An active shoaler that should be kept in groups; less aggressive than some other* Botia

species and more active during the day. May lie on its side, seemingly dead or dying, for some time; such specimens are, however, perfectly healthy and appear to be resting or asleep (some other Botia *species are also known to exhibit this behavior).*

ORANGE-FINNED LOACH (BOTIA MODESTA)

OTHER *BOTIA* SPECIES

In addition to the featured species, other *Botia* loaches are available on a more or less regular basis. All have the same basic requirements, and some exhibit the unusual "lying-on-the-side" behavior of *B. macracantha* (see p.228). The following are among the most frequently imported species. Sizes quoted are approximate maximums for wild-caught specimens.

SCIENTIFIC NAME	COMMON NAME(S)	SIZE
B. beauforti *	Beaufort's Loach	8in (20cm)
B. berdmorei *	None	10in (25cm)
B. dario	Bengal Loach	4in (10cm)
B. morleti (formerly horae)	Hora's Loach	4in (10cm)
B. striata	Zebra Loach	4in (10cm)

NOTE

*It is possible that *B. berdmorei* and *B. beauforti* may be one and the same species. However, until this matter is decided, they are generally regarded as separate species.

BEAUFORT'S LOACH (BOTIA BEAUFORTI) ▼

DIET: *As for B. helodes*

AQUARIUM: *As for B. helodes*

BREEDING: *Has been bred commercially, but only rarely in aquaria*

ORANGE-FINNED LOACH
BLUE LOACH
Botia modesta

FAMILY: Cobitidae
SUBFAMILY: Botinae

THIS IS AN UNUSUALLY, BUT MOST ATTRACTIVELY, colored species. It is sometimes confused with *B. lecontei* (Leconte's Loach). However, in Orange-finned Loach, all the fins are orange to yellow, while in *B. lecontei*, the dorsal fin is grayish blue.

DISTRIBUTION: *Malaysia, Thailand and Vietnam*

SIZE: *Up to 9½in (24cm) reported, but usually much smaller*

BEHAVIOR: *Can be timid; may be kept in a group*

DIET: *As for B. helodes*

AQUARIUM: *As for B. helodes*

BREEDING: *As for B. helodes*

CHAIN LOACH
DWARF LOACH
Botia sidthimunki

FAMILY: Cobitidae
SUBFAMILY: Botinae

THIS SMALL GEM IS AVAILABLE MORE WIDELY THAN it was during the latter decades of the 20th century. For optimum effect, it is best to maintain a shoal of a minimum of six specimens.

DISTRIBUTION: *Northern India and northern Thailand*

SIZE: *Up to 2¼in (5.5cm)*

BEHAVIOR: *An active species that likes to rest on broadleaved plants in full view. Unlike some other* Botia *species, it does not avoid bright lights.*

DIET: *As for B. helodes*

AQUARIUM: *As for B. helodes*

BREEDING: *As for B. helodes*

HORSE-FACED LOACH
LONG-NOSED LOACH
Acanthopsis choirorhynchus

FAMILY: Cobitidae
SUBFAMILY: Cobitinae

THIS DELICATELY MARKED SPECIES IS A POOR swimmer, which spends most of its time on the bottom or actually buried in the

BREEDING: *Shallow water preferred; a bubble nest is usually, but not invariably, built. Hatching takes one to two days*

COMBTAIL
Belontia signata

FAMILY: Belontiidae
SUBFAMILY: Belontiinae

ADULT SPECIMENS EXHIBIT THE EXTENDED RAYS in the caudal fin, which gives rise to the common name of this impressive species. Two subspecies are generally recognized: *B. s. signata* (the "traditional" Combtail), and *B. s. jonklaasi* (Pectoral Spot Combtail), also from Sri Lanka. There is also a dark-bodied morph named "Kottawa Forest."

DISTRIBUTION: *Sri Lanka*

SIZE: *Up to 6in (15cm) reported, but often smaller*

BEHAVIOR: *Can be quite aggressive, particularly at breeding time*

DIET: *As for* B. hasselti

AQUARIUM: *As for* B. hasselti, *but less alkaline conditions and slightly lower temperatures preferred*

BREEDING: *Basically, as for* B. hasselti. *Hatching takes about one-and-a-half days*

SLENDER BETTA
Betta bellica

FAMILY: Belontiidae
SUBFAMILY: Macropodinae

BOTH ADULT MALES AND FEMALES OF THIS SPECIES have a yellowish-brown anterior half, with bluish-green scales appearing pro-gressively down the body. The fins also have this bluish-green sheen. Males have longer, more pointed fins than do females.

DISTRIBUTION: *Mainly Perak region of peninsular Malaysia*

SIZE: *Around 4¼in (11cm)*

BEHAVIOR: *Relatively peaceful, despite its* bellica *("warlike") species name*

DIET: *Livefoods, deep-frozen and freeze-dried diets preferred, but other foods may also be accepted*

AQUARIUM: *Densely planted (including floating vegetation), with a number of shelters. Illumination not too bright. Soft, acid water. Temperature range: 75–82°F (24–28°C)*

BREEDING: *A challenging bubble-nesting species*

WINE RED FIGHTER
CLARET BETTA
Betta coccina

FAMILY: Belontiidae
SUBFAMILY: Macropodinae

THIS EXCEPTIONALLY MARKED SPECIES HAS A reddish-brown body with longitudinal bands and a central spot (not always visible). The dorsal and caudal fins are delicately edged in bluish white.

DISTRIBUTION: *Reported from southern peninsular Malaysia and central Sumatra*

SIZE: *Up to 2¼in (5.5cm) reported, but often smaller*

BEHAVIOR: *Timid, retiring; must not be kept with boisterous tankmates*

▲ COMBTAIL (BELONTIA SIGNATA)

▼ SLENDER BETTA (BETTA BELLICA)

▲ *WINE RED FIGHTER (BETTA COCCINA)*
◀ *FEMALE CRESCENT BETTA (BETTA IMBELLIS)*

DISTRIBUTION: *Western Borneo, northeast Sumatra and Malaysia*

SIZE: *Around 2in (5cm)*

BEHAVIOR: *Relatively peaceful, except at breeding time or when a new specimen is introduced into the aquarium*

DIET: *As for* B. bellica

AQUARIUM: *As for* B. bellica

BREEDING: *Easier than* B. bellica *and* B. coccina. *Male builds bubble nest under floating or submerged leaves; spawning is nonviolent, and male guards the eggs and newly hatched fry. Hatching can take up to three days*

PENANG MOUTH-BROODING BETTA

Betta pugnax

FAMILY: Belontiidae
SUBFAMILY: Macropodina

THIS WAS ONE OF THE EARLY *BETTA* SPECIES TO BE imported, arriving in 1905. It has never become widespread in the hobby, having been overshadowed by its more spectacular relative, B. splendens (Siamese Fighter). It is nevertheless a delicately colored species worthy of greater recognition. Several naturally occurring color morphs are known.

DISTRIBUTION: *Malaysia*

DIET: *As for* B. bellica

AQUARIUM: *Basically, as for* B. bellica; *lighting levels should be subdued*

BREEDING: *As for* B. bellica

CRESCENT BETTA

PEACEFUL BETTA

Betta imbellis

FAMILY: Belontiidae
SUBFAMILY: Macropodinae

THE CRESCENT FROM WHICH ONE OF THE COMMON names for this species is derived is particularly well-exhibited on the caudal fin of males in peak condition. The deep red of this crescent is also evident on the anal and pelvic fins.

SIZE: *Up to 4¾in (12cm), but usually smaller*

BEHAVIOR: *Relatively peaceful except during breeding*

DIET: *As for B. bellica*

AQUARIUM: *Basically, as for B. bellica, but slow water flow appreciated. Tannin-stained water (see Aquarium Set-up) advisable*

BREEDING: *A mouthbrooding species in which male retains the eggs and larvae in his mouth for about ten days*

EMERALD BETTA

SMARAGD BETTA/FIGHTER

Betta smaragdina

FAMILY: Belontiidae
SUBFAMILY: Macropodinae

ALTHOUGH INTRODUCED ONLY AROUND 1970, the Emerald Betta has become one of the more popular *Betta* species in the hobby. It is a truly magnificent species when in peak condition, rivaling both B. *imbellis* and B. *splendens* in beauty.

DISTRIBUTION: *Cambodia, Laos, northeastern and eàstern Thailand*

SIZE: *Up to 2¾in (7cm)*

BEHAVIOR: *Males are aggressive toward each other, but will accept several females in the same aquarium; should not be kept with boisterous tankmates*

DIET: *As for B. bellica*

AQUARIUM: *As for B. bellica*

BREEDING: *A bubble-nester that can be relatively easily bred. Nests may be built at water surface, or under submerged leaf or other surface. Male guards the eggs and newly hatched fry*

SIAMESE FIGHTER

Betta splendens

FAMILY: Belontiidae
SUBFAMILY: Macropodinae

THIS FAMOUS OLD FAVORITE WAS IMPORTED INTO Europe during the last decade of the 19th century and has been popular ever since. It was originally renowned, not just for its coloration, but for its fighting qualities. As far as the aquarium hobby is concerned, though, the species' ongoing popularity is owed to the exceptionally colorful, long-finned varieties that have been developed over the years. This is a "must keep" fish for every aquarist at some stage.

DISTRIBUTION: *Southeast Asia, but some self-sustaining populations have become established in a number of nonnative locations in, e.g., Laos, Myanmar (Burma) and Colombia*

SIZE: *Up to 2½in (6cm)*

BEHAVIOR: *Males will fight, sometimes to the death; otherwise, a slow-moving, tolerant, retiring species that should not be kept with boisterous tankmates; males become territorial during breeding and aggressive toward females after spawning*

DIET: *Wide range of livefoods and commercial formulations accepted*

AQUARIUM: *As for* B. bellica

BREEDING: *Male builds beautiful bubble nest at water surface, and guards the eggs and newly hatched fry for several days. Hatching takes about one day*

*SIAMESE FIGHTER (*Betta splendens*)*

OTHER *BETTA* SPECIES

During the 1980s and 1990s, there was a significant increase in the number of *Betta* species discovered, described, and introduced into the specialist sector of the aquarium hobby. Most of these species, while available through anabantoid societies, are rarely encountered in stores. However, as the numbers bred in captivity continue to increase, some will become better known and more widely available. Seek detailed advice before attempting to keep and breed these species (*see also* Bibliography). The list that follows includes many of the new *Betta* species, along with all the older ones that have not been featured in the main entries. Most require the same basic care outlined for the featured species.

SCIENTIFIC NAME	COMMON NAME(S)	SIZE	BREEDING
B. akarensis	Akara Betta	4¾in (12cm)	MB
B. albimarginata	Whiteseam Betta	2in (5cm)	MB?
B. anabatoides	Unspotted Betta	5in (13cm)	MB
B. balunga	Balunga Betta	5½in (14cm)	MB
B. brownorum	Brown's Red Dwarf Betta	1½in (4cm)	BN
B. chloropharynx	Greenthroat Betta	5½in (14cm)	MB
B. climacura	Ladder Betta	5½in (14cm)	MB
B. dimidiata	Dwarf Betta	2¾in (7cm)	MB
B. edithae	Edith's Betta	3⅓in (8.5cm)	MB
B. foerschi	Foersh's Betta	2¾in (7cm)	MB
B. fusca	Brown Betta	4¾in (12cm)	MB
B. livida	Selangor Red Betta	2in (5cm)	BN
B. macrostoma	Peacock Betta	5½in (14cm)	MB
B. ocellata	Eye-spot Betta	4¾in (12cm)	MB
B. persephone	Black Betta	1½in (4cm)	BN
B. picta	Javan Betta	2⅜in (6cm)	MB
B. rutilans	Red Dwarf Betta	2⅜in (6cm)	BN
B. simorum	Simor Betta	4¾in (12cm)	BN
B. taeniata	Striped Betta	3in (8cm)	MB
B. tussyae	Tussy's Betta	2⅜in (6cm)	BN

Notes:

a) In this list, BN = bubble-nester; MB = mouthbrooder

b) In the common names (which may vary from author to author), the term Betta is frequently used interchangeably with Fighter or—as in the case of oral brooders—with Mouthbrooder.

ONE-SPOT BETTA
ONE-SPOT FIGHTER

Betta unimaculata

FAMILY: Belontiidae
SUBFAMILY: Macropodinae

THIS IS A SLENDER-BODIED *BETTA* WITH THE characteristically large mouth of a mouth-brooding species. The anal and caudal fins of males exhibit intensified blue-green coloration at breeding time; a spot behind the gills becomes similarly colored.

DISTRIBUTION: *Kalimantan Timur and Sabah (Borneo)*

SIZE: *Up to 4¾in (12cm), but often smaller*

BEHAVIOR: *Generally peaceful toward conspecifics; peaceful and tolerant toward other species*

DIET: *Livefoods preferred, but other diets also accepted*

AQUARIUM: *As for* B. bellica

BREEDING: *Eggs are incubated orally by male. Hatching and subsequent release of fry takes about nine to ten days in total*

INDIAN GOURAMI
NOBLE GOURAMI, CTENOPS
Ctenops nobilis

FAMILY: Belontiidae
SUBFAMILY: Macropodinae

ALTHOUGH THE INDIAN GOURAMI WAS IMPORTED into Europe during the early decades of the 20th century, it never attained wide popularity owing to its "challenging" requirements and delicate nature. This is, undoubtedly, a species that should be kept only by experienced aquarists. Kept in appropriate conditions, it is a truly beautiful fish.

DISTRIBUTION: *Eastern India and Bangladesh*

SIZE: *Up to 4¾in (12cm), but usually smaller*

BEHAVIOR: *Shy, retiring; must not be kept with boisterous tankmates*

DIET: *Livefoods preferred, but deep-frozen, freeze-dried, and some other commercial diets, may be accepted*

AQUARIUM: *Heavily planted, tranquil, with subdued lighting and numerous bogwood shelters. Softish, neutral water advisable, with a little deviation tolerated. Temperature range: 77–86°F (25–30°C)*

BREEDING: *Very challenging and infrequent in aquaria. Small numbers of eggs are incubated orally by female who releases free-swimming fry 10–15 days after spawning*

BLACK PARADISE FISH
Macropodus concolor

SYNONYM: *Macropodus opercularis concolor*
FAMILY: Belontiidae
SUBFAMILY: Macropodinae

THERE HAS LONG BEEN CONTROVERSY REGARDING the status of this fish. Some believe it to be a subspecies of the better-known *M. opercularis* (Paradise Fish), while others see it merely as a naturally occurring morph. Most modern opinion, however, tends toward regarding it as a valid species in its own right, despite the ease with which it hybridizes with *M. opercularis* to produce the Dark Paradise Fish.

DISTRIBUTION: *Cambodia and Vietnam*

SIZE: *Males around 4¾in (12cm); females somewhat smaller*

BEHAVIOR: *Considerably less aggressive than* M. opercularis, *but territorial during breeding*

DIET: *Wide range of foods accepted*

AQUARIUM: *Spacious, well-planted, with some open areas and shelters. Water chemistry not critical. Temperature range: 68–79°F (20–26°C)*

BREEDING: *Male builds bubble nests and vigorously defends nest, eggs and subsequent fry until they are free-swimming. Hatching takes about one day*

CHINESE PARADISE FISH
ROUND-TAILED PARADISE FISH
Macropodus ocellatus

SYNONYM: *Macropodus chinensis*
FAMILY: Belontiidae
SUBFAMILY: Macropodinae

THIS EXCEPTIONALLY BEAUTIFUL SPECIES IS SEEN much less frequently than its two closest relatives. Despite one of its common names, the caudal fin of fully adult males tends to have a blunted-tip profile rather than a smoothly rounded one. This species is known to hybridize with *M. opercularis*: the hybrids are sometimes referred to as Matte's Paradise Fish.

DISTRIBUTION: *Southern China and (possibly) Korea*

SIZE: *Males around 3in (8cm); females smaller*

BEHAVIOR: *As for* M. concolor

DIET: *As for* M. concolor

AQUARIUM: *As for* M. concolor

BREEDING: *As for* M. concolor. *Temperature range: around 61°F (16°C) to 79°F (26°C)*

PARADISE FISH
Macropodus opercularis

FAMILY: Belontiidae
SUBFAMILY: Macropodinae

THIS WAS THE FIRST "TROPICAL" FISH TO BE imported into Europe (arriving in 1869). It soon became popular because of its hardiness, coloration and interesting breeding habits. Today, it is still widely available and popular in a range of colors, from the wild type, through a "blue," to an albino form. This species hybridizes easily with its two closest relatives (*see M. concolor* and *M. ocellatus*).

DISTRIBUTION: *Southern China, Vietnam, Korea, Taiwan and other islands in the region*

SIZE: *Males up to 4¾in (12cm); females smaller*

BEHAVIOR: *More aggressive and territorial than its relatives; keep only one male per aquarium*

DIET: *As for* M. concolor

AQUARIUM: *As for* M. concolor. *Temperature range: below 61°F (16°C) to 82°F (28°C)*

BREEDING: *As for* M. concolor

ORNATE GOURAMI
PARADISE FISH, MALPULUTTA, SPOTTED POINTED-TAIL GOURAMI
Malpulutta kretseri

FAMILY: Belontiidae
SUBFAMILY: Macropodinae

THIS IS A DELICATE-LOOKING SPECIES, CONSIDERED to be under some threat in the wild. It has never been available in large numbers, but captive-bred stocks from specialist aquarists, as well as from a long-term commercial government-approved project, may ensure a continued limited supply. Two subspecies are generally recognized: *M. k. kretseri* and, a bluer type, *M. k. minor*. There is also a violet-tinged morph.

DISTRIBUTION: *Sri Lanka*

PARADISE FISH (MACROPODUS OPERCULARIS)

SIZE: *Up to 3½in (9cm) reported, but most specimens less than 2½in (6cm) long*

BEHAVIOR: *Shy, retiring*

DIET: *Small livefoods preferred, but some commercial diets also accepted*

AQUARIUM: *Quiet, well-covered, well-planted, with surface plants, a number of shelters, subdued lighting, and dark substratum. Water soft and acid, though some deviation may be accepted. Temperature range: 75–82°F (24–28°C)*

BREEDING: *Male builds bubble nest under leaf or overhang, and guards the eggs and newly hatched fry. Hatching takes about two days*

LICORICE DWARF GOURAMI

LIQUORICE, or SPLENDID, DWARF GOURAMI

Parosphromenus deisneri

FAMILY: Belontiidae
SUBFAMILY: Macropodinae

THIS IS, BY FAR, THE MOST FREQUENTLY AVAILABLE of all the licorice gourami species. It has a long history in the hobby, having first been imported in 1914, but its rather demanding requirements mean that it is often not seen at its best in aquatic stores—a factor that has undoubtedly contributed to its somewhat limited occurrence in home aquaria.

DISTRIBUTION: *Banka (Indonesia), peninsular Malaysia and Sumatra*

SIZE: *Around 1¼in (4cm), although 3in (7.5cm) reported*

BEHAVIOR: *Gentle, slow-moving; must not be kept with boisterous tankmates*

DIET: *Small livefoods preferred, but some commercial diets may also be accepted*

AQUARIUM: *As for* Malpulutta kretseri

BREEDING: *Male builds bubble nest (usually in a cave), often after egg release. Hatching can take three days. Male guards the eggs and newly hatched fry*

SPIKE-TAILED PARADISE FISH

RED-EYE SPIKETAIL

Pseudosphromenus cupanus

SYNONYM: *Macropodus cupanus*
FAMILY: Belontiidae
SUBFAMILY: Macropodinae

ALTHOUGH THE OLD NAME FOR THIS SPECIES IS NOW disappearing from aquarium literature, it is still encountered from time to time. It is a relic of the days when this species and *P. dayi* were believed to be more closely related to *Macropodus opercularis* than they

---

OTHER *PAROSPHROMENUS* SPECIES

The 1980s and 1990s saw a marked increase in the number of *Parosphromenus* species discovered and described. This increase mirrored, though on a more modest scale, the *Betta* "explosion" referred to in the OTHER *BETTA* SPECIES table (*see* p.238). Most of the "new" *Parosphromenus* are generally available through specialist anabantoid societies, though a few, such as the featured species and *P. filamentosus*, are also encountered from time to time in stores. The list that follows includes some of the newer species, as well as all the older ones. There are also, in addition, several species that are awaiting description. Most have similar requirements to *P. deisneri*, but specialist advice should be sought.

SCIENTIFIC NAME	COMMON NAME(S)	SIZE
P. allani	Allan's Licorice/Liquorice Gourami	1½in (4cm)
P. anjuganensis	Anjugan Licorice/Liquorice Gourami	1½in (4cm)
P. filamentosus	Filament-tailed Licorice/Liquorice Gourami	1½in (4cm)
P. harveyi	Harvey's Licorice/Liquorice Gourami	1½in (4cm)
P. linkei	Linke's Licorice/Liquorice Gourami	1½in (4cm)
P. nagyi	Nagy's Licorice/Liquorice Gourami	1½in (4cm)
P. ornaticauda	Red-tailed Licorice/Liquorice Gourami	1¼in (3cm)
P. paludicola	Swamp Licorice/Liquorice Gourami	1½in (4cm)
P. parvulus	Small Licorice/Liquorice Gourami	1¼in (3cm)

actually are. Both *Pseudosphromenus* were also once believed to be subspecies, rather than distinct valid species.

DISTRIBUTION: *Probably from southern India, originally; now found in Sri Lanka and (possibly) Bengal, Myanmar (Burma), Sumatra and Tonkin (north Vietnam)*

SIZE: *Around 2½in (6cm)*

BEHAVIOR: *Peaceful; should not be kept with boisterous tankmates*

DIET: *Wide range of foods accepted*

AQUARIUM: *Heavily planted, with caves or other shelters, and dark substratum. Water chemistry not critical. Temperature range: around 68°F (20°C) to 82°F (28°C)*

BREEDING: *Male builds bubble nest under broad leaf or in a cave. Egg care usually undertaken by male, but female may participate. Hatching takes about two days*

DAY'S SPIKE-TAILED PARADISE FISH

BROWN SPIKE-TAILED PARADISE FISH, DAY'S SPIKETAIL

Pseudosphromenus dayi

SYNONYM: *Macropodus dayi*
FAMILY: Belontiidae
SUBFAMILY: Macropodinae

ADULT MALES OF THIS SPECIES POSSESS FINE extensions on the central rays of the caudal fin, along with bright greenish-blue fin edges. There are also two dark bands on the body, which run all the way from the

head to the caudal peduncle. Hybridization between the two *Pseudosphromenus* species is known to occur, with the resulting hybrids being fertile.

DISTRIBUTION: *Range said to include southern and western India, Sri Lanka, Vietnam, Sumatra, Myanmar (Burma) and the Malabar Coast*

SIZE: *Up to 3in (7.5cm) reported, but usually smaller*

FEMALE SPIKE-TAILED PARADISE FISH
(PSEUDOSPHROMENUS CUPANUS)

BEHAVIOR: *As for P. cupanus*

DIET: *As for P. cupanus*

AQUARIUM: *As for P. cupanus; temperature range may be even wider*

BREEDING: *Normally, a bubble-nester (like P. cupanus); but in colder parts of its range has been reported as spawning like cichlids.*

DWARF CROAKING GOURAMI
PYGMY CROAKING GOURAMI
Trichopsis pumilus

SYNONYM: *Trichopsis pumila*
FAMILY: Belontiidae
SUBFAMILY: Macropodinae

THE THREE SPECIES BELONGING TO THE GENUS *Trichopsis* are capable of producing croaking sounds, hence the common names of this species and *T. vittatus*. All three are slender species with pointed snouts resembling some of the *Parosphromenus* species, to which they are related. The Dwarf Croaking Gourami is, reportedly, capable of hybridizing with *T. schalleri*, with the resulting offspring being fertile.

DISTRIBUTION: *Indonesia, Malaysia and Thailand*

SIZE: *Up to 1½in (4cm)*

BEHAVIOR: *Peaceful; must not be kept with boisterous tankmates*

DIET: *Wide range of foods accepted*

AQUARIUM: *As for Pseudosphromenus cupanus, but water should be closer to soft, acid end of the chemistry spectrum. Temperature range: 77–82°F (25–28°C)*

BREEDING: *Bubble nest of variable quality is built, and the eggs and newly hatched fry are guarded by male. Hatching takes about two days*

SPARKLING GOURAMI
SCHALLER'S GOURAMI
Trichopsis schalleri

FAMILY: Belontiidae
SUBFAMILY: Macropodinae

THIS IS PERHAPS THE MOST BEAUTIFUL OF THE THREE *Trichopsis* species, with specimens in peak condition living up to the "sparkling" label. Sparkling Gourami is reported to produce fertile hybrids in crosses with its two close relatives.

DISTRIBUTION: *Southern Thailand*

SIZE: *Up to 2¼in (6cm)*

BEHAVIOR: *As for T. pumilus*

DIET: *As for T. pumilus*

AQUARIUM: *As for T. pumilus*

BREEDING: *As for T. pumilus*

BANDED GOURAMI (COLISA FASCIATA)

CROAKING GOURAMI
Trichopsis vittatus

SYNONYM: *Trichopsis vittata*
FAMILY: Belontiidae
SUBFAMILY: Macropodinae

SEVERAL FORMS OF THIS SPECIES ARE KNOWN IN THE wild, including a two-spot type and a blue one (sometimes referred to as *T. harrisi*). Owing to its widespread distribution and variability, some doubts remain regarding the correct identification of the various types. The Croaking Gourami is known to interbreed with *T. schalleri*, with the resulting offspring being fertile.

DISTRIBUTION: *Widely distributed in southeast Asia*

SIZE: *Up to 2¼in (7cm), but often smaller*

BEHAVIOR: *As for T. pumilus*

DIET: *As for T. pumilus*

AQUARIUM: *As for T. pumilus. Temperature range: 72–82°F (22–28°C).*

BREEDING: *As for T. pumilus. Male may build more substantial bubble nest than his T. pumilus and T. schalleri counterparts. Hatching takes about one day*

HONEY GOURAMI
HONEY DWARF GOURAMI
Colisa chuna

SYNONYM: *Colisa sota*
FAMILY: Belontiidae
SUBFAMILY: Trichogasterinae (Trichogastrinae in *Nelson* 1994—*see* Bibliography)

THE SCIENTIFIC NAME OF THIS, THE SMALLEST member of the genus *Colisa*, has oscillated over time, with current opinion settling on *Colisa chuna*. The Honey Gourami is different from the other *Colisa* species in that it lacks oblique body bands. Males in nuptial coloration are particularly impressive, especially when they "stand on their tails" during courtship displays. Golden, peach and mottled varieties are frequently available.

DISTRIBUTION: *Northeastern India and Bangladesh*

SIZE: *Up to 2¼in (7cm), but generally smaller*

BEHAVIOR: *Peaceful, retiring; should not be kept with boisterous tankmates*

DIET: *Most foods accepted*

AQUARIUM: *Heavily planted, tranquil, with surface vegetation and adequate shelter. Water chemistry not critical. Temperature range: 72–82°F (22–28°C)*

BREEDING: *Male builds good bubble nest, and guards the eggs and newly hatched fry. Hatching takes about one day*

BANDED GOURAMI
STRIPED, INDIAN, or GIANT, GOURAMI
Colisa fasciata

FAMILY: Belontiidae
SUBFAMILY: Trichogasterinae (Trichogastrinae in *Nelson* 1994—*see* Bibliography)

THIS SPECIES HAS BEEN KNOWN IN THE HOBBY FOR over 100 years. However, unlike the three other members of the genus, it has never been developed into fin or color varieties. The Banded Gourami will interbreed with its closest relatives, *C. labiosa* and *C. lalia*; the resulting hybrids from *C. labiosa* crosses are fertile.

DISTRIBUTION: *Most of India, except south and southwest; also reported from Myanmar (Burma)*

SIZE: *Up to 4¾in (12cm) reported, but usually a little smaller*

BEHAVIOR: *Peaceful toward other species, except during breeding; males somewhat less peaceful toward each other*

DIET: *As for* C. chuna

AQUARIUM: *As for* C. chuna

BREEDING: *As for* C. chuna

THICK-LIPPED GOURAMI

THICKLIP GOURAMI

Colisa labiosa

FAMILY: Belontiidae
SUBFAMILY: Trichogasterinae (Trichogastrinae in *Nelson* 1994—*see* Bibliography)

CLOSELY RELATED TO *C. FASCIATA*, THE THICK-lipped Gourami can be immediately recognized by its smaller head and (in fully mature males) the elegantly extended tip of the dorsal fin. *C. labiosa* x *fasciata* hybrids are fertile, while *C. labiosa* x *lalia* are not. A peach-colored variety is widely available.

DISTRIBUTION: *Irrawaddy River (Myanmar/Burma)*

SIZE: *Up to 4in (10cm) reported, but usually smaller*

BEHAVIOR: *As for* C. fasciata

DIET: *As for* C. chuna

AQUARIUM: *As for* C. chuna

BREEDING: *As for* C. chuna

DWARF GOURAMI

Colisa lalia

FAMILY: Belontiidae
SUBFAMILY: Trichogasterinae (Trichogastrinae in *Nelson* 1994—*see* Bibliography)

THIS IS THE MOST WIDELY KEPT *COLISA* SPECIES (*see* photo p.232). It has been developed into a number of color forms, the best

known being the Sunset (Red), Rainbow, Blue, Neon, and Multicolored. *C. lalia* will hybridize with both *C. fasciata* and *C. labiosa*, although the hybrids are infertile.

DISTRIBUTION: *Northern India*

SIZE: *Up to 2¼in (6cm), but usually smaller*

BEHAVIOR: *More tolerant of conspecific males than are* C. fasciata *and* C. labiosa

DIET: *As for* C. chuna

AQUARIUM: *As for* C. chuna

BREEDING: *As for* C. chuna; *male builds exceptional nest containing interwoven vegetation*

FALSE CHOCOLATE GOURAMI

Parasphaerichthys ocellatus

FAMILY: Belontiidae
SUBFAMILY: Trichogasterinae (Trichogastrinae in *Nelson* 1994—*see* Bibliography)

ALTHOUGH DESCRIBED AS LONG AGO AS 1929, this remains one of the rarely seen species. It is a somewhat more elongate fish than *Sphaerichthys osphromenoides* (Chocolate Gourami), with a rounded tail. Exacting in its demands, it is undoubtedly one for the specialist and best avoided by new aquarists.

DISTRIBUTION: *Mountain streams in northern Myanmar (Burma)*

SIZE: *Up to 2¼in (6cm) reported, but usually smaller*

BEHAVIOR: *Shy, retiring; can be kept only with quiet tankmates*

DIET: *Small livefoods, although some deep-frozen/freeze-dried foods may be accepted; dried formulations may be accepted only reluctantly*

AQUARIUM: *Well-planted, with surface vegetation and subdued lighting important. Soft, slightly acid to neutral water. Temperature range: 72–77°F (22–25°C)*

BREEDING: *No documented accounts available; may be a mouthbrooder like* Sphaerichthys *(see following entries)*

POINTED-MOUTHED GOURAMI

LARGE CHOCOLATE GOURAMI

Sphaerichthys acrostoma

FAMILY: Belontiidae
SUBFAMILY: Trichogasterinae (Trichogastrinae in *Nelson* 1994—*see* Bibliography)

IN ADDITION TO BEING LARGER AND POSSESSING a more pointed snout than other *Sphaerichthys* species, the Pointed-mouthed Gourami has a plainer-colored, i.e., less-patterned, body. It is also less frequently encountered than *S. osphromenoides* (*see* next entry).

DISTRIBUTION: *Borneo*

SIZE: *Up to 4in (10cm), but usually smaller*

BEHAVIOR: *Generally retiring; must not be kept with boisterous tankmates*

DIET: *As for* Parasphaerichthys ocellatus

AQUARIUM: *As for* Parasphaerichthys ocellatus, *but pH should be maintained within the acid part of the spectrum. Temperature range: 77–86°F (25–30°C)*

BREEDING: *Very challenging. Eggs are incubated orally by female*

CHOCOLATE GOURAMI

Sphaerichthys osphromenoides

FAMILY: Belontiidae
SUBFAMILY: Trichogasterinae (Trichogastrinae in *Nelson* 1994—*see* Bibliography)

THIS IS, BY FAR, THE MOST FAMOUS MEMBER OF ITS genus, having first been imported into Europe in 1905. In the late 1970s, a red-finned "Chocolate"—the Crossband Chocolate Gourami—was described and afforded subspecific status: *S. o. selatanensis*. At that point, *S. osphromenoides* became *S. o. osphromenoides*.

DISTRIBUTION: S. o. osphromenoides: *Indonesia and Malaysia;* S. o. selatanensis: *Borneo*

SIZE: *Up to 2½in (6cm), but usually smaller*

BEHAVIOR: *Retiring and peaceful; must not be kept with boisterous tankmates*

DIET: *As for* S. acrostoma

AQUARIUM: *As for* S. acrostoma

BREEDING: *Challenging in aquaria; female orally incubates the eggs and fry for up to two weeks*

VAILLANT'S CHOCOLATE GOURAMI

Sphaerichthys vaillanti

FAMILY: Belontiidae
SUBFAMILY: Trichogasterinae (Trichogastrinae in *Nelson* 1994—*see* Bibliography)

THOUGH NOT THE "YOUNGEST" OF THE *SPHAER-ichthys* species, Vaillant's Chocolate Gourami is, perhaps, the most recent one to appear with any degree of regularity. It is a beautifully marked species when in peak condition.

DISTRIBUTION: *Borneo*

SIZE: *Up to 3in (8cm), but usually smaller*

BEHAVIOR: *As for* S. acrostoma *and* S. osphromenoides

DIET: *As for* S. acrostoma *and* S. osphromenoides

AQUARIUM: *As for* S. acrostoma *and* S. osphromenoides

BREEDING: *As for* S. acrostoma *and* S. osphromenoides. *Some doubt exists regarding the sex of the mouthbrooding parent*

PEARL GOURAMI

LACE, LEERI, or MOSAIC, GOURAMI

Trichogaster leeri

FAMILY: Belontiidae
SUBFAMILY: Trichogasterinae (Trichogastrinae in *Nelson* 1994—*see* Bibliography)

ONCE SEEN, A LARGE, MATURE, MALE PEARL Gourami in full breeding regalia is never forgotten. This is another of those "must keep" fish. A golden form appeared in outdoor ponds in Florida in the early 1990s, but the colors faded and were replaced by normal wild-type coloration over a period of a few weeks once the fish were transferred to indoor aquaria.

DISTRIBUTION: *Peninsular Malaysia, Borneo, Sumatra, (possibly) Java and the area around Bangkok (Thailand)*

SIZE: *Up to 6in (15cm) reported, but usually considerably smaller*

BEHAVIOR: *Generally peaceful, except at breeding time when males become territorial*

DIET: *Most foods accepted*

AQUARIUM: *Large, covered, well-planted, with central open area. Surface vegetation also recommended, as well as subdued illumination. Water chemistry not critical. Temperature range: 73–82°F (23–28°C)*

BREEDING: *Substantial bubble nest may be built at water surface by male. The eggs and newly hatched fry are also guarded by male. Hatching takes about one day*

▲ *CHOCOLATE GOURAMI (*SPHAERICHTHYS OSPHROMENOIDES*)*   ▼ *PEARL GOURAMI (*TRICHOGASTER LEERI*)*

MOONLIGHT GOURAMI

MOONBEAM, or THINLIP, GOURAMI

Trichogaster microlepis

FAMILY: Belontiidae
SUBFAMILY: Trichogasterinae (Trichogastrinae in *Nelson* 1994—*see* Bibliography)

THIS IS AN ELEGANT, SILVERY FISH WITH extremely long filament-like pelvic fins. Neither it, nor any of the other gouramis in its genus, or within *Colisa*, should be kept with fin-nipping species, such as *Barbus tetrazona* (Tiger Barb), which would—sooner or later—damage these delicate fins.

DISTRIBUTION: *Cambodia, Malaysia, Singapore and Thailand*

SIZE: *Up to 8in (20cm) reported, but usually considerably smaller*

BEHAVIOR: *As for* T. leeri

DIET: *As for* T. leeri

AQUARIUM: *As for* T. leeri

BREEDING: *Basically, as for T. leeri. Male may tear off bits of submerged vegetation for inclusion in bubble nest*

SNAKESKIN GOURAMI

Trichogaster pectoralis

FAMILY: Belontiidae
SUBFAMILY: Trichogasterinae (Trichogastrinae in *Nelson* 1994—*see* Bibliography)

WHILE NOT SPECTACULARLY COLORED, THE BROWN shades and patterns of the Snakeskin Gourami, suffused overall with a delicate purplish sheen, make it a very attractive fish. It is much loved by the anabantoid enthusiasts that have kept and bred it.

DISTRIBUTION: *Cambodia, Vietnam and Thailand, but also introduced elsewhere in southeast Asia and other regions, including Sri Lanka and Haiti*

SIZE: *Up to 8in (20cm)*

BEHAVIOR: *Very peaceful despite its size*

DIET: *As for T. leeri*

AQUARIUM: *As for T. leeri*

BREEDING: *Basically, as for T. leeri; bubble nests can be quite small*

SPOTTED GOURAMI

TWO-SPOT, THREE-SPOT, BLUE, COSBY, OPALINE, OPAL, PLATINUM, LAVENDER, GOLDEN, AMETHYST, or BROWN, GOURAMI, HAIRFIN

Trichogaster trichopterus

FAMILY: Belontiidae
SUBFAMILY: Trichogasterinae (Trichogastrinae in *Nelson* 1994—*see* Bibliography)

THIS SPECIES, IN ITS NUMEROUS COLOR VARIETIES, is, along with the Dwarf Gourami (*Colisa lalia—see* p.242) the most widely kept of all the gouramis. Two subspecies are generally recognized: *T. t. trichopterus*, which occurs in various (nonblue) natural forms, such as the Brown and Lavender Gourami; and *T. t. sumatranus*, a blue form found exclusively in Sumatra. According to some authorities, the blue "sumatranus" is no more than yet another color morph and not a distinct subspecies.

DISTRIBUTION: *T. t. trichopterus: widely distributed in Indochina, Malaysia, Indonesia, Thailand and neighboring regions; T. t. sumatranus: restricted to Sumatra*

SIZE: *Up to 6in (15cm), but often smaller*

BEHAVIOR: *Males more intolerant of each other than are those of related species*

DIET: *Basically, as for T. leeri*

AQUARIUM: *Basically, as for T. leeri*

▲ MOONLIGHT GOURAMI (TRICHOGASTER MICROLEPIS)   ▼ SNAKESKIN GOURAMI (TRICHOGASTER PECTORALIS)

BREEDING: *Basically, as for T. leeri. Quality of nest may vary from small, single layer of bubbles to major construction*

KISSING GOURAMI

Helostoma temminckii

SYNONYM: *Helostoma rudolfi*
FAMILY: Helostomatidae

THIS LARGE SPECIES IS FAMOUS FOR ITS "KISSING" habit and fleshy lips (*see* photo p.232). The kissing, though, has little to do with affection and a great deal to do with gaining or maintaining territory; it is, in fact, a mouth-to-mouth trial of strength, which results in no damage to either party. There are three color forms available: the green or wild type, a pink-bodied version, and a mottled one.

DISTRIBUTION: *Widely distributed (and introduced) in southeast Asia*

SIZE: *Up to 12in (30cm), but usually only around half this size*

BEHAVIOR: *Generally peaceful, despite its size (and strength trials); exhibits strong appetite for delicate plants*

DIET: *All foods accepted; vegetable component recommended*

AQUARIUM: *Large, well-covered, and with a selection of hardy and/or unpalatable plants (see Aquarium Plants). A gravel substratum, with several large pieces of decor, e.g., rocks or bogwood, also recommended. Water chemistry not critical. Temperature range: 72–86°F (22–30°C)*

BREEDING: *Spawning may occur in the absence of bubble nest or in the presence of a token one. No strong egg/fry care exhibited. Hatching takes about one day, or slightly less at high temperatures*

PIKEHEAD
Luciocephalus pulcher

FAMILY: Luciocephalidae

BUILT LIKE A TORPEDO AND ARMED WITH A LARGE mouth, the Pikehead is an efficient predator. It is a fish for the specialist who can cater to its needs. A second, as yet, unidentified species, the Spotted Pikehead, was collected in the late 1990s but has not become widespread.

DISTRIBUTION: *Southeast Asia*

SIZE: *Up to 8in (20cm)*

BEHAVIOR: *Predatory; stalks its prey*

DIET: *Almost exclusively livefoods—e.g., insects, but including fish—a factor that needs due consideration prior to purchase*

AQUARIUM: *Well-covered, with adequate shelter, open spaces, and subdued lighting. Soft, slightly acid water preferred. Temperature range: 72–84°F (22–29°C)*

BREEDING: *No documented accounts currently available; assumed to be a mouthbrooder*

GIANT GOURAMI
Osphronemus goramy

SYNONYM: *Osphronemus gorami*
FAMILY: Osphronemidae

AS ITS NAME IMPLIES, THIS IS A LARGE FISH THAT can be kept on a longterm basis only by aquarists who can accommodate it. It is usually available as juveniles of various colors, including (mainly) the wild type and a golden-bodied one. The Red-finned Giant Gourami, which began becoming available in the 1990s, is probably *O. laticlavus*, originally from Sabah. The *O. septemfasciatus* (Sevenstripe Giant Gourami) is only rarely seen. Both these last species were described only during the early 1990s.

DISTRIBUTION: *Widely distributed and introduced in tropical Asia, but probably originating in Borneo, Java and Sumatra*

SIZE: *Up to 24in (60cm) or slightly larger*

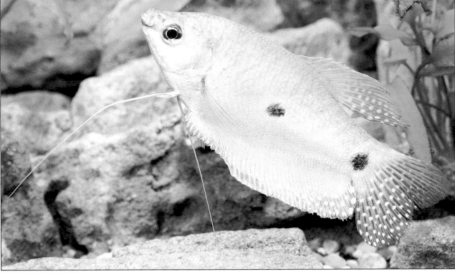

◀ SPOTTED GOURAMI (TRICHOGASTER TRICHOPTERUS)
▼ GIANT GOURAMI (OSPHRONEMUS GORAMY)

Boeseman's Rainbowfish (Melanotaenia boesemani)

Subdued lighting. Relatively soft, slightly acid water preferred. Temperature range: 72–84°F (22–29°C)

BREEDING: *Eggs are scattered—over a period of several days—among fine-leaved vegetation. Hatching can take 10 to 12 days, depending on temperature*

BOESEMAN'S RAINBOWFISH

Melanotaenia boesemani

FAMILY: Melanotaeniidae

THIS SPLENDID FISH WAS FIRST IMPORTED INTO Europe in 1980. Its strikingly unusual coloration, best seen in mature males in peak condition, quickly made it popular with aquarists. The vast majority of specimens available for aquaria are now captive-bred.

DISTRIBUTION: *Ajamaru Lakes and surrounding areas in Irian Jaya (New Guinea)*

SIZE: *Up to 4¾in (12cm) reported, but usually smaller*

BEHAVIOR: *Generally peaceful, though active, shoaler*

DIET: *Wide range of foods accepted*

AQUARIUM: *Spacious, well-planted, with large open central area. Short, fine-leaved/fronded plants, such as Java Moss (Vesicularia dubyana), may be used along bottom of swimming area. Soft, slightly acid to neutral water recommended; well-filtered, but not turbulent. Temperature range: 77–86°F (25–30°C)*

Breeding: *Eggs are scattered—over a period of a few days—among fine-leaved vegetation, e.g., Java Moss. Hatching takes approximately seven days*

LAKE TEBERA RAINBOWFISH

Melanotaenia herbertaxelrodi

FAMILY: Melanotaeniidae

FULLY MATURE SPECIMENS OF THIS SPECIES ARE very impressive, owing not just to their coloration but in addition to the depth of the body. This species was first described in 1981 and has been popular ever since this time.

DISTRIBUTION: *Lake Tebera (Papua New Guinea)*

SIZE: *Up to 5in (13cm), but usually smaller*

BEHAVIOR: *Generally peaceful shoaler*

DIET: *As for* M. boesemani.

AQUARIUM: *As for* M. boesemani, *but slightly lower temperatures and slightly higher alkalinity and hardness recommended*

BREEDING: *As for* M. boesemani

Lake Tebera Rainbowfish (Melanotaenia herbertaxelrodi)

LAKE KUTUBU RAINBOWFISH

Melanotaenia lacustris

FAMILY: Melanotaeniidae

ALTHOUGH THIS MAGNIFICENT SPECIES WAS described in 1964, it was not until the 1980s—when commercially bred stocks became more widely available—that it began to be seen on a regular basis. Mature males make a truly impressive sight in their metallic-blue and silvery white livery.

DISTRIBUTION: *Lake Kutubu (Papua New Guinea)*

SIZE: *Up to 4¾in (12cm), but usually smaller*

BEHAVIOR: *As for* M. herbertaxelrodi

DIET: *As for* M. herbertaxelrodi

AQUARIUM: *As for* M. herbertaxelrodi

BREEDING: *As for* M. herbertaxelrodi

MacCULLOCH'S RAINBOWFISH

BLACK-LINED, DWARF, or AUSTRALIAN, RAINBOWFISH

Melanotaenia maccullochi

FAMILY: Melanotaeniidae

THIS IS ONE OF THE "EARLIER" RAINBOWS, FIRST imported into Europe in 1934. It is also one of the smaller species, whose popularity has gradually been eclipsed by the more recent and more colorful additions to the range of species that are available. At least two naturally occurring forms are known.

DISTRIBUTION: *Northeast Australia and southeast Papua New Guinea*

SIZE: *Up to 2¾in (7cm)*

BEHAVIOR: *As for* M. herbertaxelrodi

DIET: *As for* M. herbertaxelrodi

AQUARIUM: *As for* M. herbertaxelrodi. *Temperature range: 68–86°F (20–30°C)*

BREEDING: *As for* M. herbertaxelrodi

PARKINSON'S RAINBOWFISH

Melanotaenia parkinsoni

FAMILY: Melanotaeniidae

THIS IS AN UNUSUALLY COLORED AND PATTERNED fish in which a sparkling bluish base color is liberally mottled in yellow, gold and orange in the posterior half of the body. The same yellow, gold, orange coloration extends into the unpaired fins. A red form is also available.

DISTRIBUTION: *Southeastern Papua New Guinea*

SIZE: *Fully mature males reported up to 5½in (14cm)*

BEHAVIOR: *As for* M. herbertaxelrodi

DIET: *As for* M. herbertaxelrodi

AQUARIUM: *As for* M. herbertaxelrodi. *Temperature range: 77–84°F (25–29°C)*

BREEDING: *As for* M. herbertaxelrodi

LAKE KUTUBU RAINBOWFISH (MELANOTAENIA LACUSTRIS)

MacCULLOCH'S RAINBOWFISH (MELANOTAENIA MACCULLOCHI)

PARKINSON'S RAINBOWFISH (MELANOTAENIA PARKINSONI)

Splendid Rainbowfish (Melanotaenia splendida)

SPLENDID RAINBOWFISH

Melanotaenia splendida

FAMILY: Melanotaeniidae

FOUR SUBSPECIES OF THIS POPULAR RAINBOW ARE known: *M. s. splendida* (Eastern Rainbowfish), *M. s. australis* (Western Rainbowfish), *M. s. inornata* (Chequered Rainbowfish) and *M. s. rubrostriata* (Red-striped Rainbowfish). All have the same basic requirements.

DISTRIBUTION: M. s. splendida: *Queensland;* M. s. australis: *Western Australia and Northern Territory;* M. s. inornata: *Daly River (Northern Territory);* M. s. rubrostriata: *Aru Island and southern New Guinea*

SIZE: M. s. splendida: *5½in (14cm);* M. s. australis: *4¼in (11cm);* M. s. inornata: *4¾in (12cm);* M. s. rubrostriata: *6in (15cm)*

BEHAVIOR: *As for* M. herbertaxelrodi

DIET: *As for* M. herbertaxelrodi

AQUARIUM: *As for* M. herbertaxelrodi. *Temperature range: 70–82°F (21–28°C)*

BREEDING: *As for* M. herbertaxelrodi

OTHER *MELANOTAENIA* SPECIES

Australian Rainbowfish of the genus *Melanotaenia* are relatively young in evolutionary terms, with the main "surge" in their evolution believed to have begun only some 10,000 years ago. It is also believed that the pace of these changes is still being maintained today, as evidenced by the large-scale variations observed in separate populations of individual species. Some of these may eventually be regarded as distinct subspecies or even species in their own right. The following are some of the species (subspecies excluded) that are more widely available. Most do well in soft to medium-hard, neutral to slightly alkaline water, with the harder/alkaline end of the spectrum being preferable as it is more resistant to chemical fluctuations. (Two exceptions are noted below.) Sizes given are approximate.

SCIENTIFIC NAME	COMMON NAME(S)	SIZE
M. affinis	Northern Rainbowfish	5½in (14cm)
M. duboulayi	Crimson-spotted Rainbowfish	4¼in (11cm)
M. exquisita	Exquisite Rainbowfish	2¾in (7cm)
M. fluviatilis	Murray River Rainbowfish	3½in (9cm)
M. goldei	Goldie River Rainbowfish	5½in (14cm)
M. gracilis	Slender Rainbowfish	2¾in (7cm)
*M. monticola**	Mountain Rainbowfish	4in (10cm)
M. nigrans	Black-banded Rainbowfish	3½in (9cm)
*M. praecox***	Dwarf Neon Rainbowfish	2½in (6cm)
M. sexlineata	Fly River Rainbowfish	3in (8cm)
*M. trifasciata****	Banded River Rainbowfish	5in (13cm)

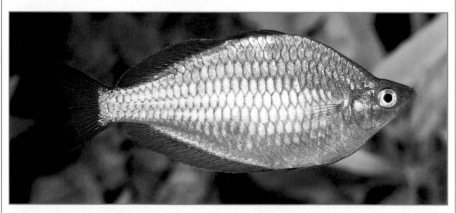

Dwarf Neon Rainbowfish (Melanotaenia praecox)

NOTES

* *M. monticola* requires slightly lower temperatures, ranging from around 61°F (16°C) to 72°F (22°C).

* * *M. praecox* requires soft, slightly acid water and should therefore not be kept in hard or alkaline conditions.

* * * *M. trifasciata* is one of the most variable of all the *Melanotaenia* species, with individual rivers having their own distinctive form of the species. The Goyder River morph—known, appropriately, as the Goyder River Rainbowfish—requires harder, more alkaline water than many of the other naturally occurring forms.

FORK-TAILED BLUE-EYE

FORK-TAILED RAINBOWFISH

Pseudomugil furcatus

SYNONYM: *Popondichthys furcatus*
FAMILY: Pseudomugilidae

OWING TO THEIR DIETARY PREFERENCES AND SMALL size, members of this genus can prove somewhat more challenging to keep than *Melanotaenia* rainbows. A good shoal in peak condition, however, is nothing short of magnificent. The Fork-tailed Blue-eye and *P. signifer* are the largest species in the genus.

DISTRIBUTION: *Eastern Papua New Guinea*

SIZE: *Up to 2¼in (6cm), but often smaller*

BEHAVIOR: *Peaceful, though active, shoaler; must not be kept with larger, more boisterous tankmates*

DIET: *Livefoods preferred, but deep-frozen, freeze-dried, and some dry formulations, may also be accepted*

AQUARIUM: *Heavily planted, with central open swimming area. Surface cover in the form of floating vegetation also recommended. Soft to medium-hard, neutral to slightly alkaline water preferred. Temperature range: 73–79°F (23–26°C)*

BREEDING: *Eggs are scattered (usually over several days) among feathery roots of floating plants or among fine-leaved vegetation. Hatching can take up to around 20 days, depending on temperature*

AUSTRALIAN BLUE-EYE (PSEUDOMUGIL SIGNIFER)

AUSTRALIAN BLUE-EYE
PACIFIC BLUE-EYE
Pseudomugil signifer

FAMILY: Pseudomugilidae

THIS SPECIES SHOWS CONSIDERABLE VARIATION throughout its range. Some populations are more colorful, or larger, or (as reported for some of the more northern ones) more aggressive than others.

DISTRIBUTION: *Queensland and Victoria (eastern Australia)*

SIZE: *Up to 2¼in (6cm) reported, but often smaller*

BEHAVIOR: *As for P. furcatus, although males from some populations can become a little aggressive*

DIET: *As for P. furcatus*

AQUARIUM: *As for P. furcatus, but slightly harder, more alkaline water accepted. Some salt (slightly less than 1oz per gal/500mg per liter) may be added to the water, but this is not essential. Temperature range: 73–82°F (23–28°C)*

BREEDING: *As for P. furcatus*

CELEBES RAINBOWFISH
SAILFISH
Marosatherina ladigesi

SYNONYM: *Telmatherina ladigesi*
FAMILY: Telmatherinidae

THIS SPECIES HAS BEEN AVAILABLE SINCE 1933, and although it has never achieved the popularity *of Melanotaenia* rainbows it has always been popular among specialist fishkeepers. It does well only in good-quality water and in the absence of larger, aggressive tankmates.

DISTRIBUTION: *Sulawesi (Indonesia)*

SIZE: *Up to 3in (7.5cm), but usually smaller*

BEHAVIOR: *Peaceful, though active, shoaler*

OTHER *PSEUDOMUGIL* SPECIES

Only one other species of *Pseudomugil—P. gertrudae*—has been widely available; others are on offer on a less regular basis. All have basically similar requirements to *P. signifer*, with two possible exceptions, noted below.

SCIENTIFIC NAME	COMMON NAME(S)	SIZE
P. connieae *	Popondetta Blue-eye	2in (5cm)
P. cyanodorsalis **	Blueback Blue-eye	1¼in (3cm)
P. gertrudae	Spotted Blue-eye	1½in (4cm)
P. mellis	Honey Blue-eye	1¼in (3cm)
P. tenellus	Delicate Blue-eye	1½in (4cm)

SPOTTED BLUE-EYE (PSEUDOMUGIL GERTRUDAE)

NOTES

* Provide tank conditions as for *P. furcatus.*

** This species requires salt in the water, i.e., it is essential rather than optional

DIET: *Wide range of livefoods and commercial diets accepted*

AQUARIUM: *Setup as for Pseudomugil furcatus. Softish, slightly acid conditions may be accepted, but seems to do better at higher pH and hardness values. Water quality must be good. Temperature range: 68–82°F (20–28°C)*

BREEDING: *Long breeding season lasting several months. Eggs are scattered among fine-leaved vegetation. Hatching takes 8 to 12 days, depending on temperature*

CELEBES RAINBOWFISH (MAROSATHERINA LADIGESI)

SUNFISH AND DARTERS

Within the sunfish, two "groups" have traditionally been recognized: the "normal" sunfish species, such as the Pumpkinseed (*Lepomis gibbosus*) and its relatives, on the one hand, and the pygmy or dwarf sunfishes like the Everglades Dwarf or Pygmy Sunfish (*Elassoma evergladei*).

At one time, both groups were deemed to be so closely related that they were regarded as subfamilies (Centrarchinae and Elassomatinae) of the family Centrarchidae. Currently, they are regarded as distinct families: Centrarchidae and Elassomatidae (referred to as Elassomidae by some authors). However, this is now being questioned as new evidence begins to indicate that they may not be even closely related. Indeed, some consider that pygmy sunfishes may be more closely related to sticklebacks (Gasterosteidae) and swamp eels (Synbranchidae) than to the Centrarchidae. Pending the resolution of this controversial matter, the classification followed here (Nelson, 1994—*see* Bibliography) assigns sunfishes to the Centrarchidae and pygmy sunfishes to the Elassomatidae.

No such controversy surrounds the darters, which belong to the family Percidae, although there is some debate regarding the splitting of this family into two subfamilies, one of which, the Percinae, is then subdivided into two tribes: Percini—including such species as the various perches (*Perca* spp.), and the Etheostomatini—which contains the darters, proper, e.g. *Etheostoma* spp.

BLUE-SPOTTED SUNFISH

Enneacanthus gloriosus

FAMILY: Centrarchidae

THIS SPARKLING SILVERY FISH WITH REFLECTIVE blue spots is probably the most attractive of the three species in its genus. It has been in the hobby since the early 1900s but, owing to its low temperature requirements, it has never acquired great popularity among tropical freshwater aquarists.

DISTRIBUTION: *Atlantic and Gulf Slope drainages of the United States, from New York in the north, southward to Florida*

SIZE: *Up to 3¾in (9.5cm)*

BEHAVIOR: *A shoaling species, except at breeding time when males become highly territorial and aggressive*

DIET: *Livefoods preferred, but deep-frozen, freeze-dried and other commercial formulations accepted*

AQUARIUM: *Spacious, heavily planted with cool-water species, and with numerous hiding places* and a coarse sand or fine-gravel substratum. Neutral to slightly alkaline, medium-hard water preferred. Temperature range: 50–72°F (10–22°C)

BREEDING: *Lowering water level to around 6in (15cm) seems to enhance chances of success. Eggs are laid in a depression dug by male, who also defends the brood*

PUMPKINSEED

Lepomis gibbosus

FAMILY: Centrarchidae

FIRST IMPORTED INTO EUROPE IN 1877, THIS stunning species, with its reflective blue speckling, is the most frequently kept of all the sunfish species. Tough and adaptable, it is capable of becoming established in most temperate habitats, so it is essential to ensure that it neither escapes nor is released into non-native waters. Such cautionary advice applies not just to the Pumpkinseed but to all other sunfishes and similarly adaptable species. Since the Pumpkinseed can attain a substantial size, it will outgrow most average-sized aquaria, a factor that requires consideration prior to purchase.

DISTRIBUTION: *Widely distributed along the Atlantic drainages of the United States; also introduced into other areas of North America, Canada and Europe where it has become established in a number of locations*

SIZE: *Up to 16in (40cm), but usually smaller*

BEHAVIOR: *Generally peaceful, but territorial and aggressive during breeding*

DIET: *As for* Enneacanthus gloriosus

AQUARIUM: *As for* E. gloriosus, *but with open swimming area. Temperature range: 39–72°F (4–22°C)*

BREEDING: *As for* E. gloriosus

LONGEAR SUNFISH

Lepomis megalotis

FAMILY: Centrarchidae

AS ITS COMMON NAME INDICATES, THIS SPECIES has long "ears"— fleshy extensions along the posterior edge of the gill cover (these extensions—but shorter—are characteristic of all *Lepomis* species). The spotted body patterning, incorporating both red and blue pigments, is striking.

DISTRIBUTION: *Widely distributed in broad band extending from the Great Lakes down to the Florida panhandle, southern Texas, New Mexico and northeast Mexico; also introduced outside its native range in the United States*

OTHER *ENNEACANTHUS* SPECIES

Two other species of *Enneacanthus* are also available. Their basic requirements are as for *E. gloriosus*, although one, *E. chaetodon* can tolerate even lower temperatures around 39°F (4°C).

SCIENTIFIC NAME	COMMON NAME(S)	SIZE
E. chaetodon	Black-banded Sunfish	3in (8cm)
E. obesus	Banded, Diamond, or Little, Sunfish	3¾in (9.5cm)

PUMPKINSEED (LEPOMIS GIBBOSUS)

SIZE: *Up to 9½in (24cm)*

BEHAVIOR: *Adults may be intolerant of each other, with males becoming territorial and aggressive at breeding time*

DIET: *As for* Lepomis gibbosus

AQUARIUM: *As for* Lepomis gibbosus

BREEDING: *As for* Lepomis gibbosus

EVERGLADES PYGMY SUNFISH

FLORIDA PYGMY SUNFISH

Elassoma evergladei

FAMILY: Elassomatidae (referred to as Elassomidae by some authors)

THE EVERGLADES PYGMY SUNFISH IS THE BEST known of the six species in the genus. It has been available for nearly three quarters of a century and is still much sought after by coldwater aquarists. It is not, however, a community fish that can be kept with other, larger, cool-water fish such as goldfish.

DISTRIBUTION: *From North Carolina to Florida, including the Everglades*

OTHER *LEPOMIS* SPECIES

There are nine other species of *Lepomis*, of which two are more frequently encountered than the others. All have similar characteristics to those outlined for the featured species, and they have wide temperature tolerance, although excessively low temperatures should be avoided (around 50°F/10°C should be regarded as a safe minimum). Sizes quoted are approximate.

SCIENTIFIC NAME	COMMON NAME(S)	SIZE
L. auritus	Redbreast Sunfish	9½in (24cm)
L. cyanellus*	Green Sunfish	12¼in (31cm)
L. gulosus	Warmouth	12¼in (31cm)
L. humilis	Orange-spotted Sunfish	6in (15cm)
L. macrochirus*	Bluegill	16in (41cm)
L. marginatus	Dollar Sunfish	4¾in (12cm)
L. microlophus	Redear Sunfish	10in (25cm)
L. punctatus	Spotted Sunfish	8in (20cm)
L. symmetricus	Bantam Sunfish	3½in (9cm)

NOTE:

* These two species are usually more frequently available than the others

ORANGE-SPOTTED SUNFISH (LEPOMIS HUMILIS) ▲
BLUEGILL (LEPOMIS MACROCHIRUS) ▶

SIZE: *Around 1¼in (3.5cm)*

BEHAVIOR: *Timid, sometimes retiring; best kept in a tank specifically set aside for it; males become territorial at breeding time*

DIET: *Livefoods preferred, but other diets also accepted*

AQUARIUM: *Heavily planted, with hiding places, open swimming area and sandy substratum. Mature, neutral to alkaline, medium-hard water preferred. Temperature range: 46–86°F (8–30°C)*

BREEDING: *Eggs are laid among fine-leaved vegetation. Hatching takes two to three days*

RAINBOW DARTER

Etheostoma caeruleum

FAMILY: Percidae

THIS BRILLIANTLY COLORED COOL-WATER SPECIES is, like many of its closest relatives, susceptible to deteriorating water quality. It is not suitable for beginners.

DISTRIBUTION: *Great Lakes and Mississippi River basin*

SIZE: *Up to 3in (7.7cm)*

BEHAVIOR: *Bottom dweller, with high oxygen demands*

DIET: *Predominantly livefood-based*

AQUARIUM: *Well-filtered, well-oxygenated, with a gravel bottom and scattered rocks. Slightly acid to slightly alkaline, medium-hard water preferred. Temperature range: 43–59°F (6–15°C)*

BREEDING: *Challenging in aquaria. Eggs are laid over gravel in fast-flowing water*

ORANGETHROAT DARTER (ETHEOSTOMA SPECTABILE)

OTHER *ELASSOMA* SPECIES

In addition to *Elassoma evergladei*, there are five other species in the genus, all with the same basic characteristics and requirements.

SCIENTIFIC NAME	COMMON NAME(S)	SIZE
E. alabamae	Spring Pygmy Sunfish	c. 1¼in (3cm)
E. boehlkei	Carolina Pygmy Sunfish	c. 1¼in (3.2cm)
E. okatie	Blue-barred Sunfish	c. 1¼in (3.4cm)
E. okefenokee	Okefenokee Pygmy Sunfish	c. 1¼in (3.4cm)
E. zonatum	Banded Pygmy Sunfish	2in (4.7cm)

ORANGETHROAT DARTER

Etheostoma spectabile

FAMILY: Percidae

THIS IS THE MOST VARIABLE OF ALL THE DARTER species. Five of these variants are regarded as subspecies: *E. s. spectabile*, *E. s. fragi*, *E. s. pulchellum*, *E. s. squamosum* and *E. s. uniporum*. All have varying degrees of orange on the throat area and on the two dorsal fins, with variations mostly occurring in the body patterning and/or coloration. *E. s. spectabile*, for example, has a row of thin dark stripes or spots on its body (depending on where in the range a particular population or race originates), while *E. s. fragi* has oblique blue-green bands. All have the same requirements in aquaria.

DISTRIBUTION: *Lake Erie and Mississippi river basins, and Gulf drainages (U.S.A)*

SIZE: *Up to 2¾in (7.2cm)*

BEHAVIOR: *As for* E. caeruleum

DIET: *As for* E. caeruleum

AQUARIUM: *As for* E. caeruleum

BREEDING: *As for* E. caeruleum

OTHER *ETHEOSTOMA* SPECIES

Although, in total, there are some 106 *Etheostoma* species, the two featured in the accompanying entries are the only ones seen with any regularity. The keeping of darters in aquaria is best reserved for specialists. Even where winter water temperatures in unheated aquaria may be tolerated, summer temperatures will often prove too high for these species, causing stress and making death likely. An aquarium water chiller/cooler is essential for keeping these fish in certain climates.

PERCH (PERCA FLUVIATILIS)

PERCH
Perca fluviatilis

FAMILY: Percidae

THIS BEAUTIFULLY MARKED SPECIES, WHILE belonging to the same subfamily (Percinae) and family as the darters, belongs to a separate tribe, the Percini. (Darters belong to the tribe Etheostomatini). Although the Perch has considerably wider temperature tolerance than darters, it is best reserved for the specialist.

DISTRIBUTION: *Europe, but also introduced elsewhere*

SIZE: *Up to 18in (45cm), but usually smaller*

BEHAVIOR: *Shoaling predator during juvenile phase, but tends to be a loner as it matures; can be kept only with tankmates too large to swallow*

DIET: *Almost exclusively livefoods (invertebrates and fish)*

AQUARIUM: *Large, well-filtered, well-oxygenated, with ample plant cover and gravel substratum. Neutral, soft to medium-hard water preferred, but some variation tolerated. Temperature range: 46–68°F (8–20°C)*

BREEDING: *Very large setup necessary. Eggs are laid among plants or rocks and may take up to three weeks to hatch*

OTHER PERCHES

Occasionally, other perch species become available in specialist "coldwater" outlets. All are predatory and none is suitable for beginners. While all will take live fish—a factor that requires serious consideration prior to purchase—most will also accept large invertebrate livefoods such as earthworms, river shrimp, etc. All require the same basic conditions listed for *Perca fluviatilis*. Sizes given are approximate for free-living specimens; aquarium specimens are likely to be smaller.

SCIENTIFIC NAME	COMMON NAME(S)	SIZE
Gymnocephalus cernuus (cernua)	Ruffe	c.12in (30cm)
Perca flavescens	Yellow Perch	16in (40cm)
Percina caprodes (3 subspecies)	Logperch	7in (18cm)
Stizostedion lucioperca	Zander	51in (130cm)
Stizostedion vitreum	Walleye	c.36in (90cm)

ZANDER (STIZOSTEDION LUCIOPERCA)

are the most appropriate; the connection with trout embodied in the third is misleading because there is none. The slightly smaller, but equally beautiful *M. adspersa*, also known as the Purple-spotted Gudgeon, from the eastern and southeastern parts of Australia, has similar requirements, but is less frequently available.

DISTRIBUTION: *Central and north Australia, New Guinea*

SIZE: *Up to 7in (17.5cm), but often smaller*

BEHAVIOR: *Males become aggressive and territorial during breeding; less so at other times*

DIET: *Livefoods preferred, but other diets accepted*

AQUARIUM: *Sufficiently spacious and planted, with open area, and with strategically placed caves or shelters around which several males can establish territories. Neutral to slightly alkaline, hardish water preferred. Temperature range: 72–86°F (22–30°C)*

BREEDING: *Eggs are laid in caves or on flat surfaces (including bogwood, or even the aquarium panes) and are guarded by male. Hatching can take five to nine days*

PEACOCK GOBY
PEACOCK GUDGEON
Tateurndina ocellicauda

FAMILY: Eleotridae (subfamily Eleotridinae—*sensu* Hoese and Gill)
SUBFAMILY: Eleotrinae or Eleotridinae (*sensu* Nelson)

THIS SPECIES, THE MOST COLORFUL OF ALL THE sleeper gobies, achieved great popularity during the mid-1980s and the 1990s. It has now been widely bred in captivity and is one of the most often seen eleotrids.

DISTRIBUTION: *New Guinea*

SIZE: *Up to 3in (7.5cm) reported, but usually smaller*

BEHAVIOR: *Peaceful; should not be kept with boisterous tankmates*

DIET: *Livefoods preferred, but a range of other diets accepted*

AQUARIUM: *Well-planted, with a number of hiding places or caves. Softish, slightly acid or neutral water preferred, though some deviation tolerated if adjustments are carried out gradually. Temperature range: 72–81°F (22–27°C)*

BREEDING: *Eggs are laid on the roof of cave or other hiding place (although spawning in the open also occurs). The eggs are guarded by male. Hatching takes about seven days*

BUMBLEBEE GOBY
GOLD-BANDED GOBY
Brachygobius nunus

SYNONYMS: *See* below
FAMILY: Gobiidae
SUBFAMILY: Gobiinae

THE GENUS *BRACHYGOBIUS* IS CLEARLY IN GREAT need of closer study, for several similar-looking species appear under a number of (often disputed) names. *B. nunus*, for example, is regarded by some as synonymous with *B. doriae*, while some doubt the validity of the most frequently encountered name, *B. xanthozona*. In addition, there is *B. aggregatus*. All species have the same basic requirements and characteristics.

DISTRIBUTION: *Southeast Asia*

SIZE: *Around 1¾in (4.5cm), but often smaller*

BEHAVIOR: *Peaceful and retiring toward other tankmates (which must be neither large nor boisterous), but territorial toward conspecifics*

◄ BUMBLEBEE GOBY (BRACHYGOBIUS NUNUS)
▼ PEACOCK GOBY (TATEURNDINA OCELLICAUDA)

DIET: *Livefoods preferred, but deep-frozen and (sometimes) waterlogged freeze-dried formulations may be accepted*

AQUARIUM: *Smallish, well-planted, with several small caves or snail shells. Hard, alkaline water with as much as one tablespoonful of salt per 1 Imp. gal (4.5–5 liters) preferred. Temperature range: 75–86°F (24–30°C)*

BREEDING: *Eggs are laid in caves or snail shells and are guarded by male. Hatching takes about four days*

KNIGHT GOBY

Stigmatogobius sadanundio

FAMILY: Gobiidae
SUBFAMILY: Gobionellinae

THIS IMPRESSIVE, STURDY LOOKING FISH IS regularly available. It can adapt to freshwater (it is often found in such habitats in the wild), but in aquaria it appears not to fare so well in the absence of salt.

DISTRIBUTION: *Indonesia and Philippines*

SIZE: *Up to 3½in (8.5cm)*

BEHAVIOR: *Males are territorial, especially toward their own species and (somewhat less so) toward other bottom-dwelling tankmates*

DIET: *Livefoods preferred, but deep-frozen, freeze-dried and other formulations may also be accepted; algal supplement recommended*

AQUARIUM: *Well-planted (with salt-tolerant species), and with a fine-grained substratum and several caves or shelters. Well-filtered, hard, alkaline water with one teaspoonful of salt per 1 Imp. gal (4.5–5 liters). Soft water must be avoided. Temperature range: 68–79°F (20–26°C)*

BREEDING: *Eggs are laid on roof of cave, and both they and the fry are protected by both parents*

BLOTCHED MUDSKIPPER

Periophthalmus barbarus

FAMILY: Gobiidae
SUBFAMILY: Oxudercinae

MUDSKIPPERS ARE FASCINATING FISH THAT LIVE in burrows on mangrove flats and spend a great deal of time out of water grazing the mud surface for microalgae and other tiny organisms. All species can prove challenging to keep and are not suitable for beginners. Male Blotched Mudskippers have spectacularly colored dorsal fins which they flick open and shut during displays. Two other species are also occasionally available: *P. papilio* (Butterfly Mudskipper) and *P. vulgaris* (Blue Flagfin); both have similar characteristics and requirements to *P. barbarus*.

DISTRIBUTION: *Widespread in estuaries in Africa, Red Sea, Madagascar, Southeast Asia, and Australia*

SIZE: *Up to 6in (15cm)*

BEHAVIOR: *Territorial; needs an exposed area on to which it can climb*

DIET: *Livefoods taken, especially from the surface of exposed substrates*

AQUARIUM: *Spacious, covered, with reduced water level and an exposed "beach" area or rocks and/or bogwood. Hard, alkaline water with a teaspoonful of salt per 1 Imp. gal (4.5–5 liters) is necessary. Ensure that a high level of humidity is maintained above the water surface. Temperature range: 77–86°F (25–30°C)*

BREEDING: *No documented accounts currently available*

EMERALD RIVER GOBY

Stiphodon elegans

FAMILY: Gobiidae
SUBFAMILY: Sicydiinae

THIS IS ONE OF THE MORE RECENT SPECIES OF goby to appear in the hobby. The lightish colored body has a few irregular dark bands extending from snout to tail, but fully mature males develop the shiny emerald coloration indicated by the name.

DISTRIBUTION: *Southeast Asia*

SIZE: *Around 1¾in (4.5cm)*

BEHAVIOR: *Active, but peaceful*

DIET: *Livefoods preferred, but other diets, including algae, accepted*

AQUARIUM: *Well-filtered, planted, with fine-grained substratum, some pebbles, and a water current (e.g. as produced by a powerhead outlet). Neutral, medium-hard water preferred, but some deviation (though not extreme) tolerated. Temperature range: 75–81°F (24–27°C)*

BREEDING: *Challenging, but achievable, in aquaria. However, no documented accounts currently available*

KNIGHT GOBY (STIGMATOGOBIUS SADANUNDIO)

placed *Epiplatys* within *Aplocheilus*. Owing to distinct body patterning and unique caudal fin color distribution, along with some skeletal and behavioral differences, Scheel also regarded *A. annulatus* to be in a sufficiently "isolated position in *Aplocheilus*" to warrant its own subgenus, *Pseudepiplatys* (considered as a valid genus by some earlier authors). Scheel's classification is being followed for all *Epiplatys* species in this book, with the alternative names acknowledged.

DISTRIBUTION: *West Africa, including Guinea, Liberia and Sierra Leone*

SIZE: *Up to 1½in (4cm), but often smaller*

BEHAVIOR: *Peaceful surface swimmer; must not be housed with larger, boisterous tankmates*

DIET: *Livefoods preferred, but other formulations may be accepted*

AQUARIUM: *Well-planted, with some floating plants, peat substratum and subdued lighting. Softish, slightly acid water preferred. Temperature range: 73–79°F (23–26°C)*

BREEDING: *Eggs are laid among fine-leaved vegetation and are ignored by the spawners (a spawning mop—see Aphyosemion australe, p.262—will also be acceptable). Hatching takes about eight to ten days*

CHAPER'S PANCHAX
Aplocheilus chaperi

SYNONYM: *Epiplatys chaperi*
FAMILY: Aplocheilidae (*sensu* Parenti and Nelson)
SUBFAMILY: Aplocheilinae (*sensu* Nelson)

TWO SUBSPECIES OF *A. CHAPERI* ARE KNOWN: Chaper's Panchax (*A. c. chaperi*) and Schreiber's Panchax (*A. c. schreiberi*). Both have varying numbers of backward-slanting, narrow, oblique dark bands that are more pronounced in females than in males. The body is somewhat sturdier than in *A. annulatus*, and the caudal fin lacks the central fin-ray extensions.

DISTRIBUTION: *Western Africa: Ghana and Ivory Coast*

SIZE: *Up to 2¾in (7cm)*

BEHAVIOR: *Peaceful, though not quite as retiring as* A. annulatus

DIET: *As for A. annulatus*

AQUARIUM: *As for A. annulatus. Temperature range: 72–82°F (22–28°C)*

BREEDING: *As for A. annulatus*

BLUE PANCHAX
Aplocheilus panchax

FAMILY: Aplocheilidae (*sensu* Parenti and Nelson)
SUBFAMILY: Aplocheilinae (*sensu* Nelson)

THE BLUE PANCHAX IS ONE OF THE EARLIEST SPECIES imported into Europe (1899). Despite this, it has never become as widespread within the hobby as its undoubted beauty deserves.

DISTRIBUTION: *Southeast Asia*

SIZE: *Up to 3in (8cm)*

BEHAVIOR: *Relatively peaceful surface swimmer, although very small fry may be regarded as food; males somewhat aggressive toward each other*

DIET: *Livefoods preferred, but other diets also accepted*

AQUARIUM: *Well-covered, spacious, with some floating plants, dense plant shelter around edges and back, and some open swimming spaces along the front. Subdued lighting also advisable, as are bogwood and other types of shelter. Water chemistry not critical, but quality must be good. Temperature range: 68–77°F (20–25°C)*

BREEDING: *Eggs are laid among fine-leaved vegetation or spawning mops (see Aphyosemion australe, p.262) over a period of days. Hatching takes up to two weeks*

PLAYFAIR'S PANCHAX
Aplocheilus (Pachypanchax) playfairi

SYNONYM: *Pachypanchax playfairii*
FAMILY: Aplocheilidae (*sensu* Parenti and Nelson)
SUBFAMILY: Aplocheilinae (*sensu* Nelson)

PLAYFAIR'S PANCHAX WAS SUBSUMED WITHIN THE genus *Aplocheilus* by Scheel (*see* Bibliography) who nevertheless regarded it as sufficiently different to retain subgeneric, i.e. (*Pachypanchax*) status.

DISTRIBUTION: *Madagascar, Seychelles and Zanzibar*

SIZE: *Males around 4in (10cm); females smaller*

BEHAVIOR: *Aggressive and territorial toward conspecifics; preys on small fish, but may be kept with similar-sized tankmates*

DIET: *Livefoods preferred, but other diets also accepted*

AQUARIUM: *As for A. panchax, but water slightly acid to neutral and soft to medium-hard. Temperature range: 72–77°F (22–25°C)*

BREEDING: *As for A. panchax*

▲ CHAPER'S PANCHAX (APLOCHEILUS CHAPERI)

▼ BLUE PANCHAX (APLOCHEILUS PANCHAX)

SIX-BARRED PANCHAX (APLOCHEILUS SEXFASCIATUS)

SIX-BARRED PANCHAX
SIX-BARRED EPIPLATYS
Aplocheilus sexfasciatus

SYNONYM: *Epiplatys sexfasciatus*
FAMILY: Aplocheilidae (*sensu* Parenti and Nelson)
SUBFAMILY: Aplocheilinae (*sensu* Nelson)

THIS SPECIES HAS SIMILAR OBLIQUE BODY BANDS TO *A. chaperi*. It is also extremely variable, both in color and body patterning, with five sub-species, each exhibiting variability depending on location.

DISTRIBUTION: *Western Africa, including Togo, Gabon, Cameroon and (at least) Taylor Creek in Nigeria*

SIZE: *Around 3in (8cm), but up to 4¼in (11cm) reported*

BEHAVIOR: *A surface-living species that may prey on very small fish*

DIET: *As for* A. annulatus

AQUARIUM: *As for* A. annulatus. *Temperature range: 72–82°F (22–28°C)*

BREEDING: *As for* A. annulatus

GÜNTHER'S NOTHOBRANCH

Nothobranchius guentheri

FAMILY: Aplocheilidae (*sensu* Parenti and Nelson)
SUBFAMILY: Aplocheilinae (*sensu* Nelson)

THIS COLORFUL ANNUAL SPECIES, IN THE HOBBY since the mid-1910s, is one of the best-known representatives of its genus. *Nothobranchius* are highly variable, thus often causing confusion with regard to precise identification. Some aquarium strains are also known. Like many other killifishes, it is only occasionally available in general aquatic outlets.

DISTRIBUTION: *Island of Zanzibar, but also reported from the Tanzanian mainland*

SIZE: *Around 2in (5cm), but larger sizes sometimes quoted*

BEHAVIOR: *Males aggressive toward each other*

DIET: *Livefoods preferred, but other diets may be accepted*

AQUARIUM: *This species is best kept in a tank set aside specifically for it and in groups of one male and several females. To keep several males, the aquarium must be large enough to accommodate non-overlapping territories. Provide several shelters and some open swimming spaces surrounded by vegetation and a dark, soft substratum (peat is ideal). Soft, slightly acid water preferred. Temperature range: 72–79°F (22–26°C)*

BREEDING: *Eggs are buried in the substratum. Treat these as for* A. filamentosum *for three to four months before resoaking. Adults die at the end of breeding season*

KORTHAUS' NOTHOBRANCH
MAFIA NOTHOBRANCH
Nothobranchius korthausae

FAMILY: Aplocheilidae (*sensu* Parenti and Nelson)
SUBFAMILY: Aplocheilinae (*sensu* Nelson)

SEVERAL COLOR FORMS OF THIS SPECIES ARE known, including one with a deep-red fin. There is a second red morph, in which the body is blue, plus two brown morphs that differ from each other in the intensity and distribution of the brown coloration, as well as in the yellow and black patterning (particularly) on the caudal fin.

DISTRIBUTION: *Mafia Island in Tanzania*

SIZE: *Around 1¾in (4.5cm), but up to 2⅓in (6cm) reported*

BEHAVIOR: *As for* N. guentheri

DIET: *As for* N. guentheri

AQUARIUM: *As for* N. guentheri. *Temperature range: 73–79°F (23–26°C)*

BREEDING: *As for* N. guentheri

OTHER *APLOCHEILUS* SPECIES

Aplocheilus (*sensu* Scheel, and thus including the species traditionally listed as *Epiplatys*, *Pseudepiplatys* and *Pachypanchax*) contains over 40 species, many of which are only infrequently seen outside specialist shops and killifish societies. As with *Aphyosemion*, aquarists wishing to keep these species should consult specialist literature (*see* Bibliography) and consider joining a specialist killifish society. Generally speaking, species listed elsewhere as *Epiplatys* or *Pseudepiplatys* have similar overall requirements and characteristics to those indicated in the accompanying entries for *Aplocheilus* (*Pseudepiplatys*) *annulatus*. For species listed elsewhere as *Pachypanchax*, the guidelines given here for *Aplocheilus* (*Pachypanchax*) *playfairi* generally apply.

KORTHAUS' NOTHOBRANCH
(NOTHOBRANCHIUS KORTHAUSAE)

PALMQVIST'S NOTHOBRANCH (NOTHOBRANCHIUS PALMQVISTI)

PALMQVIST'S NOTHOBRANCH
Nothobranchius palmqvisti

FAMILY: Aplocheilidae (*sensu* Parenti and Nelson)
SUBFAMILY: Aplocheilinae (*sensu* Nelson)

THIS IS ONE OF SEVERAL SPECIES IN WHICH THE caudal fin is blood-red throughout. As in so many other *Nothobranchius* species, the body coloration shows variation, depending on locality of origin.

DISTRIBUTION: *Coastal regions of southern Kenya and Tanzania*

SIZE: *Up to 2in (5cm)*

BEHAVIOR: *Males are particularly aggressive toward each other*

DIET: *Sometimes very reluctant to accept non-livefoods*

AQUARIUM: *As for* N. guentheri

BREEDING: *As for* N. guentheri

OTHER *NOTHOBRANCHIUS* SPECIES

Some 50 species and subspecies, plus a few hybrids, of *Nothobranchius* are known. The males of all the various types are beautifully colored. When kept in appropriate conditions (as described for *N. guentheri*), they hold their fins erect for much of the time, which makes for a dazzling display despite their relatively small size. One of the main reasons that *Nothobranchius* killifishes are not more widely available is that they are annual and therefore die at the end of the breeding season. It often takes eight to twelve weeks for males to develop their full coloration (females are generally drab-colored), which means that by the time such fish can be sold most are already about one quarter through their average lifespan. Owing to their long diapause and tough, resistant outer layers, *Nothobranchius* eggs are often exchanged between killie enthusiasts at club meetings or even by post. These hobbyists are among the best sources of supply, particularly of the less-frequently encountered species. Aquarists contemplating keeping *Nothobranchius* killifish would therefore be well-advised to seek membership of a killifish society.

RACHOW'S NOTHOBRANCH
Nothobranchius rachovii

FAMILY: Aplocheilidae (*sensu* Parenti and Nelson)
SUBFAMILY: Aplocheilinae (*sensu* Nelson)

SEVERAL COLOR FORMS ARE KNOWN TO EXIST IN the wild, along with a few aquarium-bred forms. Scheel (*see* Bibliography) states that the chromosomes of this species are the most specialized in the genus and that males from the northern parts of the range are the most colorful.

DISTRIBUTION: *From Quelimane (southern Mozambique) southward to northern parts of Krüger National Park (Republic of South Africa)*

SIZE: *Around 2in (5cm)*

BEHAVIOR: *Generally less aggressive than some other* Nothobranchius

DIET: *As for* N. guentheri

AQUARIUM: *As for* N. guentheri

BREEDING: *As for* N. guentheri

ARGENTINE PEARL
Cynolebias bellotti (but see box, opposite)

FAMILY: Aplocheilidae (*sensu* Nelson); Rivulidae (*sensu* Parenti)
SUBFAMILY: Rivulinae (*sensu* Nelson)

MIRRORING THE LIFESTYLE OF ITS OLD WORLD relatives belonging to the genus *Nothobranchius*, the Argentine Pearl and other *Cynolebias* species are annual fishes. Their reproductive behavior is virtually identical.

ARGENTINE PEARL (CYNOLEBIAS BELLOTTI)

BLACK-FINNED ARGENTINE PEARL (CYNOLEBIAS NIGRIPINNIS)

WHITE'S PEARL (CYNOLEBIAS WHITEI)

The Argentine Pearl was among the first New World killifish to be introduced into the hobby almost 100 years ago.

DISTRIBUTION: *Rio de la Plata basin (Argentina)*

SIZE: *Males up to 2¾in (7cm); females smaller*

BEHAVIOR: *Males, in particular, are active and sometimes aggressive*

DIET: *Livefoods preferred, but other diets also accepted*

AQUARIUM: *Single-species aquarium, with peat substratum and some clumps of vegetation as cover for females. Soft, slightly acid, good-quality water important. Temperature range: 59–72°F (15–22°C); extremely low temperatures, e.g. 39°F (4°C), and high temperatures, e.g. 86°F (30°C), will be temporarily tolerated*

BREEDING: *Use one male to two or three females. Eggs are buried in the peat, which should then be squeezed gently to remove excess water and stored in a small polythene bag or tub (in the dark) for three to four months, ensuring that the peat remains moist. When the eggs are then resoaked in aquarium water they will begin hatching, sometimes within hours. Females must be removed immediately after spawning, since they will be harassed by the male, which is able to spawn again straightaway*

BLACK-FINNED ARGENTINE PEARL

DWARF ARGENTINE PEARL

Cynolebias nigripinnis

FAMILY: Aplocheilidae (*sensu* Nelson); Rivulidae (*sensu* Parenti)
SUBFAMILY: Rivulinae (*sensu* Nelson)

MANY AUTHORS RECOGNIZE TWO SUBSPECIES OF *C. nigripinnis*: *C. n. nigripinnis* (Black-finned, or Dwarf, Argentine Pearl) and *C. n. alexandri* (Entre Rio Argentine Pearl). Others (perhaps a majority) consider each a valid species in its own right. While being overall similar to each other, *C. n. alexandri* males have brownish, almost vertical bands on the body; *C. n. nigripinnis*

lacks these bands but has the characteristic black fins indicated in both the scientific and common names.

DISTRIBUTION: *Argentina. C. n. alexandri: Entre Rio Province (near Gualeguaychu); C. n. nigripinnis: Paraná (near Rosario de Santa Fe)*

SIZE: *Males up to 2in (5cm); females smaller*

BEHAVIOR: *Similar to C. bellotti*

DIET: *As for C. bellotti*

AQUARIUM: *As for C. bellotti. Temperature range: 64–77°F (18–25°C) recommended, but slightly higher and lower temperatures tolerated. C. n. alexandri prefers the higher end of the temperature scale*

BREEDING: *As for C. bellotti*

WHITE'S PEARL

Cynolebias whitei

FAMILY: Aplocheilidae (*sensu* Nelson); Rivulidae (*sensu* Parenti)
SUBFAMILY: Rivulinae (*sensu* Nelson)

AS IN THE OTHER SPECIES FEATURED, THE BODY IN male *C. whitei* is spangled with numerous white/cream/bluish "pearls." Males also exhibit a brownish base body color and elongated dorsal and anal fins. An aquarium-bred albino form is occasionally available.

DISTRIBUTION: *Near Rio de Janeiro (Brazil)*

SIZE: *Males up to 3in (8cm); females smaller*

BEHAVIOR: *As for C. bellotti*

OTHER *CYNOLEBIAS* SPECIES

The genus *Cynolebias* contains around 35 species. In addition to the ones featured here, only a few others are seen with any regularity. While availability will vary according to season and from country to country, the most frequently encountered of these other species are probably: *C. adloffi* (Banded Pearl), *C. boitonei* (Brazilian Pearl/Lyretail), *C. constanciae* (Featherfin Pearl), *C. dolichopterus* (Sicklefin Pearl), and *C. melanotaenia* (Fighting Gaucho). Some of the best sources of these and other *Cynolebias* species are members of killifish societies, although some of the more specialized retail outlets will also stock *Cynolebias*. The eggs of *C. melanotaenia* and *C. brucei* (Turner's Gaucho) are fertilized internally and then released. All *Cynolebias* species have similar aquarium requirements, with temperatures around 72–75°F (22–24°C) being generally acceptable. However, seek specialist advice for individual species. *Cynolebias* can be classified as *Austrolebias*, *Nematolebias* or *Simpsonichthys* by some authors

FIGHTING GAUCHO (CYNOLEBIAS MELANOTAENIA)

DIET: *Livefoods preferred; dried food accepted only reluctantly*

AQUARIUM: *As for* C. bellotti. *Temperature range: 68–73°F (20–23°C)*

BREEDING: *As for* C. bellotti

LACE-FINNED KILLIFISH

Pterolebias zonatus

FAMILY: Aplocheilidae (*sensu* Nelson); Rivulidae (*sensu* Parenti)
SUBFAMILY: Rivulinae (*sensu* Nelson)

THIS IS A TRULY MAGNIFICENT SPECIES, WITH brownish speckling and body bands on a light metallic blue base color. Fully mature males have an almost sail-like anal fin and substantial caudal fin. Of the other four species in the genus, *P. longipinnis* (Long-finned Killifish) is the most frequently encountered; it has similar requirements to Lace-finned Killifish.

DISTRIBUTION: *Venezuela*

SIZE: *Up to 6in (15cm) reported, but usually much smaller*

BEHAVIOR: *Males are aggressive toward each other; less so as they age*

DIET: *Predominantly livefoods; other diets usually accepted only with reluctance*

AQUARIUM: *As for* C. bellotti. *Temperature range: 64–73°F (18–23°C)*

BREEDING: *As for* C. bellotti

MAGDALENA SPOT-FINNED KILLIE

Rachovia brevis

FAMILY: Aplocheilidae (*sensu* Nelson): Rivulidae (*sensu* Parenti)
SUBFAMILY: Rivulinae (*sensu* Nelson)

OF THE SIX SPECIES IN THE GENUS (ALL ANNUALS), *R. brevis* is generally most available. Both males and females of this sturdy-looking species are attractively, though not spectacularly, colored.

DISTRIBUTION: *Colombia (largely, on coastal plains)*

SIZE: *Males around 3in (7.5cm); females slightly smaller*

BEHAVIOR: *Generally peaceful toward other fish, but males somewhat aggressive toward each other*

DIET: *Livefoods preferred, but other formulations—primarily deep-frozen and fresh—accepted*

AQUARIUM: *As for* C. bellotti. *Temperature range: around 77–81°F (25–27°C)*

BREEDING: *As for* C. bellotti. *Store eggs for about six weeks*

GREEN RIVULUS

BROWN, or CUBAN, RIVULUS

Rivulus cylindraceus

FAMILY: Aplocheilidae (*sensu* Nelson): Rivulidae (*sensu* Parenti)
SUBFAMILY: Rivulinae (*sensu* Nelson)

UNLIKE SOME OF THE OTHER MEMBERS OF THE family, *Rivulus* species do not bury their eggs. If pools dry out in the wild, the eggs of some species may withstand desiccation for a while—but do not go into the extended diapause exhibited by annual species. *Rivulus* species tend to live for 18 months or more, with Green Rivulus having a lifespan of up to four years.

DISTRIBUTION: *Cuba (in mountain streams)*

SIZE: *Around 2¼in (5.5cm)*

BEHAVIOR: *Generally peaceful, though active; exhibits good jumping ability*

DIET: *Predominantly livefoods, but other diets also accepted*

AQUARIUM: *Well-covered, with dark substratum, some clumps of fine-leaved vegetation, and subdued lighting. Water chemistry not critical, but neutral, medium-hard water preferred. Temperature range: 22–24°C (72–77°F) with some deviation either side*

BREEDING: *Use a trio of one male and two females. Eggs are laid, mainly, on fine-leaved vegetation or spawning mop (see Aphyosemion australe, p.262); spawning may occur on top of the mop, and the exposed eggs may survive exposure for a week or more. Hatching of submerged eggs takes 12–14 days*

▲ LACE-FINNED KILLIFISH (*PTEROLEBIAS ZONATUS*)

▼ GREEN RIVULUS (*RIVULUS CYLINDRACEUS*)

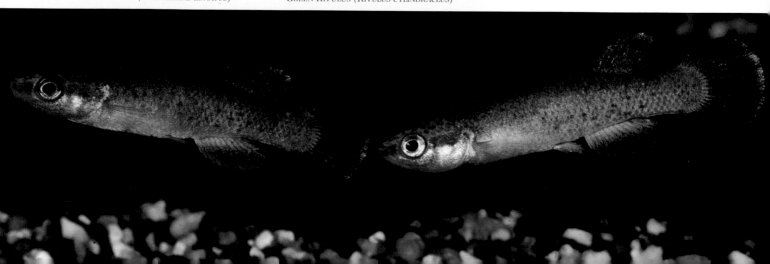

BAR-TAILED RIVULUS

Rivulus magdalenae

FAMILY: Aplocheilidae (*sensu* Nelson): Rivulidae (*sensu* Parenti)
SUBFAMILY: Rivulinae (*sensu* Nelson)

BAR-TAILED RIVULUS IS ONE OF THE FIVE LARGEST species in the genus (the largest, *R. igneus*—Firebelly Rivulus—can attain 6in/15cm). While coloration will vary, depending on location, the body is always covered in numerous small reddish-brown spots and there is a distinct light-colored posterior edge to the caudal fin. The lifespan of this species is around two-and-a-half years.

DISTRIBUTION: *Colombia: Magdalena river basin, Caqueta tributaries, and (possibly) Cauca river basin*

SIZE: *Males up to 3½in (9cm); females smaller*

BEHAVIOR: *As for* R. cylindraceus

DIET: *As for* R. cylindraceus

AQUARIUM: *As for* R. cylindraceus

BREEDING: *Basically, as for* R. cylindraceus. *Hatching may take up to 35 days*

BLUE-STRIPED RIVULUS
BAND-TAILED RIVULUS

Rivulus xiphidius

FAMILY: Aplocheilidae (*sensu* Nelson): Rivulidae (*sensu* Parenti)
SUBFAMILY: Rivulinae (*sensu* Nelson)

THIS IS PROBABLY THE MOST SPECTACULARLY colored of all the *Rivulus* species. It is also one of the smallest and more challenging members of the genus—not a fish for beginners. It has a lifespan of about two-and-a-half years.

DISTRIBUTION: *French Guyana (forest springs); Amazon region (Brazil); also (possibly) Suriname, although the species found here may be R. frenatus*

SIZE: *Up to 1¾in (4.5cm), but often smaller*

BEHAVIOR: *Retiring, placid, with good jumping ability*

DIET: *Almost exclusively livefoods*

AQUARIUM: *Well-covered, with subdued lighting and some plant thickets. Soft, slightly acid water important. Temperature range: 72–79°F (22–25°C)*

BREEDING: *Challenging in aquaria, but, basically, as for* R. cylindraceus. *Hatching takes around 14 days*

GOLDEN TOP MINNOW
GOLDEN-EARED KILLIFISH

Fundulus chrysotus

FAMILY: Fundulidae (*sensu* Nelson and Parenti)

THIS SPECIES HAS A CHARACTERISTIC GOLDEN patch on the gill cover, directly behind the

OTHER *RIVULUS* SPECIES

There are about 110 species in the genus *Rivulus* (defined in its broadest sense, i.e. including Parenti's "Rivulus"—*see* Bibliography). Few, however, are kept regularly in aquaria, more through lack of availability than difficulty of upkeep. A few species, e.g., *R. stellifer* (Stellate Rivulus) and *R. compactus* may be annual species that bury their eggs, as in *Nothobranchius* and *Cynolebias*; all others are longer-lived (average lifespan around three years). *R. urophthalmus* (The Golden Rivulus) may live for more than five years. Another long-lived species, *R. ocellatus* (Ocellate Rivulus)—traditionally referred to as *R. marmoratus*—is famous for being a hermaphrodite. While most species of *Rivulus* may be kept and bred following the general guidelines outlined for *R. cylindraceus*, detailed information should be sought from specialist literature (*see* Bibliography) and/or via membership of a killifish society.

BLUE-STRIPED RIVULUS (RIVULUS XIPHIDIUS)

eyes, hence its common names. In males, the greenish body is liberally covered in small reddish-brown spots; females are drabber but have numerous glistening light-colored spots.

DISTRIBUTION: *Gulf Coast plain of North America, including South Carolina and Florida and westward to the Trinity River drainage in Texas*

SIZE: *Up to 3in (7.5cm)*

BEHAVIOR: *Reasonably tolerant; rivalry intensifies between males at breeding time*

DIET: *Livefoods preferred, but other formulations, particularly deep-frozen ones, accepted*

AQUARIUM: *Spacious, well-covered, with surface vegetation, plant thickets and pieces of bogwood. Water chemistry not critical; a small amount of salt (about 1 teaspoonful per 1 Imp. gal./4.5–5 liters) may be added for stocks that originate from brackish-water regions. Temperature range: 64–72°F (18–22°C), with some deviation at either end*

BREEDING: *Use one male and two or more females. Eggs—which are laid, over a period of about a week, among fine-leaved vegetation—are ignored by the spawners. Hatching takes several days*

BLUEFIN KILLIFISH

Lucania goodei

FAMILY: Fundulidae (*sensu* Nelson and Parenti)

OF THE TWO MEMBERS OF THE GENUS, BLUEFIN Killifish is occasionally encountered in the hobby. It is a beautiful fish possessing blue coloration in both the dorsal and anal fins. The dorsal fin may also exhibit a small orange-red patch at the back, with similar coloration on the caudal and pelvic fins.

DISTRIBUTION: *Widespread in Florida*

SIZE: *Up to 2½in (6cm)*

BEHAVIOR: *An active shoaling species*

DIET: *Livefoods preferred, but some commercial diets—particularly deep-frozen ones—accepted*

AQUARIUM: *Well-covered, with some open space. Softish, slightly acid to neutral water preferred; partial water changes required about once a week/two weeks. Temperature range: 64–72°F (18–22°C), with some deviation at either end*

BREEDING: *Similar to B. chrysotus*

OTHER *APLOCHEILICHTHYS* SPECIES

Of the 40* or so *Aplocheilichthys* species, subspecies and undescribed types (sometimes offered for sale with a "code" added—as in *A. sp. aff. maculatus* "K86/1"), relatively few are encountered regularly in aquatic retail outlets. Of these, the following are among those most frequently seen. Their aquarium requirements are, basically, those described for *A. luxophthalmus*. Sizes given are approximate.

SCIENTIFIC NAME	COMMON NAME(S)	SIZE
A. johnstoni	Johnston's Lampeye	3½in (8.5cm)
A. katangae	Blackstripe, or Katanga, Lampeye	1¾in (4.5cm)
A. (Congopanchax) myersi	Myer's, or Hummingbird, Lampeye	1in (2.5cm)
A. normani	Norman's Lampeye/Blueye	1½in (4.0cm)
A. rancureli	Rancurel's, or Filamentosus, Lampeye	1½in (4.0cm)
A. scheeli	Scheel's Lampeye	1⅜in (3.5cm)

NOTE:

*This figure includes the species referred to as "*Aplocheilichthys*" by Parenti (1981)—see Bibliography.

NORMAN'S LAMPEYE (APLOCHEILICHTHYS NORMANI)

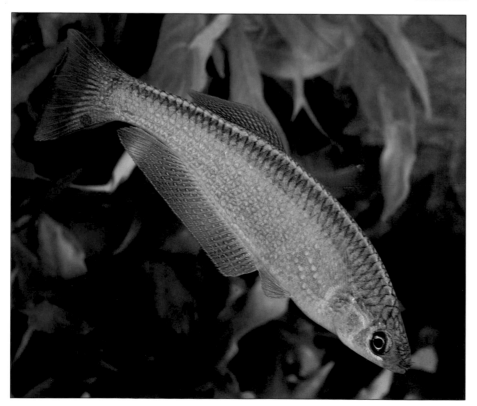

TANGANYIKA PEARL KILLIFISH
(LAMPRICHTHYS TANGANICUS)

BANDED LAMPEYE

Aplocheilichthys spilauchen

FAMILY: Poeciliidae
SUBFAMILY: Poeciliinae

AT FIRST SIGHT, THIS LAMPEYE DOES NOT APPEAR to belong within the genus *Aplocheilichthys*: it looks a little more like some *Aplocheilus* species than either of the two previous *Aplocheilichthys* featured. Skeletal and other characteristics, however, prove otherwise. The vertical bands on the body and caudal fin help make the Banded Lampeye a very visually pleasing and desirable fish.

DISTRIBUTION: *Western Africa: from Senegal to lower Congo (Zaire), taking in Liberia, Gambia and northern Angola*

SIZE: *Up to 2¾in (7cm)*

BEHAVIOR: *Active shoaler*

DIET: *Livefoods preferred, but other diets accepted*

AQUARIUM: As for *A. luxophthalmus*. *Add 1 teaspoonful of salt per 1 Imp. gal (4.5–5 liters) of water. Temperature range: 75–90°F (24–32°C)*

BREEDING: *Similar to* A. luxophthalmus, *but add salt as above*

TANGANYIKA PEARL KILLIFISH

Lamprichthys tanganicus

FAMILY: Poeciliidae
SUBFAMILY: Aplocheilichthyinae

THIS EXCEPTIONALLY BEAUTIFUL SPECIES IS THE sole representative of its genus and the largest of the Aplocheilichthyinae. It is a streamlined fish with a series of lines of small, metallic-blue scales that are particularly resplendent in reflected light. It can prove challenging to keep in peak condition.

DISTRIBUTION: *Lake Tanganyika (Africa)*

SIZE: *Up to 5in (13cm)*

BEHAVIOR: *Active shoaler*

DIET: *Livefoods preferred, but other formulations also accepted*

AQUARIUM: *Spacious, covered, with some plant thickets and ample swimming space, and at least one group of rocks or blocks of bogwood, placed closely together to provide crevices. Top-quality alkaline medium-hard to hard water important. Temperature range: 72–77°F (22–25°C)*

BREEDING: *Eggs are generally deposited in cracks or crevices in rocks or bogwood and are best left to develop in the dark for over a week*

GREEN LAMPEYE
BLUE-GREEN LAMPEYE
Procatopus aberrans

FAMILY: Poeciliidae
SUBFAMILY: Aplocheilichthyinae

OF THE THREE SPECIES IN THE GENUS, GREEN Lampeye is probably the one that is most often seen. Mature males in peak condition are particularly impressive, with their characteristic blue-green body coloration and red fin edges. The Large-finned Lampeye (*P. nototaenia*) and the Variable Lampeye (*P. similis*)—both from different locations within Cameroon—are also very attractive and worth searching for. None, however, is recommended for beginners.

DISTRIBUTION: *Western and southwestern Cameroon*

SIZE: *Around 2½in (6cm)*

BEHAVIOR: *Active, peaceful shoaler*

DIET: *As for* Lamprichthys tanganicus

AQUARIUM: *As for* Lamprichthys tanganicus

BREEDING: *As for* Lamprichthys tanganicus

KNIFE LIVEBEARER

Alfaro cultratus

FAMILY: Poeciliidae
SUBFAMILY: Poeciliinae

WHILE NOT THE MOST COLORFUL OF THE poeciliines, Knife Livebearer makes a dazzling display when kept in a shoal (but *see* below). The "knife" consists of a series of scales on the lower edge of the body between the vent and the beginning of the caudal fin. *A. huberi* (Orange Rocket), from Guatemala, Honduras and Nicaragua, has a central body spot, is smaller (around 2¾in/7cm), and is less frequently available.

DISTRIBUTION: *Costa Rica, Nicaragua and Panama*

SIZE: *Males reported up to 3½in (9cm); females slightly larger*

BEHAVIOR: *Can be shy and easily frightened in sparsely decorated aquaria. Males can sometimes be aggressive toward each other, but not excessively so when kept in a shoal that includes several other males; aggression is highest when only two males are present*

DIET: *Livefoods preferred, but other diets also accepted*

AQUARIUM: *Spacious, well-planted, and covered, with some open swimming spaces and shelters. Neutral or slightly alkaline medium-hard, well-filtered water with some movement (as produced by a powerhead outlet) recommended. Temperature range: 75–82°F (24–28°C)*

BREEDING: *Fertilization is internal. Females give birth to as many as 100 fry every four to five weeks (although broods are generally much smaller than this)*

PIKE TOP LIVEBEARER
PIKE TOP MINNOW/KILLIFISH
Belonesox belizanus

FAMILY: Poeciliidae
SUBFAMILY: Poeciliinae

THIS STREAMLINED, BEAK-MOUTHED, SABRE-toothed species has been in the hobby for nearly 100 years. One of the livebearers "with character," it is undoubtedly for the specialist who likes something a little different. Two subspecies are sometimes recognized: *B. b. belizanus* and *B. b. maxillosus* (Yellow Pike Top Livebearer) from the Yucatán in Mexico. Some authorities doubt the validity of the second subspecies.

DISTRIBUTION: *B. b. belizanus: from Veracruz (Mexico), southward to Guatemala, Honduras and Nicaragua; B. b. maxillosus: Yucatán Peninsula (Mexico)*

SIZE: *Males up to 4¾in (12cm); females 8in (20cm)*

BEHAVIOR: *Predatory; must be housed only with similar-sized tankmates; large females may even prey on small males of their own species*

DIET: *Livefoods, deep-frozen and freeze-dried diets*

AQUARIUM: *Spacious, covered, well-planted, with some shelters and well-filtered water. Neutral to alkaline hard water with 1 teaspoonful of salt per 2 Imp. gal (9–10 liters) preferred. Temperature range: 79–86°F (26–30°C) or slightly higher*

BREEDING: *Up to 100 large fry (up to 1in/2.5cm) produced every 4½–7 weeks, following internal fertilization*

THE BISHOP

Brachyraphis episcopi

FAMILY: Poeciliidae
SUBFAMILY: Poeciliinae

THE BISHOP IS PERHAPS THE BEST KNOWN OF THE nine or so *Brachyraphis* species (the total number is uncertain because some are awaiting scientific description). This is a distinctive fish, with netlike scale patterning, a red line and dark spots running down the body, red-edged dorsal fin, and the characteristic "Brachy" black spot around the vent and extending into the

KNIFE LIVEBEARER (ALFARO CULTRATUS)

anal fin. It is challenging to maintain in peak condition.

DISTRIBUTION: *Both oceanic slopes of Panama*

SIZE: *Males up to 1⅜in (3.5cm); females 2in (5cm)*

BEHAVIOR: *Relatively aggressive toward smaller and even some similar-sized tankmates; exhibits fin-nipping tendencies, but may be kept as a shoal*

DIET: *Predominantly livefoods, but other diets accepted (flakes often rejected)*

AQUARIUM: *Well-planted and well-filtered. Neutral to alkaline medium-hard water preferred. Temperature range: 75–79°F (24–26°C)*

BREEDING: *Small broods of around 20 fry produced every four weeks or so*

BANDED WIDOW
STUART'S LIVEBEARER
Carlhubbsia stuarti

FAMILY: Poeciliidae
SUBFAMILY: Poeciliinae

THIS LARGE-EYED SPECIES HAS ATTRACTIVE, THIN, black vertical stripes along the body—more pronounced in males than females; males have a black gonopodium with a white tip. A second species, *C. kidderi* (Kidder's Livebearer)—from Mexico and Guatemala—is similar but lacks the very well-marked stripes of Banded Widow. These stripes also distinguish Banded Widow from *Phallichthys amates* (*see* p.278).

DISTRIBUTION: *Rio Polochic system, Dulce and Sebol rivers, and Laguna Izabal (Guatemala)*

SIZE: *Males up to 2in (5cm); females up to 2⅜in (6cm), but usually smaller*

BEHAVIOR: *Can be a little timid, particularly in sparsely planted aquaria; should be kept as a shoal*

DIET: *Livefoods preferred, but some other diets also accepted*

AQUARIUM: *Well-planted, covered, with subdued lighting. Slightly alkaline hardish water preferred, but softer, more acid conditions also tolerated. Temperature range: 75–82°F (24–28°C)*

BREEDING: *Broods of between 10 and 50 fry are produced every five to seven weeks. Males of this genus have dextrally (right-handedly) or sinistrally (left-handedly) asymmetrical gonopodia*

TEN-SPOT LIVEBEARER
Cnesterodon decemmaculatus

FAMILY: Poeciliidae
SUBFAMILY: Poeciliinae

DEPENDING ON LOCALITY OR MOOD, THIS SPECIES can exhibit the ten spots (which are more like very short vertical bands than spherical marks) either brilliantly or not at all. The number of spots may also vary, from 7 to 11. Of the three species in the genus,

---

OTHER *BRACHYRAPHIS* SPECIES

Once the undescribed species (sometimes referred to in aquarium literature by a code, e.g. *Brachyraphis* sp. "FU35") have been named and the nature of others, e.g. *Brachyraphis cf. roseni* has been determined, this genus could end up with over 15 species. Currently, though, the following are fully recognized (in addition to *B. episcopi*) and are available with varying degrees of regularity from specialist aquatic outlets or from members of livebearer societies. All have the same basic characteristics and requirements as *B. episcopi*, but specialist literature should be consulted (*see* Bibliography). Sizes given are approximate, with that of males listed first.

SCIENTIFIC NAME	COMMON NAME(S)	SIZE
B. cascajalensis	Cascajal Brachy/Bishop	2⅜in (6cm); 3in (7.5cm)
B. hartwegi	Hartweg's Brachy/Bishop	1⅜in (3.5cm); 2in (5cm)
B. holdridgei	Holdridge's Brachy/Bishop	1⅝in (4cm); 2in (5cm)
B. parisima	Parisima Brachy/Bishop	1¾in (4.5cm); 2in (5cm)
B. punctifer	Spotted Brachy/Bishop	1¼in (3cm); 2in (5cm)
B. rhabdophora	Lace Brachy, Regan's Bishop	1⅝in (4cm); 2¾in (7cm)
B. roseni	The Cardinal, Cardinal Brachy	2in (5cm); 2⅝in (6.5cm)
B. terrabensis	Sailfin Brachy, Terraba Bishop	2in (5cm); 2⅝in (6.5cm)

---

only *C. carnegiei* (Carnegie's Livebearer) from southeastern Brazil and Uruguay is likely to be encountered in the hobby.

DISTRIBUTION: *Argentina, Bolivia, Brazil, Paraguay and Uruguay*

SIZE: *Males around 1in (2.5cm); females around 1¾in (4.5cm)*

BEHAVIOR: *Should be kept as a shoal in a species tank or only with other small nonaggressive species*

DIET: *Small livefoods preferred, but other diets may be accepted*

AQUARIUM: *Well-planted, covered, with well-oxygenated water; carry out regular partial water changes. Neutral, moderately soft water preferred, but a little deviation on either side is tolerated. Temperature range: 64–77°F (18–25°C)*

BREEDING: *Broods of around 20 fry are produced every four to six weeks*

BLACKLINE MOSQUITOFISH
Flexipenis vittata

SYNONYMS: *Flexipenis vittatus, Gambusia vittata*
FAMILY: Poeciliidae
SUBFAMILY: Poeciliinae

THERE IS CONSIDERABLE DEBATE REGARDING THE true identity of this beautiful fish. Some authorities believe it to be the single representative of the genus *Flexipenis*, while others (probably a majority) believe it to be a *Gambusia*.

DISTRIBUTION: *Atlantic side of Mexico*

SIZE: *Males around 1¾in (4.5cm); females around 2⅜in (6cm)*

BEHAVIOR: *Surprisingly unaggressive for a "Gambusia-type" species; may be kept in a shoal*

DIET: *Wide range of foods accepted*

AQUARIUM: *Well-planted, well-lit, covered. Neutral, softish water, with some deviation on either side, accepted. Temperature range: 72–77°F (22–25°C)*

BREEDING: *Broods of around 20 fry produced every four to six weeks*

WESTERN MOSQUITOFISH
Gambusia affinis

SYNONYM: *Gambusia affinis affinis*
FAMILY: Poeciliidae
SUBFAMILY: Poeciliinae

TOGETHER WITH ITS CLOSEST RELATIVE, G. HOL-*brooki* (Eastern Mosquitofish), this is undoubtedly the most widely distributed of all the livebearers, having been introduced into numerous tropical and subtropical regions as a biological means of malaria control. While effective in this role—by eating large quantities of malaria mosquito larvae—both these species have proved very invasive and have often displaced native species. Melanic (black or black-mottled) morphs of *G. holbrooki* are commonly found in the wild.

DISTRIBUTION: *G. affinis: From northern Veracruz (Mexico) northward to southern Indiana and eastward to Alabama; G. holbrooki: From central Alabama eastward to Florida and northward up to New Jersey. Both species also exist as exotic populations in numerous other locations*

SIZE: *Males up to 1⅝in (4cm); females up to 2¾in (7cm)*

BEHAVIOR: *Distinct fin-nipping tendencies; voracious appetite toward anything of a swallowable size. Both these species should be kept as a shoal*

DIET: *Livefoods preferred, but wide range of other diets also accepted*

AQUARIUM: *Well-planted, covered, and with surface vegetation with feathery roots (to offer protection for fry). Water chemistry not critical, but quality must be good. Temperature range: from below 50°F (10°C) to above 86°F (30°C)*

BREEDING: *Broods can vary from 10–80 fry and are produced every five to eight weeks during the warmer months. Parents are highly cannibalistic toward their offspring*

GOLDEN GAMBUSIA
GOLDEN MOSQUITOFISH
Gambusia aurata

FAMILY: Poeciliidae
SUBFAMILY: Poeciliinae

THIS VERY ATTRACTIVE SPECIES, WITH GOLDEN body color and rows of fine black body spots, is one of the stockier-looking representatives of the genus.

DISTRIBUTION: *State of Tamaulipas (Mexico)*

SIZE: *Males around 1in (2.5cm); females around 1½in (4cm)*

BEHAVIOR: *As for G. affinis*

DIET: *As for G. affinis*

AQUARIUM: *As for G. affinis, but temperatures should not go below 15°C (59°F) for extended periods*

BREEDING: *Broods of 10–20 fry produced every 4–6 weeks*

OTHER *GAMBUSIA* SPECIES

There are around 35 species of *Gambusia* so far described, with the possibility that this figure may rise slightly as some outstanding taxonomical queries are resolved. Most are hardy and relatively easy to keep and breed following the guidelines given for *G. affinis*, though not all exhibit the keen cannibalistic and fin-nipping characteristics of this species. Although most are comfortable at temperatures in the 72–77°F (22–25°C) range, quite a number can tolerate considerably lower temperatures, while a few, e.g. *G. luma* (Clawed Gambusia or Mosquitofish) from Guatemala and *G. nicaraguensis* (Nicaragua Gambusia or Mosquitofish) require warmer water in the 75–84°F (24–29°C) range. Before obtaining any *Gambusia* species, expert advice should be sought, both from specialist literature (*see* Bibliography) and specialist livebearer aquarists and societies.

MARSH'S GAMBUSIA
MARSH'S MOSQUITOFISH
Gambusia marshi

FAMILY: Poeciliidae
SUBFAMILY: Poeciliinae

THE YELLOWISH-BROWN BASE BODY COLOR, AND the distinct dark band that runs from the head to the caudal peduncle, make this species easily recognizable.

DISTRIBUTION: *Cuatro Ciénegas basin in Coahuila (Mexico)*

SIZE: *Males around 1⅜in (3.5cm); females up to 2¼in (6cm)*

BEHAVIOR: *One of the more peaceful of the genus; should be kept in a shoal*

DIET: *Wide range of foods accepted*

AQUARIUM: *As for G. affinis. Temperature range: 72–77°F (22–25°C)*

BREEDING: *As for G. aurata*

GIRARDINUS TOPMINNOW
METALLIC, or BLACK-BELLIED METALLIC, TOPMINNOW
Girardinus metallicus

FAMILY: Poeciliidae
SUBFAMILY: Poeciliinae

THIS IS THE MOST FREQUENTLY SEEN OF THE EIGHT species making up this genus. In some males, the gonopodium has black coloration that extends forward into the chest area (hence the "black-bellied" part of one of the common names). Both males and females have a metallic sheen and vertical black body bands.

DISTRIBUTION: *Most of Cuba*

SIZE: *Males up to 2in (5cm); females up to 3½in (9cm)*

BEHAVIOR: *Lively shoaler*

GIRARDINUS TOPMINNOW (GIRARDINUS METALLICUS)

OTHER *GIRARDINUS* SPECIES

In addition to *G. metallicus*, seven other species are cited in current aquatic literature. All exhibit similar characteristics and have similar requirements to those outlined for *G. metallicus*, but specialist literature should be consulted (*see* Bibliography) or advice sought from experts. Sizes given below are approximate, that of males being listed first.

SCIENTIFIC NAME	COMMON NAME(S)	SIZE
G. creolus *	Creole Topminnow	1½in (4cm); 2¾in (7.5cm)
G. cubensis **	Cuban Topminnow	1¼in (3cm); 1¾in (4.5cm)
G. denticulatus	Toothy Topminnow	1½in (4cm); 2⅜in (6cm)
G. falcatus *	Goldbelly Topminnow	1½in (4cm); 2¾in (7cm)
G. microdactylus	Smallfinger Topminnow	1⅜in (3.5cm); 2⅜in (6cm)
G. serripensis	Taco Taco, or Serrated, Topminnow	1½in (4cm); 2½in (6.5cm)
G. uninotatus	Singlespot Topminnow	2in (5cm); 3in (8cm)

NOTE

* These two species are generally seen more frequently than the others listed

**There is some doubt regarding the validity of this species

DIET: *Wide range of foods accepted*

AQUARIUM: *Planted, covered, well-filtered, with some gentle water movement. Slightly alkaline, medium-hard water preferred. Temperature range: 72–84°F (22–29°C)*

BREEDING: *At the higher temperatures, broods of up to 100 fry (but usually fewer) are produced every five weeks or so*

MOSQUITO FISH

DWARF LIVEBEARER, DWARF TOPMINNOW, LEAST KILLIFISH

Heterandria formosa

FAMILY: Poeciliidae
SUBFAMILY: Poeciliinae

OF THE COMMON NAMES CITED, THE LAST SHOULD cease to be used because this delightful, minute species is not a killifish at all. It ranks among the smallest vertebrates known to science. A fish for the specialist, it should be regarded as a "must" by any aquarist who develops the appropriate level of husbandry skills.

DISTRIBUTION: *From southeastern North Carolina southward, including eastern and southern Georgia, Florida, the Gulf Coast (as far as New Orleans) and Louisiana*

SIZE: *Males up to ¾in (2cm); females up to 1¼in (3cm)*

BEHAVIOR: *Peaceful shoaler, best kept in a tank set up exclusively for it*

DIET: *Small livefoods preferred, but other diets also accepted; a regular vegetable supplement recommended*

AQUARIUM: *Thickly planted, covered. Alkaline hardish water preferred, but other conditions*

also accepted. Temperature range: from 61°F (16°C) to around 84°F (29°C)

BREEDING: *Small numbers of relatively large fry are released on an almost daily basis over a period of 10–14 days (this is known as superfetation)*

MILLER'S FLYER

Heterophallus milleri

SYNONYM: *Gambusia milleri*
FAMILY: Poeciliidae
SUBFAMILY: Poeciliinae

AS THE TWO SCIENTIFIC NAMES INDICATE, THERE is some debate regarding the true identity of this attractively finned species. In addition to the glistening coloration of some of the fins, the caudal—at least, in some specimens—has three rounded tips: one at the top, one in the middle and one on the bottom, the latter being slightly extended in some mature males. Two other species also occasionally available are: *H. echeagarayi* (Palenque Flyer) and *H. rachovii* (Rachow's Flyer)—both also from Mexico.

DISTRIBUTION: *Mainly Teapa river in Tabasco (Mexico)*

SIZE: *Males around 1in (2.5cm); females up to 1½in (4cm)*

BEHAVIOR: *Active shoaler*

DIET: *Livefoods preferred, but other diets may also be accepted*

AQUARIUM: *Thickly planted, with some water movement. Carry out regular partial water changes. Neutral, softish water seems to be preferred but*

MOSQUITO FISH (*HETERANDRIA FORMOSA*)

▲ DOMINICAN LIMIA (LIMIA DOMINICENSIS); SEE BOX P.278   ▼ HUMPBACKED LIMIA (LIMIA NIGROFASCIATA)

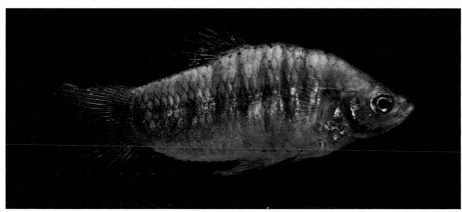

HUMPBACKED LIMIA

BLACK-BARRED LIMIA

Limia nigrofasciata

SYNONYM: *Poecilia nigrofasciata*
FAMILY: Poeciliidae
SUBFAMILY: Poeciliinae

THE HUMPED BACK OF ONE OF THE COMMON names is particularly evident in fully mature males, a group of which create an impressive sight in any aquarium. Hybridization with closely related species is not uncommon. Two very similar species: *L. grossidens* (Largetooth Limia) and *L. miragoanensis* (Miragoane Limia)—both also from Lake Miragoane—are thought by some authors to be synonymous with Humpbacked Limia.

DISTRIBUTION: *Lake Miragoane in Haiti*

SIZE: *Males around 2¼in (5.5cm); females up to 2½in (6cm)*

BEHAVIOR: *A peaceful shoaler*

DIET: *As for* L. melanogaster

AQUARIUM: *As for* L. melanogaster, *but water need not be as hard and alkaline. Temperature range: 75–82°F (24–28°C)*

BREEDING: *Temperature appears to affect the sex ratio of fry, with the higher end of the scale reportedly resulting in more females. Broods of around 60 fry are produced every four to ten weeks*

CUBAN LIMIA

Limia vittata

SYNONYM: *Poecilia vittata*
FAMILY: Poeciliidae
SUBFAMILY: Poeciliinae

THIS IS ANOTHER EXTREMELY ATTRACTIVE *LIMIA* species that hybridizes easily with its closest relatives. It is also highly variable, with some specimens having very little spotting, while others—particularly some of the aquarium-bred strains—being richly spotted in yellow and black.

DISTRIBUTION: *Cuba; some populations occur in brackish waters*

SIZE: *Males up to 2½in (6.5cm); females up to 4¾in (12cm), but usually smaller*

BEHAVIOR: *As for* L. melanogaster

DIET: *As for* L. melanogaster

AQUARIUM: *As for* L. melanogaster. *A little salt—about 1 teaspoonful per 1 Imp. gal (4.5–5 liters) may be added to the aquarium water, but this is not essential. Temperature range: 75–82°F (24–28°C)*

BREEDING: *Large broods of up to 100 fry are produced every four to six weeks*

some deviation acceptable. Temperature range: 64–84°F (18–29°C)

BREEDING: *Small broods (usually fewer than 20 fry) produced every four to six weeks*

BLACK-BELLIED LIMIA

Limia melanogaster

SYNONYM: *Poecilia melanogaster*
FAMILY: Poeciliidae
SUBFAMILY: Poeciliinae

IN PEAK CONDITION, THIS A SUPERB LITTLE FISH for a community aquarium. Males have a bluish sheen and yellow coloration in the caudal and dorsal fins, and females have a large black belly patch. Males, in particular, are always on the move, displaying to each other and attempting to mate, both with females of their own species and with those of closely related ones (when fertile hybrids may be produced).

DISTRIBUTION: *Jamaica*

SIZE: *Males up to 1¾in (4.5cm); females up to 2¼in (6cm)*

BEHAVIOR: *Active shoaler*

DIET: *Wide range of foods accepted; regular vegetable component important*

AQUARIUM: *Well-planted, covered, with open swimming area, and good illumination to encourage growth of green encrusting algae (a natural source of vegetable food) on the aquarium panes (leave the sides and back unscraped during aquarium maintenance). Alkaline, hardish, good-quality water preferred. Temperature range: 72–82°F (22–28°C)*

BREEDING: *Broods of about 20 fry are produced every five to eight weeks. Considerable variation, however, exists, both in the size and frequency of these broods*

CUBAN LIMIA (LIMIA VITTATA)

OTHER *LIMIA* SPECIES

In addition to the featured species (plus the two mentioned in the *L. nigrofasciata* entry), there are 15 other limias currently recognized. Characteristics and requirements are generally similar, with all species preferring water conditions on the alkaline and harder end of the pH and hardness spectra and temperatures in the 75–82°F (24–28°C) region. The following are the most likely species to be encountered. Sizes given are approximate, that of males being listed first.

SCIENTIFIC NAME	COMMON NAME(S)	SIZE
L. dominicensis	Dominican, Haiti, or Tiburón Peninsula, Limia	1¼in (3cm); 2in (5cm)
L. ornata	Ornate Limia	2in (5cm); 2½in (6cm)
L. perugiae	Perugia's Limia	2¾in (7cm); 3⅓in (8.5cm)
L. sulphurophila	Sulphur Limia	1⅓in (3.5cm); 1⅓in (3.5cm)
L. tridens	Tiburón Limia	1¼in (3cm); 1¾in (4.5cm)
L. zonata	Striped, or Zoned, Limia	1⅓in (3cm); 2½in (6cm)

NOTE:

Some *Limia* species interbreed easily, in some cases producing fertile hybrids, so to maintain genetic "purity," it is important not to keep species together in the same aquarium.

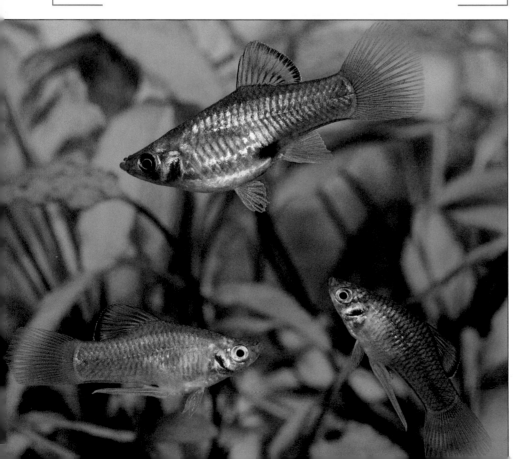

MERRY WIDOW (PHALLICHTHYS AMATES)

PICTA

Micropoecilia picta

SYNONYM: *Poecilia picta*
FAMILY: Poeciliidae
SUBFAMILY: Poeciliinae

THIS TINY FISH IS SUPERFICIALLY SIMILAR TO (*Poecilia reticulata—see* p.279). Males are brilliantly colored and highly variable, as are those of the other species in the genus. Of these, the most frequently encountered is *M. branneri* (Branner's Livebearer) from Brazil. Neither species is suitable for beginners.

DISTRIBUTION: *Guyana and Trinidad*

SIZE: *Males up to 1¼in (3cm); females up to 2in (5cm)*

BEHAVIOR: *Active shoaler; should not be kept with large boisterous tankmates*

DIET: *Range of small foods accepted; vegetable component required*

AQUARIUM: *Thickly planted, covered. Add 1 teaspoonful salt per 1 Imp. gal (4.5–5 liters) of water for longterm health. Temperature range: 75–82°F (24–28°C)*

BREEDING: *Challenging; fewer than 20 fry may be produced every four to five weeks*

MERRY WIDOW

Phallichthys amates

SYNONYM: *Phallichthys amates amates*
FAMILY: Poeciliidae
SUBFAMILY: Poeciliinae

SUPERFICIALLY, MALES OF THIS SPECIES RESEMBLE those of *Carlhubbsia stuarti* (Banded Widow—*see* p.274), but lack the bold vertical body bands of the latter. Two other species are also occasionally available: *P. fairweatheri* (Elegant Widow) from Guatemala and *P. pittieri* (Orange-dorsal Widow) from Costa Rica, western Panama and Nicaragua.

DISTRIBUTION: *Atlantic slope of southern Guatemala and northern Honduras*

SIZE: *Males up to 1½in (4cm); females up to 2¾in (7cm)*

BEHAVIOR: *Quiet shoaler; must not be kept with active tankmates*

DIET: *Range of foods accepted; vegetable component necessary*

AQUARIUM: *Thickly planted, with little or no water movement and subdued lighting. Water chemistry not critical, but extremes must be avoided. Temperature range: 72–82°F (22–28°C)*

BREEDING: *Up to 150 fry may be produced by large females every four to six weeks*

ONE-SPOT LIVEBEARER

GOLDEN ONE-SPOT, SPOTTED, or
GOLDEN SPOTTED, LIVEBEARER, THE
CAUDO

Phalloceros caudimaculatus

SYNONYMS: *Phalloceros caudimaculatus auratus* and *P. c. a. reticulatus*
FAMILY: Poeciliidae
SUBFAMILY: Poeciliinae

OWING TO ITS GREAT VARIABILITY, WITH SOME specimens bearing one body spot, others none at all and yet others being golden and/or mottled (reticulated), this species has a wide range of both common and scientific names. Modern-day thinking is that all are representatives of a highly variable single species, *P. caudimaculatus.*

DISTRIBUTION: *Southern Brazil, Paraguay and Uruguay; introduced into some locations outside its range, e.g. Malawi and western Australia*

SIZE: *Males around 1¼in (3cm); females up to 2in (5cm)*

BEHAVIOR: *A peaceful shoaler*

DIET: *Range of foods accepted; vegetable component required*

AQUARIUM: *Well-planted, well-illuminated. Water chemistry not critical, but alkaline, medium-hard conditions preferred. Temperature range: 64–82°F (18–28°C)*

BREEDING: *Up to 80 fry may be produced every five to six weeks*

SAILFIN MOLLY

Poecilia latipinna

FAMILY: Poeciliidae
SUBFAMILY: Poeciliinae

DESPITE ITS COMMON NAME, NOT ALL WILD MALES of this species develop the full sail-like dorsal fin. The pure wild form of the species is hardly ever seen within the hobby. Instead, either cultivated color varieties or, more frequently, fertile hybrids between sailfins and two of their closest relatives, *P. sphenops* and *P. velifera—see* separate entries—are encountered.

DISTRIBUTION: *The Carolinas, Florida, Texas, Virginia and Atlantic coast of Mexico*

SIZE: *Males around 4in (10cm); females around 4¾in (12cm)*

BEHAVIOR: *Peaceful shoaler; males constantly display toward each other*

DIET: *Range of foods accepted; vegetable component essential*

AQUARIUM: *Spacious, planted, with some open swimming space. Alkaline, medium-hard water with 1 teaspoonful salt per 1 Imp. gal (4.5–5*

liters) important for longterm health. Temperature range: 77–82°F (25–28°C)

BREEDING: *Broods of well over 100 fry are common every eight to ten weeks*

GUPPY

MILLIONS FISH

Poecilia reticulata

FAMILY: Poeciliidae
SUBFAMILY: Poeciliinae

IN THE HOBBY SINCE THE EARLY 1900S, THE Guppy is one of the best known and popular aquarium fishes of all time. It is an adaptable, hardy fish whose inherent genetic variability has been exploited over the years to produce a bewildering array of fin and color permutations. As a result, the original short-finned wild type of the species is hardly ever seen, except in the aquaria of specialist livebearer enthusiasts. Endler's Livebearer is a particularly beautiful wild form.

DISTRIBUTION: *Widely distributed north of the Amazon and extensively introduced into tropical and subtropical regions outside of the range*

SIZE: *Wild males up to 1¼in (3cm); wild females around 2in (5cm); cultivated varieties generally larger*

BEHAVIOR: *Peaceful shoaler; should not be kept with boisterous or fin-nipping tankmates, e.g. Barbus tetrazona (Tiger Barb)*

DIET: *Wide range of foods accepted; vegetable component recommended*

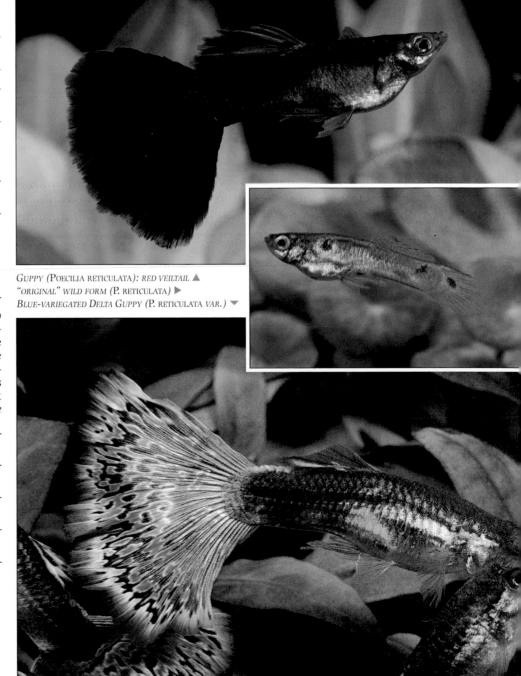

GUPPY (POECILIA RETICULATA): RED VEILTAIL ▲
"ORIGINAL" WILD FORM (P. RETICULATA) ▶
BLUE-VARIEGATED DELTA GUPPY (P. RETICULATA VAR.) ▼

AQUARIUM: *Well-planted, well-illuminated, with some open swimming space. Water chemistry not critical, but alkaline, medium-hard conditions preferred. Temperature range: 64–82°F (18–28°C)*

BREEDING: *Large females can produce over 150 fry every four to six weeks*

SPHENOPS MOLLY

Poecilia sphenops
GREEN, BLACK, LIBERTY, MEXICAN, or POINTED-MOUTH, MOLLY

FAMILY: Poeciliidae
SUBFAMILY: Poeciliinae

THIS HIGHLY VARIABLE, WIDELY DISTRIBUTED species has given rise to a vast array of cultivated varieties (many through hybridization), the best known of which is the Black Molly. According to some authorities, it is the closely related—and very similar—*P. mexicana* (Atlantic Molly) that is the true ancestor of the aquarium strains. The confusion seems to have arisen from both species' being regarded as one and the same. The Liberty Molly, a form of Sphenops Molly, possesses a short, but very attractively colored and patterned dorsal fin. Both *P. mexicana* and Sphenops Molly hybridize with *P. latipinna* and *P. velifera* (*see* p.279 and below).

DISTRIBUTION: *From Texas southward along both Mexican coasts, as far as Colombia; also introduced elsewhere*

SIZE: *Males around 2¼in (6cm); females around 3¼in (8cm)*

BEHAVIOR: *Peaceful shoaler*

DIET: *Wide range of foods accepted; vegetable component essential*

AQUARIUM: *As for* P. latipinna

BREEDING: *Broods of around 80 fry produced every five to seven weeks*

YUCATÁN MOLLY

SAILFIN MOLLY
Poecilia velifera

FAMILY: Poeciliidae
SUBFAMILY: Poeciliinae

WILD SPECIMENS OF THIS SPECIES LOOK SIMILAR to those of *P. latipinna* (*see* p.279). However, Yucatán Molly is larger, and has a fuller sail-like dorsal fin, with a higher number of fin rays (18 or 19, as opposed to 14). Ease of hybridization between this species, *P. latipinna* and/or *P. sphenops* has resulted in a spectacular range of aquarium varieties.

BLACK MOLLY
(POECILIA VELIFERA VAR.)

DISTRIBUTION: *Yucatán Peninsula (Mexico)*

SIZE: *Males up to 6in (15cm); females up to 7in (18cm)*

BEHAVIOR: *As for* P. latipinna

DIET: *As for* P. latipinna

AQUARIUM: *As for* P. latipinna

BREEDING: *Broods numbering 100 fry—and produced every six to eight weeks—are not uncommon*

OTHER *POECILIA* SPECIES

There are about 35 species in the genus *Poecilia*, most of which are only rarely available. However, stocks of most species are maintained by members of livebearer associations throughout the world. For a full listing of all the known species, as well as for specific guidance on aquarium care, consult specialist literature (*see* Bibliography). The following are the species most likely to be encountered. Sizes given are approximate, with that of males listed first.

SCIENTIFIC NAME	COMMON NAME(S)	SIZE
P. butleri	Pacific Molly	2¾in (7cm); 3in (8cm)
P. caucana	South American Molly	1¼in (3cm); 1½in (4cm)
P. chica	Dwarf Molly	1¼in (3cm); 1½in (3.5cm)
P. dominicensis	Santo Domingo Molly	1½in (3.5cm); 2½in (6cm)
P. "formosa" *	Amazon Molly	—*; 2½in (6cm)
P. gillii	Gill's Molly	1½in (4cm); 2in (5cm)
P. latipunctata	Tamesí Molly	2in (5cm); 2½in (6cm)
P. maylandi	Mayland's Molly	4in (10cm); 4¾in (12cm)
P. petenensis	Petén Molly	4in (10cm); 3in (8cm)
P. salvatoris	Salvator Molly	3in (8cm); 4in (10cm)
P. vivipara	One-spot Molly	2in (5cm); 2½in (6cm)

NOTE

* This is not a true species, but a hybrid in which eggs appear to develop after they are "penetrated" by sperm, but without fertilization actually taking place (gynogenesis). The species involved are generally thought to be *P. latipinna* and *P. mexicana*, but males of a number of species are known to produce the same effect. All *P. "formosa"* are females; males reported from time to time have not been unequivocally confirmed

▲▲▲ SOUTH AMERICAN MOLLY (POECILIA CAUCANA)
▲▲ DWARF MOLLY (POECILIA CHICA) ▲ GILL'S MOLLY (POECILIA GILLII)

ORANGE AND BLACK SAILFIN MOLLY (POECILIA VELIFERA VAR.)

and a "keel" running from the vent to the base of the caudal fin. *P. intermedia* (Oaxacan Blue-eye), from Oaxaca (Mexico) and *P. olmecae* (Olmecan Blue-eye), from around Veracruz (Mexico) are also occasionally available; the latter has very attractive fins with a good deal of orange coloration.

DISTRIBUTION: *Chiapas (Mexico)*

SIZE: *Males up to 1¾in (4.5cm); females 2¾in (7cm)*

BEHAVIOR: *Active shoalers with excellent jumping ability. (They are known to catch flying insects in the wild)*

DIET: *Strong preference for livefoods, but other formulations accepted*

AQUARIUM: *Spacious, planted and covered, with open swimming areas and water movement (as produced via the outlet of a powerhead or power filter). Clean, well-oxygenated water essential. Extremes of pH and hardness must be avoided. Temperature range: 72–82°F (22–28°C)*

BREEDING: *Up to 30 fry may be produced every four to eight weeks*

PORTHOLE LIVEBEARER

Poeciliopsis gracilis

FAMILY: Poeciliidae
SUBFAMILY: Poeciliinae

THIS SILVERY-SIDED SPECIES HAS A NUMBER OF black spots along the body, which can vary in number (from 4 to 11) and in intensity.

DISTRIBUTION: *Southern Mexico to Honduras, along both the Atlantic and Pacific coasts*

SIZE: *Males up to 1½in (4cm); females reported up to 2¾in (7cm)*

BEHAVIOR: *Active shoaler*

DIET: *Livefoods preferred, but other diets accepted; vegetable component recommended*

AQUARIUM: *Well-planted, covered, with some open swimming space. Neutral to slightly alkaline, well-oxygenated, medium-hard water preferred. Temperature range: 72–82°F (22–28°C)*

BREEDING: *A few fry are produced every day over a period of some ten days (superfetation); up to 60 fry may be produced over this period*

MAYAN BLUE-EYE

SLAB-SIDED BLUE-EYE

Priapella compressa

FAMILY: Poeciliidae
SUBFAMILY: Poeciliinae

LIKE THE TWO OTHER MEMBERS OF ITS GENUS, *P. compressa* has beautiful blue eyes. It also has a compressed, beige-orange body,

TWO-SPOT LIVEBEARER

COMMON TWIN-SPOT LIVEBEARER, SPOT-TAILED MOSQUITOFISH, PSEUDO HELLERI

Pseudoxiphophorus bimaculatus

SYNONYM: *Heterandria bimaculata*
FAMILY: Poeciliidae
SUBFAMILY: Poeciliinae

WITH THE POSSIBLE EXCEPTION OF *POECILIA velifera* (*see* p.280), this is the largest of the poeciliid livebearers. In peak condition, it is a truly impressive species. *P. joinesii* (Northern Twin-spot Livebearer)—also from Mexico, and the only other species seen with any frequency in the hobby—does not possess the same intensity of coloration, but it is about half the size of *P. bimaculata* and therefore a little easier to maintain.

DISTRIBUTION: *From southern Veracruz and Oaxaca (Mexico), to Belize, Guatemala and Honduras*

SIZE: *Males around 2¾in (7cm); females 6in (15cm)*

BEHAVIOR: *Highly aggressive and predatory, but can be kept as a shoal of similar-sized individuals, as well as with similar-sized tankmates of other species*

DIET: *Livefoods strongly preferred, but some other formulations may be accepted*

AQUARIUM: *Spacious, well-planted, covered, with some open swimming areas and water current (as produced via a powerhead or power filter outlet). Clean, well-oxygenated water important, and extremes of pH and hardness should be avoided. Temperature range: 72–79°F (22–26°C)*

BREEDING: *Broods of over 100 fry are produced every four to eight weeks*

OTHER *POECILIOPSIS* SPECIES

There are just over 20 species in this genus, but only *P. gracilis* is seen on a regular basis. Several of these are spotted and can be easily confused with *P. gracilis*. Advice should therefore be sought, both from specialist literature and hobbyists (also the best source of supply). The following are probably the most frequently available of these. Sizes are approximate, with that of males listed first.

SCIENTIFIC NAME	COMMON NAME(S)	SIZE
P. baenschi *	Baensch's Topminnow	1¼in (3cm); 1¼in (3cm)
P. hnilickai *	Comitan Topminnow	1⅖in (3.5cm); 2in (5cm)
P. infans	Black Topminnow, or Rio Lerma, Mosquitofish	1⅖in (3.5cm); 2in (5cm)
P. latidens*	Broad-toothed Topminnow	1¼in (3cm); 2in (5cm)
P. prolifica	Prolific Topminnow	¾in (2cm); 1⅖in (3.5cm)
P. turrubarensis *	Pacific, or Costa Rican, Topminnow	1⅖in (4cm); 3in (8cm)
P. viriosa	Robust Topminnow	1⅖in (3.5cm); 2½in (6cm)

NOTE:

* These are some of the spotted species referred to in the opening paragraph.

BLACK-BARRED LIVEBEARER
BARRED TOPMINNOW
Quintana atrizona

FAMILY: Poeciliidae
SUBFAMILY: Poeciliinae

IN PEAK CONDITION, THIS IS A DELIGHTFUL SPECIES with black body bars, black patches in the dorsal fin, light blue in the pelvic and anal fins, and silvery chest and belly.

DISTRIBUTION: *Western Cuba*

SIZE: *Males up to 1in (2.5cm); females up to 1½in (4cm)*

BEHAVIOR: *Retiring shoaler; must not be kept with boisterous tankmates*

DIET: *Livefoods preferred, but other diets accepted; vegetable component recommended*

AQUARIUM: *Densely planted, with surface vegetation and little water movement. Clean, slightly alkaline, medium-hard water preferred. Temperature range: 75–82°F (24–28°C)*

BREEDING: *Broods numbering, on average, around 25–30 fry are produced every five to eight weeks*

SHEEPHEAD SWORDTAIL
Xiphophorus birchmanni

FAMILY: Poeciliidae
SUBFAMILY: Poeciliinae

THIS IS ONE OF THE "NEWER" SPECIES OF SWORDtail and Platy described since the mid-1980s. It is a stocky fish in which males have a magnificent rounded dorsal fin and very short sword. Mature males also have a characteristic thickened (hump) area on the head, hence the common name.

DISTRIBUTION: *Southern part of the Pánuco river basin, San Pedro river system, Montezuma and Tuxpan rivers—all in Mexico*

SIZE: *Males around 2½–3in (6–8cm); females around 2¾in (7cm)*

BEHAVIOR: *Somewhat timid shoaler; either one male, or a group, should be maintained (if only two males are kept, one is likely to suffer)*

DIET: *Livefoods preferred, but other diets also accepted; vegetable component important*

AQUARIUM: *Heavily planted, covered, with some open space. Alkaline medium-hard water preferred. Temperature range: 70–77°F (21–25°C)*

BREEDING: *About 30 fry produced every four to five weeks*

PUEBLO PLATY
Xiphophorus evelynae

FAMILY: Poeciliidae
SUBFAMILY: Poeciliinae

THE "PEPPER-DUST" SPOTTING EXHIBITED BY THIS fish makes it very attractive. It is not dissimilar in overall body shape to the *X. variatus—see* p.283.

DISTRIBUTION: *Nexaca, and Tecolutla river system (Mexico)*

SIZE: *Males up to 1¾in (4.5cm); females around 2in (5cm)*

BEHAVIOR: *Peaceful shoaler (keep as outlined for X. birchmanni)*

DIET: *As for X. birchmanni*

AQUARIUM: *As for X. birchmanni*

BREEDING: *Around 50 fry are produced every four to five weeks*

SWORDTAIL
Xiphophorus helleri

FAMILY: Poeciliidae
SUBFAMILY: Poeciliinae

TRUE WILD-TYPE SWORDTAILS ARE HARDLY EVER seen within the general hobby today. Considerable numbers of this highly variable species are, however, kept by livebearer enthusiasts who represent the best source of such specimens. Elsewhere, the vast majority of swordtails are available in a wide range of color and fin varieties developed over many decades. Many of these cultivated fish are the result of crosses between Swordtail and one or other of two of its close relatives, *X. maculatus* and *X. variatus—see* separate entries.

DISTRIBUTION: *Atlantic drainages in central America from Mexico to northwestern Honduras; also introduced into numerous locations outside its range, including Sri Lanka and South Africa*

SIZE: *Males around 4in (10cm), excluding the sword; females around 4in (10cm); larger sizes also reported but generally not attained*

BEHAVIOR: *Active shoaler; males can be scrappy among themselves; keep as outlined for X. birchmanni*

DIET: *As for X. birchmanni*

AQUARIUM: *As for X. birchmanni*

BREEDING: *Up to 200 fry are produced every four to six weeks*

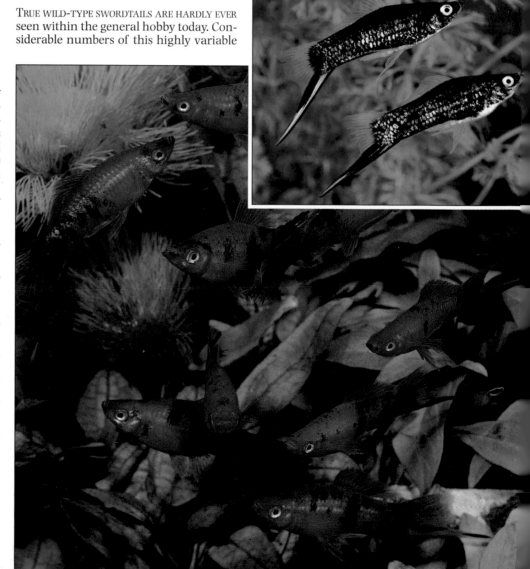

MARBLED RED SWORDTAIL (XIPHOPHORUS HELLERI VAR.)
(Inset) *BLACK SWORDTAIL (XIPHOPHORUS HELLERI VAR.)*

SOUTHERN PLATY
MOONFISH
Xiphophorus maculatus

FAMILY: Poeciliidae
SUBFAMILY: Poeciliinae

JUST LIKE ITS FAMOUS RELATIVE, *X. HELLERI*, THIS species is inherently highly variable and has been developed into numerous color varieties. It has also been hybridized with both *X. helleri* and *X. variatus*. The best source of true wild-type specimens is specialist livebearer societies (*see* photo p.3).

DISTRIBUTION: *From Veracruz in Mexico, to Belize and Guatemala*

SIZE: *Males to 1½in (4cm); females up to 2¼in (6cm); cultivated varieties and hybrids may be larger*

BEHAVIOR: *Placid shoaler*

DIET: *As for* X. birchmanni

OTHER *XIPHOPHORUS* SPECIES

There are around 30 species in the genus *Xiphophorus*, relatively few of which are available in aquatic outlets with any regularity. Some species are under threat in the wild, but most (including the threatened ones) are kept and bred by members of livebearer societies in various countries. These societies are the best sources of supply for such species, as well as of maintenance and breeding information. Within the genus, some species are referred to as platies and some as swordtails, but the distinction between the two is not clear-cut. Numerous reports of sex reversal in swordtails may be found in aquarium literature, but these need to be regarded with great caution, since—in all cases that have been studied—the "females" that have apparently changed into males have all been late-developing males. The following are among the best known species. Sizes given are approximate, with that of males listed first. (In the case of swordtails, the length quoted excludes the sword).

SCIENTIFIC NAME	COMMON NAME(S)	SIZE
X. alvarezi	Upland Swordtail	2⅜in (6cm); 3in (7.5cm)
X. andersi	Ander's Platy	1¾in (4.5cm); 2⅛in (5.5cm)
X. clemenciae	Yellow Swordtail	1½in (4cm); 2⅛in (5.5cm)
X. cortezi *	Cortés Swordtail	1¾in (4.5cm); 2⅜in (6cm)
X. couchianus	Monterrey Platy	2in (5cm); 2⅜in (6cm)
X. gordoni	Cuatro Ciénegas Platy	1⅜in (3.5cm); 1⅝in (4cm)
X. malinche	Highland Swordtail	2in (5cm); 2in (5cm)
X. milleri	Catemaco Swordtail	1in (2.5cm); 1¾in (4.5cm)
X. multilineatus	High-backed Pygmy Swordtail	2in (5cm); 2in (5cm)
X. nezahualcoyotl	Northern Mountain Swordtail	2in (5cm); 2⅛in (5.5cm)
X. nigrensis	El Abra Pygmy Swordtail	2⅛in (5.5cm); 2⅛in (5.5cm)
X. pygmaeus **	Slender Pygmy Swordtail	1⅜in (3.5cm); 1⅝in (4cm)
X. signum	Comma Swordtail	3in (8cm); 4in (10cm)
X. xiphidium ***	Spiketail Platy	1¼in (3cm); 1⅝in (4cm)

NOTES:

* *X. cortezi* has traditionally been known as the Montezuma Swordtail, but this common name should be reserved for *X. montezumae*

** Two naturally occurring color forms of *X. pygmaeus* are officially recognized: "Yellow" and "Blue"

*** *X. xiphidium* hybridizes easily with some other *Xiphophorus* species, such as *X. maculatus*, *X. alvarezi* and *X. nigrensis*. A naturally occurring hybrid with *X. variatus* is generally known as *X. "kosszanderi"*

MONTERREY PLATY (XIPHOPHORUS COUCHIANUS)

AQUARIUM: *As for* X. birchmanni. *Temperature range: 64–77°F (18–25°C)*

BREEDING: *Around 50 fry are produced every four to six weeks*

MONTEZUMA SWORDTAIL
Xiphophorus montezumae

FAMILY: Poeciliidae
SUBFAMILY: Poeciliinae

MALES OF THIS SLENDER-BODIED SPECIES PRODUCE an exceptionally long sword, making a shoal of such fish an unforgettable sight. A number of zigzag body stripes, plus speckling (not seen in all populations or specimens) add to the attraction of this species, particularly among livebearer enthusiasts.

DISTRIBUTION: *Mainly Tamesi river basin (Tamaulipas) and Panuco river basin (San Luis de Potosi) in Mexico*

SIZE: *Males up to 2⅜in (6cm)—excluding the sword; females up to 7.5 cm (3in); larger sizes also reported*

BEHAVIOR: *Active shoaler; keep as outlined for* X. birchmanni

DIET: *As for* X. birchmanni

AQUARIUM: *As for* X. birchmanni

BREEDING: *Up to 50 fry (but usually fewer) are produced every four to eight (usually four to five) weeks*

SUNSET PLATY
VARIATUS PLATY
Xiphophorus variatus

FAMILY: Poeciliidae
SUBFAMILY: Poeciliinae

THIS FISH IS MORE SLENDER THAN X. MACULATUS (*see* above) and carries a number of bars on its body (lacking in *X. maculatus*). Many aquarium Variatus specimens are hybrids between these two platy species or between *X. variatus* and *X. helleri*. At least one such variety even exhibits a pronounced sword, which is a characteristic of *X. helleri*, but not of either platy species.

DISTRIBUTION: *Atlantic slope of Mexico*

SIZE: *Males up to 2¼in (5.5cm); females approximately 2¾in (7cm); cultivated varieties may be larger*

BEHAVIOR: *A peaceful shoaler*

DIET: *As for* X. birchmanni

AQUARIUM: *As for* X. birchmanni. *Temperature range: 61–81°F (16–27°C)*

BREEDING: *Around 50 fry (but up to 100) produced every four to six weeks*

▲ MONO (MONODACTYLUS ARGENTEUS)

▼ SPOTTED PUFFER (TETRAODON SCHOUTEDENI). SEE BOX

and is referred to as *S. "rubrifrons"* or *S. argus atromaculatus*. However, it is generally accepted that it is just a naturally occurring color variety of *S. agrus. S. tetracanthus* (African Scat) is only rarely seen in the hobby. *Selenotoca multifasciata* (Silver Scat) from Australia—also known as Striped Butterfish or Striped Scat—is occasionally available and has similar characteristics and requirements. In the wild, adult Scats are generally estuarine or saltwater fish. Juveniles enter freshwater, and it is these that are usually available in shops.

DISTRIBUTION: *Widely distributed in brackish and marine waters in the Indian and Pacific oceans*

SIZE: *Up to 12in (30cm)*

BEHAVIOR: *Lively, peaceful shoaler*

DIET: *All foods accepted; vegetable component essential*

AQUARIUM: *Large, deep, with clumps of salt-tolerant (or artificial) plants*, and substantial open swimming areas. Well-filtered, alkaline, hard water important. Add 1 teaspoonful of salt per 1 Imp. gal (4.5–5 liters) to aquaria housing juveniles, gradually doubling this concentration as they grow. Eventually, nearly (or fully) saline conditions*

should be provided for adults. Temperature range: 68–82°F (20–28°C)

BREEDING: *No documented accounts available*

*NOTE: *It has been reported that the Java Fern (Microsorum pteropus) is toxic to Scats*

MONO
MOON, or FINGER, FISH, SILVER BATFISH, BUTTER BREAM
Monodactylus argenteus

FAMILY: Monodactylidae

USUALLY SOLD AS JUVENILES, MONOS WILL—given appropriate conditions—eventually grow into large fish. Juveniles often occur in freshwater, but adults require brackish conditions. As juveniles grow, they lose their pelvic fins either partially or entirely. In *Psettus (Monodactylus) sebae* (Seba Mono), the body is deeper than long, particularly in young specimens. It is also a little less tolerant of freshwater conditions than the Mono.

DISTRIBUTION: *Widely distributed in brackish-water tropical regions from Africa to Asia and Australia*

SIZE: *Up to 10in (25cm), but usually smaller*

BEHAVIOR: *Peaceful shoaler, but larger specimens may prey on small fish*

DIET: *As for* Scatophagus argus

AQUARIUM: *As for* Scatophagus argus

BREEDING: *As for* Scatophagus argus

GREEN PUFFER
Tetraodon fluviatilis

FAMILY: Tetraodontidae

THIS IS PROBABLY THE SPECIES OF PUFFER MOST frequently seen in shops. As its species name indicates, this species can be found in at least some freshwater habitats in the wild. However, for peak longterm health, brackish conditions are recommended.

DISTRIBUTION: *Freshwater and brackish regions in southeast Asia*

SIZE: *Up to 6¾in (17cm)*

BEHAVIOR: *Increasingly intolerant and aggressive with age, particularly toward conspecifics; exhibits fin-nipping tendencies*

DIET: *Wide range of foods accepted, including aquatic snails and succulent plants*

AQUARIUM: *Spacious, with several shelters, fine-grained substratum, and tough and/or unpalatable plants (see Aquarium Plants)—or their artificial equivalents—arranged in clumps along sides and back, leaving open swimming area along front. Neutral to alkaline hard water with about 1 teaspoonful of salt per 1 Imp. gal (4.5–5 liters) recommended. Temperature range: 75–82°F (24–28°C)*

BREEDING: *Challenging in aquaria; brackish conditions important. Eggs are laid on stone and are guarded by male. Hatching takes around six to seven days*

SIAMESE TIGER
Datnioides microlepis

FAMILY: Lobotidae

THIS BEAUTIFULLY MARKED BRACKISH-WATER species grows to a large size and is therefore unsuitable for many aquaria. A second Siamese Tiger (*D. quadrifasciatus*), which is smaller (12in/30cm) and not as boldly marked, is also occasionally available.

DISTRIBUTION: *Borneo, Cambodia, Sumatra and Thailand*

SIZE: *Up to 16in (40cm), but usually much smaller*

BEHAVIOR: *Stalking predator; but can be kept with similar-sized tankmates*

DIET: *Predominantly large livefoods, including fish (a factor that requires consideration prior to purchase); it may be weaned off such foods and onto chunky deep-frozen, meaty and freeze-dried formulations*

OTHER PUFFER SPECIES

Several other species of puffer fish are available with varying degrees of regularity. They vary in size, requirements and behavior, so the main features of some of these species are listed below. Sizes given are approximate. Tank layouts should be as for *T. fluviatilis*.

SCIENTIFIC NAME	COMMON NAME(S)	SIZE	TEMPERATURE RANGE	NOTES
Carinotetraodon (Tetraodon) lorteti	Red-bellied Puffer	Up to 2¾in (7cm)	75–82°F (24–28°C)	Aggression increases with age; slightly acid, medium-hard water; no salt
Monotretus travanconicus	Red-green Dwarf Puffer	Around ¾in (2cm)	72–79°F (22–26°C)	A tiny shoaling species; slightly acid to slightly alkaline, softish water; no salt
Tetraodon biocellatus	Figure-of-eight Puffer	Up to 7in (18cm)	72–81°F (22–27°C)	Aggression increases with age; water as for *T. fluviatilis*
T. cutcutia	Mosaic Puffer	6in (15cm)	72–77°F (22–25°C)	Characteristics and water as for *T. fluviatilis*
T. mbu	Giant Puffer	Up to 12in (30cm)	75–82°F (24–28°C)	Keep alone; water conditions as for *T. fluviatilis*; no salt
T. schoutedeni	Spotted Congo Puffer	4in (10cm)	72–79°F (22–26°C)	One of the most peaceful species; tank as for *T. fluviatilis*; no salt
T. steindachneri	Steindachner's Puffer	2½in (6cm)	72–79°F (22–26°C)	Aggressive and intolerant; avid planteater; tank as for *T. fluviatilis*; no salt

ELEPHANTNOSE (GNATHONEMUS PETERSII)

AQUARIUM: *As for* Tetraodon fluviatilis.
Temperature range: 72–79°F (22–26°C)

BREEDING: *No documented accounts of aquarium breeding available*

BUTTERFLYFISH

Pantodon buchholzi

FAMILY: Pantodontidae

THIS CHALLENGING FISH, KNOWN IN THE HOBBY since the early 1900s, has never been available in large numbers. Contrary to reports, this species does not fly, i.e. it does not flap its wing-like pectoral fins. It is, however, able to glide for short distances.

DISTRIBUTION: *West Africa: Cameroon, Zaire and Nigeria*

SIZE: *Up to 10cm (4in)*

BEHAVIOR: *Surface predator; can be aggressive toward other surface swimmers but tolerant toward tankmates that occupy the lower levels of the aquarium*

DIET: *Predominantly livefoods, but will take deep-frozen and freeze-dried diets, and may accept some floating dry formulations,*

AQUARIUM: *Spacious, well-covered, with large open surface areas—but also incorporating some floating vegetation. Soft, slightly acid water, preferably tannin-stained (see Aquarium Setup), preferred, but some deviation tolerated. Temperature range: 73–86°F (23–30°C)*

BREEDING: *Challenging in aquaria; floating eggs are produced over several days. Hatching takes one-and-a-half to two days*

ELEPHANTNOSE

PETER'S ELEPHANTNOSE

Gnathonemus petersii

FAMILY: Mormyridae

ELEPHANTNOSES USE WEAK ELECTRICAL PULSES TO communicate with each other and to find their way around in the often-murky waters of their natural habitat. All species are challenging to keep, although modern-day foods and a deeper understanding of these somewhat unusual fish make their upkeep much easier than it used to be.

DISTRIBUTION: *Central and West Africa*

SIZE: *Up to 9in (23cm) reported, but usually smaller*

BEHAVIOR: *Predominantly bottom dwelling; crepuscular and nocturnal; territorial toward conspecifics; burrows in substratum in search of food*

DIET: *Distinct preference for livefoods, but will also accept other formulations, particularly deep-frozen and freeze-dried diets*

AQUARIUM: *Spacious, well-filtered, with clumps of vegetation, open spaces and fine-grained substratum (very important!). A "moonlight" fluorescent tube to facilitate nighttime viewing*

Endangered Species (CITES). However, this species is now bred in such large numbers in captivity that current demand can be satisfactorily met. There are three main color varieties: silver/green, gold and—the most highly sought and expensive—red. Several other varieties have now been added and more are likely to follow. An Australian species, *S. jardinii* (Gulf Saratoga) is also now being bred in captivity, while another Australian species, *S. leichardti*

(Spotted Saratoga), is only rarely seen.

DISTRIBUTION: *Widely distributed in Southeast Asia*

SIZE: *Up to 35in (90cm)*

BEHAVIOR: *As for* Osteoglossum bicirrhosum

DIET: *As for* Osteoglossum bicirrhosum

AQUARIUM: *As for* Osteoglossum bicirrhosum

BREEDING: *As for* Osteoglossum bicirrhosum

FIRE EEL (MASTACEMBELUS ERYTHROTAENIA)

OTHER SPINY EELS

Spiny eel classification is still, after many years of study, in a slightly confused state, with *Macrognathus* and *Mastacembelus*, and *Afromastacembelus* and *Caecomastacembelus*, often being used interchangeably. Doubts also exist about the identification and validity of some species. The following are among the most frequently encountered spiny eels (but the number is increasing). All have the same basic characteristics and aquarium requirements described for *Macrognathus aculeatus*. Sizes quoted are approximate.

SCIENTIFIC NAME	COMMON NAME(S)	SIZE
Caecomastacembelus (Afromastacembelus) ellipsifer	Big-spot Spiny Eel	6in (15cm)
C. (A.) frenatus	Ladderback Spiny Eel	6in (15cm)
C. (A.) moorii	Mottled Spiny Eel	6¼in (16cm)
C. (A.) ophidium	Snaky Spiny Eel	4in (10cm)
C. (A.) tanganikae	Tanganyikan Spiny Eel	6in (15cm)
Macrognathus aral	Lesser Spiny Eel	12in (30cm)
M. circumcinctus	Banded, or Half-banded, Spiny Eel	10in (25cm)
M. maculatus	Spotted, or Black-spotted, Spiny Eel	18in (45cm)
M. pancalus	Common, Deep-bodied, or Spotted, Spiny Eel	8in (20cm)
M. siamensis	Clown, Spot-finned, or Siamese, Spiny Eel	14in (35cm)
M. zebrinus	Zebra Spiny Eel	18in (45cm)
Mastacembelus armatus	Giant, White-spotted Car-track, or Tire-track, Spiny Eel	30in (75cm)

LESSER SPINY EEL

Macrognathus aculeatus

FAMILY: Mastacembelidae

THIS SPECIES IS CHARACTERIZED BY A NUMBER OF prominent eyespots along the base of the dorsal fin and a series of darker and lighter bands running from snout to caudal peduncle. As in all spiny eels, the dorsal fin is preceded by numerous isolated small spines that can be raised, hence the common name for these interesting fish.

DISTRIBUTION: *Southeast Asia*

SIZE: *Up to 14in (35cm) reported, but usually smaller*

BEHAVIOR: *Aggressive toward conspecifics when kept as pairs or trios; aggression subsides when kept in large groups of around ten specimens; a burrower that is most active at dusk and during the night; may prey on small fish*

DIET: *Bottom-dwelling livefoods preferred, but some commercial sinking formulations, e.g. deep-frozen, freeze-dried also accepted; may reluctantly accept pellet/tablet diets*

AQUARIUM: *Spacious, well-covered (spiny eels are expert escape artists), with fine-grained substratum, numerous hiding places, and clumps of plants protected from burrowing activities (see Aquarium Plants). A "moonlight" fluorescent tube will facilitate nighttime viewing. Neutral or slightly alkaline, soft to medium-hard water recommended. A small amount of salt, i.e. 1 teaspoonful per 2 Imp. gal (9–10 liters) may be added but is not essential. Temperature range: 73–82°F (23–28°C)*

BREEDING: *Rare in aquaria. Eggs are scattered and hatch in about three days*

FIRE EEL

SPOTTED FIRE, or ASIAN FIRE, EEL

Mastacembelus erythrotaenia

FAMILY: Mastacembelidae

THIS IS THE BEST KNOWN AND MOST COLORFUL OF all the spiny eels. It is also among the largest and perhaps the most sensitive to poor water conditions and parasitic infections and injuries. Special care must hence be taken to ensure that its aquarium requirements are scrupulously met.

DISTRIBUTION: *Southeast Asia*

SIZE: *Up to c.39in (1m) reported, but usually smaller*

BEHAVIOR: *As for* Macrognathus aculeatus

DIET: *As for* Macrognathus aculeatus

AQUARIUM: *As for* Macrognathus aculeatus

BREEDING: *No documented accounts currently available*

AFRICAN LUNGFISH

Protopterus annectens

FAMILY: Protopteridae

THIS TOUGH, LARGE FISH IS, LIKE ALL OTHER lungfishes, able to tolerate a wide range of conditions. As their native pools dry up in the wild, all the African species bury into the substratum and secrete a mucus cocoon within which they aestivate (i.e. undergo a period of summer dormancy) until the rains return. The pectoral and pelvic fins of African Lungfish are long and whip-like rather than fin-like.

DISTRIBUTION: *Widespread in Africa*

SIZE: *Up to 28in (70cm) reported*

BEHAVIOR: *Intolerant and predatory*

DIET: *Large livefoods, including fish; chunky meat-based or fish-based formulations also accepted*

AQUARIUM: *Large, well-covered, well-filtered, with fine-grained substratum and large shelters and pieces of bogwood. Water chemistry not critical. Temperature range: 77–88°F (25–30°C)*

BREEDING: *No documented reports of aquarium breeding currently available*

BOWFIN

Amia calva

FAMILY: Amiidae

FOSSILS OF MEMBERS OF THIS FAMILY OCCUR IN rocks that are up to 180 million years old.

OTHER LUNGFISH SPECIES

There are only five other lungfish species living today, although these primitive fish (some authorities question whether they are fish at all) have a long fossil history going back perhaps 270–350 million years. All are rarely seen, other than in public aquaria, and all except *Neoceratodus forsteri* (*see* Notes below) have the same basic requirements and habits.

FAMILY	SPECIES	SIZE
Ceratodontidae*—one species	*Neoceratodus forsteri* * * (Australian Lungfish)	Up to c.60in (150cm)
Lepidosirenidae—one species	*Lepidosiren paradoxa* (South American Lungfish)	Up to c.50in (125cm)
Protopteridae—three species (in addition to *Protopterus annectens*, *see* main entry)	*P. aethiopicus* (Ethiopian Lungfish) *P. amphibius* (no common name) *P. dolloi* (Spotted Lungfish)	Up to c.80in (200cm) Over 40in (100cm) 33in (85cm)

NOTES:

*Referred to as Neoceratodontidae by some authors

* * *Neoceratodus forsteri* possesses only one lung, while the others possess two; its pectoral and pelvic fins are fin-like, rather than fleshy filaments; its newly hatched larvae lack the external gills possessed by the larvae of the other species; it does not build a cocoon and cannot therefore survive the summer by going into aestivation (dormancy); it has occasionally been bred in public aquaria.

Today, though, the family has just this one representative, which still retains some primitive features. Among these is a lung-like swimbladder, a heterocercal caudal fin, i.e. one that (at least, internally) has a longer upper lobe, and the remains of a spiral valve (a spiral infolding of the wall of the intestine—as found in true sharks). The dorsal fin is also interesting in that it extends more than half the length of the back.

DISTRIBUTION: *Widely distributed in eastern half of North America, extending as far north as the Great Lakes and a little beyond*

SIZE: *Males reported up to 20in (50cm); females larger*

BEHAVIOR: *Solitary predator; can only be kept with tankmates that are too large to swallow*

DIET: *Large livefoods, including fish; some chunky meat-based of fish-based formulations may be accepted*

AQUARIUM: *Large, with numerous shelters, clumps of stout vegetation, and subdued lighting. Water chemistry not critical, but avoid extremes of pH and hardness. Temperature range: from below 54°F (12°C) to around 68°F (20°C)*

BREEDING: *No documented accounts of aquarium breeding available*

REEDFISH

ROPE, or SNAKE, FISH

Erpetoichthys calabaricus

SYNONYM: *Calamoichthys calabaricus*
FAMILY: Polypteridae

CLOSELY RELATED TO THE BIRCHIRS (*POLYPTERUS* —*see* next entry), with which it shares several characteristics, such as the possession of a number of dorsal finlets (7–13)

REEDFISH (ERPETOICHTHYS CALABARICUS)

ORNATE BIRCHIR (POLYPTERUS ORNATIPINNIS)

rather than a single fin, and the ability to use its swimbladder as an auxiliary respiratory organ. It is distinguished from its relatives by its extremely elongated snake-like body and the lack of pelvic fins. Reedfish can survive out of water for several hours, as long as the air is humid.

DISTRIBUTION: *Cameroon and Nigeria*

SIZE: *Up to 16in (40cm) reported, but usually smaller*

BEHAVIOR: *Peaceful toward tankmates that are too large to swallow; likes to burrow; active mainly at dusk and during the night*

DIET: *Livefoods and chunky or meaty formulations*

AQUARIUM: *Large, well-covered, with several shelters/hiding places and fine-grained substratum. Protect plants against burrowing (see Aquarium Plants). A "moonlight" fluorescent tube to facilitate nighttime viewing recommended. Slightly acid, medium-hard water preferred. Temperature range: 72–82°F (22–28°C)*

BREEDING: *No documented accounts available*

ORNATE BIRCHIR

Polypterus ornatipinnis

FAMILY: Polypteridae

THIS IS THE MOST WIDELY AVAILABLE MEMBER OF ITS genus. While having several characteristics in common with *Erpetoichthys calabaricus* (*see* previous entry), birchirs do not possess a snake-like body and do not lack a pelvic fin. Several other species are occasionally available: *P. congicus* (Congo Birchir), mainly from Zaire, *P. delhezi* (Armored Birchir), also from Zaire, *P. palmas* (Marbled Birchir), from Guinea, Liberia, Sierra Leone and Zaire, and *P. senegalus* (Cuvier's or Senegal Birchir), from Senegal, Gambia, the Niger, White Nile and several major lakes, such as

Lakes Albert, Chad and Rudolf. All have similar requirements.

DISTRIBUTION: *Widely distributed in central Africa*

SIZE: *Up to 18in (46cm) reported*

BEHAVIOR: *Generally tolerant of large tankmates, but less so of conspecifics; will prey on small fishes*

DIET: *Large livefoods, including live fish; chunky, meaty formulations also accepted*

AQUARIUM: *As for* Erpetoichthys calabaricus. *Temperature range: 79–82°F (26–28°C)*

BREEDING: *Tight spawning embraces—usually among vegetation—are accompanied by egg release and fertilization. Eggs are abandoned, and they hatch in four days*

LONGNOSED GAR

Lepisosteus osteus

FAMILY: Lepisosteidae

THIS IS A SLIM-BODIED SPECIES WITH A LONG, pointed mouth. Along with several other gar species, it is strictly a fish for specialists who can provide sufficiently large aquaria and an appropriate diet. Among the other gars occasionally on offer are the following: *L. oculatus* (Spotted Gar)—47in (120cm); *L. platostomus* (Shortnosed Gar)—24in (60cm); *Atractosteus (L.) spatula* (Alligator Gar)—118in (300cm); *Atractosteus (L.) tristoechus* (Cuban Gar)—reported up to 118in (300cm); and *L. platyrhincus* (Florida Gar)—52in (132cm), of which a golden variety is sometimes available.

DISTRIBUTION: *Atlantic slope of U.S.A. down to Florida; Great Lakes (except Lake Superior), Gulf Coast from Florida to Rio Grande; Texas and Mexico*

SIZE: *Up to 72in (183cm) reported*

BEHAVIOR: *Stalking predator; can only be kept with other large tankmates*

DIET: *As for* Datnioides microlepis

AQUARIUM: *Very large, covered, well-planted aquarium essential. Large decor, shelters and robust plants recommended. Temperature range: 54–64°F (12–18°C)*

BREEDING: *Very challenging in aquaria. Eggs are scattered among vegetation*

SHOVELNOSED STURGEON

Scaphirhynchus platorynchus

FAMILY: Acipenseridae

MOST STURGEONS CAN GROW TO VERY LARGE sizes—e.g. *Huso huso* (Beluga) can reach around 26ft (8m)—and are therefore totally unsuitable for aquaria. However, the Shovelnosed Sturgeon, along with *Acipenser ruthenus* (Sterlet) and *A. stellatus* (Stellate Sturgeon), are smaller, and can be housed in aquaria as long as these are spacious enough. One of the reasons for their growth in popularity in certain countries—beginning in the late 1980s/early 1990s—has been the expansion of the pondkeeping/watergardening hobby, in general, and that of Koi keeping in particular: Shovelnoses, Sterlets and Stellate Sturgeons are transferred to outside ponds once they outgrow their aquaria.

DISTRIBUTION: *Mississippi river basin, Mobile Bay drainage and upper Rio Grande, U.S.A.*

SIZE: *Around 39in (1m), but often smaller*

BEHAVIOR: *Peaceful; burrows in the substratum in search of food, and may prey on small fish*

DIET: *Chunky livefoods, deep-frozen and freeze-dried preparations, as well as sinking pellets and tablets*

AQUARIUM: *Very large, well-filtered, with open swimming areas and fine-grained substratum. Neutral, medium-hard water preferred, but some*

SHOVELNOSED STURGEON
(SCAPHIRHYNCHUS PLATORYNCHUS)

deviation accepted. Temperature range: 50–68°F (10–20°C)

BREEDING: *No documented accounts of aquarium breeding available*

OCELLATED STINGRAY

PEACOCK-EYE, or MOTORO, STINGRAY

Potamotrygon motoro

SYNONYM: *Potamotrygon laticeps*
FAMILY: Potamotrygonidae

THIS IS AN EXTREMELY VARIABLE SPECIES, WHICH, along with other members of the family, is becoming increasingly popular. Stingrays are most definitely not suitable for new aquarists and should in any case be treated with caution owing to the dangers posed by the sting. Seek specialist advice and consult specialist literature (*see* Bibliography) before purchase.

DISTRIBUTION: *Widespread in tropical South America*

SIZE: *Up to 20in (50cm)*

BEHAVIOR: *Tolerant; may be kept in a group; spends much time buried in the substratum with only the eyes showing*

DIET: *Bottom-dwelling livefoods, chunky meat-based or fish-based formulations, and sinking deep-frozen diets*

AQUARIUM: *Large, well-filtered, with some floating vegetation, well-bedded rocks or bogwood pieces, and deep fine-grained substratum. Slightly acid to neutral, soft to medium-hard water accepted. Temperature range: 75–79°F (24–26°C)*

BREEDING: *No documented accounts of aquarium breeding currently available*

OCELLATED STINGRAY (POTAMOTRYGON MOTORO)

Giant Catfish 129
Giant Cichlid 112
Giant Danio 178, *178*
Giant Elodea 79
Giant Gourami 46, 233, 241, 245, *245*
Giant Hygrophila 81
Giant Puffer 291
Giant Scissortail 182
Giant Spiny Eel 294
gill fluke infection 65
Gill's Molly *280*
Giraffe Catfish 46, 129, 132, *132*
Girardinichthys viviparus 59, 285
Girardinus 276
  G. creolus 276
  G. cubensis 276
  G. denticulatus 276
  G. falcatus 276
  G. metallicus 275, *275*
  G. microdactylus 276
  G. serripensis 276
  G. uninotatus 276
Girardinus Topminnow 275, *275*
Glandulocaudinae (subfamily) 188
Glass Bloodfin 211, *211*
Glass Bloodfish 211
Glass Catfish 129, 130, 162, *162*
Classy/Glass Tetra 206, *206*
Glossolepis 249
  G. incisus 248, *248*, 249
  G. maculosus 249
  G. multisquamatus 249, *249*
  G. wanamensis 249
Glowlight Rasbora 183, 184, *185*
Glowlight Tetra 198
Glyptoperichthys gibbiceps 150, *150*
Gnathonemus:
  G. elephas 292
  G. petersii 36, 291, *291*
  G. tamandua 292
gobies 258-61
Gobiidae (family) 164, 258
Gobiinae (subfamily) 258
Gobio gobio 164, 180
Gobioidei (suborder) 258
Gobioninae (subfamily) 164
Goby Cichlid 119
Goeld's Hemiodus/
  Hemiodopsis 220
Gold Ghost Koi Carp *177*
Gold Sawfin Goodeid 20, 22
Gold Seam/Saum 85, *85*
Gold-band Neolebias 215
Gold-banded Goby 260
Gold-breasted Ilyodon 286
Gold-cheeked Theraps 126
Golden Barb 169, *169*
Golden Bumblebee Goodeid 284
Golden Dwarf Acara 106, *107*
Golden Dwarf Barb 167, *168*
Golden Dwarf Cichlid/
  Apistogramma 89
Golden Gambusia 275
Golden Gourami 244
Golden Lake Malawi Cichlid 84
Golden Lamprologus 102, *102*
Golden Leporinus 192
Golden Medaka 289
Golden Minnow 182
Golden Mosquitofish 275
Golden Neon Tetra 200
Golden One-spot Livebearer 279
Golden Orfe 181, *181*
Golden Otocinclus 152
Golden Pencilfish 223
Golden Pheasant 263
Golden Rasbora 185
Golden Rivulus 269
Golden Sleeper Goby/
  Gudgeon 295
Golden Spotted Livebearer 279
Golden Tench 187
Golden Tetra 199
Golden Top Minnow 269
Golden Trahira 217, *217*
Golden Zebra 158
Golden Zebra Danio *172*
Golden-eared Killifish 269
Golden-eyed Dwarf Cichlid 106
Goldenline Neolebias 215
Goldfin Barb 169
Goldfish *16*, 50, 164, 173, *173-5*
goldfish aquaria 43-4, 173
Goldfoil Barb 169
Goldie River Rainbowfish 252
Gold-tip Cichlid 110
Goodea:
  G. atripinnis 285
  G. toweri 285
Goodeidae (family) 19, 20, 60, 284
Goodeinae (subfamily) 284, 287
goodeids 284-7

Goshiki Koi Carp *177*
Gosse's Dwarf Cichlid 89
gouramis 232-47
Graceful Catfish 147
Graceful Lamprologus 108
Graceful Pim 159
Grant's Leporinus 192
Gray's Distichodus 214
Gray-lined Anostomus/
  Headstander 191
Greater Scissortail 182, *183*
Green Barb 169
Green Chromide 97, *98*
Green Cabomba 75
Green Discus 119, *120*
Green Goodeid 286
Green Knifefish 293, *293*
Green Lampeye 273
Green Molly 280
Green Neon Tetra *199*, 200, 208, *208*
Green Puffer 290
Green Rivulus 268, *268*
Green Sunfish 255
Green Terror 85, *85*
Greenthroat Betta 238
Guatemala Gold Cichlid 122
Gudgeon 180
Günther's Krib 92
Günther's Nothobranch 265
Guppy *75*, 279, *279*
Guyana Aequidens/Acara 85
Gymnocoronis sp. 80
Gymnocorymbus ternetzi 197, *197*
Gymnogeophagus:
  G. balzanii 99
  G. gymnogenys 99
Gyrinocheilidae (family) 226
Gyrinocheilus:
  G. aymonieri 23, 76, 226, 231, *231*

habitats *see* aquaria; natural habitats
Hair Grass 79
Haiti Cichlid 107
Haiti Limia 278
Hajiro Koi Carp *177*
Half-banded Spiny Eel 294
halfbeaks 288
Half-black Angel *116*
Half-lined Hemiodus 220
Half-striped Barb 169
Half-striped Leporinus 192
Half-stroke/Half-striped
  Pyrrhulina 225
Hamanishiki Goldfish *175*
Hancock's Catfish 145, *145*
Hanna Shushui Carp *177*
Haplochromis 19
  H. brownae 99
  H. psittacus 99
Haplochromis Borleyi 94
Haplochromis Borleyi Eastern 94
Haplochromis Chrysonotus 94
Haplochromis Electric Blue 119
Haplochromis Labrosus 103
Haplochromis Munnae 94
Haplochromis Quads 94, *94*
Hara hara 130, 163, *163*
Harald Schultz's Corydoras 141
hard/soft water 39-41, 43, 45, 53
Hard-bellied Silver Dollar 207
Hard-lipped Barb 182
Harlequin 9, 58, 184, *184*
Harrison's Pencilfish 224
Hartweg's Brachy/Bishop 274
Hartweg's Cichlid 125
Harvey's Licorice/Liquorice
  Gourami 240
Hasemania nana 188, 197, *197*
hatchetfishes 189
Head-and-tail Light Tetra 199
health/health management 25, 62-*1*, 71
  disease 62-6
  medicine/vaccines 62, 63-*7*
  quarantining new fish 51
  signs of health 49-50, 50
Heckel Discus 120, *120*
Heller's Cichlid 123
Helostoma temminckii 244, *245*
Helostomatidae (family) 233
Hemianthus 80
  H. micranthemoides 80
Hemichromis 84
  H. bimaculatus 99, *99*
  H. lifalili 100
Hemigrammopetersius caudalis 197
Hemigrammus 200
  H. bellottii 200, *200*
  H. bleheri 1, 198
  H. boesemani 200
  H. caudovittatus 198, *198*
  H. coeruleus 200
  H. erythrozonus 198
  H. hyanuary 200, *200*
  H. levis 200
  H. luelingi 200

H. marginatus 200
H. mininus 200
H. ocellifer 199
H. pulcher 199, *199*
H. rodwayi 199
H. schmardae 200
H. stictus 200
H. ulreyi 199, *199*
H. unilineatus 200
Hemiodontidae (family) 189
Hemiodopsis 220
  H. argenteus 220
  H. goeldii 220
  H. gracilis 219, *219*
  H. immaculatus 220
  H. microlepis 220, *220*
  H. quadrimaculatus quadrimaculatus 220
  H. q. vorderwinkieri 220
  H. semitaeniatus 220
  H. sterni 220
Hemiodus unimaculatus 220, *220*
Hemirhamphodon 288
  H. pogonognathus 288
Hemisorubim platyrhynchos 158, *158*
Hemisynodontis membranaceus 154
Hepsetidae (family) 189
Hepsetus odoe 221, *221*
Herichthy 126
  H. cyanoguttatus 84, 100, *100*
Heros 126
  H. severus 100
Heterandria formosa 59, 60, 276, *276*
Heteranthera zosterifolia 80
Heterophallus milleri 276
Heteropneustes fossilis 128, 129, 147
Heteropneustidae (family) 129
Hi-fin Whiptail 150
High-backed Headstander 189, *189*
High-backed Pygmy
  Swordtail 283
High-fin Shark Catfish 131
High-head Pearlscale Goldfish *175*
Highland carp 284-7
Highland Swordtail 283
Hikarimono Koi Carp *177*
Hikarimono-mono Koi Carp *177*
Hikari-utsurimono Koi Carp *177*
Hilsa Herring 227
Hi-spot Rasbora 182
Hockey Stick Pencilfish 223
Hoehne's Nannacara 85
Hog-nosed Brochis 136, *136*
Hoignei Dwarf Cichlid 89
Holdridge's Brachy/Bishop 274
Homaloptera orthogoniata 226, 227, *227*
Homoalopteridae (family) 226
Honey Blue-eye 253
Honey Dwarf Gourami 241
Honey Gourami 241
Honeycomb Combtail 235
Hong Kong Pleco 227
Hongsloi Dwarf Cichlid 89
Hoplerythrinus unitaeniatus 217, *217*
Hoplias malabaricus 188, 217, *218*
Hoplosternum 58
  H. littorale 142
Hora's Loach 229
Horaichthys setnai 59
Hornet Cichlid 114, *115*
Hornwort 79
Horseface Cichlid 97
Horse-faced Loach *54*, 229, *230*
Hottonia:
  H. inflata 80
  H. palustris 80
Hubbsina turneri 287
Hujeta 216, *216*
Humbug Catfish 146
Humpbacked Limia *277*, 277
Hydrilla verticillata 80
Hydrocharis morsus-ranae 77
Hydrocotyle verticillata 77
Hygrophila 35, 80, *80*
  H. difformis 75
Hygrorhiza aristata 77
Hypancistrus zebra 150, *151*
Hyphessobrycon 200, 203
  H. agulha 203
  H. amandae 203
  H. bentosi 200
  H. copelandi 203
  H. erythrostigma 201, *201*
  H. flammeus 201
  H. georgettae 201
  H. herbertaxelrodi 201, *201*
  H. heterorhabdus 202
  H. loretoensis 202
  H. peruvianus 203
  H. pulchripinnis 45, *45*, 202, *202*

H. reticulatus 203
H. saizi 203
H. scholzeri 202
H. socolofi 203
H. takesei 203
H. vilmae 203, *203*
Hypoptopoma thoracatum 150
Hypostomus 76, 129
  H. plecostomus 150, *151*
  H. punctatus 151, *151*
Hypselecara coryphaenoides 100
Hyseleotris 259
  H. aureus/aurea 259
  H. compressa 259, *259*
  H. cyprinoides 259
  H. ejuncida 259
  H. galii 259
  H. kimberleyensis 259
  H. klunzingeri 259
  H. regalis 259

ichthyophthiriasis 65, *65*
Ictaluridae (family) 129
Ictalurus:
  I. melas 147
  I. nebulosus 147, *147*
  I. punctatus 129, 147
Ictiobinae (subfamily) 164
Ide 164, 181
Idotropheus sprengerae 101
Iguanodectes spilurus 202, *203*
Iguanodectinae (subfamily) 188
Ilyodon furcidens 286
Imitator Corydoras 141
India 19, 164
Indian Ctenops 239
Indian Fern *77*, 77
Indian Glass Barb 172
Indian Glass Hatchet 172
Indian Glassfish *1*, 289
Indian Gourami 239, 241
Indian Najad 81
Indian Snakehead 246
Indian Stonebiter 230
Indonesia 23
Inirida Dwarf Cichlid 89
Inpaichthys kerri 203, *204*
International Union for the
  Conservation of Nature
  (IUCN): Red List 20
introduced species 21, *21*
Iodotropheus sprengerae 100
Irian Jaya 19
Iriatherina werneri 249, *249*
Iridescent Corydoras 141
Iridescent Lampeye 271
Iridescent Shark 157
Island Barb 170
Israel 25
Ivy Leaf 81

Jack Dempsey 106, *106*
Jaguar Catfish 145
Jaguar Cichlid 105
January Tetra *199*, 200
Japan 24-5, 28
  see also Koi Carp
Japanese Cress 79
Japanese Fountain Plant 81
Japanese Medaka 289
Japanese Ricefish 289
Japanese "Rush" 78
Japanese Spatterdock 74, 81
Japanese Weather Loach 230
Java Combtail 235
Java Fern 46, 73, 80, *80*
Java Moss 36, 73, 81
Javan Betta 238
jawless fishes 12
Jelly Bean Tetra 204
Jenynsia 60, 270
  J. multidentata 271
Jewel Cichlid 99, *99*
Jewel Goodeid 287
Johanni Mbuna 103
Jordanella floridae 1, 287
Julidochromis 19
  J. dickfeldi 101, *101*
  J. marlieri 101
Julii Corydoras 141
Jumbo Aulonocara/Peacock 91
Jumping Tetra/Characin 221
Jurua Dwarf Cichlid 89
"Jurupari" 118

Kawarimono Koi Carp *177*
Kennyi Mbuna 114, *115*
Kerr's Danio 171
Keyhole Cichlid 93
Ki-goi Koi Carp *177*
killifishes 262-9
Kinginrin Koi Carp *177*
Kissing Gourami 233, 244, *245*
knife fishes 36
Knife Livebearer 273, *273*
Knight Goby 261, *261*
Kohaku Koi Carp 25, *177*
Koi Carp 24-5, 44, 57, 164, 176, *176*, 177, *177*
Koromo Koi Carp *177*
Korthaus' Nothobranch 265, *265*
Kottelat's Halfbeak 288

Krib 111, *112*
Kribensis Cichlid 111
Kryptopterus bicirrhis 129, 130, 162, *162*
Kuhli Loach 231
Kullander's Dwarf Cichlid 89

Labeo 164
  L. chrysophekadion 181
Labeotropheus 84
  L. fuelleborni 101, *101*
  L. trewavasae 102
Labidochromis caeruleus 44, 102, *102*
Labidochromis Electric
  Yellow Tanganicae 44, 102, *102*
Labyrinthfishes 19, 21, 22, 232
Lace Brachy/Bishop 274
Lace Gourami 243
Lace-finned Killifish 268, 268
Ladder Betta 238
Ladderback Spiny Eel 294
Ladigesia roloffi 204
Laetacara curviceps 102
Lagarosiphon major 80
Lake Kutubu Rainbowfish 251, *251*
Lake Malawi 18, 19, 61, 84
Lake Tanganyika 18, *18*, 19, 60, 84
Lake Tebera Rainbowfish 250, *250*
Lake Victoria 18-19, *21*
Lake Wanam rainbowfish 249
Lampeye Panchax 271, *271*
Lamprichthys tanganicus 272, *272*
Lamprologus 19, 60
  L. ocellatus 102, *102*
Lamprologus "Kavala" Ubwari
  Buescheri 109
Lamprologus Finialimus 109
Lamprologus Nkambae 103
Lamprologus Zambia 109
Large Chocolate Gourami 242
Large-scaled Barb 164
Large-scaled Elephantnose/
  Whale 292
Lates niloticus 21, *21*
Latimeria chalumnae 20
Lavender Gourami 244
Lavender Mbuna 112
Least Killifish 276
Lebiasina astrigata 222
Lebiasinidae (family) 189
Lebiasininae (subfamily) 188
Leeri Gourami 243
Leiarius pictus 158, *158*
Leiocassis siamensis 133, *133*
Lemna sp. 71, 78
Lemon Cichlid 108, *109*
Lemon Tetra 45, *45*, 202, *202*
Leopard Corydoras 141
Leopard Ctenopoma 234, *234*
Leopard Danio 171
Leopard Goodeid 287
Leopold's Angel 116
Lepidocephalus thermalis 230
Lepidolamprologus kendalli 103
Lepidosiren paradoxa 295
Lepidosirenidae (family) 295
Lepisosteus osteus 296
Lepomis 255
  L. auritus 255
  L. cyanellus 255
  L. gibbosus 254, *255*
  L. gulosus 255
  L. humilis 255, *255*
  L. macrochirus 255, *255*
  L. marginatus 255
  L. megalotis 254
  L. microlophus 255
  L. punctatus 255
  L. symmetricus 255
Leporinus 192
  L. affinis 191, *191*
  L. agassizi 192
  L. desmotes 192
  L. friderici/frederici 192
  L. granti 192
  L. maculatus 192
  L. megalepis 192
  L. melanopleura 192
  L. melanosticus 192
  L. moralesi 192
  L. nigrotaeniatus 192
  L. octofasciatus 192
  L. pellegrini 192
  L. striatus 191
Lesser Bleeding Heart Tetra 203
Lesser Loach 230
Lesser Spiny Eel 294
Lethoplosternum pectorale 142
Leucaspius delineatus 181
Leuciscus 164
  L. idus 181, *181*
Liberty Molly 280
Licorice Dwarf Gourami 240
Lifalili Cichlid 100
lighting *see* aquaria lighting

Lilaeopsis:
  L. brasiliensis 80
  L. novaezelandiae 80
Limia 278
  L. dominicensis 277, 278
  L. melanogaster 277
  L. nigrofasciata 277, *277*, 278
  L. ornata 278
  L. perugiae 278
  L. sulphurophila 278
  L. tridens 278
  L. vittata 277, 278
  L. zonata 278
Limnobium laevigatum 78
Limnophila sp. 80
Linam's Pim Pim 160
Lined Citharinid 213, *213*
Linke's Licorice/Liquorice
  Gourami 240
Linker's Dwarf Cichlid 89
Lionhead Goldfish *174*
Lipingu Aulonocara/Peacock 91
Liposarcus anisisti 151, *151*
Lisa 191, *191*
Little Lake Cichlid 107
Little Sunfish 254
Livebearing Barb 170
Liver Catfish 147
Livingstoni 110, *110*
Lizard's Tail 81
loaches 226-31
Lobelia cardinalis 80
Logperch 257
Loiselle's Cichlid 107
Long-banded Rasbora 185, *185*
Longear Sunfish 254
Longfin Barb 165
Longfin Pyrrhulina 225
Long-finned Angel 116
Long-finned Brochis 136
Long-finned Characin 195, *195*
Long-finned Lamprologus 109
Long-nosed Gar 296
Long-nosed Halfbeak 288
Long-nosed Loach 229
Long-nosed Synodontis 157
Longsnout Mbuna 103
Long-snouted Halfbeak 288
Loreto Tetra 202
Loricaria sp. 45
Loricariidae (family) 129
Loricariichthys sp. 45
Lucania goodei 269
Luciocephalus pulcher 232, 245
Ludwigia sp. 35, 80
Lueling's Dwarf Cichlid/
  Apistogramma 89
Lueling's Tetra 200
lungfish 295
lymphocystis 63, *63*
Lyretail 262, *262*
Lyretail Checkerboard Cichlid 96
Lyretail Lamprologus 108
Lyretailed Panchax 262
Lysmachia nummularia 80

MacCulloch's Rainbowfish 249, 251
Macmaster's Dwarf Cichlid 88, *88*
Macrognathus 36, 294
  M. aculeatus 294
  M. aral 294
  M. circumcinctus 294
  M. maculatus 294
  M. pancalus 294
  M. siamensis 294
  M. zebrinus 294
  see also Mastacembelus
Macropodus 58
  M. concolor 239
  M. ocellatus 239
  M. opercularis 28, 58, 232, 239, *239*
Mafia Nothobranch 265
Magara Shell Dweller 109
Magdalena Spot-finned Killie 268
Malachite Green (medication) 66
Malapteruridae (family) 130
Malapterurus electricus 130
Malatengo Cichlid 123
Malawi Blue Dolphin 96, *96*
Malawi Butterfly 90
Malawi Eye-biter 97, *97*
Malawi Golden Cichlid 103
Malayan Halfbeak 288
Malaysian Shark 165
Malpulutta 239
Malpulutta kretseri 19, 21, 22, 239
Managua Cichlid 105, *105*
mangrove swamps 19, *19*
Malaysia 25
Many-banded Dwarf
  Lamprologus 109
Many-banded Leporinus 191, *191*

Many-pointed Cichlid 107
Many-spined Bushfish 235
Many-spotted Corydoras 141
Many-spotted Distichodus 214
Many-spotted Synodontis 156
Marakely 111
Marbled Hatchetfish *38*, 218
Marbled Pike Cichlid 95
Marbled Red Swordtail *282*
Marbled Sleeper 258
Marbled Vieja 126
March Trefoil 80
Marcusenius:
  M. angolensis 292
  M. brachyistius 292
  M. longianalis 292
  M. macrolepidotus 292
Marlier's Julie 101
Marosatherina ladigesi 253, *253*
Marsh's Gambusia 275
Marsh's Mosquitofish 275
Marsilea crenata 80
Mastacembelus 36, 294
  M. armatus 294
  M. erythrotaenia 46, 294, *294*
  see also Macrognathus
Mato Grosso Aequidens/
  Acara 85
Mayan Blue-eye 281
Maylandia 104
  M. zebra 9
Mayland's Molly 280
Medaka *see* Rice Fish
medicine/vaccines 62, 63-7
  administration 66-7
  anaesthesia 67
  dosages 66-7
  euthanasia 67
Megaladoras irwini 146
Megalamphodus:
  M. megalopterus 204, *204*
  M. sanctaefilomenae 206
  M. sweglesi 204, *204*
Megalechis thoracata 143, *143*
Meinken's Dwarf Cichlid 89
Mekong Catfish 129
Melanochromis 19, 103
  M. auratus 103, 84
  M. chipokae 103
  M. dialeptos 103
  M. interruptus 103
  M. joanjohnsoni 103
  M. johanni 103
  M. labrosus 103
  M. loriae 103
  M. melanopterus 103
  M. parallelus 103
  M. robustus 103
  M. simulans 103
  M. sp. "Auratus Dwarf" 103
  M. vermivorus 103
  M. xanthodigma 103
Melanchromis Red 103
Melanotaenia 248, 252
  M. affinis 252
  M. boesemani 250, *250*
  M. duboulayi 252
  M. exquisita 252
  M. fluviatilis 252
  M. goldei 252
  M. gracilis 252
  M. herbertaxelrodi 250, *250*
  M. lacustris 251, *251*
  M. maccullochi 251, *252*
  M. monticola 252
  M. nigrans 252
  M. parkinsoni 251, *252*
  M. praecox 252, *252*
  M. sexilineata 252
  M. splendida 252, *252*
  M. trifasciata 252
Melanotaeniidae (family) 248
Melapterurus electricus 154, *154*
Melon Barb 170
Mendez's Dwarf Cichlid 89
Merry Widow 278, *278*
Mesonauta festivus 103, *104*
Meta Aequidens/Acara 85
Meta Satanoperca 118
Meta Tetra 222, *222*
Metallic Topminnow 275
Metriaclima 104
  M. zebra 9, 84, 104, *104*
Metynnis:
  M. argenteus 205, *205*
  M. hypsauchen 205, *205*
Mexican Livebearer 19
Mexican livebearers 284-7
Mexican Molly 280
Mexican Oak Leaf 81
Mexican Tetra 194
Mexico 19, 20, 188
Mia's Cichlid 107
Michael's Cichlid 85
Microctenopoma sp. 235
Microgeophagus:
  M. altispinosus 104
  M. ramirezi 84, 104, *105*
Microglanis theringi 159
Micropoecilia picta 278

Microsorum pteropus 46, 73, 80, 80
Midas Cichlid 86, 86
Midget Sucker Catfish 152
Midnight Catfish 129, 131, 132
Milfoil 81
Miller's Flyer 276
Millions Fish 279
Minnow Sleeper Goby/ Gudgeon 259
minnows 164
Minutus 115
Misgurnus 226
  M. anguillicaudatus 230, 230
Moae Dwarf Cichlid 89
Mochokidae (family) 128, 130
Mochokiella paynei 155, 155
Moderlieschen 181
Modest Lamprologus 109
Moenkhausia:
  M. oligolepis 206, 206
  M. pittieri 39, 206
Mogurnda mogurnda 259, 259
Mondabu Lamprologus 109
Moneywort 80
Mono 45, 290, 290
Monocirrhus 232
  M. polyacanthus 56, 247, 247
Monodactylus 19, 45
  M. argenteus 290, 290
Monotretus travancoricus 291
Montezuma Swordtail 283
Moon Fish 290
Moonbeam Gourami 243
Moonfish 283
Moonlight Gourami 243, 244
Moor Goldfish 174
Moore's Lamprologus 109
Moorii 124
Mormyridae (family) 292
Mormyrus longirostris 292
Mosaic Catfish 126
Mosaic Gourami 243
Mosaic Puffer 291
Mosquito Fish 21, 28, 276, 276
Mosquitofish 275
Motagua Cichlid 107
Mother of Pearl Killifish 287
Mottley Lamprologus 109
Motoro Stingray 297
Mottled Catfish 133
Mottled Ctenopoma 235, 235
Mottled Dwarf Cichlid 89
Mottled Spiny Eel 294
Mountain Asian Bagrid 134
Mountain Rainbowfish 252
Moustache Synodontis 154
mouth fungus 64, 64
Mouthbrooding Krib 92
Mozambique Mouthbrooder 110, 111, 114, 115
Muddy Lamprologus 109
mudskippers 46
Multifasciatus Big Eye 109
Multispot Aulonocara/ Peacock 91
Murray River Rainbowfish 252
mussels 58
Mustax 109
Myanmar 164
Myer's Hatchetfish 218
Myer's Hillstream Loach 227
Myer's Loach 231, 231
Myleus rubripinnis 206, 207
Mylossoma duriventre 207, 207
Myriophyllum sp. 61, 81
Mystus 134
  M. micracanthus 133
  M. montanus 134
  M. nemurus 134
  M. tengara 134, 134
  M. vittatus 134, 134
  M. wyckii 134
Myxocyprinus asiaticus 226, 227, 227

Nagy's Licorice/Liquorice Gourami 240
Najas indica 81
Nandidae (family) 232
Nandopsis 107
  N. bartoni 107
  N. beani 107
  N. dovii 107, 107
  N. facetum 107
  N. festae 105
  N. friedrichsthalii 105, 105
  N. grammodes 107
  N. haitiensis 107
  N. istlanum 107
  N. labridens 107
  N. loisellei 107
  N. managuense 105, 105
  N. motaguense 107
  N. octofasciatus 106, 106
  N. ornatus 107
  N. parilus 107
  N. ramsdeni 107
  N. salvini 106, 106

N. steindachneri 107
N. tetracanthus 107
N. umbriferus 107
N. urophthalmus 107
N. vombergae 107
Nandus nandus 247
Nannacara 84
  N. anomala 106, 107
Nannaethiops unitaeniatus 215
Nannostomus:
  N. beckfordi 223, 223
  N. bifasciatus 223
  N. digrammus 223
  N. eques 223
  N. espei 224
  N. harrisoni 224
  N. marginatus 224, 224
  N. trifasciatus 224
  N. unifasciatus 224, 224
Nanochromis parilus 106, 107
Narrow Hatchetfish 213, 213
Narrow-wedged Rasbora 183
Nastus Cichlid 110
Natterer's Corydoras 141
natural habitats 17-19
natural history 10-25
Nyasa Blue Cichlid 104
Nyassa Peacock 91
Nyassa Syndontis 157
Nyphaea 74
  N. maculata 81
Nymphoides aquatica 81

Ocean Voice International 22
Ocellate Rivulus 269
Ocellated Stingray 297, 297
Odessa Barb 168
Ogon Koi Carp 177
Okefenokee Pygmy Sunfish 256
Old World Rivulines 262
Olive Lamprologus 109
Ompok:
  O. bimaculatus 162
  O. eugeniatus 163
One-banded African Tetra 215
One-lined Pencilfish 224
One-sided Livebearer 60, 271
One-spot Betta 238
One-spot Bushfish 235
One-spot Fighter 238
One-spot Geophagus 118
One-spot Hemiodus 220, 220
One-spot Livebearer 279
One-spot Molly 280
One-spot Synodontis 157
One-spotted Hemiodus/ Hemiodopsis 220
One-striped African Characin 215
Onion Plant 72, 74, 79
Opal Gourami 244
Opaline 181
Opaline Gourami 244
Ophiopogon japonicus 81
Opthalmotilapia:
  O. boops 110
  O. heterodonta 110
  O. nasuta 110
  O. ventralis 110
Oranda Goldfish 174
Orange Barb 170
Orange and Black Sailfin Molly 201
Orange Bushfish 234
Orange Chromide 45, 97, 97
Orange-finned Barb 185
Orange-finned Loach 229, 229
Orange-spotted Sunfish 255, 255
Orange-tailed Goodeid 286, 286
Orangethroat Darter 256, 256
Orchid Lily 78
Oreochromis mossambicus 110, 111
Orfe 164
organophosphates (medication) 66
Orinoco Geophagus 118
Ornament Cichlid 107
Ornate Birchir 296, 296
Ornate Gourami 239
Ornate Limia 278
Ornate Pim 160
Ornate Pointed-tail Gourami 233
Ornate Pseudogastomyzon 227
Ortmann's Dwarf Cichlid 89
Oryzias 61
  O. latipes 28, 59, 289
Oscar 45, 84, 90, 90
Osphronemidae (family) 233
Osphronemus goramy 46, 233, 245, 245
Osteichthyes (class) 13
Osteochilus hasselti 182
Osteoglossidae (family) 20, 294
Osteoglossum 47, 58
  O. bicirrhosum 293, 293, 294
Otocinclus 76
  O. affinis 152
oviparity 59
  see also breeding
Oxyeleotris 76
  O. marmoratus 258
Oxyzygonectinae (subfamily) 270

Pachypanchax Sp. 265
Pacific Blue-eye 253
Pacific Molly 280
Pacific Topminnow 281
Pacu 205
Paddlefish 20
Painted Talking Catfish 144
Pakistani Loach 228, 228
Pale Bushfish 235
Pale Chub 187
Palmqvist's Nothobranch 266, 266
Panaque nigrolineatus 130, 152, 152
Panda Corydoras 140, 140
Panda Dwarf Cichlid 88, 88
Pangasianodon gigas 129
Pangasiidae (family) 130
Pangasius sutchi 130, 157
Pangio:
  P. myersi 231, 231
Pantanai Geophagus 118
Panther Vacuum-mouthed Corydoras 133
Pantodon bucholzi 293
Papua New Guinea 19
Parabramis sp. 164
Paracheirodon:
  P. axelrodi 23-4, 24, 39, 45, 188, 208, 208
  P. innesi 188, 208, 208
  P. simulans 208, 208
Paradise Fish 28, 58, 232, 239, 239
Paradontine (subfamily) 189
Paraguay Eartheater 99
Parambassis 19
  P. ranga 1, 289
Parasphaerichthys ocellatus 242
Parastremma sp. 188
Paratheraps sp. 126
Paratilapia polleni 111
Parauchenoglanis macrostoma 134
Parisima Brachy/Bishop 274
Parkinson's Rainbowfish 251, 251
Parosphromenus 58, 240
  P. allani 240
  P. anjunganensis 240
  P. deisneri 240
  P. filamentosus 240
  P. harveyi 240
  P. linkei 240
  P. nagyi 240
  P. ornaticauda 240
  P. paludicola 240
  P. parvulus 240
Parotocinclus maculicauda 1, 152
Parrot Cichlid 93, 99
Passion Cichlid 123
Payne's Synodontis 155, 155
Peaceful Betta 237
Peacock Bass 95
Peacock Betta 238
Peacock Cichlid 92, 93
Peacock Coby 260, 260
Peacock Gudgeon 260
Peacock-eye Cichlid 45, 84, 90, 90
Peacock-eye Stingray 297
Pearl Bushfish 235
Pearl Cichlid 98, 98, 100
Pearl Danio 171, 171
Pearl Gourami 243, 243
Pearl of Likoma 103
Pearl Satanoperca 118
Pearl-lined Lamprologus 109
Pearly Compressiceps 85, 86
Pearly Rasbora 185
Peckoltia pulcher 153
Pectorosus Hatchetfish 219
Pellegrin's Bushfish 235
Pelteobagrus:
  P. fluvidraco 134
  P. ornatus 135
Pelvicachromis 84
  P. humilis 111, 111
  P. pulcher 111, 112
  P. roloffi 112
  P. subocellatus 112
  P. taeniatus 112
Penang Mouth-brooding Betta 237
pencilfishes 189
Penguin Fish 213
Pennywort 77
Pepper Tetra 194
Perca fluviatilis 257, 257
Perch 257, 257
Percidae (family) 254
Percinae (subfamily) 254
Percini (tribe) 254
Percoidei (suborder) 232
Periophthalmus 46
  P. barbarus 261
personal hygiene 67
Pertensis Dwarf Cichlid 89
Peru Altum 118
Perugla's Limia 278
Peruvian Tetra 205
Peten Cichlid 112, 122, 122
Peten Molly 280

Peten Thorichthys 122
Petenia splendida 112, 113
Peter's Elephantnose 291
Petheric's Bushfish 235
Petitella georgia 210
Petricola 109
Petrocephalus catostoma 292
Petrotilapia Tridentiger 100
Petrotilapia tridentiger 112
Phago maculatus 216, 216
Phallichthys amates 278, 278
Phalloceros caudimaculatus 279
Phenacogrammus interruptus 210, 210
phosphate levels 52
photosynthesis 70, 70, 71
Phoxinus 164
  P. erythrogaster 181, 181
Phractocephalus hemioliopterus 46, 130, 159, 159
Phractura 129
  P. ansorgii 130, 130
Physoriella leptophylla 81
Picoted Goodeid 287
Picta 278
Pike Characin 216
Pike Cichlid 84
Pike Top Livebearer 6, 273
Pike Top Minnow/Killifish 273
Pikehead 232, 245
Pilea cadieri 71, 81
Pimelodella:
  P. dorseyi 160
  P. gracilis 159
  P. laticeps 160
  P. linami 160
Pimelodid sp. 160
Pimelodidae (family) 12, 128, 130
Pimelodus 130, 160
  P. albofasciatus 160
  P. biochi 160
  P. maculatus 160
  P. ornatus 160
  P. pictus 160, 160
Pimephales promelas 182
Pink-tailed Chalseus 195
Pink-tailed Characin 195, 195
Pin-striped Panaque 152
Pirarucu 294
Pirhana 188
Pistia stratiotes 78
Placidochromis electra 113, 113
Plain Metynnis/Pacu 205
plants see aquarium plants
Platinum Gourami 244
Platydoras costatus 146, 146
Platystoma sp. 130
Platystomatichthys sturio 160, 161
Playfair's Panchax 264
Pleco 150, 151
Plotosus (genus) 128
Plumed Killifish 262
Poecilia 280
  P. butleri 280
  P. caucana 280, 280
  P. chica 280, 280
  P. dominicensis 280
  P. "formosa" 280
  P. gillii 280, 280
  P. latipunctata 280
  P. latipinna 279
  P. maylandi 280
  P. petenensis 280
  P. reticulata 25, 75, 279, 279
  P. salvatoris 280
  P. sphenops 76, 280
  P. velifera 76, 280
  P. velifera var. 280
  P. vivipara 280
Poeciliidae (family) 20, 59, 270
poeciliids 270-83
Poeciliopsis 59, 281
  P. baenschi 281
  P. gracilis 281
  P. hnilickai 281
  P. infans 281
  P. latidens 281
  P. prolifica 281
  P. turneri 60
  P. turrubarensis 281
  P. viriosa 281
Poecilocharax weitzmani 210
Pointed-mouth Molly 280
Pointed-mouthed Gourami 242
Polka Dot Synodontis 155
Polleni 111
Pollimyrus nigripinnis 292
pollution problems 71
Polycentrus 232
  P. schomburgki 247
Polyodon spathulae 20
Polypterus ornatipinnis 296, 296
Polystigma 110
Pompadour 120

Pongol Sword 79
Popondetta Blue-eye 253
Port Acara 93
Port Cichlid 93
Port Hoplo 143, 143
Porthole Antenna Catfish 158
Porthole Catfish 141, 142
Porthole Livebearer 281
Potamogeton crispus 81
Potamotrygon motoro 297, 297
Powder Blue Hap 119
Pretty Peckoltia 153
Pretty Tetra 199, 199
Priapella compressa 281
Princess of Burundi 108
Princess of Zambia 108
Prince Regent Sleeper Goby/ Gudgeon 259
Prionobrama filigera 211, 211
Pristella maxillaris 211
Procatopus aberrans 273
Prochilodontinae (subfamily) 188
Prolific Topminnow 281
protein skimmers 47
Protomelas:
  P. annectens 114
  P. fenestratus 113, 113
  P. ornatus 114
  P. similis 114
  P. spilonotus 114
  P. taeniolatus 114
Protopteridae (family) 295
Protopterus:
  P. aethiopicus 295
  P. annectens 295
  P. amphibius 295
  P. dolloi 295
protozoan infections 55, 55
Pseudacanthicus spinosus 153, 153
Pseudepiplatys sp. 265
Pseudo Helleri 281
Pseudocrenilabrus 84
  P. multicolor 114, 114
  P. philander 114, 115
Pseudotropheus 19
  P. aurora 114, 115
  P. crabro 114
  P. lombardoi 114
  P. macrophthalmus 115
  P. minutus 115
  P. socolofi 115
Pseudodoras niger 46, 146, 146
Pseudogastromyson myersi 227
Pseudomugil 253
  P. connieae 253
  P. cyanodorsalis 253
  P. furcatus 252, 253
  P. gortrudae 253, 253
  P. mellis 253
  P. signifer 253, 253
  P. tenellus 253
Pseudomugilidae (family) 248
Pseudoplatystoma fasciatum 161
Pseudosphromenus 58
  P. cupanus 240, 240
  P. dayi 240
Pseudotropheus sp. 84, 116
  P. crabro 115
  P. lombardo 115
  P. macrophthalmus 115
  P. socolofi 116
Pseudoxiphophorus bimaculatus 281
Psilorhynchinae (subfamily) 164
Psilorhynchoides sp. 164
Psilorhynchus sp. 164
Pterolebias zonatus 268, 268
Pterophyllum 60, 84, 118
  P. altum 116, 117, 118
  P. dumerilii 118
  P. eimekei 118
  P. leopoldi 116
  P. scalare 24, 84, 116, 117
Pterygoplichthys spp. 76
Pueblo Platy 282
puffer 291
Pulchra Dwarf Cichlid 89, 89
Pumpkinseed 254, 255
Pungitius sp. 58
Puntius sp. 170
Purple Cichlid 111
Purple Mbuna 103
Purple-headed Barb 168
Purple-spotted Sleeper Goby/Gudgeon 259
Purple-striped Sleeper Goby 259, 259
Pygmy Catfish 129
Pygmy Croaking Gourami 241
Pygmy Green-eyed Cichlid 107
Pygmy Hatchetfish 218
Pygmy Leopard Synodontis 157
Pygmy Rasbora 171
Pygocentrus:
  P. rhombeus 212
  P. nattereri 211, 211

Pyjama Synodontis 156
Pyrrhulina 225
  P. brevis 225
  P. eleanori 225
  P. filamentosa 225
  P. laeta 225
  P. rachoviana 225, 225
  P. spilota 225
  P. vittata 225
  P. zigzag 225
Pyrrhulininae (subfamily) 189

Quadrimaculatus 94
Quetzal 126, 126
Quintana atrizona 282

Rabaut's Corydoras 141
Rachovia brevis 268
Rachow's Nothobranch 266
Rainbow Dace 176
Rainbow Darter 256
Rainbow Emperor Tetra 207
Rainbow Goodeid 285
Rainbow Shark 179
Rainbow Snakehead 246
rainbowfish 248-53
Ram 84, 104, 105
Ramirez's Dwarf Cichlid 104
Ramsden's Cichlid 107
Ranchu Goldfish 175
Rasbora 185
  R. argyrotaenia 185
  R. borapetensis 182, 182
  R. caudimaculata 182, 183
  R. cephalotaenia 185
  R. daniconius 185, 185
  R. dorsiocellata 182
  R. einthovenii 185, 185
  R. elegans 183, 183
  R. espei 183, 185
  R. heteromorpha 9, 58, 184, 184
  R. kalochroma 184
  R. pauciperforata 184, 185
  R. reticulata 185
  R. somphongsi 185
  R. taeniata 185
  R. trilineata 185
  R. urophthalma 185
  R. vaterifloris 185, 185
Rasborinae (subfamily) 164
Rathbun's Bloodfin 193, 193
"Real/True" Thomasi 149
Red Aphyosemion 263
Red Base Tetra 200
Red Devil 86, 86
Red Dwarf Betta 238
Red Horse Minnow 176
Red Kadango 94
Red Lamprologus 102
Red Line Torpedo 170
Red Oranda 43
Red Parrot Cichlid 9, 93
Red Phantom 204, 204
Red Rasbora 184
Red Shiner 176
Red Snakehead 246, 246
Red Snook 112
Red Tench 187
Red Terror 105
Red Top Afra 95
Red Veiltail 279
Red Whiptail Catfish 130, 130
Red and White Goldfish 175
Red and White Tench 187
Red-bellied Piranha 211, 211
Red-bellied Puffer 291
Redbreast Sunfish 255
Redear Sunfish 255
Red-eye 186
Red-eye Spiketail 240
Red-eyed Lionhead Goldfish 174
Red-eyed Tetra 193, 194, 206
Redfin Otocinclus 1, 152
Red-finned Cichlid 102
Red-finned Straight Distichodus 214, 214
Red-finned Shark 179
Red-green Dwarf Puffer 291
Redhook Metynnis 206
Redhook Pacu 206, 207
Red-hump Geophagus 98
Redlip Geophagus 118
Red-line Rasbora 184
Red-seam Killifish 262
Redside Barb 165
Red-spotted Angel 118
Red-spotted Characin 221
Red-spotted Cichlid 126
Red-spotted Copeina 221, 221
Red-spotted Rachow's Pyrrhulina 225, 225
Red-striped Rasbora 184
Red-tail Theraps 126
Red-tailed Black Shark 179, 179
Red-tailed Catfish 46, 159, 159
Red-tailed Cichlid 126
Red-tailed Dwarf Cichlid 88, 88
Red-tailed Flag Tetra 203
Red-tailed Goodeid 286

Red-tailed Hemiodus/
  Hemiodopsis 220, *220*
Red-tailed Labeo 179
Red-tailed Licorice/Liquorice
  Gourami 241
Red-tailed Rasbora 182,
  182
Red-topped Cichlid 102
Reedfish 295, *295*
Regal Peacock 91
Regan's Cichlid 126
Resti Dwarf Cichlid 89
Reticulated Corydoras 141
Reticulated Leporinus 192
Reticulated Tetra 203
Rhoadsiinae (subfamily) 188
Rhoadsia sp. 188
Rhodeus 58, 60, 164
  R. sericeus 186
Rice Fish 59
Riccia 35
  R. fluitans 73, 78
Rineloricaria fallax 153
Rio Grande Perch 100
Rio Ixtia Cichlid/Istianum 107
Rio Lerma Mosquitofish 281
Rio Meta Corydoras 139
Rio Palala Aspidoras 135
Rio Salinas Cory 139
Rivulinae (subfamily) 262
Rivulus 269
  R. compactus 269
  R. cylindraceus 268, 269
  R. magdalenae 7, 269
  R. marmoratus 269
  R. ocellatus 269
  R. stellifer 269
  R. urophthalmus 269
  R. xiphidius 269, *269*
Roach 164
Robina's Corydoras 141
Robust Topminnow 281
Rocket Panchax 263
Roloff's Krib 112
Rope Fish 295
Rosy Barb 166, *166*
Rosy Red 182
Rosy Tetra 200
Rotala sp. 81
Rough Fish 227
Round-banded Barb 170
Round-tailed Paradise Fish
  239
Royal Farlowella 154
Royal Panaque 152
Royal Whiptail 154
Ruby Barb 1, 19, 21, 168
Ruby Shark 179
Rudd 164, 186, *186*
Ruffe 257
Ruki Synodontis 157
Rusty Cichlid 100, *101*
Rutilus sp. 164
Ryukin Goldfish *174*

Saccobranchidae (family)
  129
Saddle Cichlid 85
Saddled Hillstream Loach
  226, 227, 227
Sagittaria sp. 72, 81
Sailfin Brachy 274
Sail-fin Brochis/Corydoras/
  Catfish 136
Sailfin Characin 210
Sailfin Marbled Catfish 158,
  158
Sailfin Molly 279, 280
Sailfin Pin 158
Sailfin Suckermouth Catfish
  150
Sailfin Tetra 210
Sailfish 253
Sajica's Cichlid 89
salamanders 12, *12*
Salmon Red Rainbowfish
  248, *248*
salt/brackish water 19, 45-6
Salt-and-pepper Corydoras
  139
Salvator Molly 280
Salvina sp. 35, 78
Salvin's Cichlid 106, *106*
Salz's Tetra 203
Samolus 81
  S. parviflorus 81
Sandpaper Shiner 176
Sanke Koi Carp 177
Sanshoku Koi Carp 177
Santo Domingo Molly 280
Sapaya Aequidens/Acara 85
Sarasa Comet Goldfish *173*
Satanoperca 99
  S. acuticeps 118
  S. daemon 118, *118*
  S. jurupari 118
  S. sp. jurupari 118
  S. leucosticta 118
  S. sp. leucostica 118
  S. sp. leucostitca 118
  S. lilith 118
  S. mapiritensis 118
  S. pappaterra 118
  S. sp. "Redlip" 118
Saururus cernuus 81
Savoryi 109
Scalare 116
Scalare Angelfish 84
Scaleblotch Pyrrhulina 225
Scaphirhynchus platorynchus
  296, *297*

Scardinius 164
  S. erythrophthalmus 186,
    186
Scat 45, 289, *289*
Scatophagus 19, 45
Schaller's Gourami 241
Schilbe mystus 130, 162
Schilbeidae (family) 130
Schmard Tetra 200
Schomburgk's Leaf Fish 247
Schreyen's Lamprologus
  109
Schubert's Barb 169
Schwanenfeld's Barb 169
Schwarzer Neolobias 215
Sciaenochromis fryeri 119
Scissortail 185
Scleropages formosus 20,
  21-2, *22*, 46, 58, 293,
  294
Sealhead Goldfish *174*
Selangor Red Betta 238
Semaprochilodus taeniurus
  217, 217
Sentani Rainbowfish 249
Sepik Rainbowfish 249, *249*
septicaemia 64
Serrasalminae (subfamily)
  188
Severum Cichlid 100
Shark-tailed Distichodus 214,
  214
Sheephead Swordtail 282
Sheepshead Angel 118
Shinnersia rivularis 81
Short-bodied Brochis/
  Corydoras/Catfish 136
Short-faced Elephantnose/
  Whale 292
Short-lined Pyrrhulina 225
Short-striped Thayeria 213
Shovelnosed Sturgeon 296,
  297
Showa Koi Carp 177
Shusui Koi Carp 177
Siamese Algae Eater 176
Siamese Fighter 232, 237,
  238
Siamese Flying Fox 76, 176
Siamese Shark 157
Siamese Spiny Eel 294
Siamese Stone-lapping
  Sucker 180, *180*
Siamese Tiger 290
Sicklefin Pearl 267
Sierra Leone Dwarf Characin
  204
Sieve Cichlid 107
Siluridae (family) 129, 130
Siluriformes (order) 129
Silurus Glanis 129
Silver Arowana 293, *293*
Silver Batfish 290
Silver Distichodus 214, *214*
Silver Dollar 205, *205*
Silver Hatchetfish 218, 219
Silver Hemiodus 220
Silver Leporinus 192
Silver Mylossoma 207, *207*
Silver Ogon Koi Carp 177
Silver Prochilodus 217, *217*
Silver Rasbora 185
Silver Seam/Saum 85, *85*
Silver Shark 165, *165*
Silver Shark Catfish 131
Silver Vieja 126
Silver-tipped Tetra 197, *197*
Silver-tipped Zebra 188
Simor Betta 238
Singapore 21, 22, 25
Sisoridae (family) 130
Six-barred Epiplatys 265
Six-barred Panchax 265, *265*
Skiffia
  S. multipunctata 286
  S. francescae 20, 22
skin fluke infections 65
Skunk Corydoras 138
Slab-sided Blue-eye 281
sleepers 258-61
Slender Elephantnose/Whale
  292
Slender Betta 236, *236*
Slender Hemiodus/Hemio-
  dopsis 219, *219*, 220
Slender Mbuna 124
Slender Pygmy Swordtail
  283
Slender Rainbowfish 252
Slender Sleeper Goby/
  Gudgeon 259
Slender Tetra 202, *203*
Slim Harlequin 183, *184*
Slimy Loach 231
Small Licorice/Liquorice
  Gourami 240
Small Tailspot Bushfish 235
Smaragd Betta/Fighter 237
Smooth-breasted Snakehead
  246
Snail-eating Doradid 146
Snake Fish 295
snakeheads 46
Snakeskin Gourami 244, *244*
Snaky Spiny Eel 294
Snow King Plec/Pleco 151,
  151
Snowflake Bristlenose 148
Snowflake Woodcat 132
Socolof's Cichlid 123

soft water *see* hard/soft
  water
Sorubim 130
South African
  Mouthbrooder 114
South American Leaf Fish
  56, 247, *247*
South American Lungfish
  295
South American Molly *280*
South American Tiger Fish
  217
Southern Green Corydoras
  141
Southern Platy 2-3, *283*
Southern Red-belly Dace
  181, *181*
Spade Leaf Plant 80
Spanner Barb 168, *168*
Sparkling Geophagus 118
Sparkling Gourami 241
Spathiphyllum wallisii 81
Spathodus erythrodon 119
species *see* fish classification
Speckled Sawfin Goodeid
  286
Sphaerichthys 58
  S. acrostoma 242
  S. osphromenoides 242,
    243
  S. vaillanti 243
Sphenops Molly 280
Spider Plant 71, 79
Spiketail Platy 283
Spike-tailed Paradise Fish
  240, *240*
Spined Weather Loach 230
spiny eels 36, 294
Spiny Plec/Pleco 153, *153*
Splashing Tetra/Characin
  221, *222*
Splendid Dwarf Gourami 240
Splendid Rainbowfish 249,
  252, *252*
Spotfin Lamprologus 109
Spot-finned Spiny Eel 294
Spotlight Mini Cory 139
Spot-line Aspidoras 135, *135*
Spot-tailed Leporinus 192
Spot-tailed Mosquitofish 281
Spot-tailed Scissortail 182
Spotted Aspidoras 135
Spotted Barb 170, *170*
Spotted Blue-eye 253, *253*
Spotted Brachy/Bishop 274
Spotted Bristlenose 148
Spotted Cachorro 192
Spotted Catfish 147
Spotted Congo Puffer *290*,
  291
Spotted Ctenopoma 234
Spotted Danio 171, *172*
Spotted Doradid 144, *144*
Spotted Elephantnose/
  Whale 292
Spotted Fire Eel 294
Spotted Goby 258
Spotted Goodeid 6, 285
Spotted Gourami 244
Spotted Hatchetfish 218
Spotted Headstander 191
Spotted Hoplo 142
Spotted Hypostomus 151,
  151
Spotted Leporinus 192, *192*
Spotted Livebearer 279
Spotted Lungfish 295
Spotted Pike Characin 216
Spotted Pim 160
Spotted Piranha 212
Spotted Pleco 150, *150*, 151
Spotted Pointed-tail Gourami
  239
Spotted Rainbowfish 249
Spotted Rasbora 171
Spotted Shovelnosed Catfish
  158, *158*
Spotted Snakehead 246
Spotted Spiny Eel 294
Spotted Sunfish 255
Spotted Talking Catfish 144
Spotted Weather Loach 230
Spraying Tetra/Characin 221
Spring Pygmy Sunfish 256
spring viraemia 63
Squarehead Geophagus 99
squid 12
Sri Lanka 19, 21, 22
Star-gazing Doradid 145
Starry Growler 145
Steatocranus casuarius 119,
  119
Steel-blue Killifish 263
Steindachner's Dwarf Cichlid
  88, 107
Steindachner's Puffer 291
Stellate Rivulus 269
Stevardia riisei 59, 212, *212*
Stick Catfish 129, 149, *149*
sticklebacks 58, 254
Stigmatogobius sadanundio
  261, *261*
Stinging Catfish 147
Stiphodon elegans 261
Stizostedion
  S. lucioperca 257, *257*

S. vitreum 257
stocking levels 48-9
Stoliczk's/Stoliczka's Barb
  170
Stone Loach 226, 227
Strawberry Tetra 201
Striped Anostomus 190, *190*
Striped Barb 170
Striped Betta 238
Striped Catfish 134
Striped Dwarf Cichlid 112
Striped Four-eyed Fish 270
Striped Gobi Cichlid 97
Striped Gourami 241
Striped Headstander 190
Striped Krib 112
Striped Lamprologus 109
Striped Leporinus 191
Striped Limia 278
Striped Pike Cichlid 95, *95*
Striped Pyrrhulina 225
Striped Rasbora 185, *185*
Striped Schilbe Catfish 130,
  162
Striped Sleeper Goby 258,
  258
Striped Snakehead/Murrei
  246
Striped Synodontis 156
Stripe-tailed Catfish 142
Stuart's Livebearer 274
Sturgeon Catfish 154, 160,
  161
Sturisoma panamense 154
suckers 226-31
Sucking Loach 23, 76, 226,
  231
Sulphur/Sulfur-head Aulono-
  cara/Peacock 91, *92*
Sumatra Barb 169
sunfish 254-7
Sunset Platy 283
Sunshine Peacock 90
Suriname Swordtail 283
sustainable fishing industry
  22
Sutrisoma sp. 58
swamp eels 254
Swamp Licorice/Liquorice
  Gourami 240
Sweet Flag 78
Swegles' Tetra 204
Swordgold 60, 71, 72, 74,
  75, 79, 79
Swordtail 76, 282
Symphysodon 84
  S. aequifasciatus 24, 119,
    120
  S. discus 24, 120, *120*
Synbranchidae (family) 254
Syngonium podophyllum 81
Synodontis 130, 157
  S. alberti 157
  S. angelicus 155, *155*, 157
  S. batesii 157
  S. brichardi 155
  S. budgeti 157
  S. camelopardalis 157
  S. congicus 157
  S. decorus 156
  S. eupterus 156, *156*
  S. flavitaeniatus 156
  S. longirostris 157
  S. multipunctatus 156
  S. nigrita 157
  S. nigriventris 156, *157*
  S. njassae 157
  S. notatus 157
  S. ornatipinnis 157
  S. petricola 157
  S. pleurops 157
  S. schoutedeni 157
  S. victoriae 156

Taenia Dwarf Cichlid 89
Taeniacara candidi 121
Tail-bar Cichlid 125
Tail-light Tetra 195
Tailspot Bushfish 234
Tail-spot Corydoras 141
Tail-spot Tiger Cichlid 107
Talking Catfish 129, 145
Tamesi Molly 280
Tanakia sp. 164
Tancho Koi Carp 177
Tancho Sanke Koi Carp 177
Tanganyika Humphead 96
Tanganyika Lampeye 271,
  271
Tanganyika Pearl Killifish
  272, *272*
Tanganyikan Spiny Eel 294
Tanichthys albonubes 28,
  186, *186*
tapwater 37
Tateurndina ocellicauda 260,
  260
Tatia lupogypia 132
Tawny Dragon Catfish 134
taxonomy *see* fish
  classification
T-bar Cichlid 89, *89*
Telanthera 78
Teleogramma brichardi 121
Telmatherinidae (family) 248
Telmatochromis:
  T. bifrenatus 121
  T. brichardi 121
  T. burgeoni 121

T. dhonti 121
T. caninus 121
T. sp. "temporalis shell"
  121
T. sp. "vittatus shell" 121
T. temporalis 121
T. vittatus 121
Temporalis Cichlid/Telmat
  121
Temporalis Telmat "Shell" 121
Tench 44, 164, 186
Ten-spot Livebearer 274
Terete Lamprologus 108
Ternetz's Anostomus 190,
  190
Ternetz's Headstander 190
Terraba Bishop 274
Tetra Loreto 202
Tetraodon:
  T. biocellatus 291
  T. cutcutia 291
  T. fluviatilis 290, 291
  T. lorteti 291
  T. mbu 291
  T. schoutedeni 290, 291
  T. steindachneri 291
Tetragonopterinae (sub-
  family) 188
Texas Cichlid 84, 100, *100*
Thailand 23, 164
Thayeria:
  T. boehlkei 212, *212*
  T. obliqua 213
Theraps sp. 126
Thick-lipped Apistogramma
  89
Thick-lipped Cichlid 86, *86*
Thick-lipped Gourami 242,
  242
Thinlip Gourami 243
Thoracocharax securis 219
Thorichthys:
  T. affinis 122, *122*
  T. aureus 122, *122*
  T. callalepis 123
  T. ellioti 123
  T. helleri 123
  T. meeki 122, *122*
  T. pasionis 123
  T. socolofi 123
Threadfin Rainbowfish 249,
  249
Threadjaw Halfbeak 288
threatened species *see* fish
  conservation
Three-lined Corydoras 141
Three-lined Neolebias 215
Three-lined Pencilfish 224
Three-lined Rasbora 185
Three-spot Anostomus 190
Three-spot Gourami 233
Three-spot Demonfish 118
Three-spot Eartheater 118
Three-spot Geophagus 118,
  118
Three-spot Gourami 244
Three-spot Headstander
  190
Three-spot Rasbora 184
Three-spot Tetra 196
Three-striped Dwarf Cichlid
  89
Three-striped Pencilfish 223
Tiburón Limia 278
Tiburón Peninsula Limia 278
Ticto/Tic-tac-toe Barb 170
Tiger Barb 25, 39, 169
Tiger Cichlid 105
Tiger Loach 228
Tiger Shovelnosed Catfish
  161
Tiger Tilapia 123
Tilapia:
  T. buttikoferi 123
  T. mariae 123, *123*
  T. zillii 124
Tinca 164
  T. tinca 44, 186, *187*
Tinfoil Barb 169, *169*
Toa Lamprologus 109
Tomeurus gracilis 59
Tondanichthys kottelati 288
Tooth-lipped Cichlid 107
Torpedo Fish 220
Torporitora 164
Toxotes 19, 46
  T. jaculatrix 1, 289
Translucent Bloodfin 211
Trapa natans 78
Trewavas' Cichlid 102
Trewavas' Neolebias 215
Triangle Cichlid 125
trichlorphon (medication)
  66
trichodiniasis 65
Trichogaster 19, 58, 61
  T. leeri 243, *243*
  T. microlepis 243, *244*
  T. pectoralis 244, *244*
  T. trichopterus 244
Trichogasterinae (subfamily)
  233
Trichopsis pumilus 61, 241
Trichopsis 58
  T. schalleri 241
  T. vittatus 241
Tricolor Cichlid 124
Tri-color Shark 165
Trigonostigma:
  T. heteromorpha 9, 184
  T. somphongsi 185

Triportheus angulatus 213,
  213
Tropheops:
  T. elongatus 124
  T. tropheops 124, *124*
Tropheops Bright Yellow
  115, *115*
Tropheus 116
  T. brichardi 124
  T. duboisi 124, *125*
  T. moorii 124
trophonematra 60
tropical lilies 74
Tropheus 116
Turner's Gaucho 267
Turner's Sailfish Goodeid 287
Turquoise Danio 178
Tussy's Betta 238
Tuyra/Tuyre Cichlid 123
Twig Catfish 129, 149
Twin-spot Flag Cichlid 85
Twin-spotted Pencilfish 223
Two-banded Telmat *121*
Two-lined Pencilfish 223
Two-spot Barb 165
Two-spot Cichlid 95
Two-spot Gourami 244
Two-spot Livebearer 281
Two-spot Rasbora 183, 184
Two-striped Cichlid 126

Uape Dwarf Cichlid 89
Uaru amphiacanthoides 84,
  125, *125*
Uaru Cichlid 84, 125, *125*
Ulrey's Tetra 199, *199*
ulcers 64, *64*
ultraviolet sterilization 62,
  62
Umbrella Dwarf Cichlid 87, *87*
Umbrella Plant 79
United States 19, 25, 188
Unspotted Betta 238
Upland Swordtail 283
urchins 12, 12
Utricularia sp. 81
Utsurimono Koi Carp 177

vaccines *see* medicine/
  vaccines
Vaillant's Butter Catfish *163*
Vaillant's Chocolate Gourami
  243
Vallisneria 35, 72, 81, *81*
  V. americana 74
  V. gigantea 74
Variatus Platy 283
Veiltail Goldfish *174*
Velvet Cichlid 45, 84, 90, *90*
venomous stings 128
Ventralis Cichlid 110
Venustus 110
Vermiculated Synodontis 157
Vesicularia 61
  V. dubyana 35, 73, 81
Victoria Synodontis 157
Vieja 126
  V. argentea 126
  V. bifasciatus 126
  V. breidohri 126
  V. fenestrata 126
  V. guttulatum 126
  V. hartwegi 125
  V. heterospila 126
  V. maculicauda 125, *126*
  V. melanurus 126
  V. regani 126
  V. synspilum 126
  V. tuyrensis 126
  V. zonatus 126
Viejita Dwarf Cichlid 89, *89*
Villavicencio Apistogramma
  87, 88
Vilma's Tetra 203, *203*
viral infections 63, *63*
viviparity 59-60
Vorderwinkler's Hemiodus/
  Hemiodopsis 220

Walking Catfish 144, *144*
Walking Perch 233
Walleye 257
Warmouth 255
Waroo Cichlid 125
Water Cabbage 81
water chemistry 37-41, *37*,
  52-3
  acidity/alkalinity 19, 37,
    38-9, 43, 53,
  chlorine content 37
  hardness 39-41, 43, 45,
    53
  oxygen content 232
  phosphate levels 52
  tapwater 37
Water Chestnut 78
water conditions:
  blackwater treatments 45
  salt/brackish 19, 45-6
  see also aquaria
water filters 29-32, 30-31,
  42, 45, 62, 67
Water Goldfinch 211
water heaters/thermostats
  31, 33-5, *34*, 42, 47
Water Hedge 79
Water Hyacinth 74, *74*, 77,
  79
Water Lettuce 78
Water Rose 81
Water Sprite 77, *77*
Water Stargrass 80

Water Violet 80
Water Wisteria 75
waterlilies 74
Wauthion's Lamprologus
  Zambia 109
Weberian apparatus 128
Weise's Dwarf Cichlid 121
Weitzman's Predator Tetra
  259
Wel's Catfish 129
Western Carp/Gudgeon
  259
Western Mosquitofish 274
Whale 292
Whale-faced Marcusenius
  292
whales 292
Whiptail 58-9
White Cloud Mountain
  Minnow 28, 186, *186*
White Piranha 212
white spot 65, *65*
White Top Afra 95
White's Pearl 267, *267*
White-barred Synodontis
  157
Whiteseam Betta 238
Whiteseam Pyrrhulina 225
White-spotted Car-track/
  Tire-Track Spiny Eel 294
White-spotted Chaetostoma
  149, *149*
White-spotted Cichlid 124,
  125
White-spotted Doradid 144
White-spotted Duboisi 124
White-spotted/striped Pim
  160
White-star Tetra 194
White-top Aulonocara/
  Peacock 91
wild-caught specimens 23
  see also commercial
  breeding
Willow Moss 79
Window Cichlid 126
Wine Red Fighter 236, *237*
Wolf Cichlid 107, *107*
Wolf Fish 217, 218
worm infections 65, *65*
Wrestling Halfbeak 288, *288*

Xanoophorus captivus 286
Xenomystus nigri 292, *292*
Xenopoecilus sp. 61
Xenotoca:
  X. eiseni 286, *286*
  X. variata 287
Xiphophorus 283
  X. alvarezi 283
  X. andersi 283
  X. birchmanni 282
  X. clemenciae 283
  X. cortezi 283
  X. couchianus 283, *283*
  X. evelynae 282
  X. gordoni 283
  X. helleri 76, 282, *282*
  X. "kosszanderi" 283
  X. maculatus 2-3, 76, 283
  X. malinche 283
  X. milleri 5, 283
  X. montezumae 283
  X. multilineatus 283
  X. nezahualcoyotl 283
  X. nigrensis 283
  X. pygmaeus 283
  X. signum 283
  X. variatus 76, 283
  X. xiphidium 283
X-ray Fish 211
X-ray Tetra 211

Yellow Krib 111, *111*
Yellow Peacock 90
Yellow Perch 91, 257
Yellow Swordtail 283
Yellow-banded Tetra 206
Yellow-cheeked
  Apistogramma 89
Yellow-finned Xenotilapia 126
Yellow-tailed Conga Tetra
  197
Yellow-tailed Hemiodus 220
Y-Loach 228
Yucatán Molly 280

Zacco 187
Zacco platypus 187
Zamora Catfish 129
Zamora Woodcat 131
Zander 257, *257*
Zebra Cichlid 9, 88, 84, 104,
  104
  aquaria for 44-5
Zebra Danio 25, 172, *172*
Zebra Loach 229
Zebra Peckoltia 150, *151*
Zebra Pleco 150
Zebra Spiny Eel 294
Zebra Tilapia 123
Zenarchopterus 288
  Z. beauforti 288
  Z. dispar 288
Zig-zag Pyrrhulina 225
Zilli's Cichlid 40, 124
Zoned Limia 124
Zoogoneticus quitzeoensis
  287
zoonoses 67
Zygatus Corydoras 141